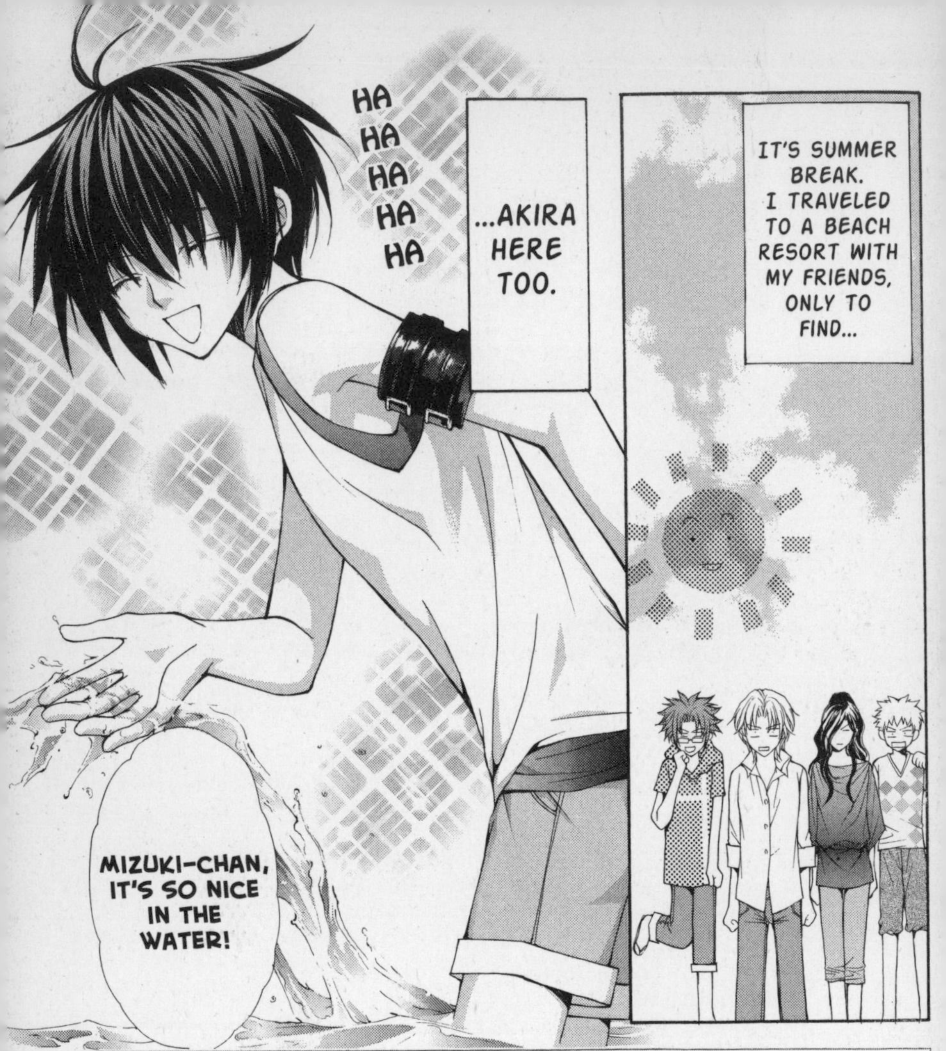
IT'S SUMMER BREAK. I TRAVELED TO A BEACH RESORT WITH MY FRIENDS, ONLY TO FIND...
...AKIRA HERE TOO.
HA HA HA HA HA
MIZUKI-CHAN, IT'S SO NICE IN THE WATER!

Ai Ore! volume 6!!

We're already up to volume 6. This volume will be published in Japan in winter, but the stories are all set in midsummer. (laugh) I've been wanting to do a summer story arc, so I'm glad I was able to. Basically I always start with storylines I want to do for *Ai Ore!*, so I'm always excited to draw the manga. In this volume I wanted to have a story that highlighted Ran because he didn't play that big of a role in volume 5.

I think the Ran fans will be happy about this. I want to do some cool chapters about Rui next. There are so many things I still want to write about in the *Ai Ore!* series. I want to add new characters, and I would also like to do a side story featuring Sho and Takumi, who turned out to be surprisingly popular with readers. I don't know how much I'll be able to do, but I really love this series.

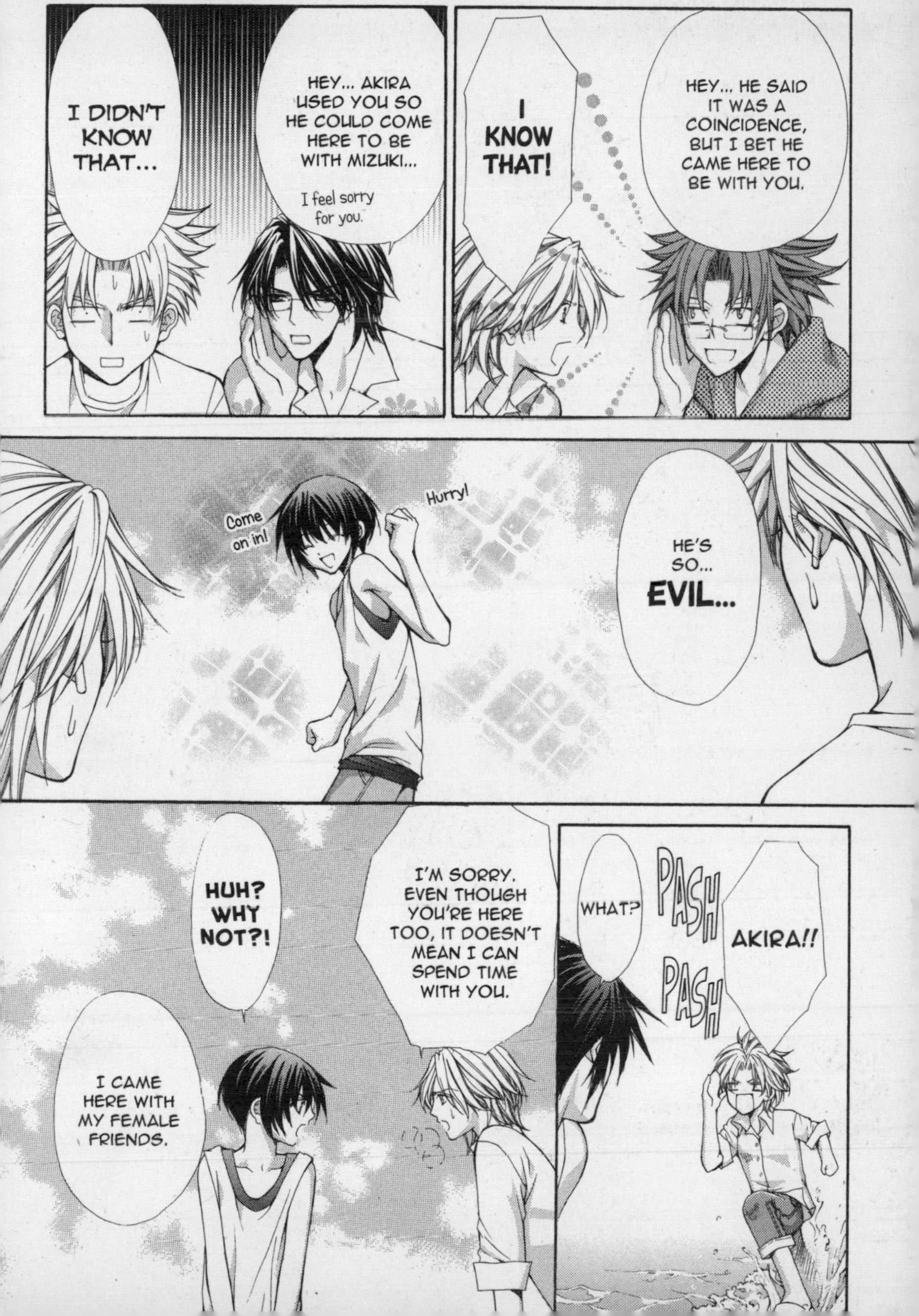
HEY... HE SAID IT WAS A COINCIDENCE, BUT I BET HE CAME HERE TO BE WITH YOU.
I KNOW THAT!
HEY... AKIRA USED YOU SO HE COULD COME HERE TO BE WITH MIZUKI...
I feel sorry for you.
I DIDN'T KNOW THAT...
HE'S SO... EVIL...
Hurry!
Come on in!
AKIRA!!
PASH
PASH
WHAT?
I'M SORRY. EVEN THOUGH YOU'RE HERE TOO, IT DOESN'T MEAN I CAN SPEND TIME WITH YOU.
HUH? WHY NOT?!
I CAME HERE WITH MY FEMALE FRIENDS.

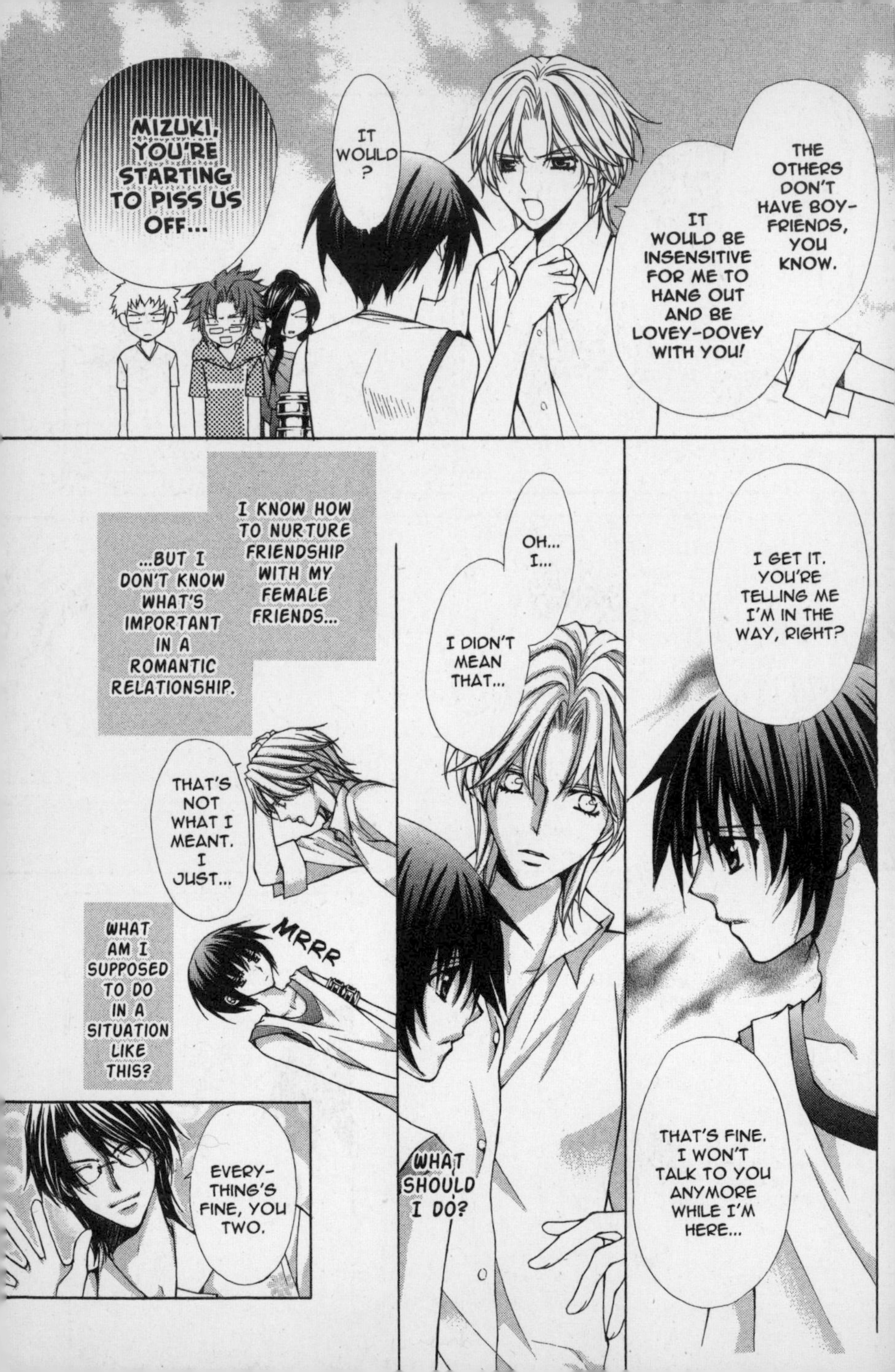
THE OTHERS DON'T HAVE BOY-FRIENDS, YOU KNOW.
IT WOULD BE INSENSITIVE FOR ME TO HANG OUT AND BE LOVEY-DOVEY WITH YOU!
IT WOULD?
MIZUKI, YOU'RE STARTING TO PISS US OFF...
I GET IT. YOU'RE TELLING ME I'M IN THE WAY, RIGHT?
THAT'S FINE. I WON'T TALK TO YOU ANYMORE WHILE I'M HERE...
OH... I...
I DIDN'T MEAN THAT...
WHAT SHOULD I DO?
I KNOW HOW TO NURTURE FRIENDSHIP WITH MY FEMALE FRIENDS...
...BUT I DON'T KNOW WHAT'S IMPORTANT IN A ROMANTIC RELATIONSHIP.
THAT'S NOT WHAT I MEANT. I JUST...
WHAT AM I SUPPOSED TO DO IN A SITUATION LIKE THIS?
MRRR
EVERY-THING'S FINE, YOU TWO.

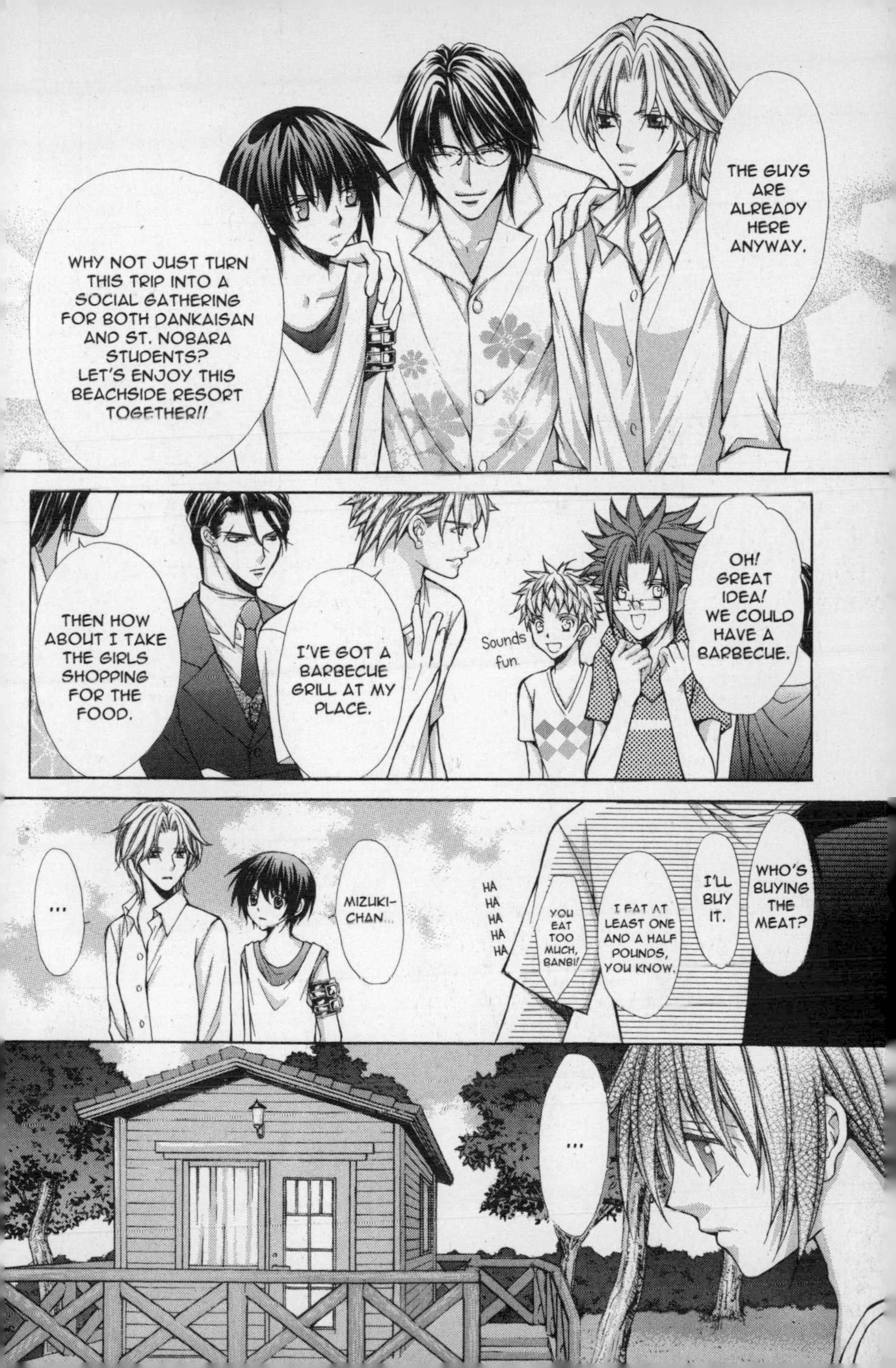
THE GUYS ARE ALREADY HERE ANYWAY.
WHY NOT JUST TURN THIS TRIP INTO A SOCIAL GATHERING FOR BOTH DANKAISAN AND ST. NOBARA STUDENTS? LET'S ENJOY THIS BEACHSIDE RESORT TOGETHER!!
OH! GREAT IDEA! WE COULD HAVE A BARBECUE.
Sounds fun.
I'VE GOT A BARBECUE GRILL AT MY PLACE.
THEN HOW ABOUT I TAKE THE GIRLS SHOPPING FOR THE FOOD.
WHO'S BUYING THE MEAT?
I'LL BUY IT.
I EAT AT LEAST ONE AND A HALF POUNDS, YOU KNOW.
YOU EAT TOO MUCH, BANBI!
HA HA HA HA HA
MIZUKI-CHAN...
...
...

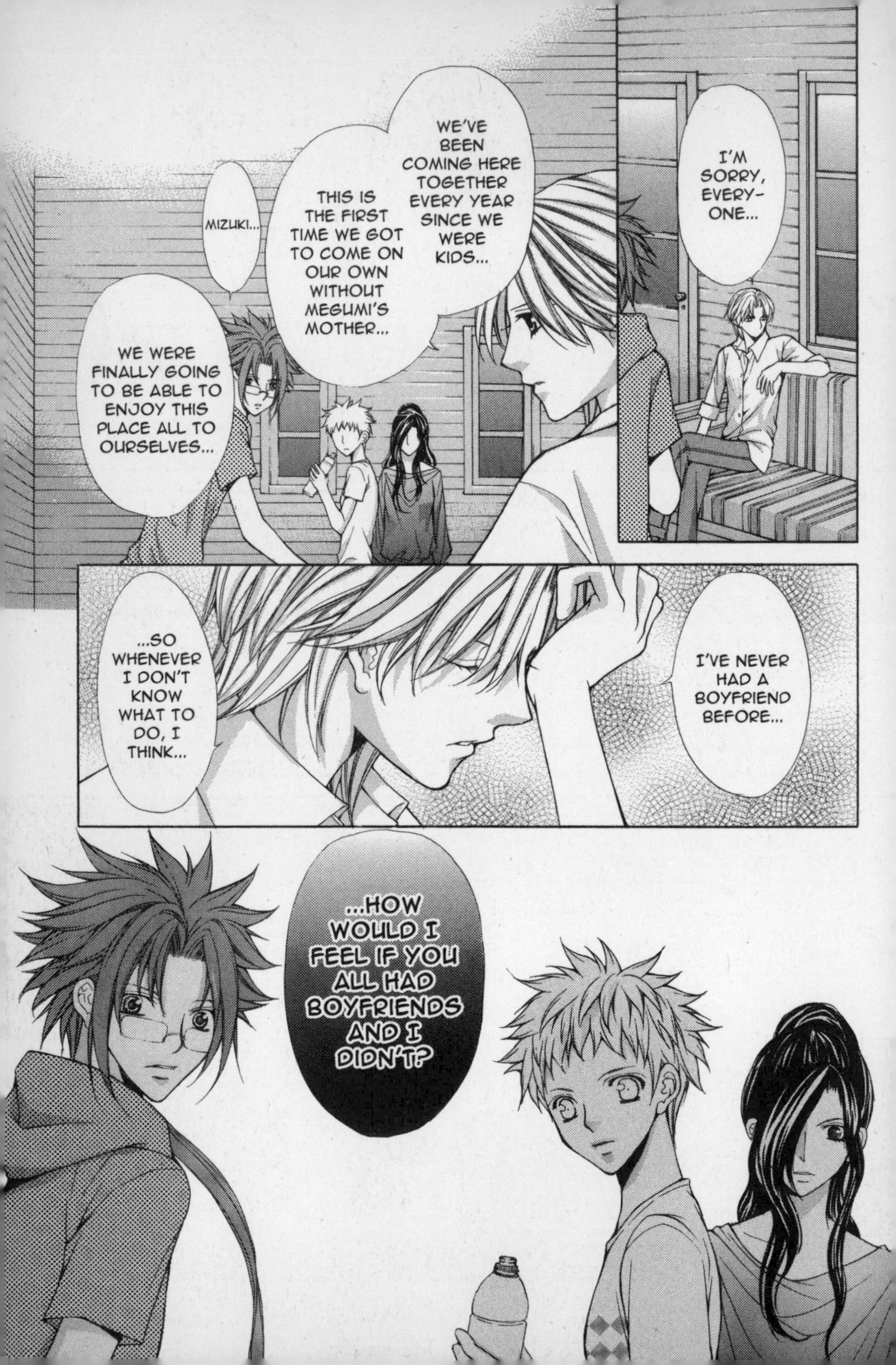
I'M SORRY, EVERYONE...
WE'VE BEEN COMING HERE TOGETHER EVERY YEAR SINCE WE WERE KIDS...
THIS IS THE FIRST TIME WE GOT TO COME ON OUR OWN WITHOUT MEGUMI'S MOTHER...
MIZUKI...
WE WERE FINALLY GOING TO BE ABLE TO ENJOY THIS PLACE ALL TO OURSELVES...
I'VE NEVER HAD A BOYFRIEND BEFORE...
...SO WHENEVER I DON'T KNOW WHAT TO DO, I THINK...
...HOW WOULD I FEEL IF YOU ALL HAD BOYFRIENDS AND I DIDN'T?

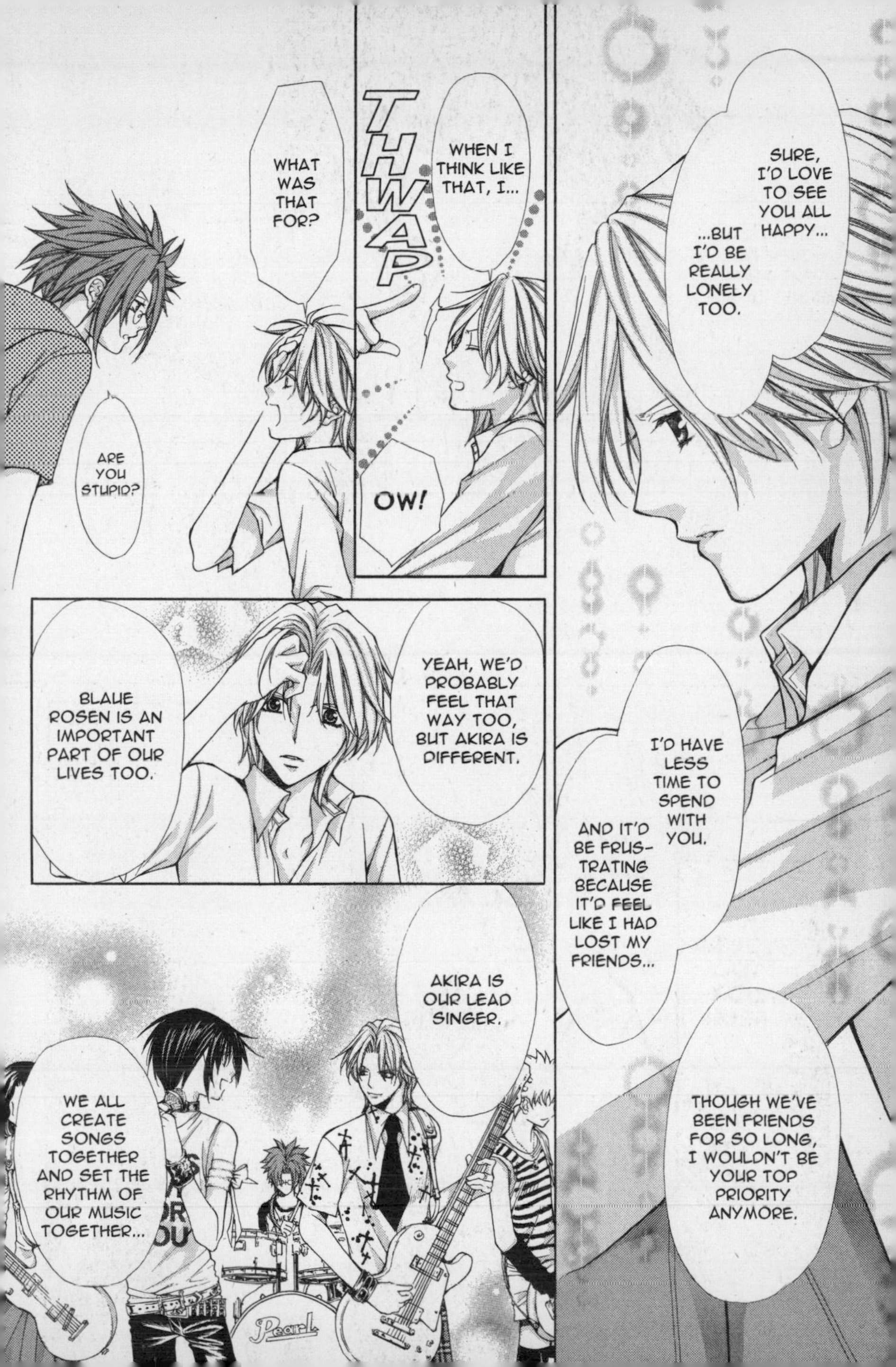
SURE, I'D LOVE TO SEE YOU ALL HAPPY...
...BUT I'D BE REALLY LONELY TOO.
I'D HAVE LESS TIME TO SPEND WITH YOU.
AND IT'D BE FRUS-TRATING BECAUSE IT'D FEEL LIKE I HAD LOST MY FRIENDS...
THOUGH WE'VE BEEN FRIENDS FOR SO LONG, I WOULDN'T BE YOUR TOP PRIORITY ANYMORE.
WHEN I THINK LIKE THAT, I...
THWAP
OW!
WHAT WAS THAT FOR?
ARE YOU STUPID?
YEAH, WE'D PROBABLY FEEL THAT WAY TOO, BUT AKIRA IS DIFFERENT.
BLAUE ROSEN IS AN IMPORTANT PART OF OUR LIVES TOO.
AKIRA IS OUR LEAD SINGER.
WE ALL CREATE SONGS TOGETHER AND SET THE RHYTHM OF OUR MUSIC TOGETHER...

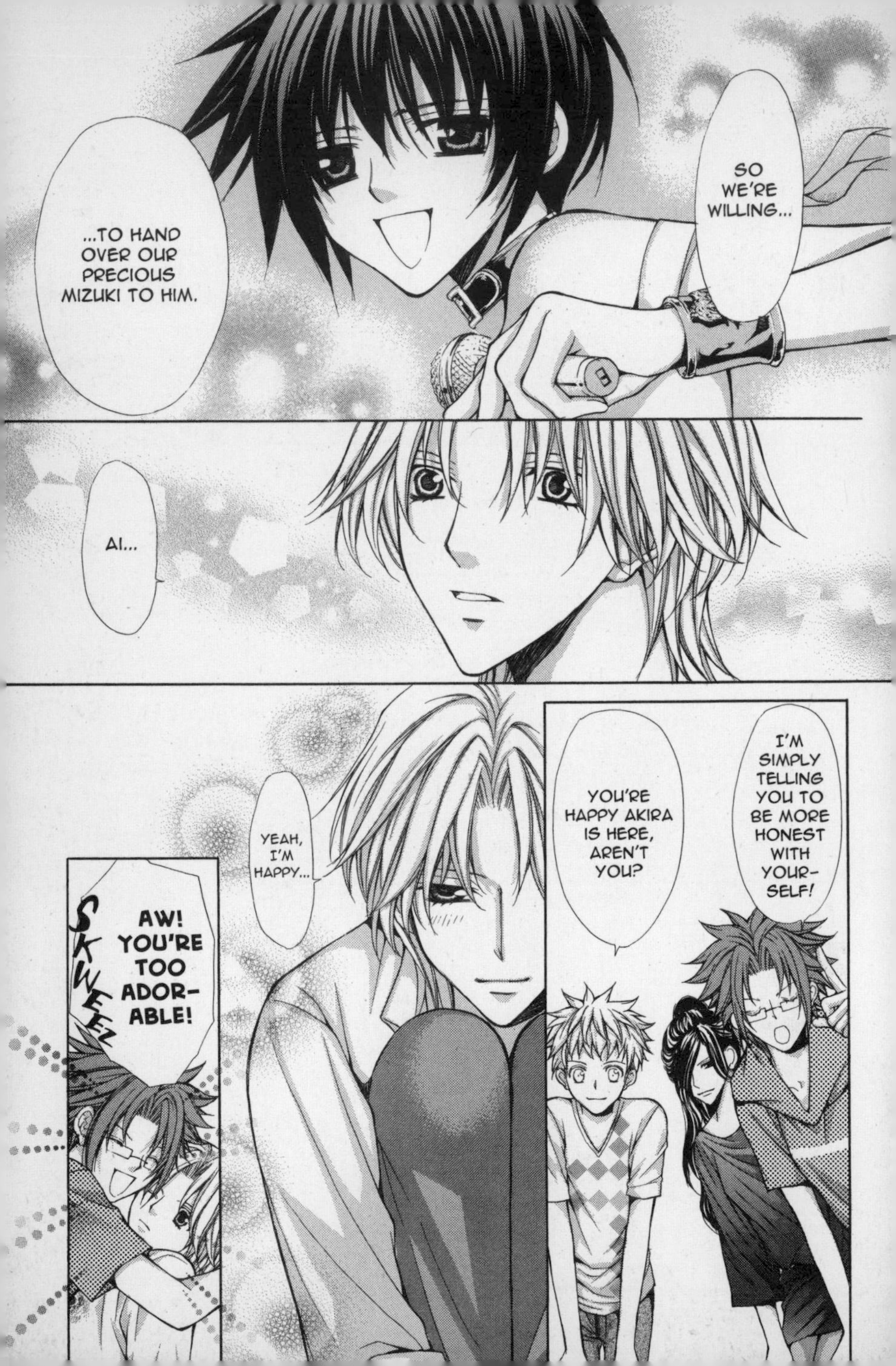
SO WE'RE WILLING...
...TO HAND OVER OUR PRECIOUS MIZUKI TO HIM.
AI...
I'M SIMPLY TELLING YOU TO BE MORE HONEST WITH YOUR-SELF!
YOU'RE HAPPY AKIRA IS HERE, AREN'T YOU?
YEAH, I'M HAPPY...
AW! YOU'RE TOO ADOR-ABLE!
SKWEEZ

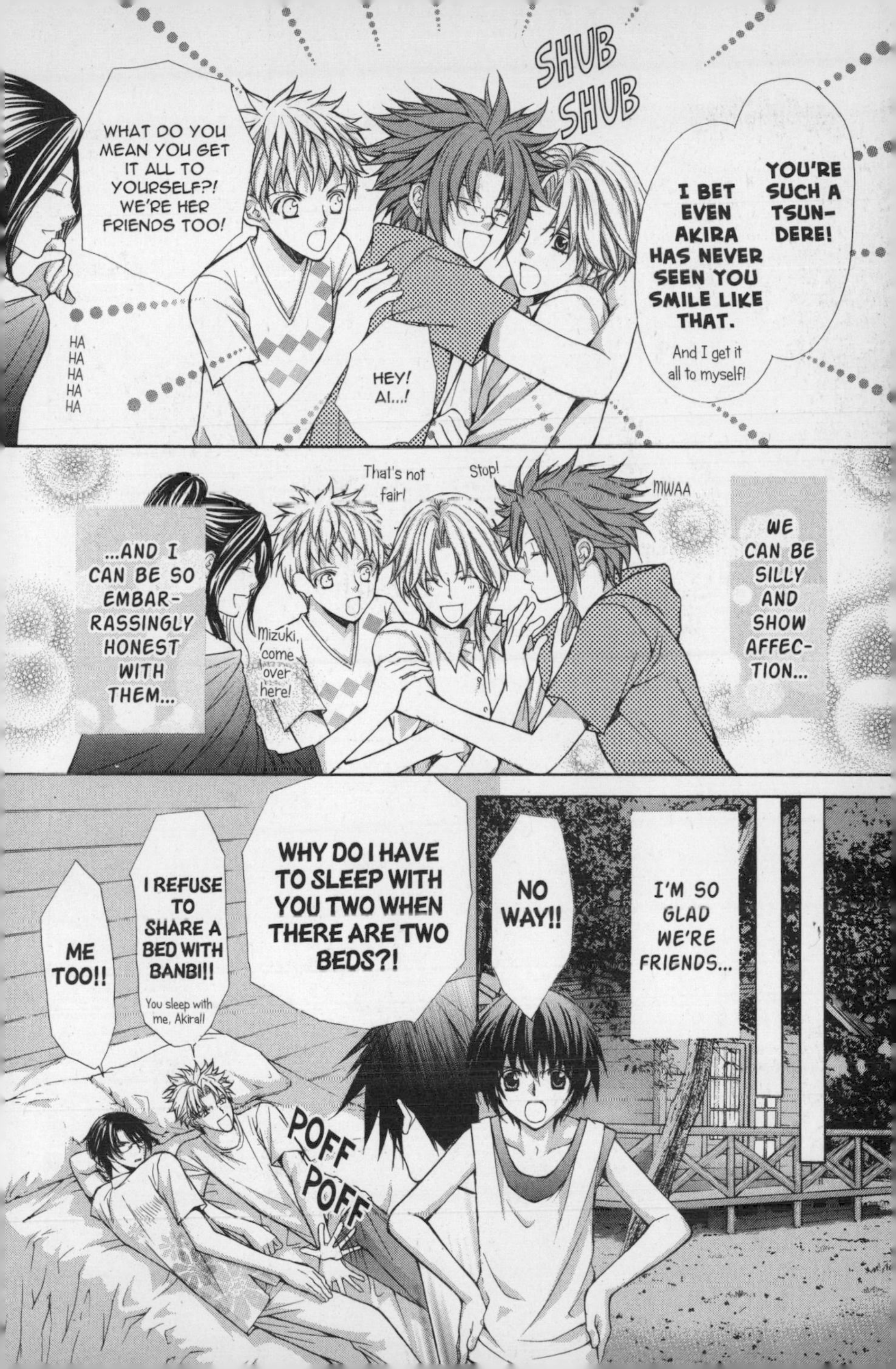
SHUB SHUB
YOU'RE SUCH A TSUN-DERE!
I BET EVEN AKIRA HAS NEVER SEEN YOU SMILE LIKE THAT.
And I get it all to myself!
HEY! AI...!
WHAT DO YOU MEAN YOU GET IT ALL TO YOURSELF?! WE'RE HER FRIENDS TOO!
HA HA HA HA HA
WE CAN BE SILLY AND SHOW AFFEC-TION...
MWAA
Stop!
That's not fair!
Mizuki, come over here!
...AND I CAN BE SO EMBAR-RASSINGLY HONEST WITH THEM...
I'M SO GLAD WE'RE FRIENDS...
NO WAY!!
WHY DO I HAVE TO SLEEP WITH YOU TWO WHEN THERE ARE TWO BEDS?!
I REFUSE TO SHARE A BED WITH BANBI!!
You sleep with me, Akira!!
ME TOO!!
POFF POFF

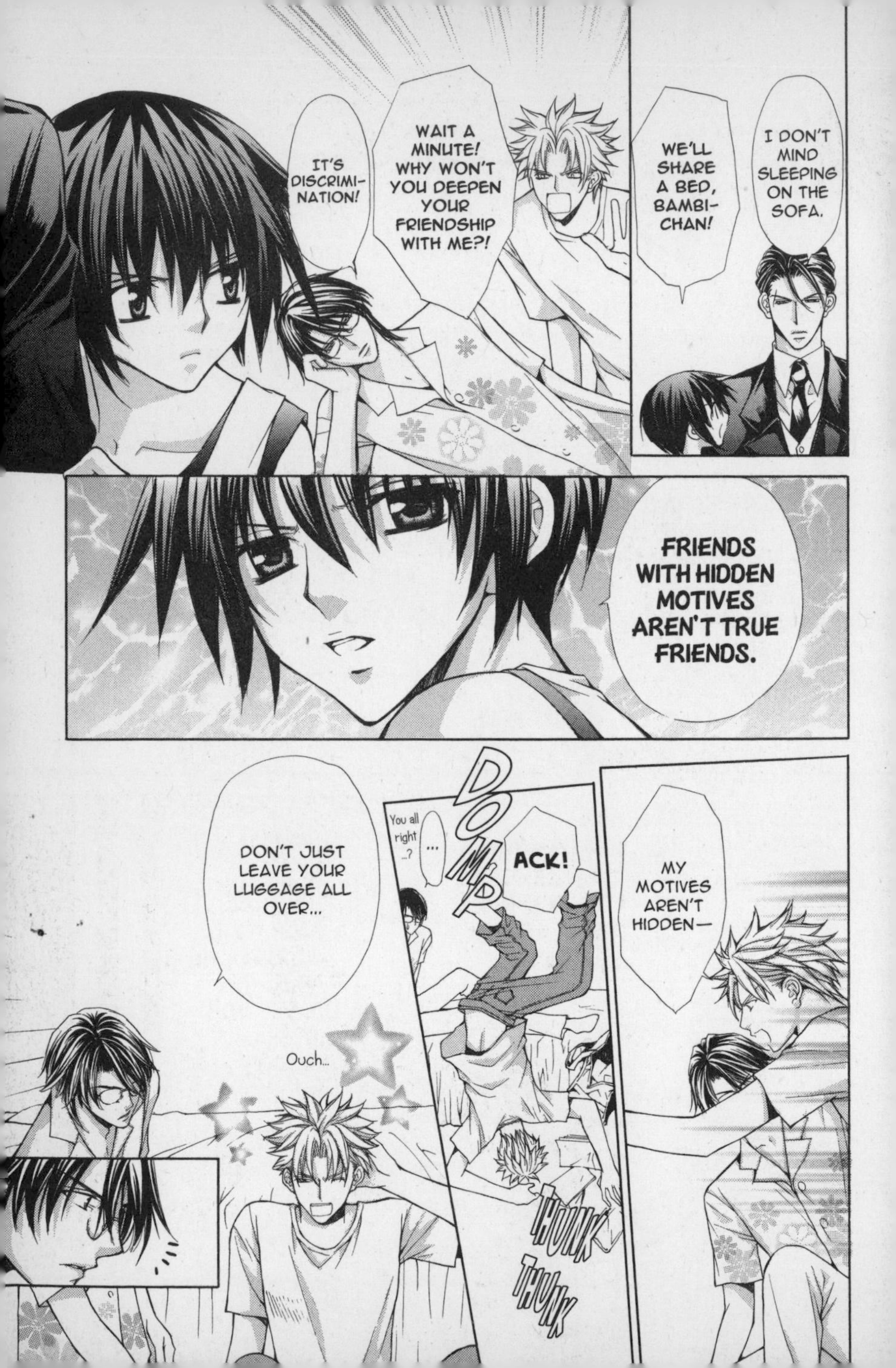

I DON'T MIND SLEEPING ON THE SOFA.
WE'LL SHARE A BED, BAMBI-CHAN!
WAIT A MINUTE! WHY WON'T YOU DEEPEN YOUR FRIENDSHIP WITH ME?!
IT'S DISCRIMI-NATION!
FRIENDS WITH HIDDEN MOTIVES AREN'T TRUE FRIENDS.
MY MOTIVES AREN'T HIDDEN—
ACK!
DOMP
You all right ...?
...
THUNK
THUNK
DON'T JUST LEAVE YOUR LUGGAGE ALL OVER...
Ouch...

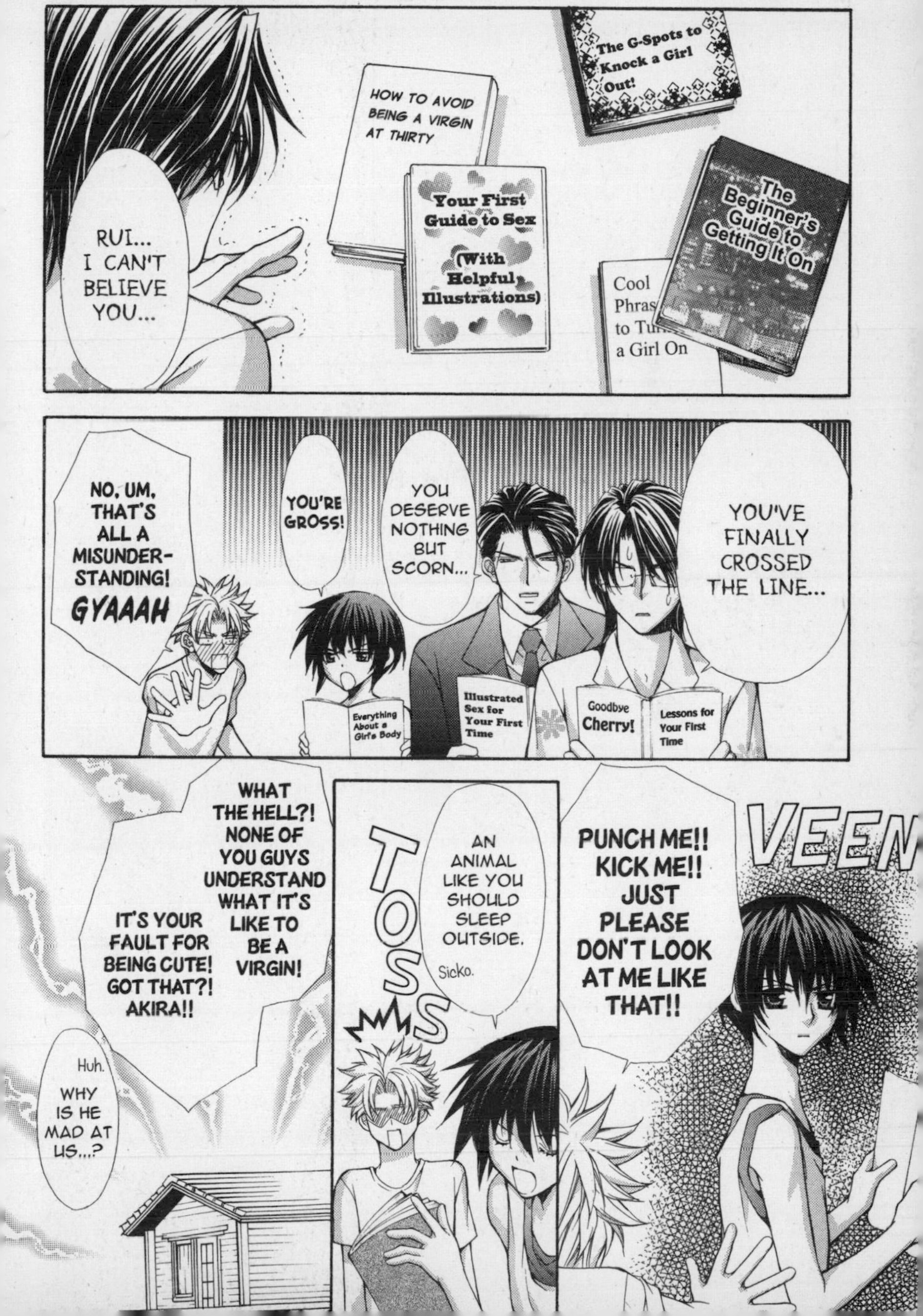
The G-Spots to Knock a Girl Out!
The Beginner's Guide to Getting It On
HOW TO AVOID BEING A VIRGIN AT THIRTY
Your First Guide to Sex (With Helpful Illustrations)
Cool Phras to Tur a Girl On
RUI... I CAN'T BELIEVE YOU...
YOU'VE FINALLY CROSSED THE LINE...
Goodbye Cherry!
Lessons for Your First Time
YOU DESERVE NOTHING BUT SCORN...
Illustrated Sex for Your First Time
YOU'RE GROSS!
Everything About a Girl's Body
NO, UM, THAT'S ALL A MISUNDER-STANDING!
GYAAAH
VEEN
PUNCH ME!! KICK ME!! JUST PLEASE DON'T LOOK AT ME LIKE THAT!!
TOSS
AN ANIMAL LIKE YOU SHOULD SLEEP OUTSIDE.
Sicko.
WHAT THE HELL?! NONE OF YOU GUYS UNDERSTAND WHAT IT'S LIKE TO BE A VIRGIN!
IT'S YOUR FAULT FOR BEING CUTE! GOT THAT?! AKIRA!!
Huh.
WHY IS HE MAD AT US...?

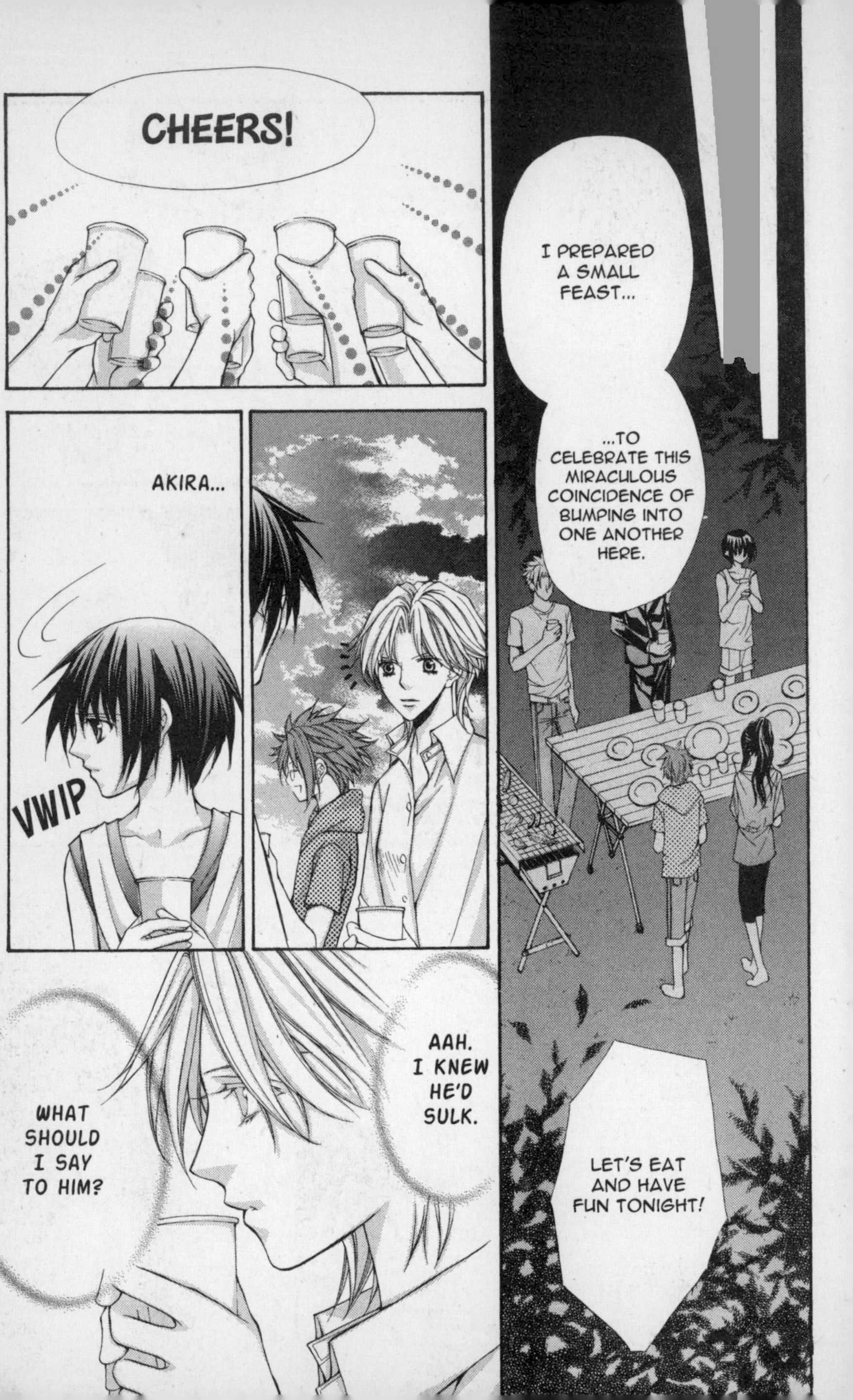
I PREPARED A SMALL FEAST...
...TO CELEBRATE THIS MIRACULOUS COINCIDENCE OF BUMPING INTO ONE ANOTHER HERE.
LET'S EAT AND HAVE FUN TONIGHT!
CHEERS!
AKIRA...
VWIP
AAH. I KNEW HE'D SULK.
WHAT SHOULD I SAY TO HIM?

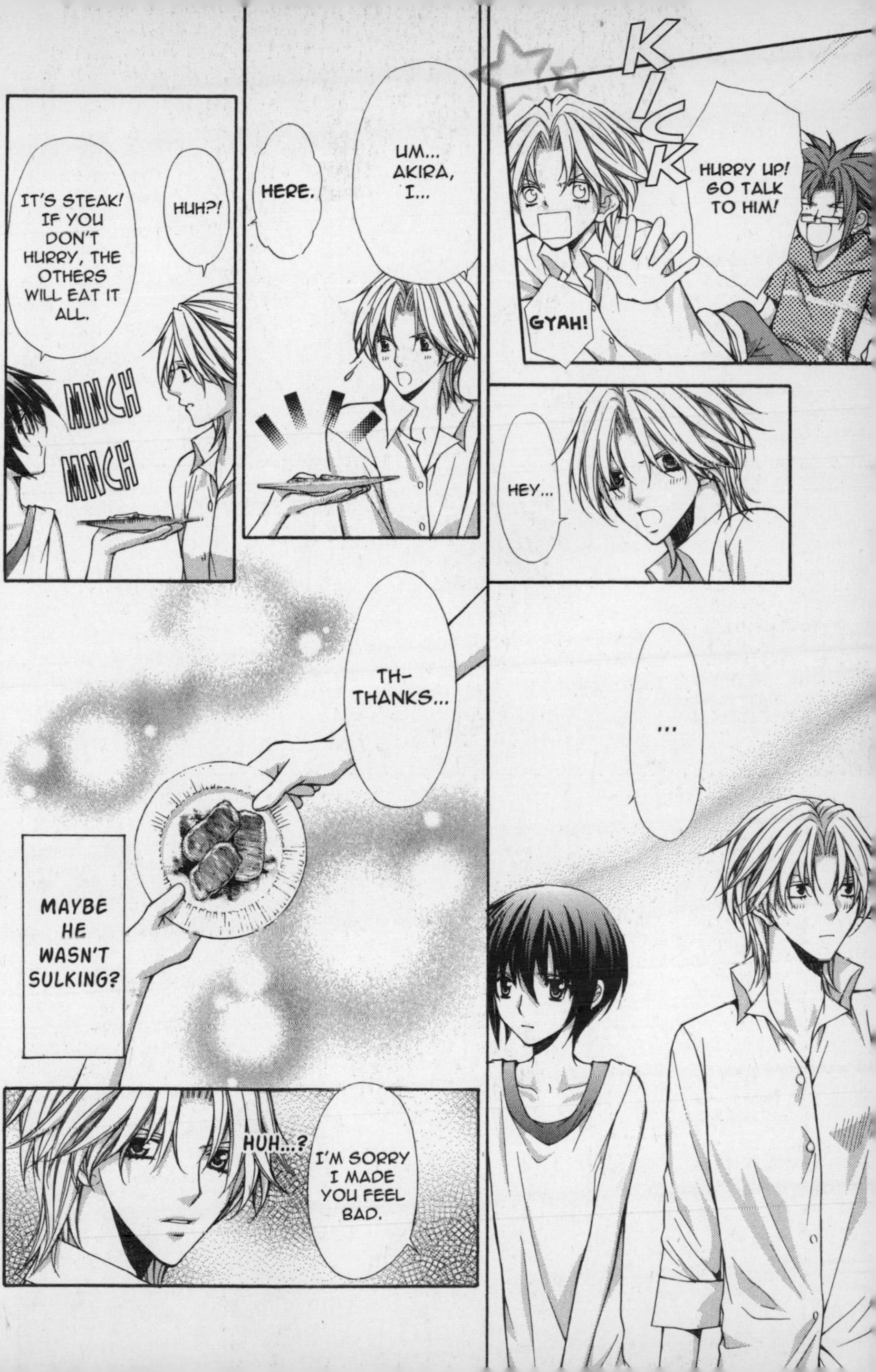
HURRY UP! GO TALK TO HIM!
KICK
GYAH!
HEY...
...
UM... AKIRA, I...
HERE.
HUH?!
IT'S STEAK! IF YOU DON'T HURRY, THE OTHERS WILL EAT IT ALL.
MNCH
MNCH
TH-THANKS...
MAYBE HE WASN'T SULKING?
I'M SORRY I MADE YOU FEEL BAD.
HUH...?

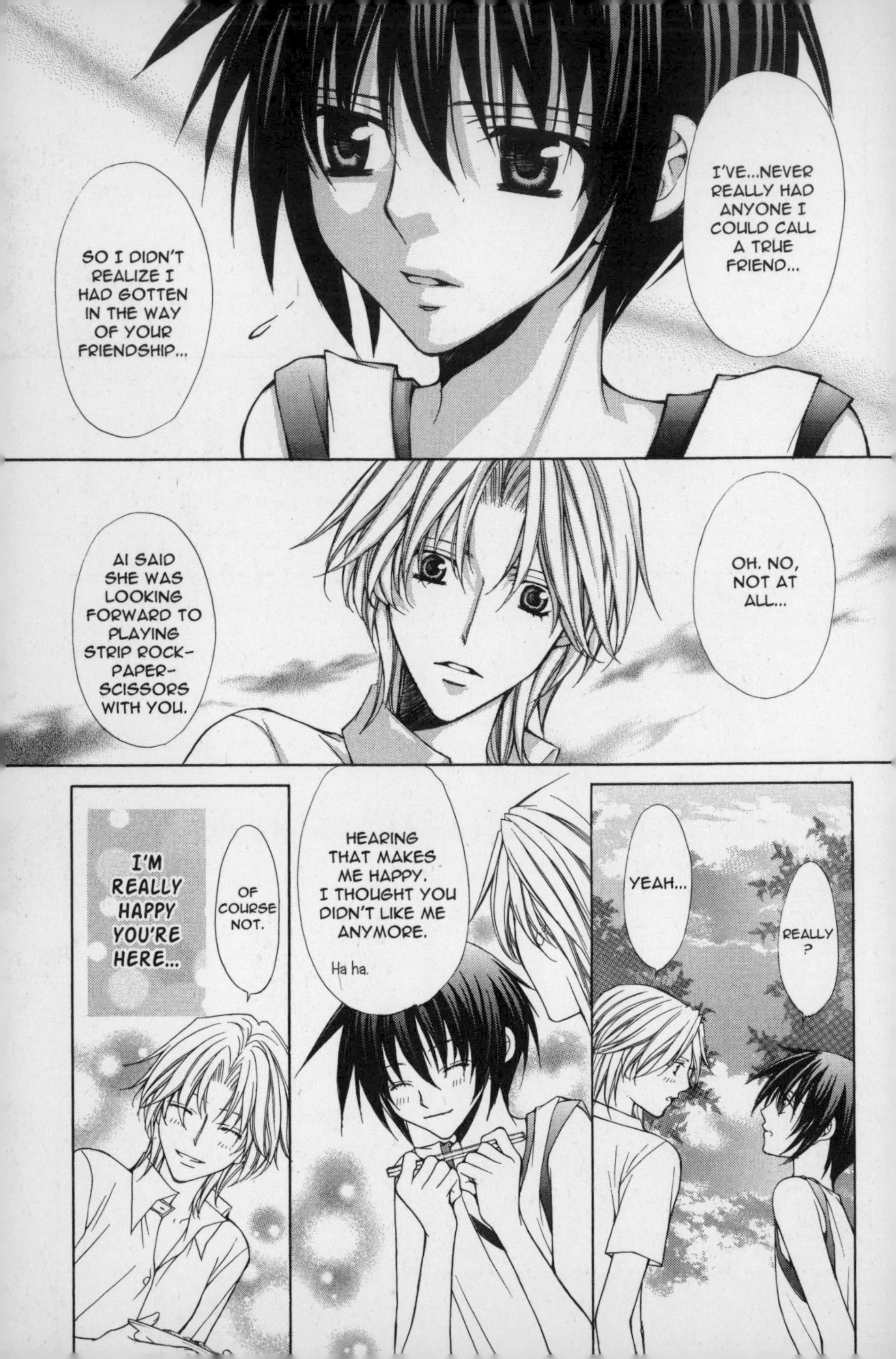
I'VE...NEVER REALLY HAD ANYONE I COULD CALL A TRUE FRIEND...
SO I DIDN'T REALIZE I HAD GOTTEN IN THE WAY OF YOUR FRIENDSHIP...
OH. NO, NOT AT ALL...
AI SAID SHE WAS LOOKING FORWARD TO PLAYING STRIP ROCK-PAPER-SCISSORS WITH YOU.
REALLY?
YEAH...
HEARING THAT MAKES ME HAPPY. I THOUGHT YOU DIDN'T LIKE ME ANYMORE.
Ha ha.
OF COURSE NOT.
I'M REALLY HAPPY YOU'RE HERE...

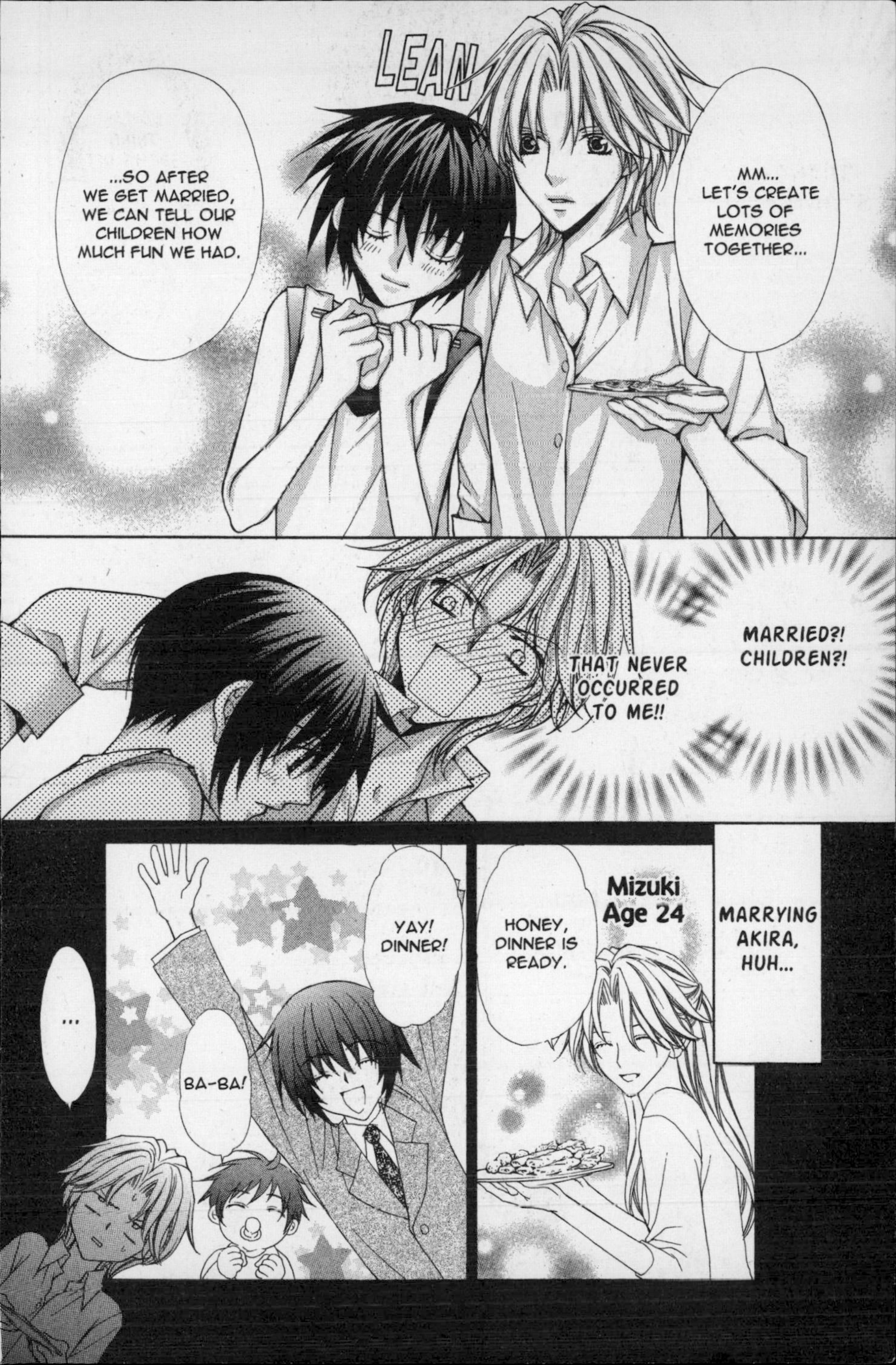
LEAN
MM... LET'S CREATE LOTS OF MEMORIES TOGETHER...
...SO AFTER WE GET MARRIED, WE CAN TELL OUR CHILDREN HOW MUCH FUN WE HAD.
MARRIED?! CHILDREN?!
THAT NEVER OCCURRED TO ME!!
MARRYING AKIRA, HUH...
Mizuki Age 24
HONEY, DINNER IS READY.
YAY! DINNER!
BA-BA!
...

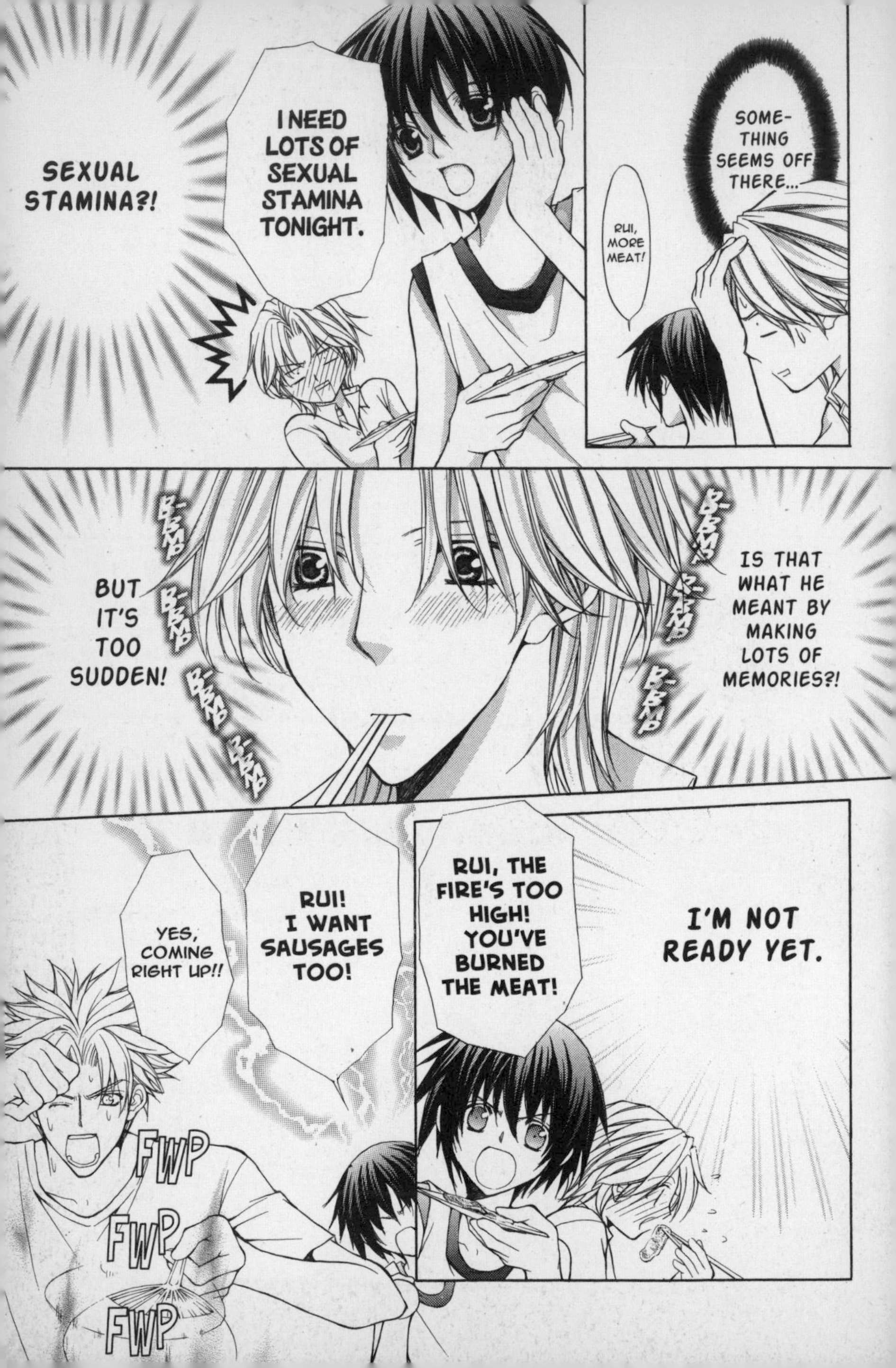
SOME-THING SEEMS OFF THERE...
RUI, MORE MEAT!
I NEED LOTS OF SEXUAL STAMINA TONIGHT.
SEXUAL STAMINA?!
B-BMP B-BMP B-BMP
IS THAT WHAT HE MEANT BY MAKING LOTS OF MEMORIES?!
B-BMP B-BMP B-BMP B-BMP
BUT IT'S TOO SUDDEN!
I'M NOT READY YET.
RUI, THE FIRE'S TOO HIGH! YOU'VE BURNED THE MEAT!
RUI! I WANT SAUSAGES TOO!
YES, COMING RIGHT UP!!
FWP
FWP
FWP

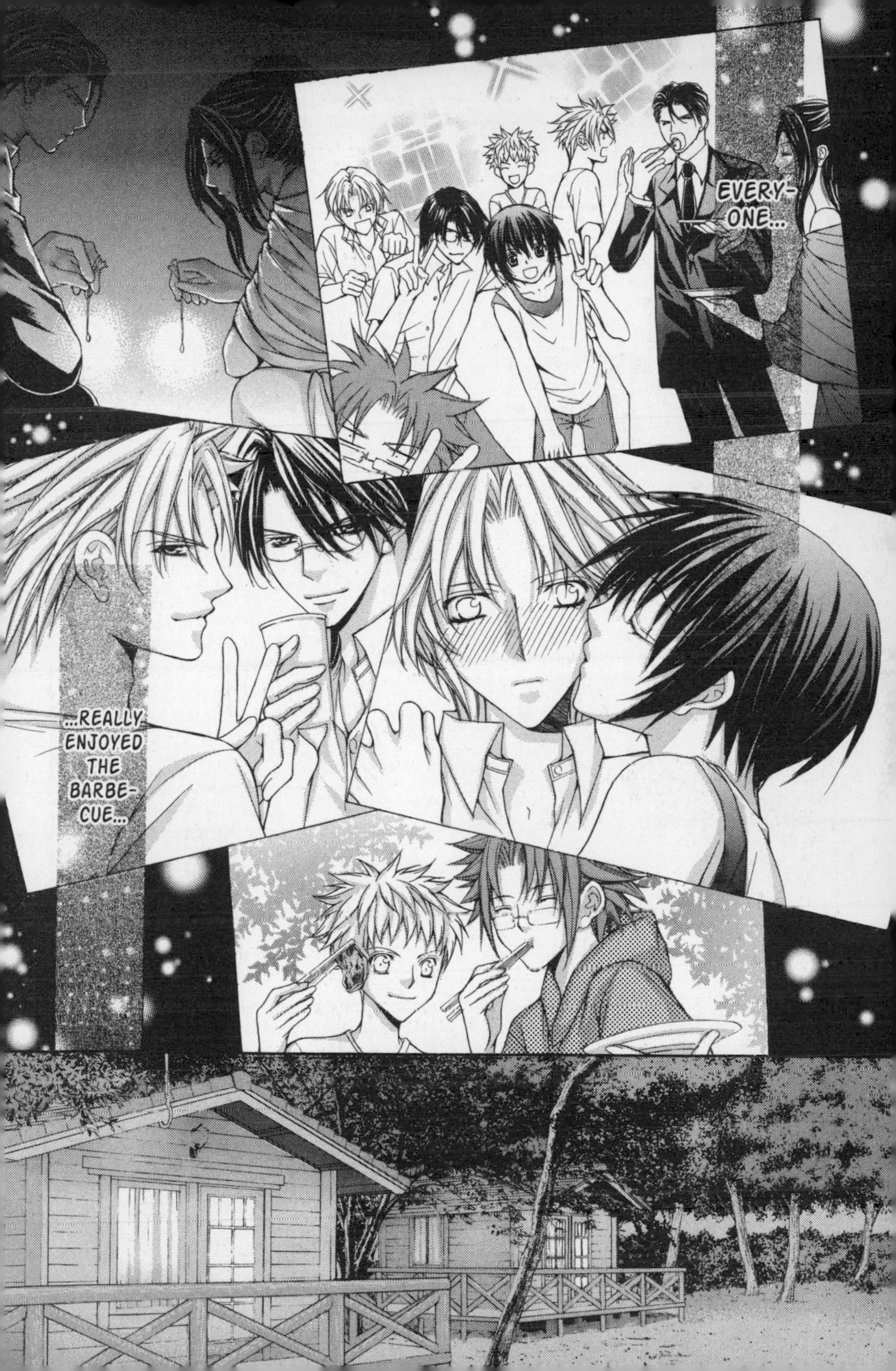
EVERY-ONE...
...REALLY ENJOYED THE BARBE-CUE...

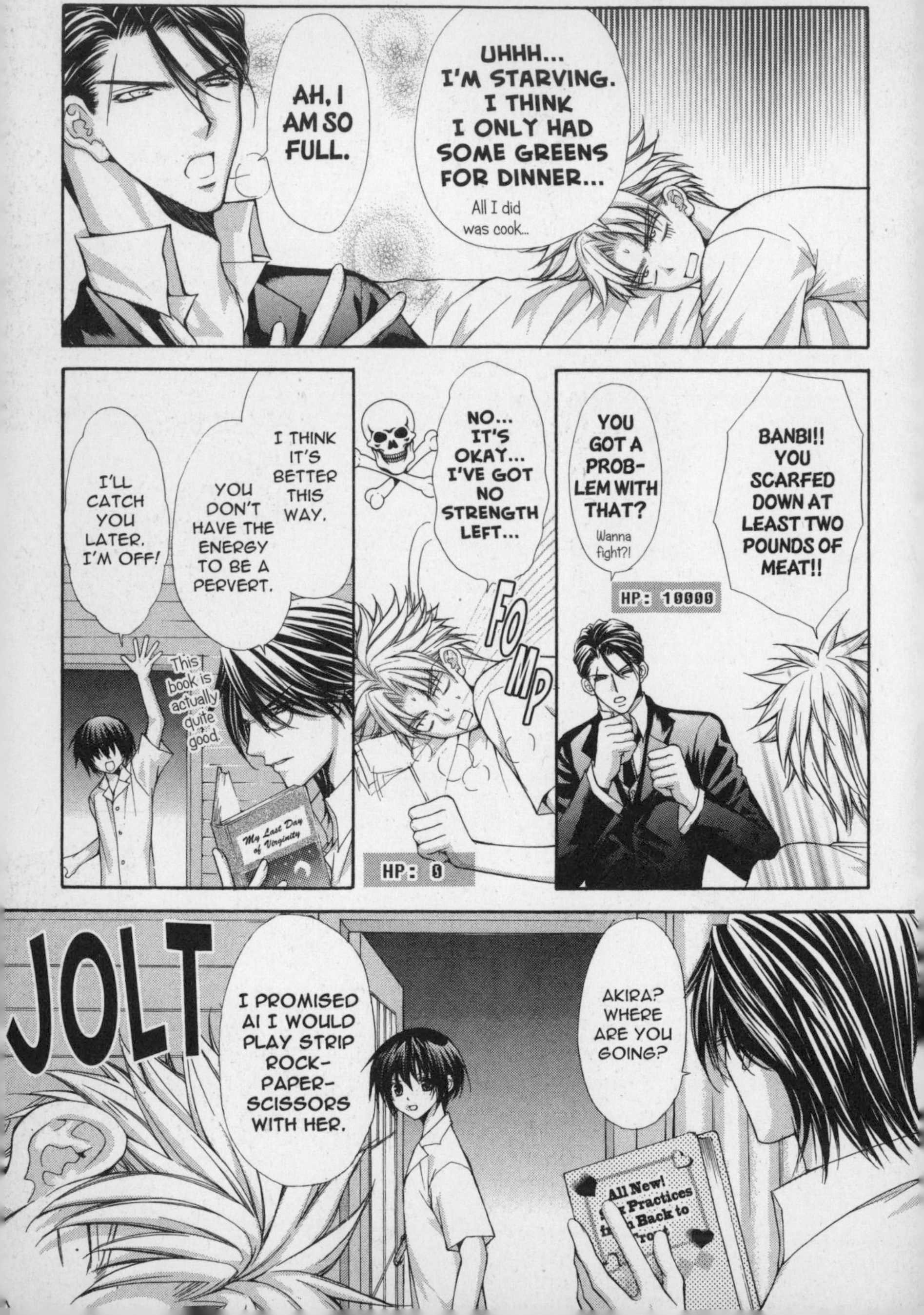
UHHH... I'M STARVING. I THINK I ONLY HAD SOME GREENS FOR DINNER...
All I did was cook...
AH, I AM SO FULL.
BANBI!! YOU SCARFED DOWN AT LEAST TWO POUNDS OF MEAT!!
YOU GOT A PROB-LEM WITH THAT?
Wanna fight?!
HP : 10000
NO... IT'S OKAY... I'VE GOT NO STRENGTH LEFT...
FOMP
HP : 0
I THINK IT'S BETTER THIS WAY.
YOU DON'T HAVE THE ENERGY TO BE A PERVERT.
I'LL CATCH YOU LATER. I'M OFF!
This book is actually quite good.
My Last Day of Virginity
AKIRA? WHERE ARE YOU GOING?
I PROMISED AI I WOULD PLAY STRIP ROCK-PAPER-SCISSORS WITH HER.
JOLT
All New!
Practices
Back to

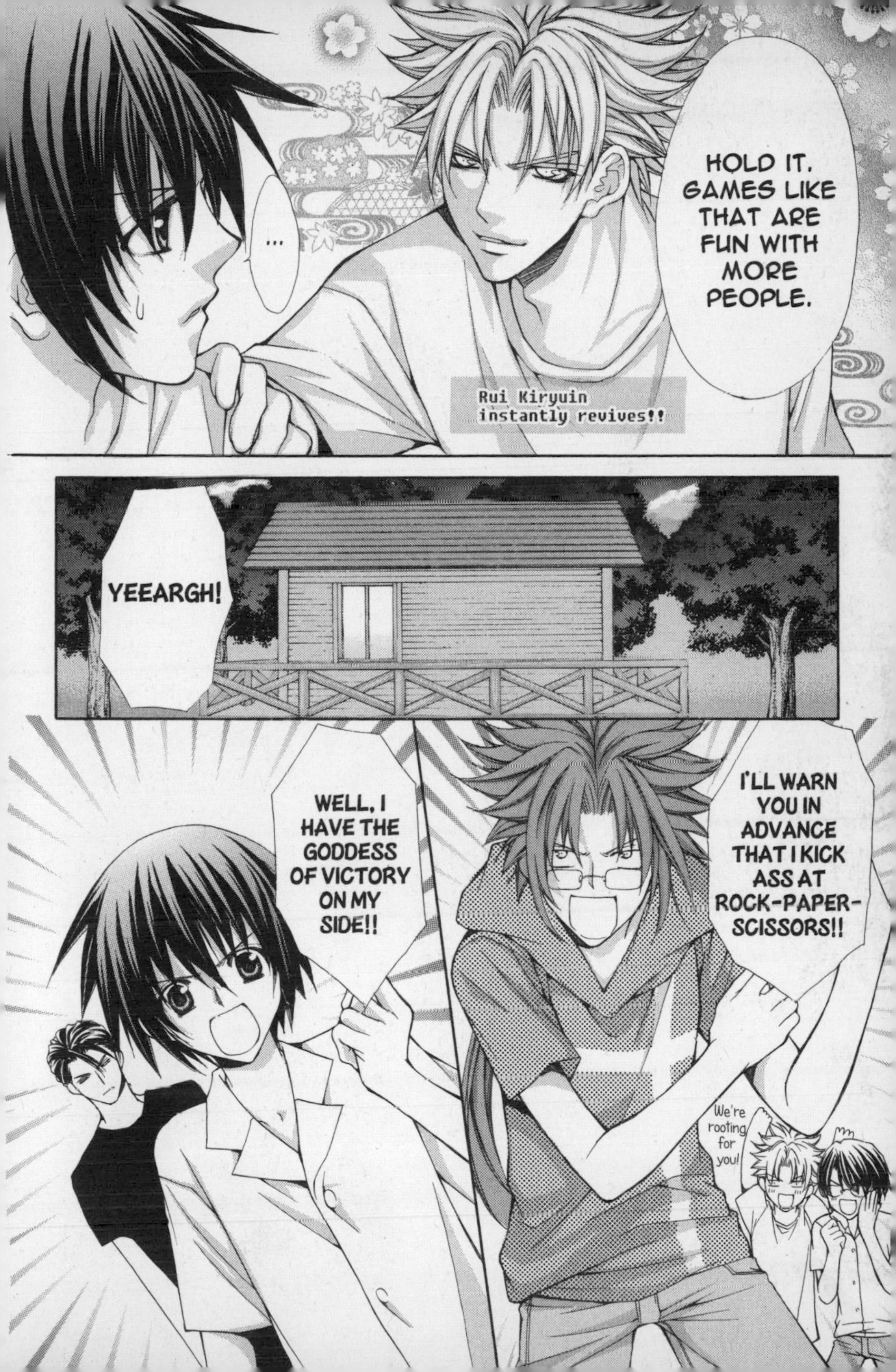
HOLD IT. GAMES LIKE THAT ARE FUN WITH MORE PEOPLE.
...
Rui Kiryuin instantly revives!!
YEEARGH!
I'LL WARN YOU IN ADVANCE THAT I KICK ASS AT ROCK-PAPER-SCISSORS!!
We're rooting for you!
WELL, I HAVE THE GODDESS OF VICTORY ON MY SIDE!!

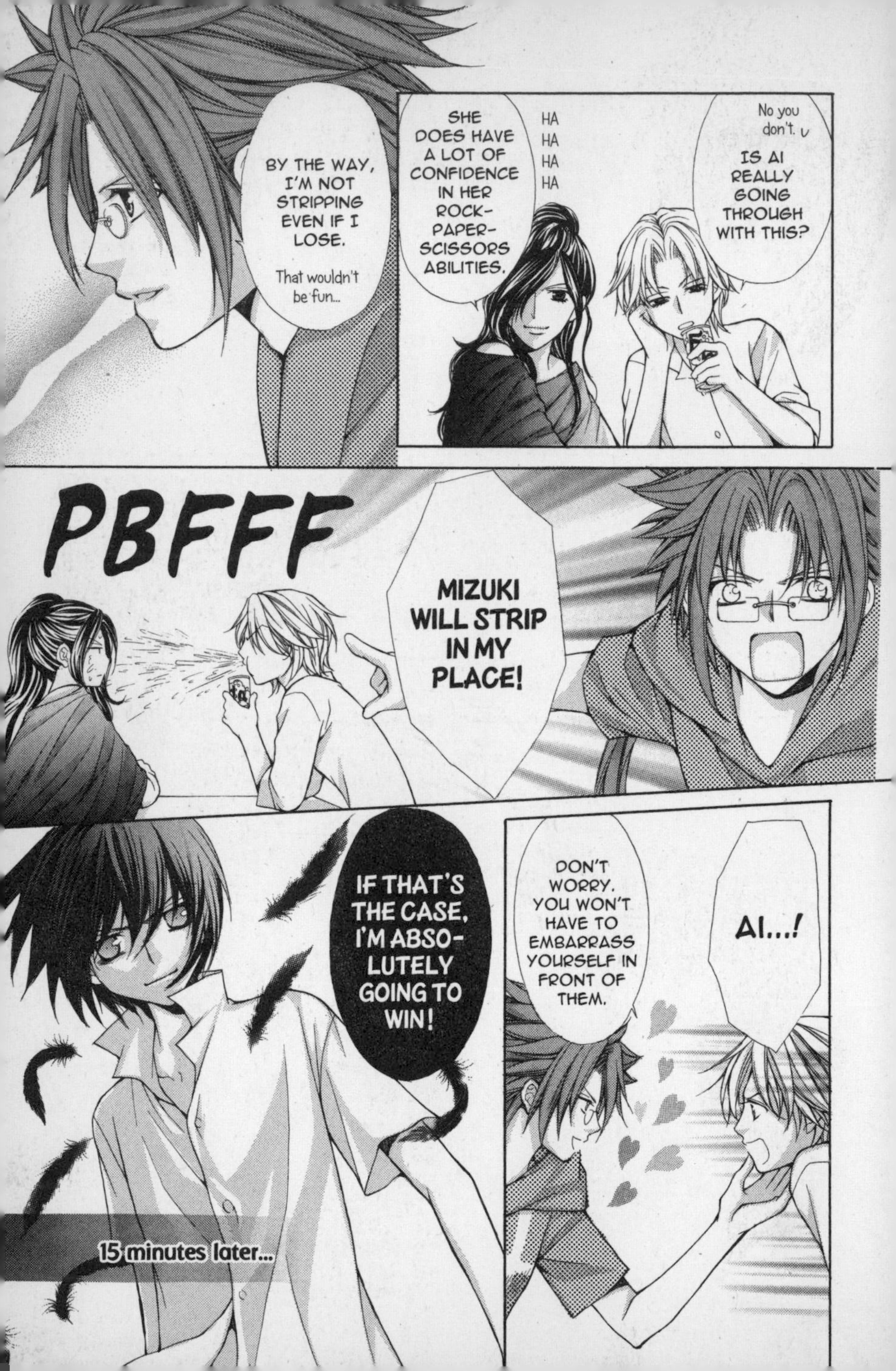
No you don't.
IS AI REALLY GOING THROUGH WITH THIS?
HA HA HA HA
SHE DOES HAVE A LOT OF CONFIDENCE IN HER ROCK-PAPER-SCISSORS ABILITIES.
BY THE WAY, I'M NOT STRIPPING EVEN IF I LOSE.
That wouldn't be fun...
MIZUKI WILL STRIP IN MY PLACE!
PBFFF
AI...!
DON'T WORRY. YOU WON'T HAVE TO EMBARRASS YOURSELF IN FRONT OF THEM.
IF THAT'S THE CASE, I'M ABSO-LUTELY GOING TO WIN!
15 minutes later...

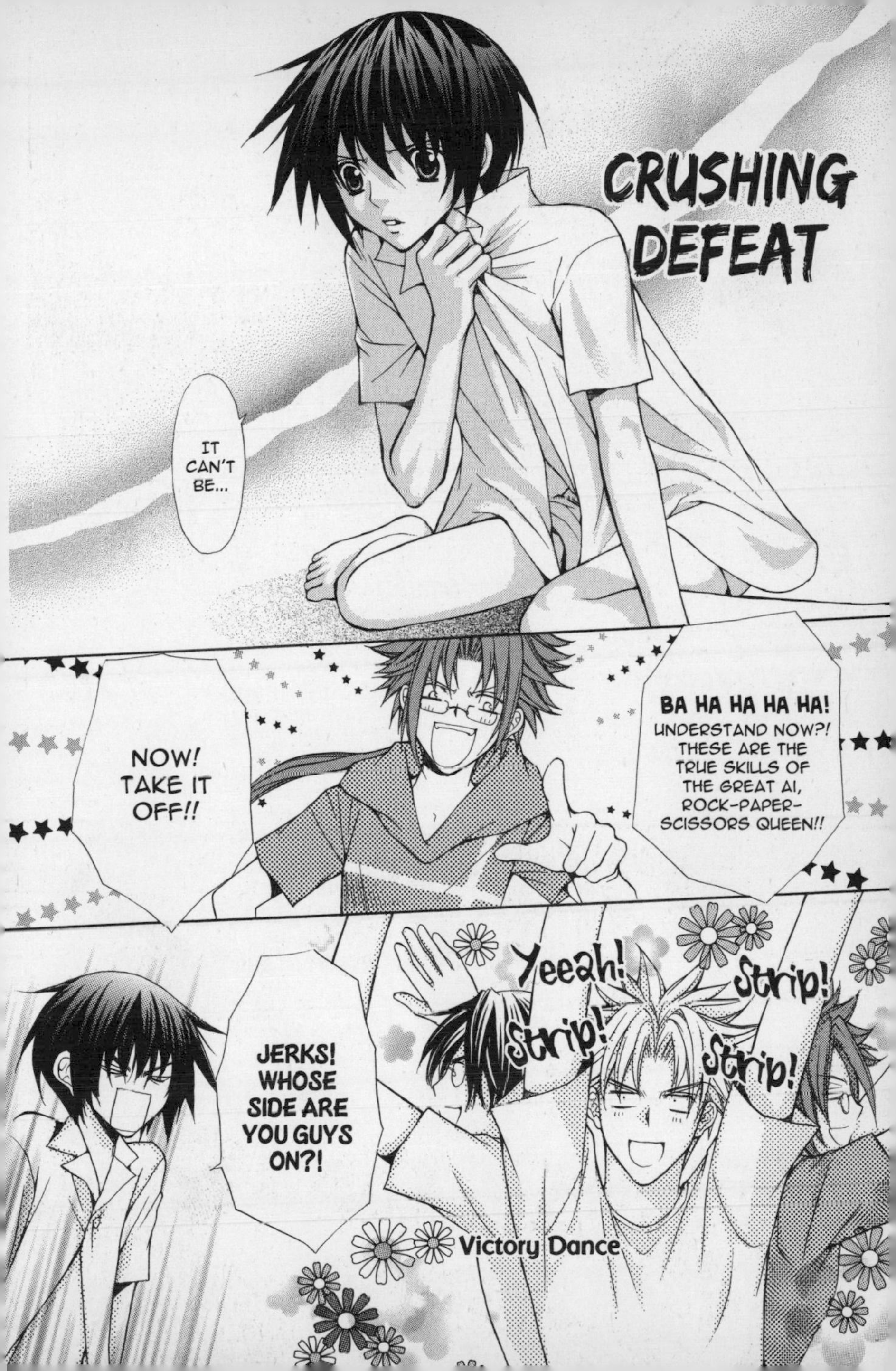
CRUSHING DEFEAT
IT CAN'T BE...
BA HA HA HA HA! UNDERSTAND NOW?! THESE ARE THE TRUE SKILLS OF THE GREAT AI, ROCK-PAPER-SCISSORS QUEEN!!
NOW! TAKE IT OFF!!
Strip!
Yeeah!
Strip!
Strip!
JERKS! WHOSE SIDE ARE YOU GUYS ON?!
Victory Dance

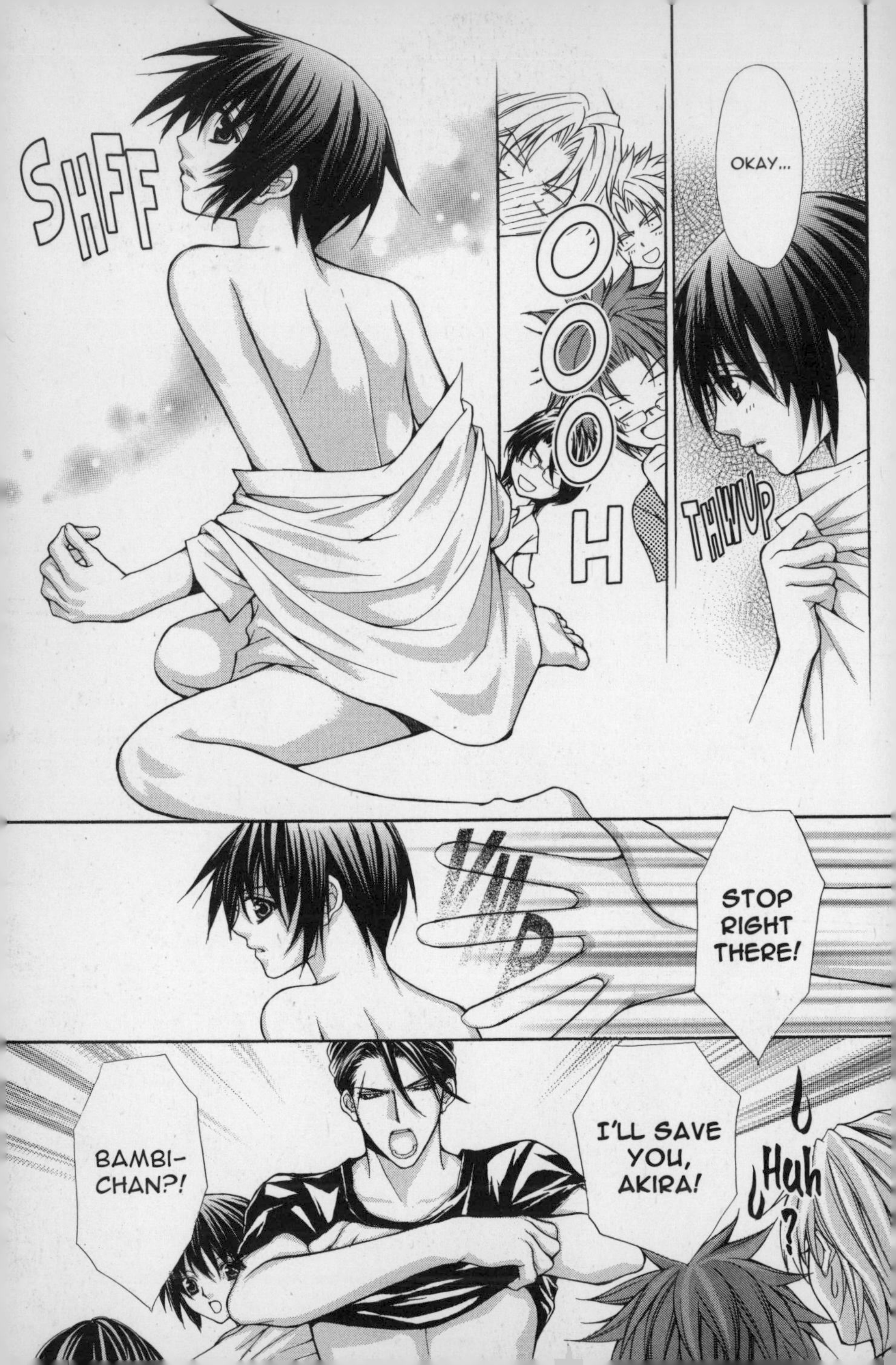
OKAY...
THWUP
OOOOH
SHFF
WHIP
STOP RIGHT THERE!
Huh?
I'LL SAVE YOU, AKIRA!
BAMBI-CHAN?!

Bambi-
chan...

SATIS-
FIED?

WHOOOO

Maybe I
shouldn't
look...?

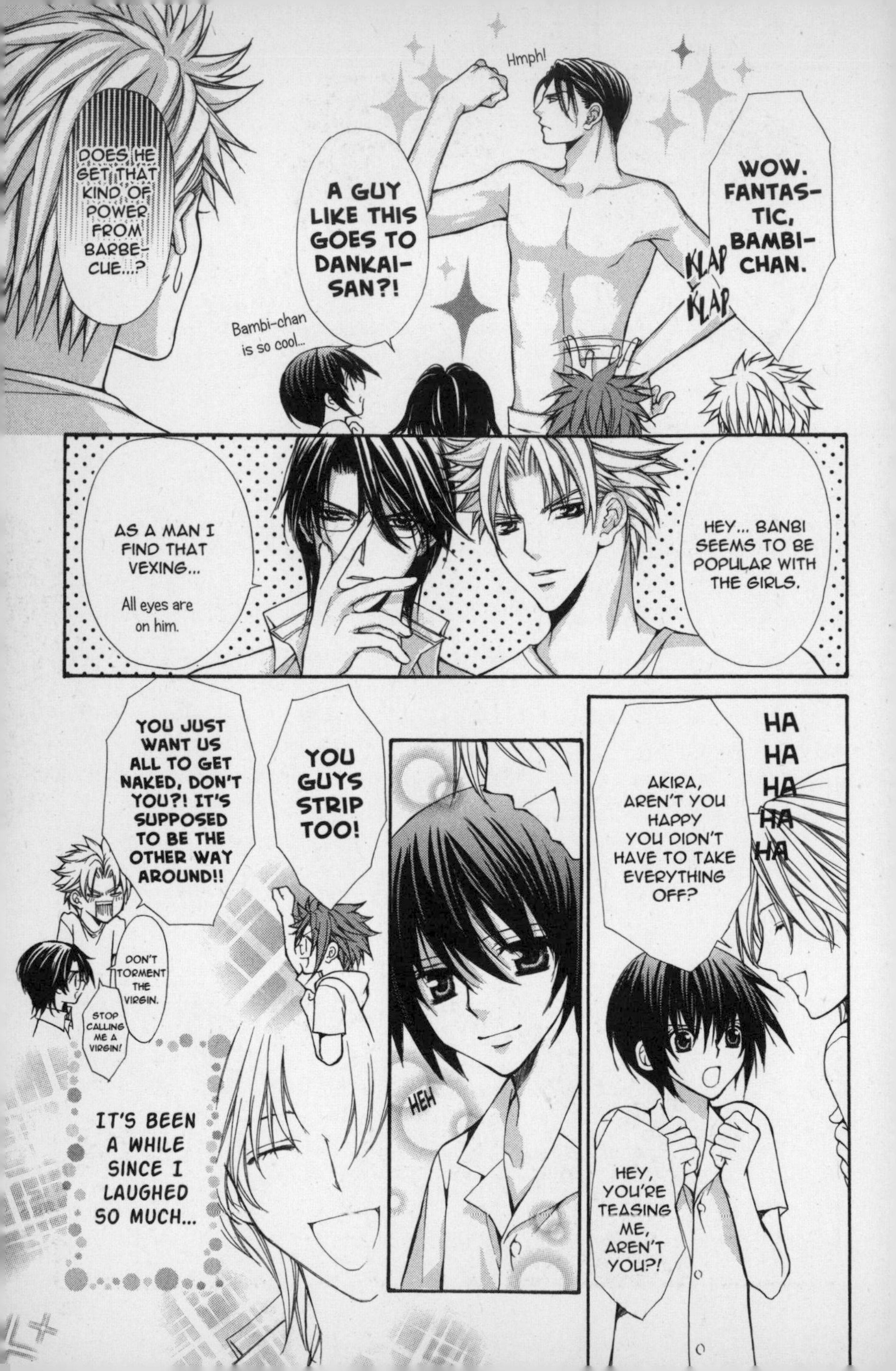
WOW. FANTASTIC, BAMBI-CHAN.
KLAP KLAP
Hmph!
A GUY LIKE THIS GOES TO DANKAI-SAN?!
Bambi-chan is so cool...
DOES HE GET THAT KIND OF POWER FROM BARBECUE...?
HEY... BANBI SEEMS TO BE POPULAR WITH THE GIRLS.
AS A MAN I FIND THAT VEXING...
All eyes are on him.
HA HA HA HA HA
AKIRA, AREN'T YOU HAPPY YOU DIDN'T HAVE TO TAKE EVERYTHING OFF?
HEY, YOU'RE TEASING ME, AREN'T YOU?!
HEH
YOU GUYS STRIP TOO!
YOU JUST WANT US ALL TO GET NAKED, DON'T YOU?! IT'S SUPPOSED TO BE THE OTHER WAY AROUND!!
DON'T TORMENT THE VIRGIN.
STOP CALLING ME A VIRGIN!
IT'S BEEN A WHILE SINCE I LAUGHED SO MUCH...

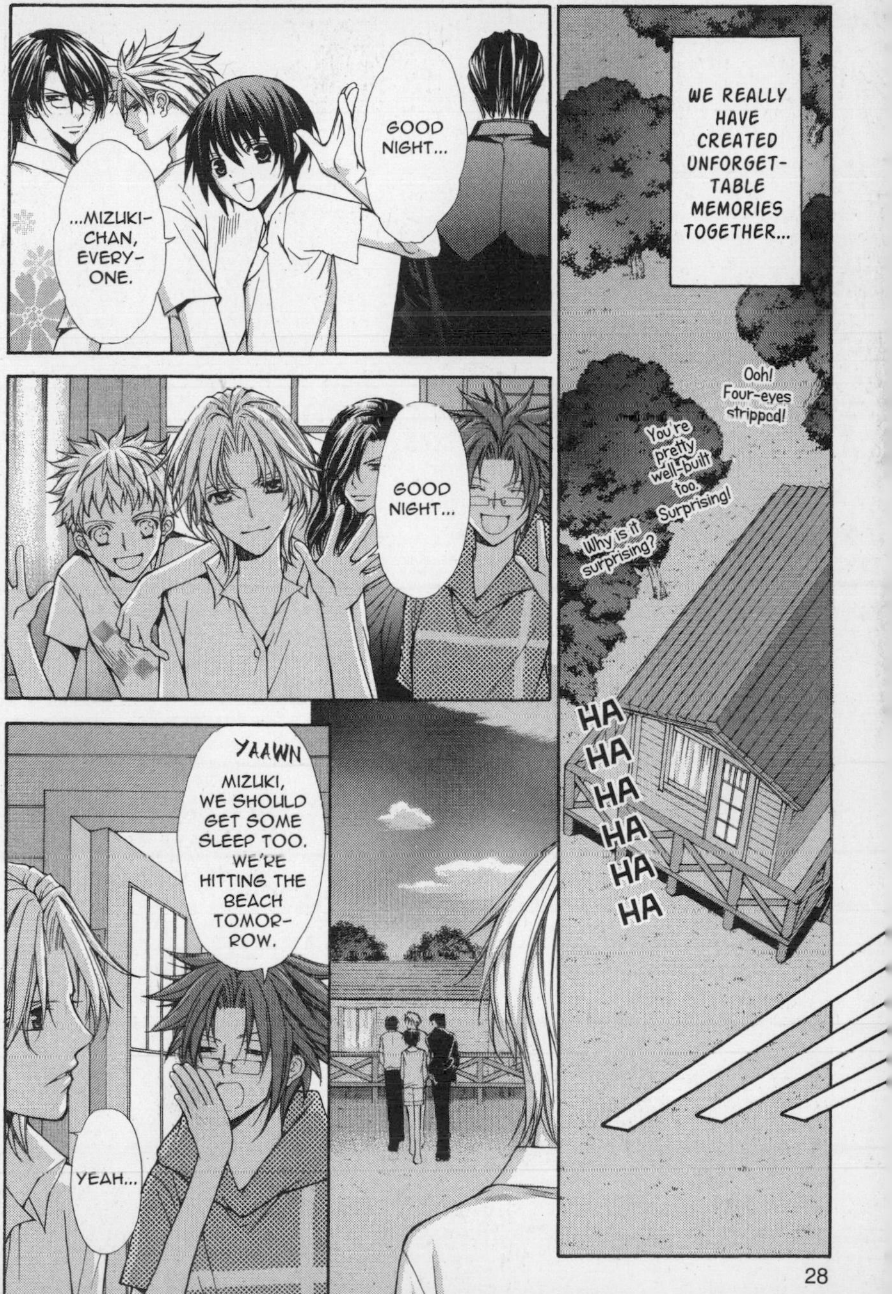
WE REALLY HAVE CREATED UNFORGET-TABLE MEMORIES TOGETHER...
Ooh! Four-eyes stripped!
You're pretty well-built too. Surprising!
Why is it surprising?
HA HA HA HA HA HA
GOOD NIGHT...
...MIZUKI-CHAN, EVERY-ONE.
GOOD NIGHT...
YAAWN
MIZUKI, WE SHOULD GET SOME SLEEP TOO. WE'RE HITTING THE BEACH TOMOR-ROW.
YEAH...

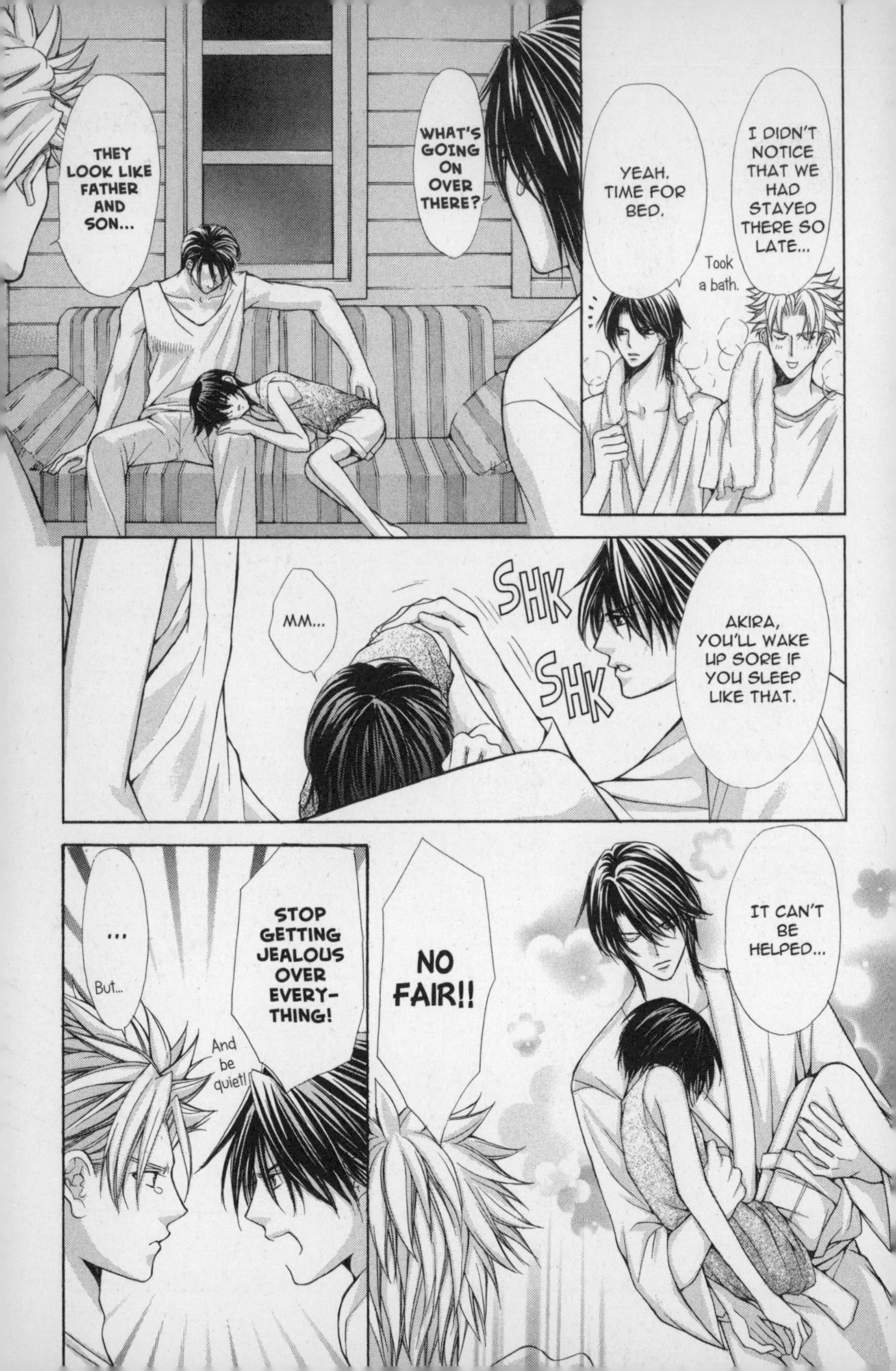
I DIDN'T NOTICE THAT WE HAD STAYED THERE SO LATE...
Took a bath.
YEAH. TIME FOR BED.
WHAT'S GOING ON OVER THERE?
THEY LOOK LIKE FATHER AND SON...
AKIRA, YOU'LL WAKE UP SORE IF YOU SLEEP LIKE THAT.
SHK
SHK
MM...
IT CAN'T BE HELPED...
NO FAIR!!
STOP GETTING JEALOUS OVER EVERY-THING!
And be quiet!
...
But...

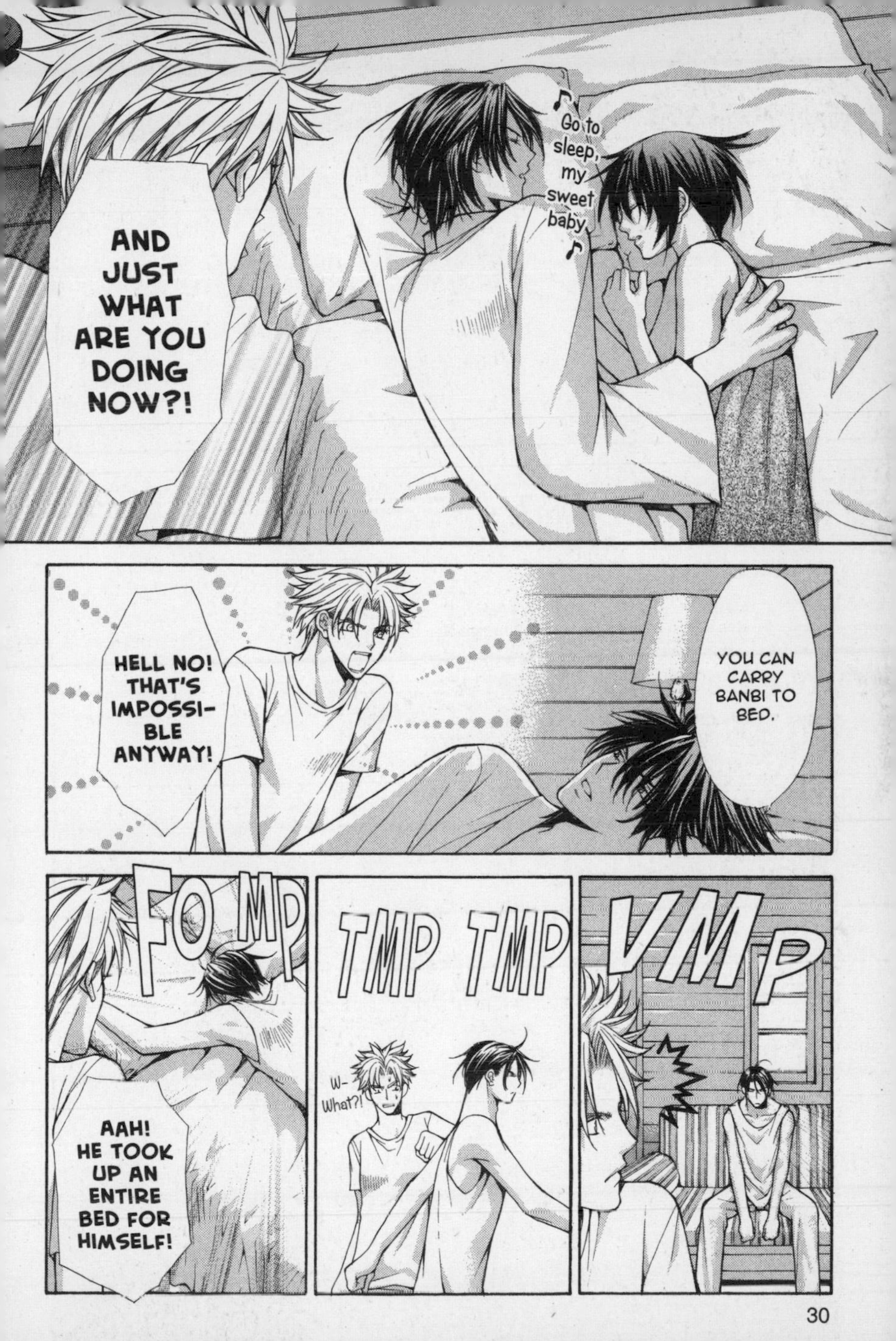
Go to sleep, my sweet baby ♪
AND JUST WHAT ARE YOU DOING NOW?!
YOU CAN CARRY BANBI TO BED.
HELL NO! THAT'S IMPOSSI-BLE ANYWAY!
VMP
TMP TMP
W-What?!
FOMP
AAH! HE TOOK UP AN ENTIRE BED FOR HIMSELF!

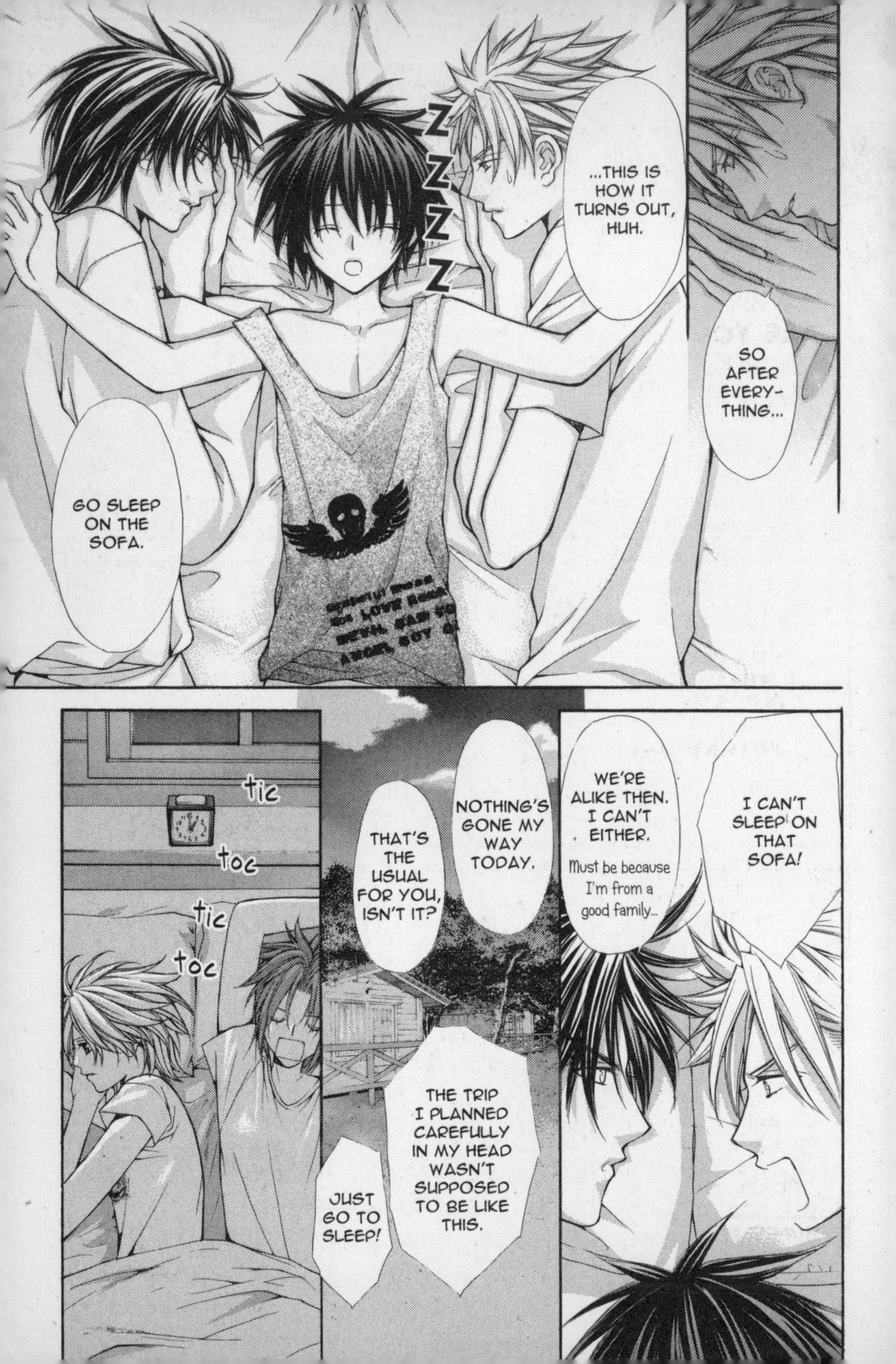
SO AFTER EVERY-THING...
...THIS IS HOW IT TURNS OUT, HUH.
Z Z Z Z
GO SLEEP ON THE SOFA.
I CAN'T SLEEP ON THAT SOFA!
WE'RE ALIKE THEN. I CAN'T EITHER.
Must be because I'm from a good family...
NOTHING'S GONE MY WAY TODAY.
THAT'S THE USUAL FOR YOU, ISN'T IT?
THE TRIP I PLANNED CAREFULLY IN MY HEAD WASN'T SUPPOSED TO BE LIKE THIS.
JUST GO TO SLEEP!
tic
toc
tic
toc

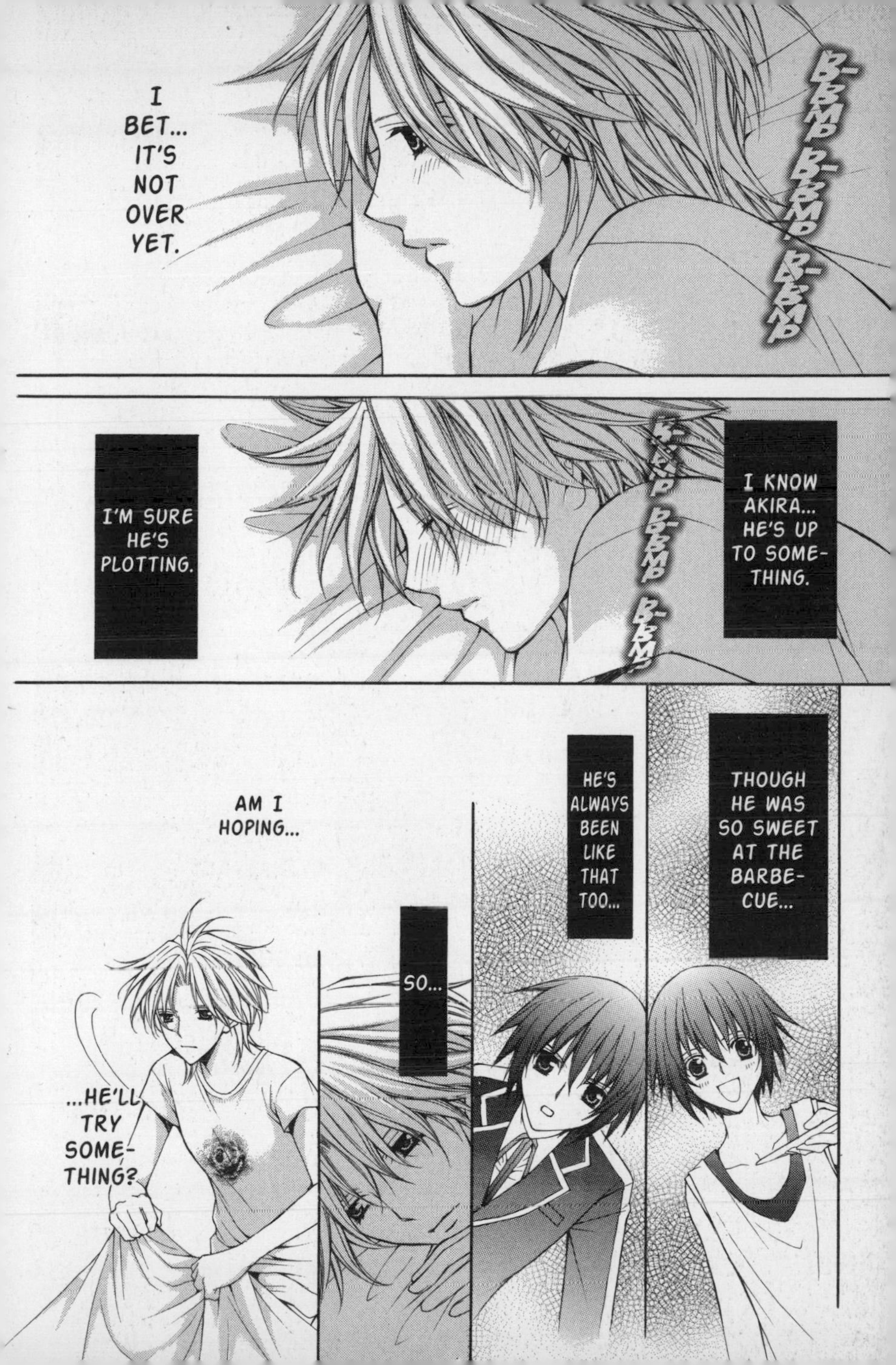

B-BMP B-BMP B-BMP
I BET... IT'S NOT OVER YET.
I KNOW AKIRA... HE'S UP TO SOME-THING.
B-BMP B-BMP
I'M SURE HE'S PLOTTING.
THOUGH HE WAS SO SWEET AT THE BARBE-CUE...
HE'S ALWAYS BEEN LIKE THAT TOO...
SO...
AM I HOPING...
...HE'LL TRY SOME-THING?

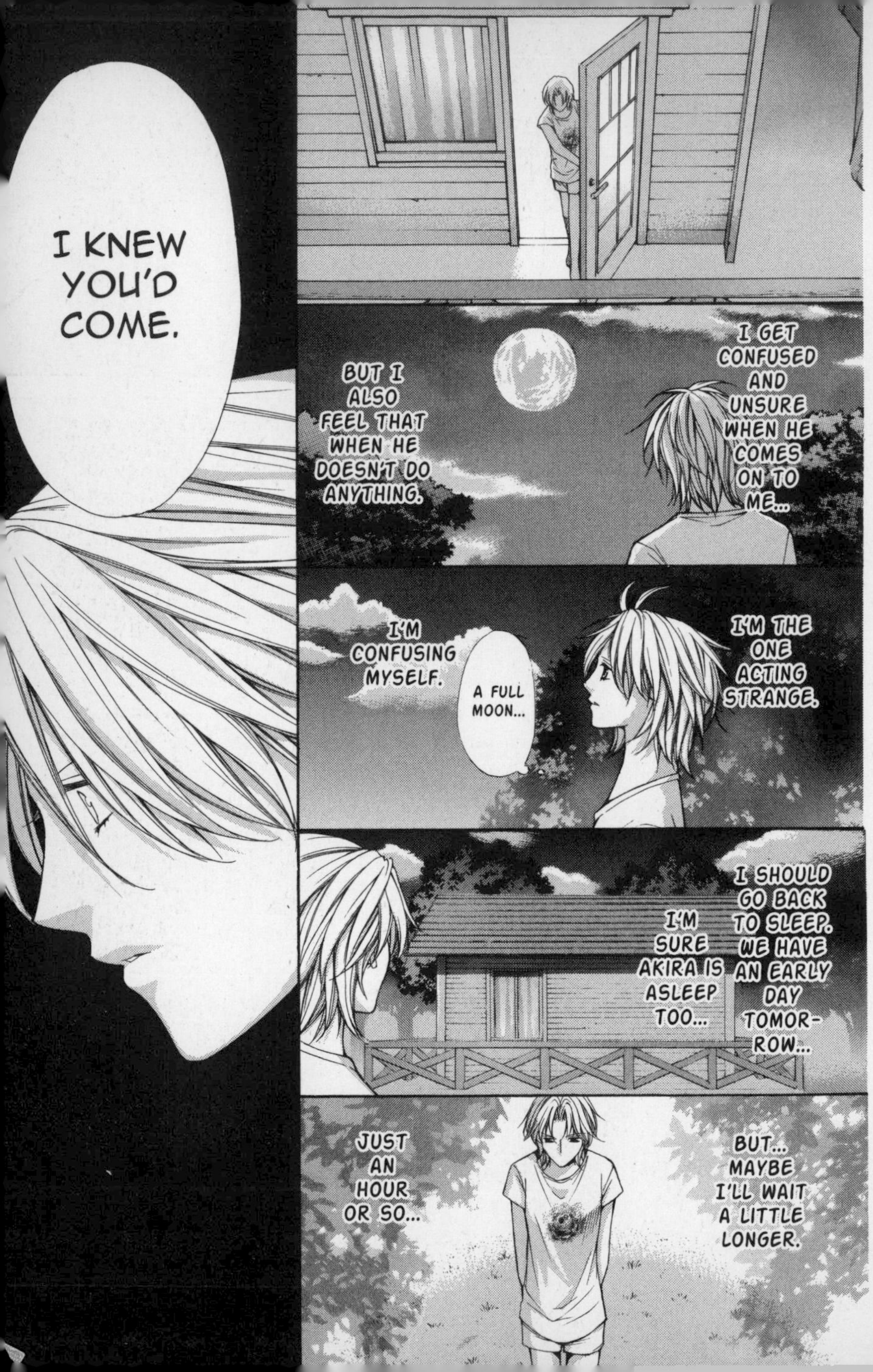
I GET CONFUSED AND UNSURE WHEN HE COMES ON TO ME...
BUT I ALSO FEEL THAT WHEN HE DOESN'T DO ANYTHING.
I'M THE ONE ACTING STRANGE.
I'M CONFUSING MYSELF.
A FULL MOON...
I SHOULD GO BACK TO SLEEP. WE HAVE AN EARLY DAY TOMOR-ROW...
I'M SURE AKIRA IS ASLEEP TOO...
BUT... MAYBE I'LL WAIT A LITTLE LONGER.
JUST AN HOUR OR SO...
I KNEW YOU'D COME.

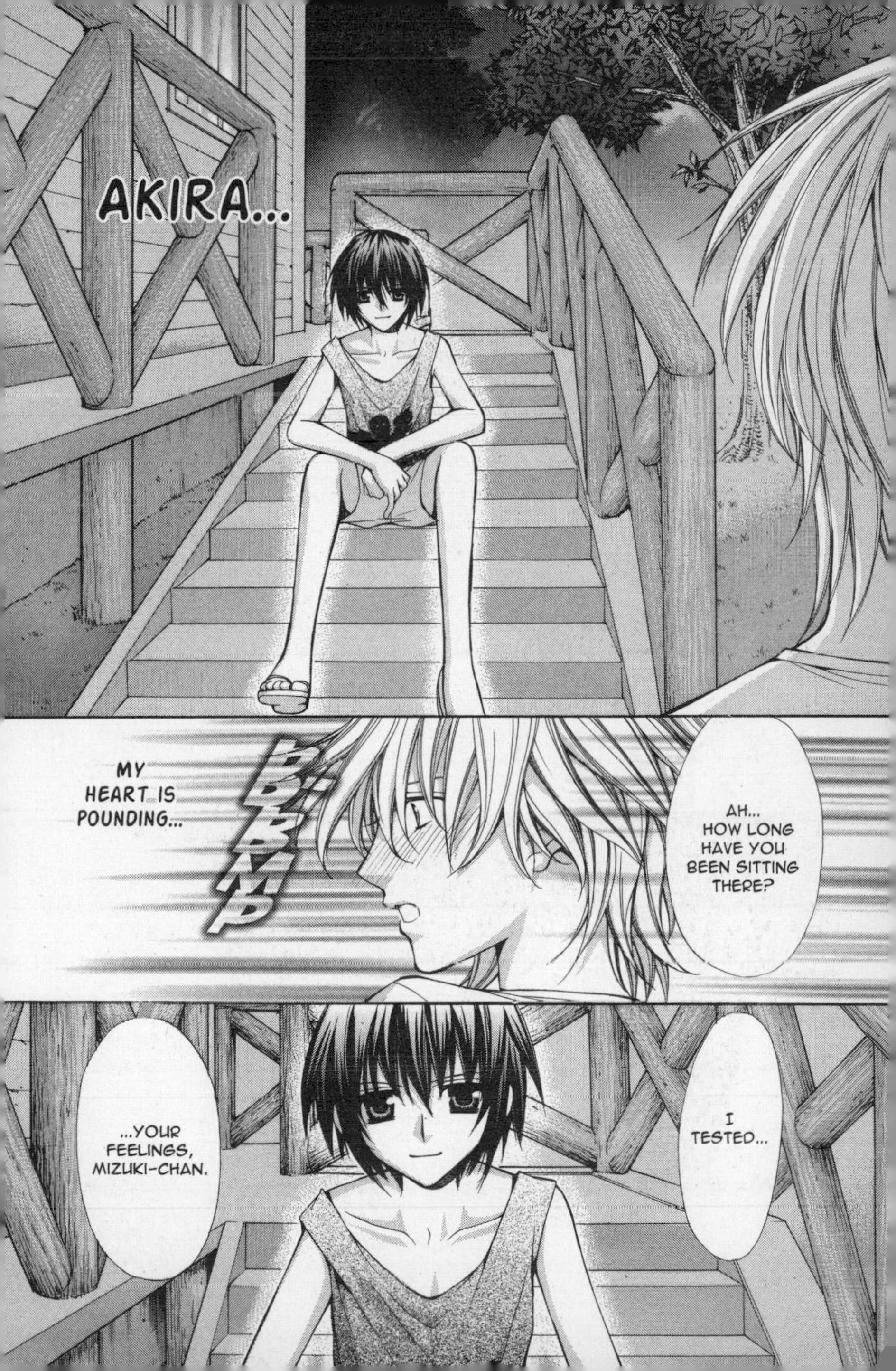
AKIRA...
AH... HOW LONG HAVE YOU BEEN SITTING THERE?
MY HEART IS POUNDING...
I TESTED...
...YOUR FEELINGS, MIZUKI-CHAN.

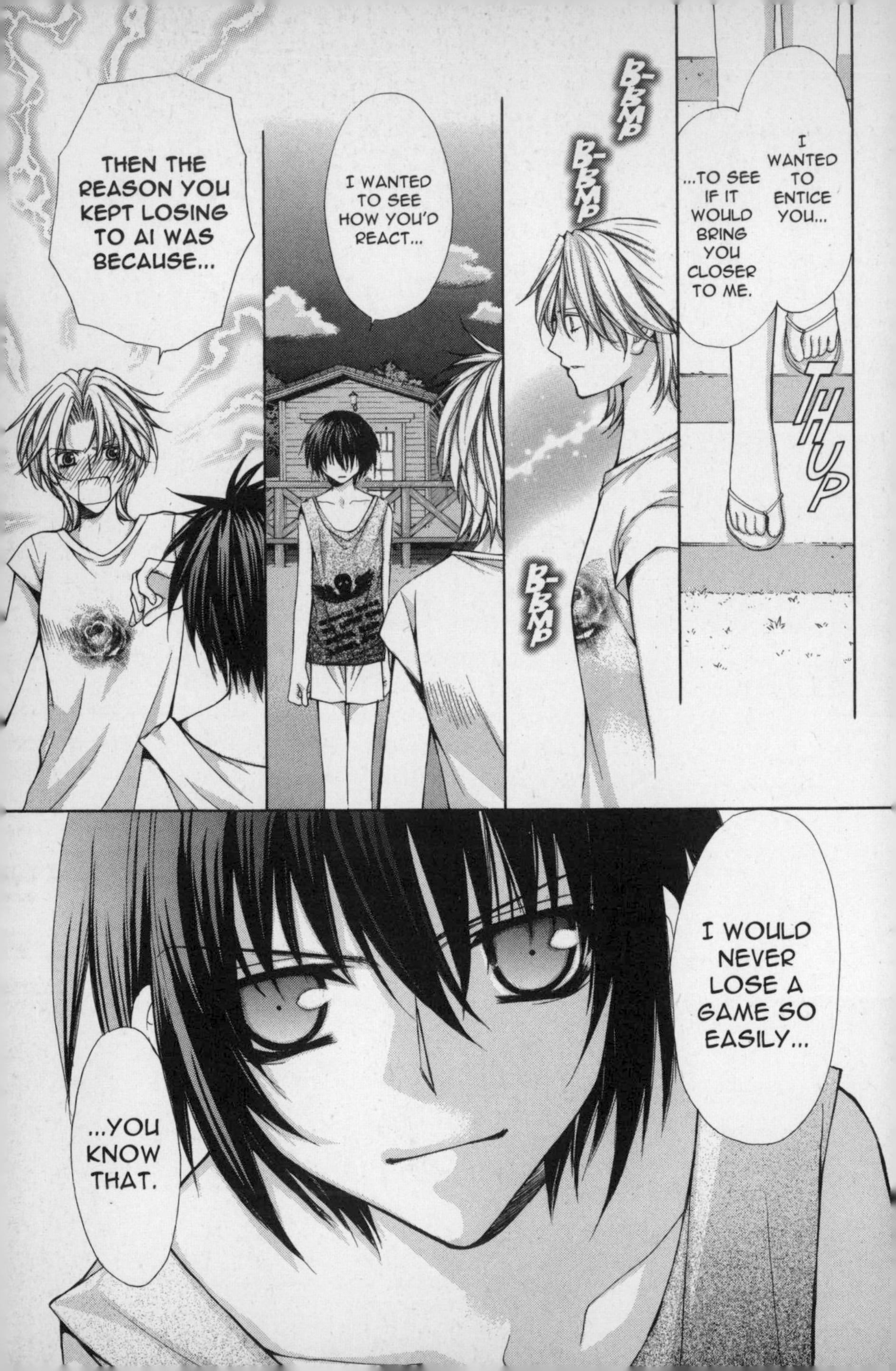
I WANTED TO ENTICE YOU...
...TO SEE IF IT WOULD BRING YOU CLOSER TO ME.
THUP
B-BMP
B-BMP
B-BMP
I WANTED TO SEE HOW YOU'D REACT...
THEN THE REASON YOU KEPT LOSING TO AI WAS BECAUSE...
I WOULD NEVER LOSE A GAME SO EASILY...
...YOU KNOW THAT.

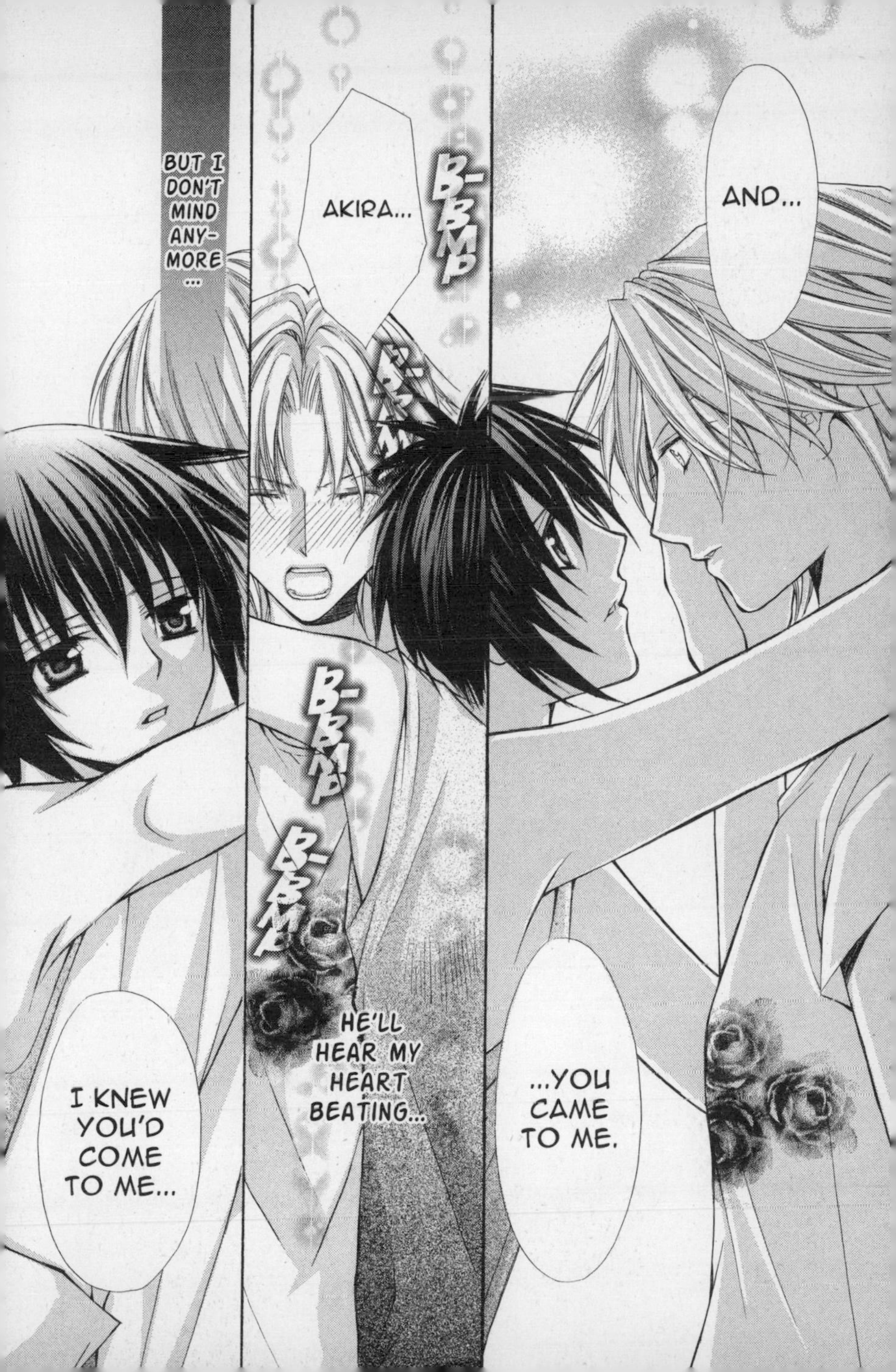
AND...
...YOU CAME TO ME.
AKIRA...
B-BMP
B-BMP
B-BMP
HE'LL HEAR MY HEART BEATING...
BUT I DON'T MIND ANY-MORE...
I KNEW YOU'D COME TO ME...

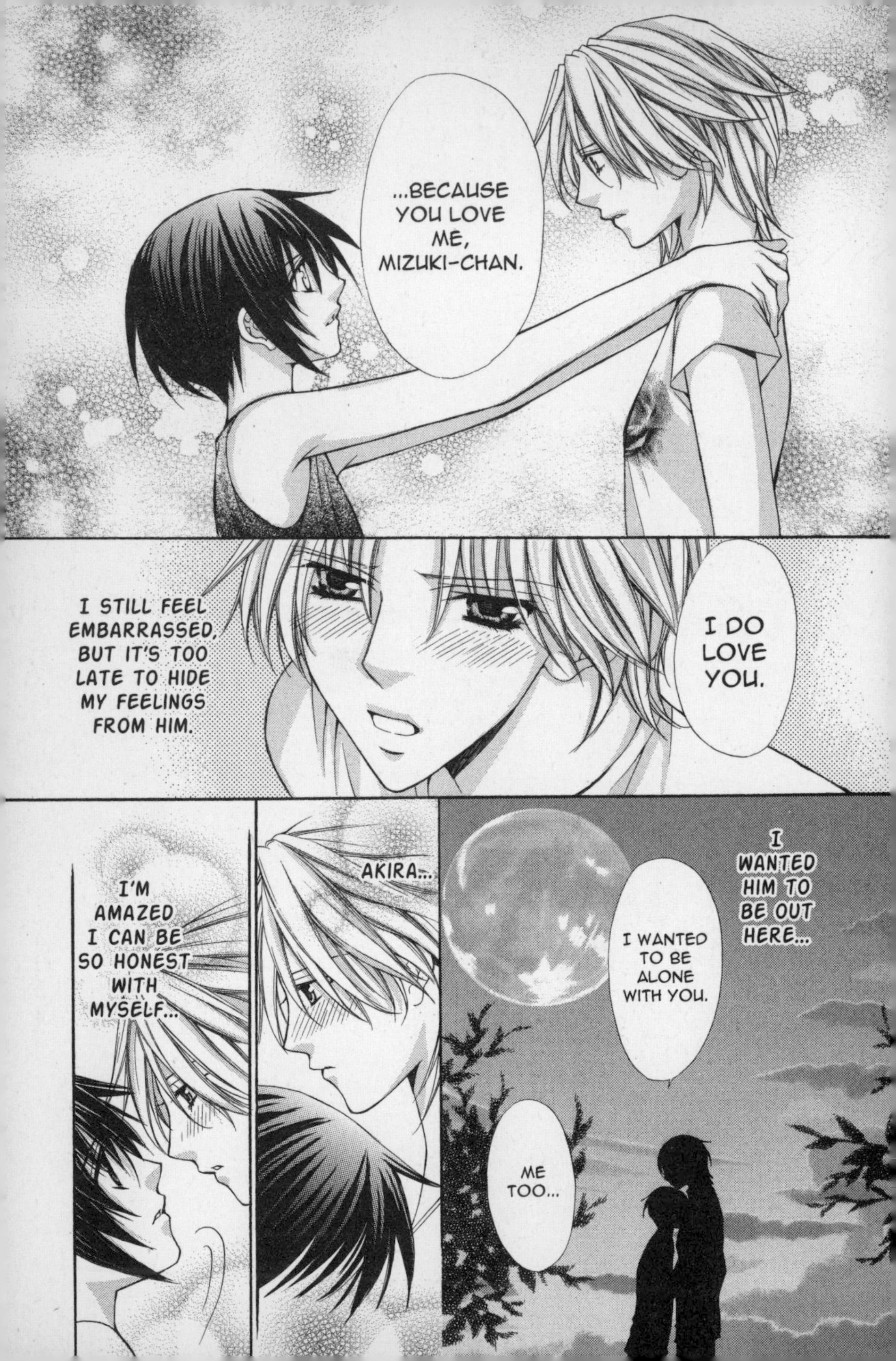
...BECAUSE YOU LOVE ME, MIZUKI-CHAN.
I DO LOVE YOU.
I STILL FEEL EMBARRASSED, BUT IT'S TOO LATE TO HIDE MY FEELINGS FROM HIM.
I WANTED HIM TO BE OUT HERE...
I WANTED TO BE ALONE WITH YOU.
ME TOO...
AKIRA...
I'M AMAZED I CAN BE SO HONEST WITH MYSELF...

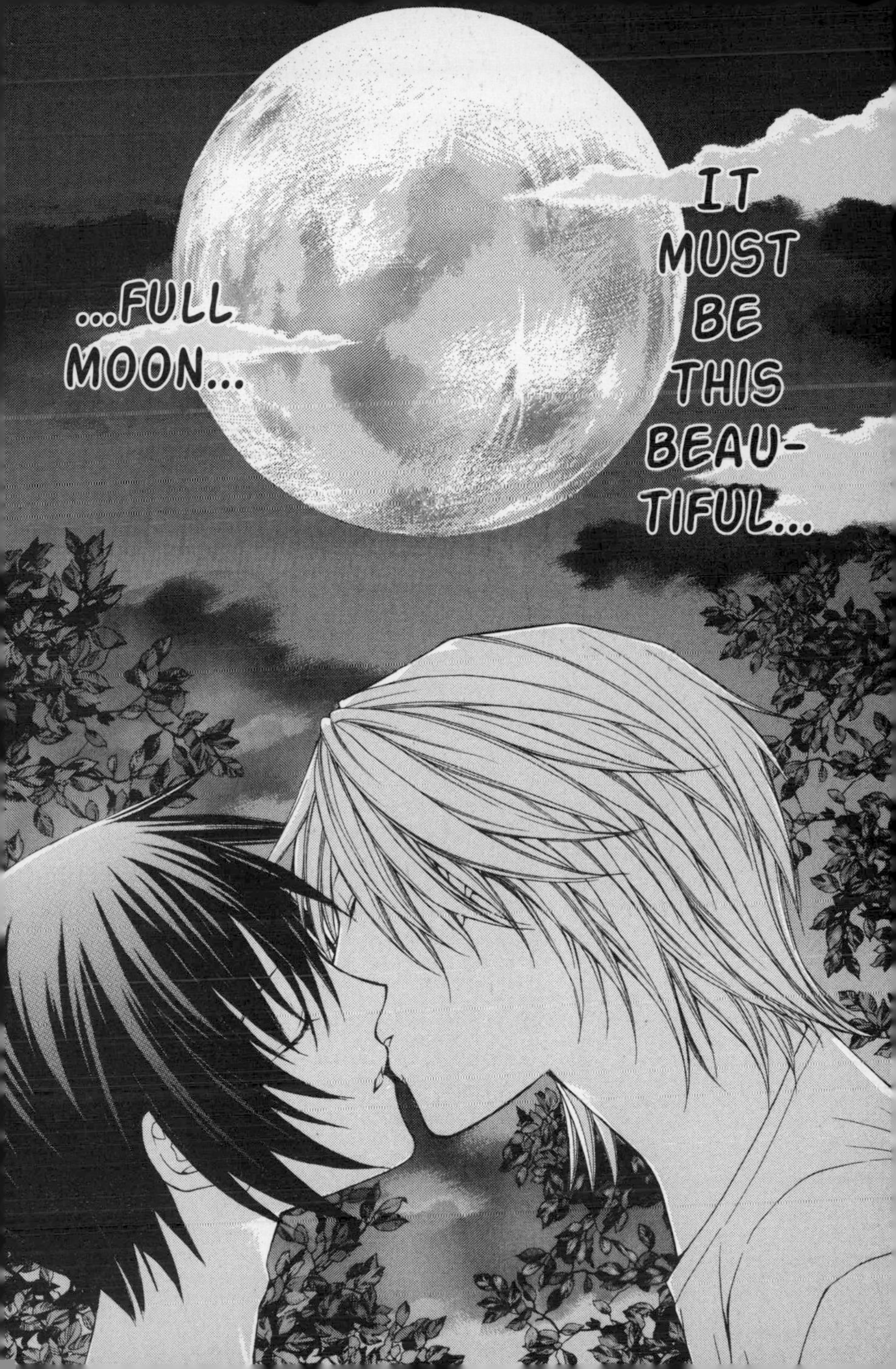
IT MUST BE THIS BEAU-TIFUL...
...FULL MOON...

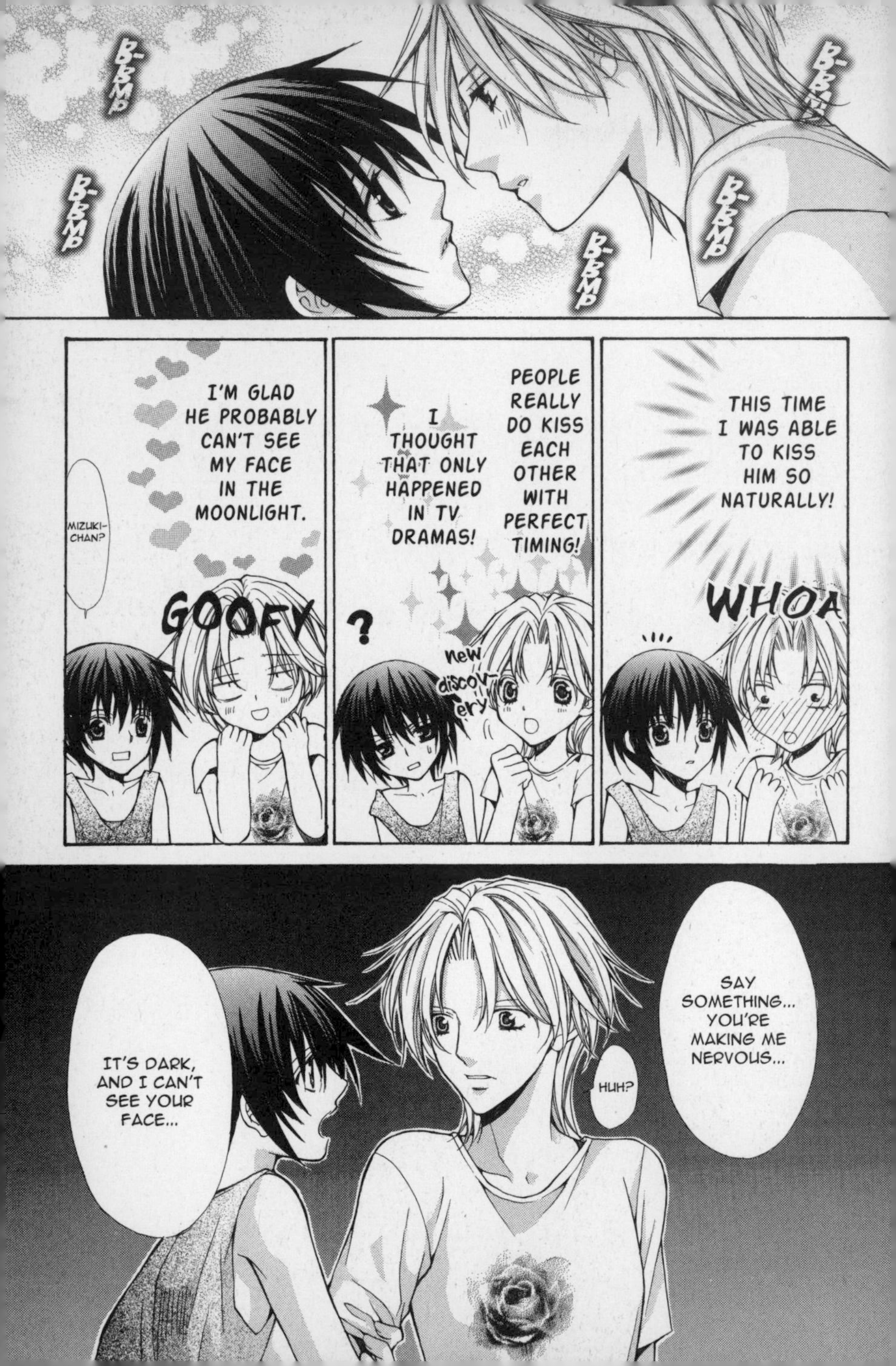
B-BMP
B-BMP
B-BMP
B-BMP
B-BMP
THIS TIME I WAS ABLE TO KISS HIM SO NATURALLY!
WHOA
PEOPLE REALLY DO KISS EACH OTHER WITH PERFECT TIMING!
I THOUGHT THAT ONLY HAPPENED IN TV DRAMAS!
new discovery
?
I'M GLAD HE PROBABLY CAN'T SEE MY FACE IN THE MOONLIGHT.
GOOFY
MIZUKI-CHAN?
SAY SOMETHING... YOU'RE MAKING ME NERVOUS...
HUH?
IT'S DARK, AND I CAN'T SEE YOUR FACE...

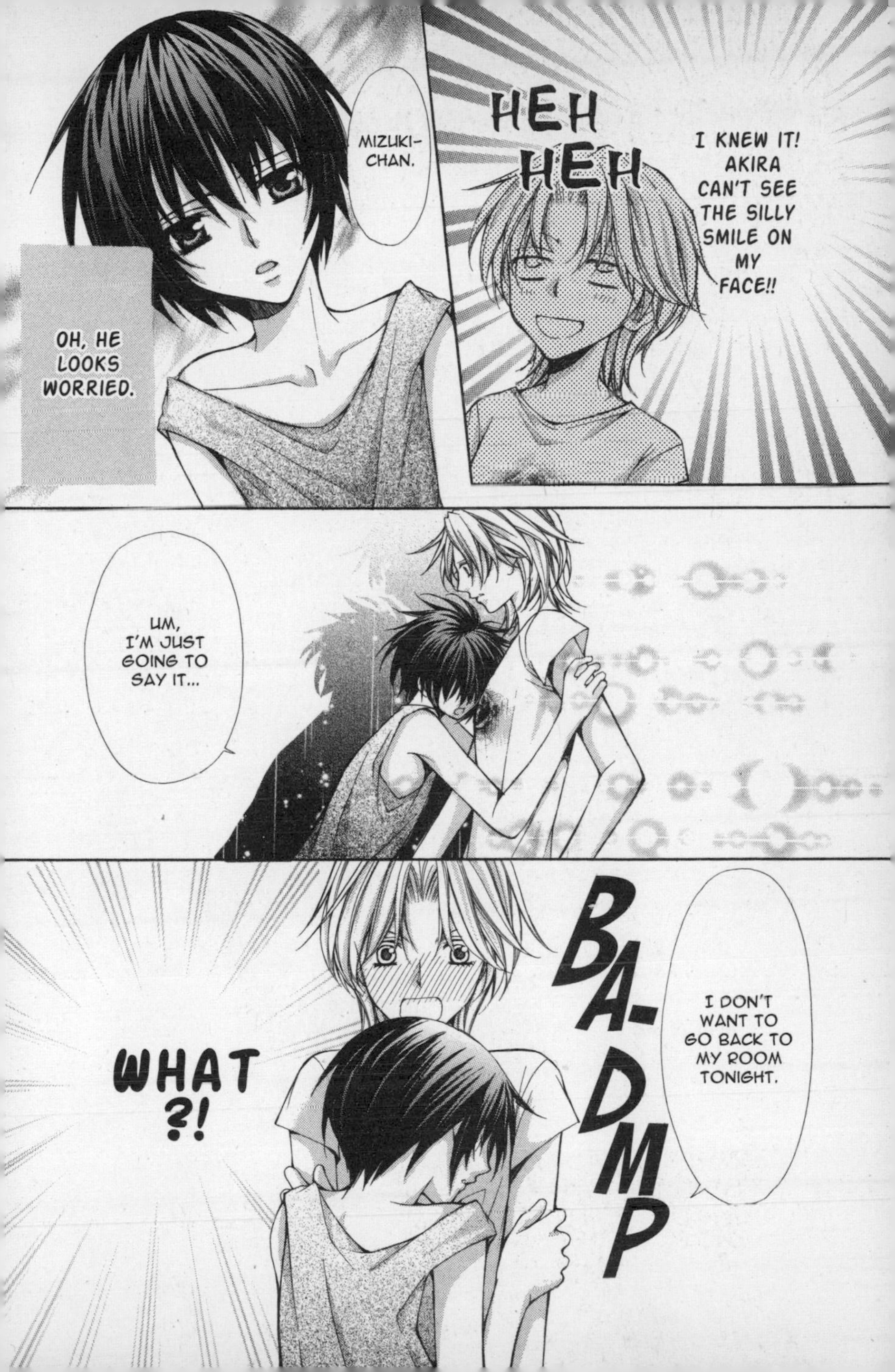

I KNEW IT! AKIRA CAN'T SEE THE SILLY SMILE ON MY FACE!!
HEH HEH
MIZUKI-CHAN.
OH, HE LOOKS WORRIED.
UM, I'M JUST GOING TO SAY IT...
I DON'T WANT TO GO BACK TO MY ROOM TONIGHT.
BA-DMP
WHAT?!

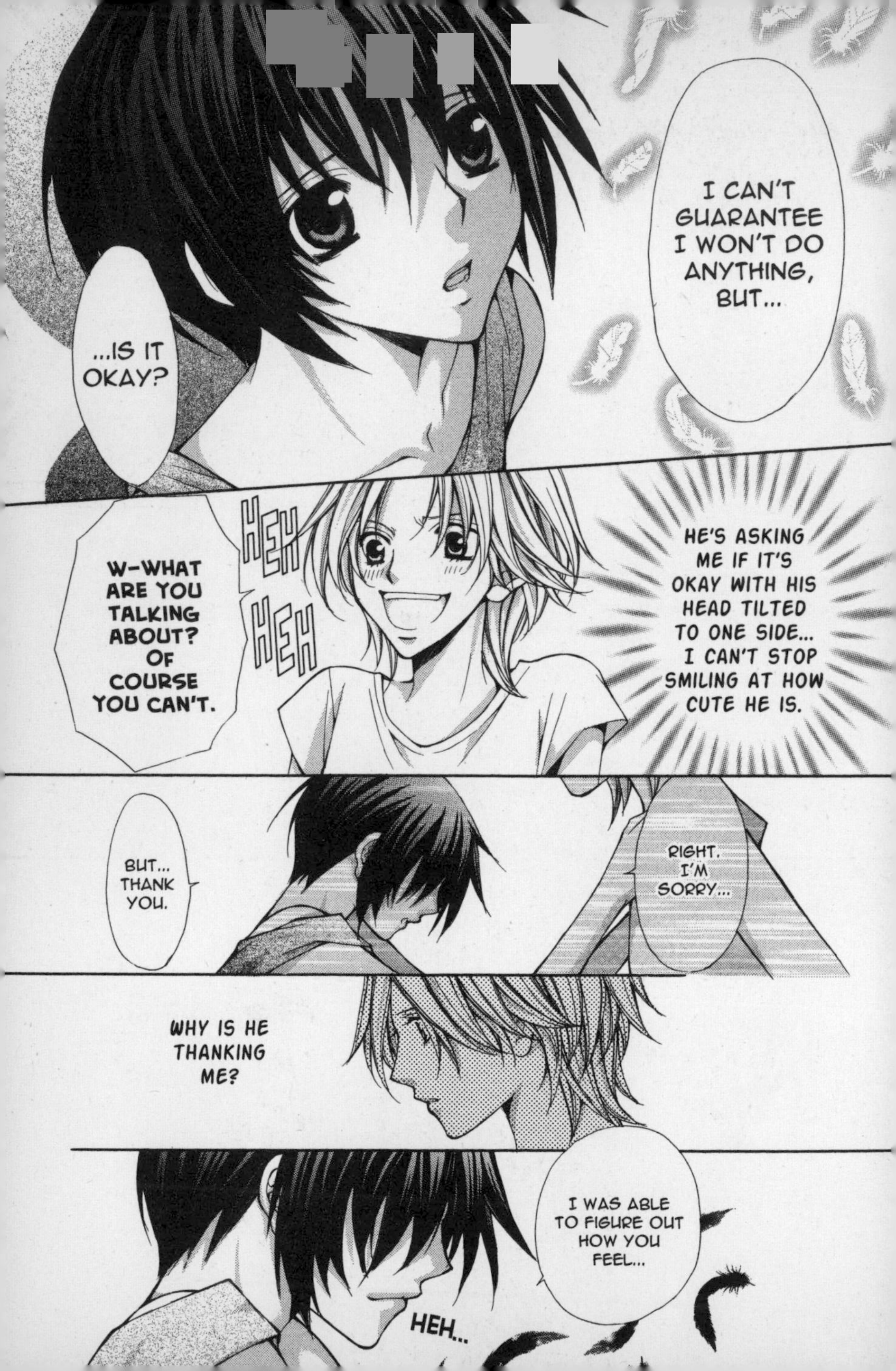
I CAN'T GUARANTEE I WON'T DO ANYTHING, BUT...
...IS IT OKAY?
HE'S ASKING ME IF IT'S OKAY WITH HIS HEAD TILTED TO ONE SIDE... I CAN'T STOP SMILING AT HOW CUTE HE IS.
HEH HEH
W-WHAT ARE YOU TALKING ABOUT? OF COURSE YOU CAN'T.
RIGHT. I'M SORRY...
BUT... THANK YOU.
WHY IS HE THANKING ME?
I WAS ABLE TO FIGURE OUT HOW YOU FEEL...
HEH...

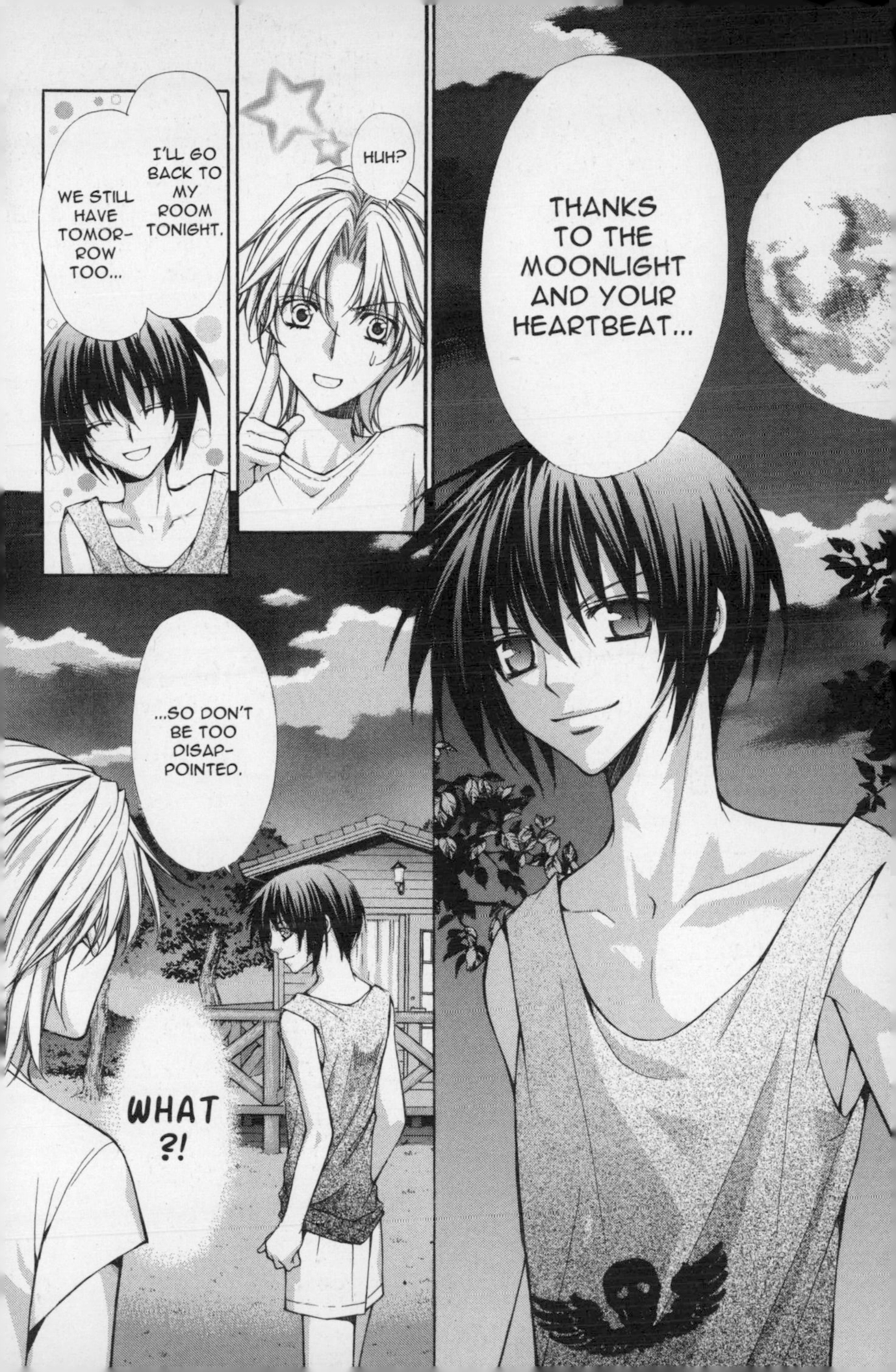
THANKS TO THE MOONLIGHT AND YOUR HEARTBEAT...
HUH?
I'LL GO BACK TO MY ROOM TONIGHT.
WE STILL HAVE TOMOR-ROW TOO...
...SO DON'T BE TOO DISAP-POINTED.
WHAT ?!

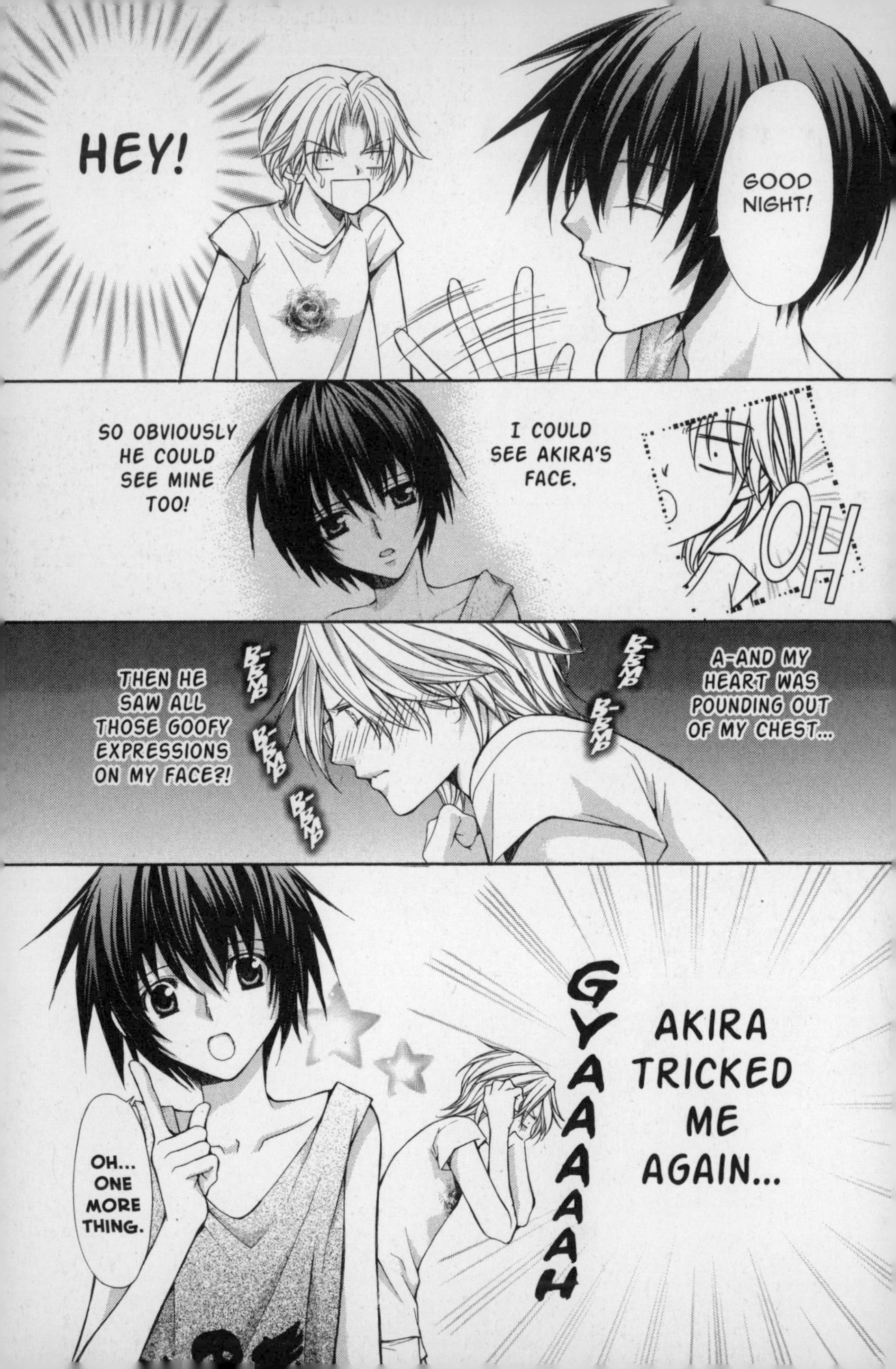

GOOD NIGHT!
HEY!
OH
I COULD SEE AKIRA'S FACE.
SO OBVIOUSLY HE COULD SEE MINE TOO!
A-AND MY HEART WAS POUNDING OUT OF MY CHEST...
B-BMP
B-BMP
B-BMP
B-BMP
B-BMP
THEN HE SAW ALL THOSE GOOFY EXPRESSIONS ON MY FACE?!
AKIRA TRICKED ME AGAIN...
GYAAAAAAH
OH... ONE MORE THING.

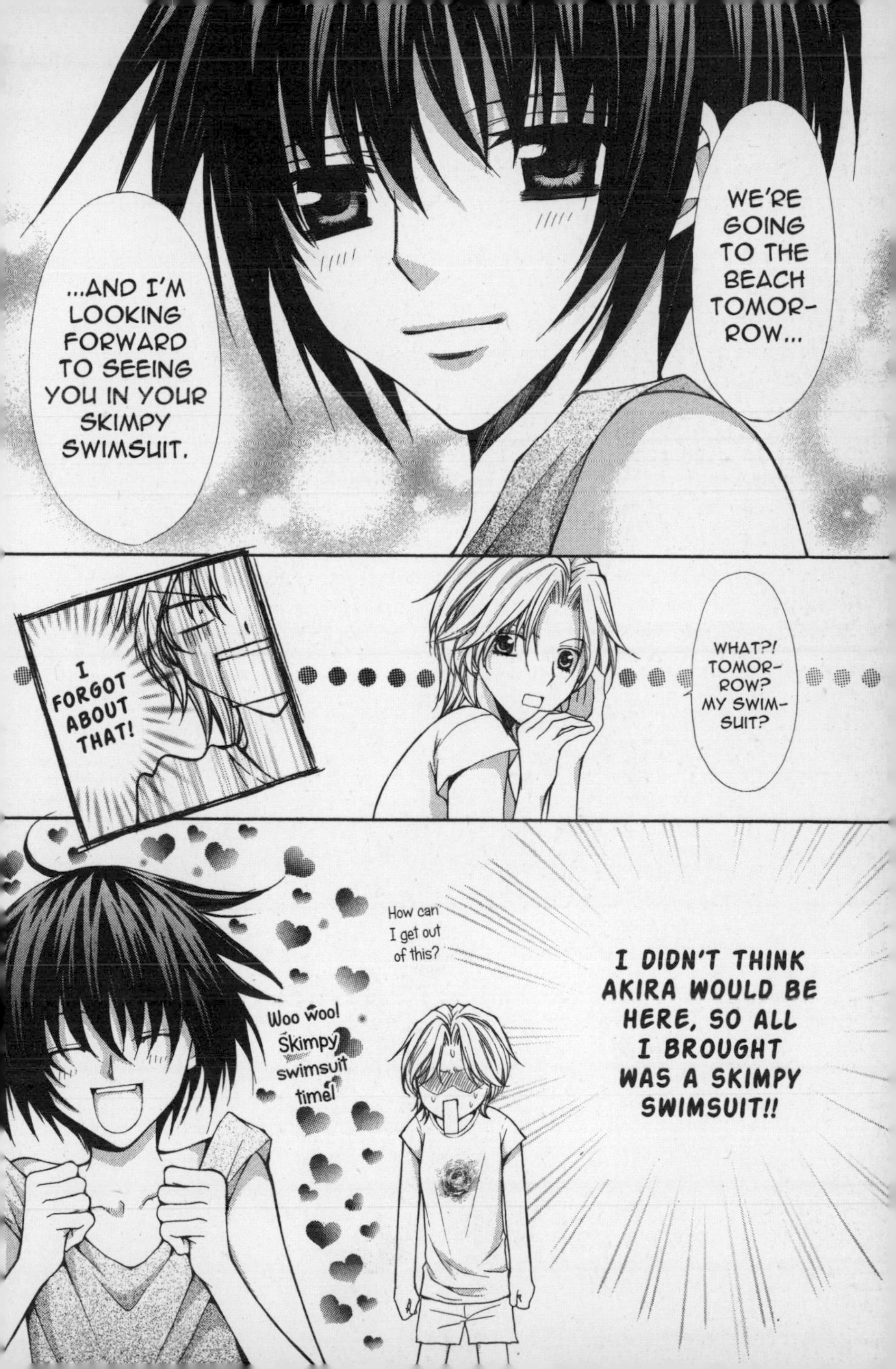
WE'RE GOING TO THE BEACH TOMORROW...
...AND I'M LOOKING FORWARD TO SEEING YOU IN YOUR SKIMPY SWIMSUIT.
WHAT?! TOMORROW? MY SWIMSUIT?
I FORGOT ABOUT THAT!
I DIDN'T THINK AKIRA WOULD BE HERE, SO ALL I BROUGHT WAS A SKIMPY SWIMSUIT!!
How can I get out of this?
Woo woo! Skimpy swimsuit time!

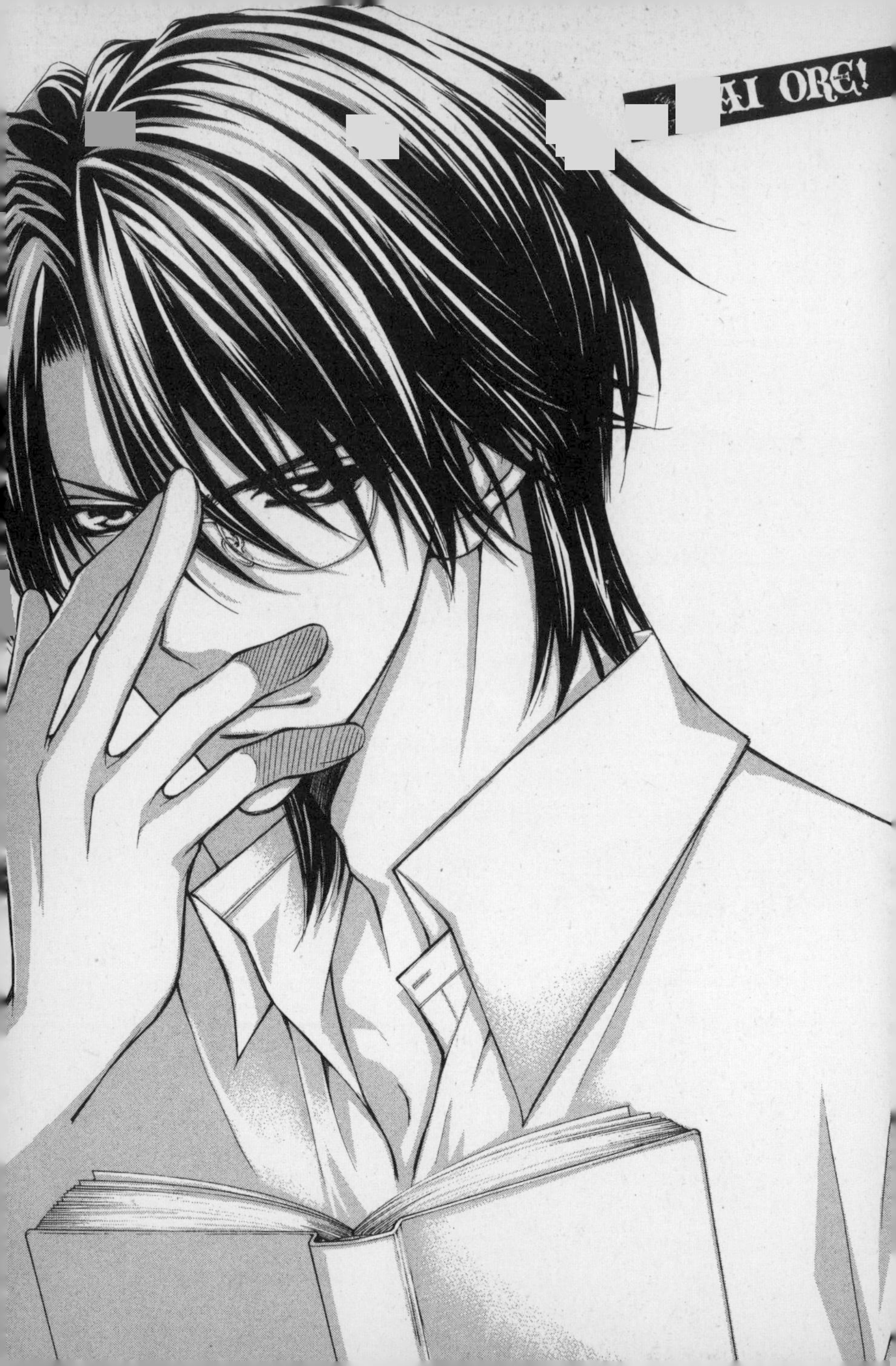
AI ORE!

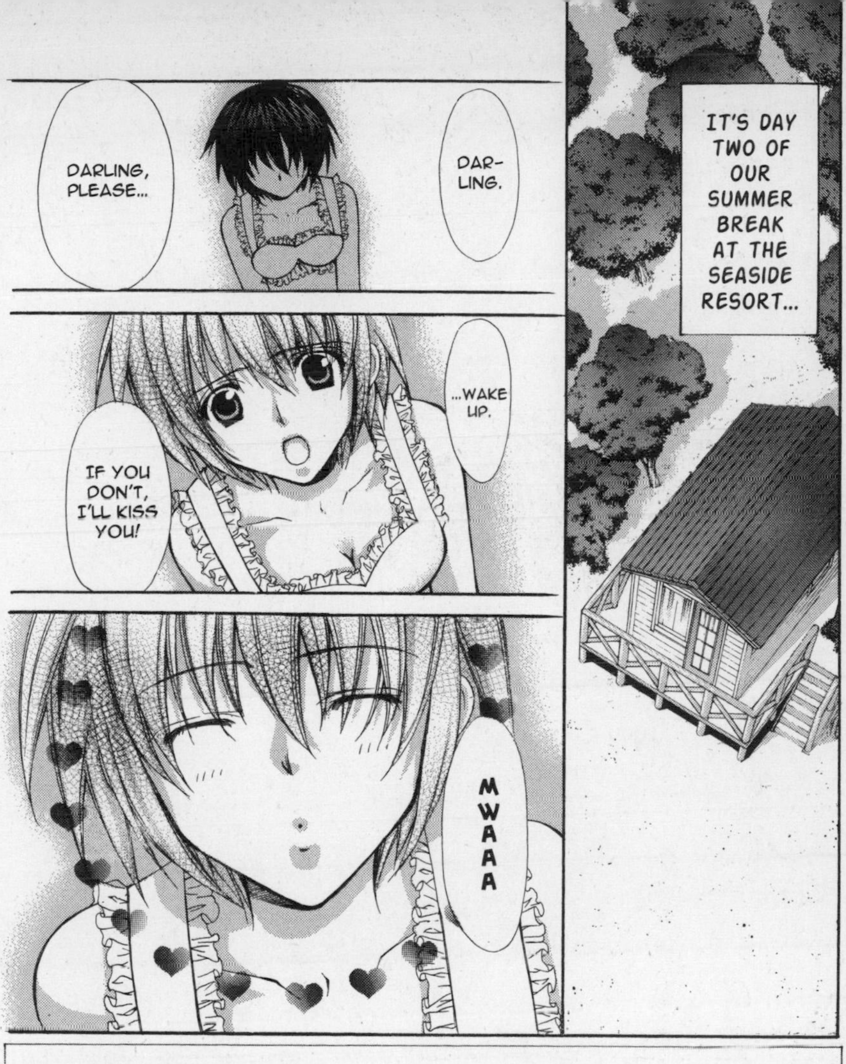
IT'S DAY TWO OF OUR SUMMER BREAK AT THE SEASIDE RESORT...
DAR-LING.
DARLING, PLEASE...
...WAKE UP.
IF YOU DON'T, I'LL KISS YOU!
MWAAAA

If *Ai Ore!*...

I often talk with my friends about casting a live-action *Ai Ore!*
First of all, casting Akira would be very difficult. In the past, I said I wanted to see an elementary school student play his part, but the people around me thought the idea was awful and didn't like it... ♢ Who should I choose, then?! I kept it in mind every time I watched TV. And... I found him!! A boy I thought would be perfect.
It's Ryosuke Yamada of "Hey! Say! JUMP."
What do you think? What do you think? What do you think? No? Personally I would like to see him in drag, and I would like to see his dark side too.
He's good at acting and singing. (After all, he's the main vocalist in the band and that's important.) I think he's perfect...

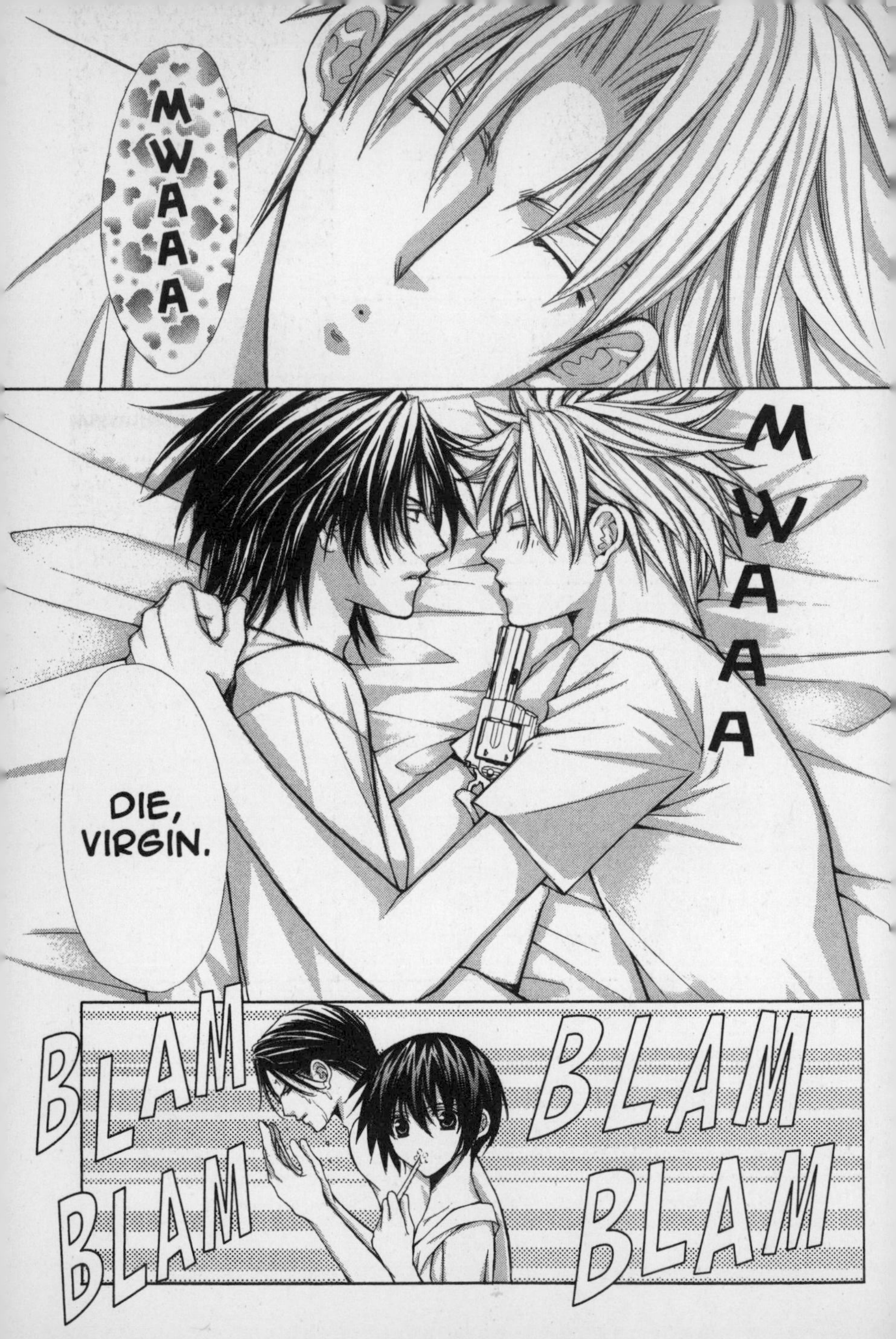

MWAAA
MWAAA
DIE, VIRGIN.
BLAM BLAM
BLAM BLAM

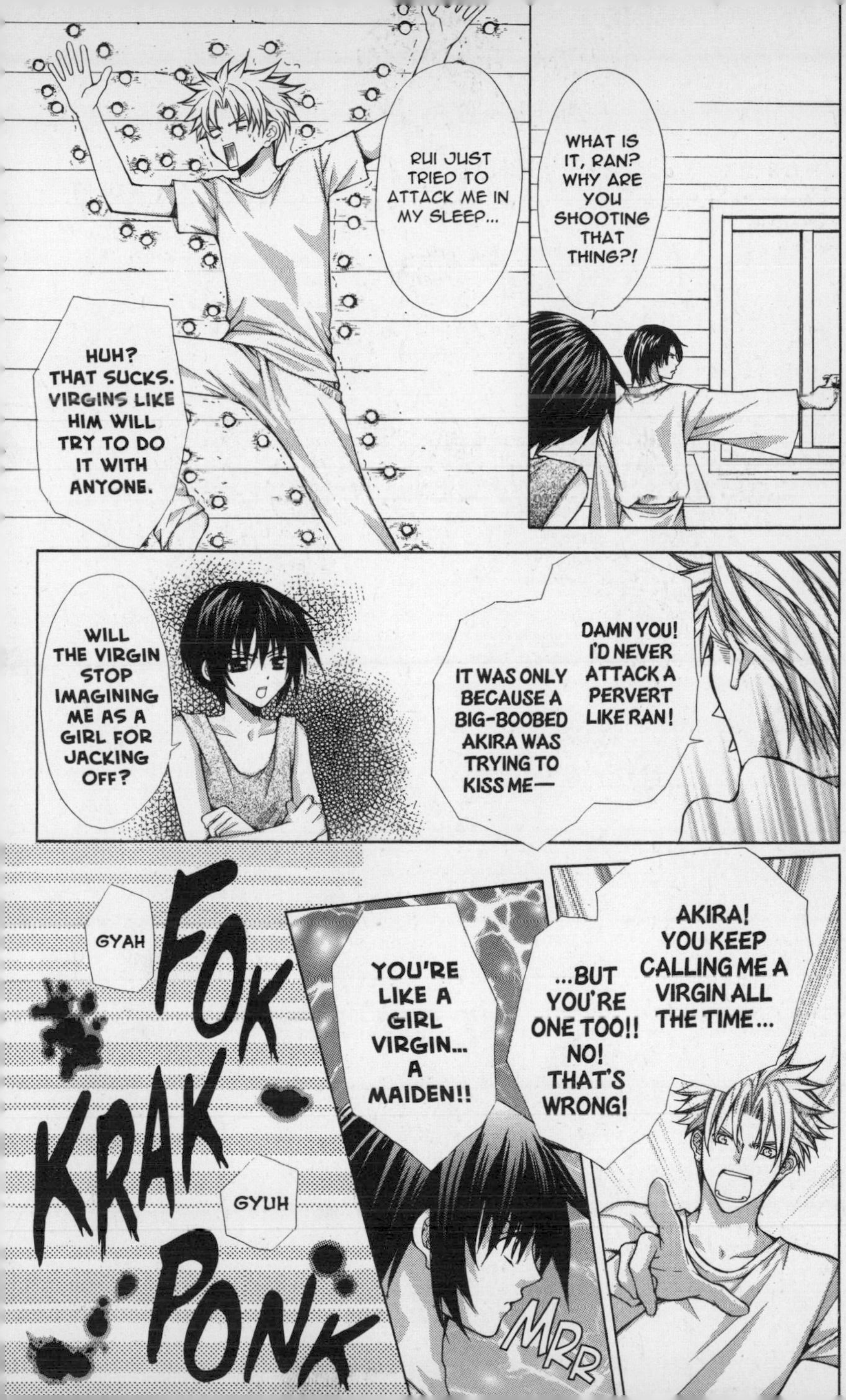
WHAT IS IT, RAN? WHY ARE YOU SHOOTING THAT THING?!
RUI JUST TRIED TO ATTACK ME IN MY SLEEP...
HUH? THAT SUCKS. VIRGINS LIKE HIM WILL TRY TO DO IT WITH ANYONE.
DAMN YOU! I'D NEVER ATTACK A PERVERT LIKE RAN!
IT WAS ONLY BECAUSE A BIG-BOOBED AKIRA WAS TRYING TO KISS ME—
WILL THE VIRGIN STOP IMAGINING ME AS A GIRL FOR JACKING OFF?
AKIRA! YOU KEEP CALLING ME A VIRGIN ALL THE TIME...
...BUT YOU'RE ONE TOO!! NO! THAT'S WRONG!
YOU'RE LIKE A GIRL VIRGIN... A MAIDEN!!
MRR
FOK
GYAH
KRAK
GYUH
PONK

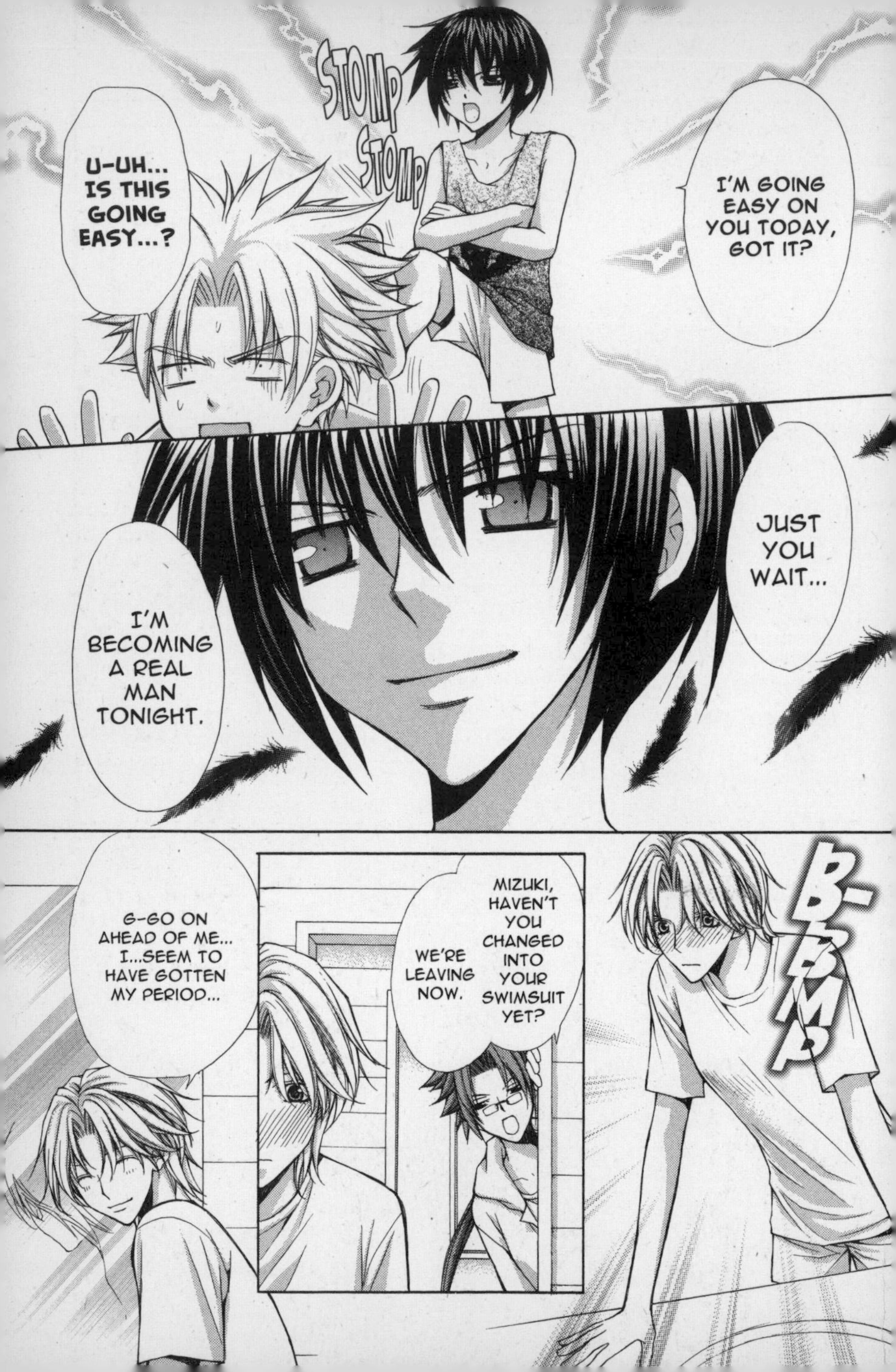
I'M GOING EASY ON YOU TODAY, GOT IT?
STOMP STOMP
U-UH... IS THIS GOING EASY...?
JUST YOU WAIT...
I'M BECOMING A REAL MAN TONIGHT.
B-BUMP
MIZUKI, HAVEN'T YOU CHANGED INTO YOUR SWIMSUIT YET?
WE'RE LEAVING NOW.
G-GO ON AHEAD OF ME... I...SEEM TO HAVE GOTTEN MY PERIOD...

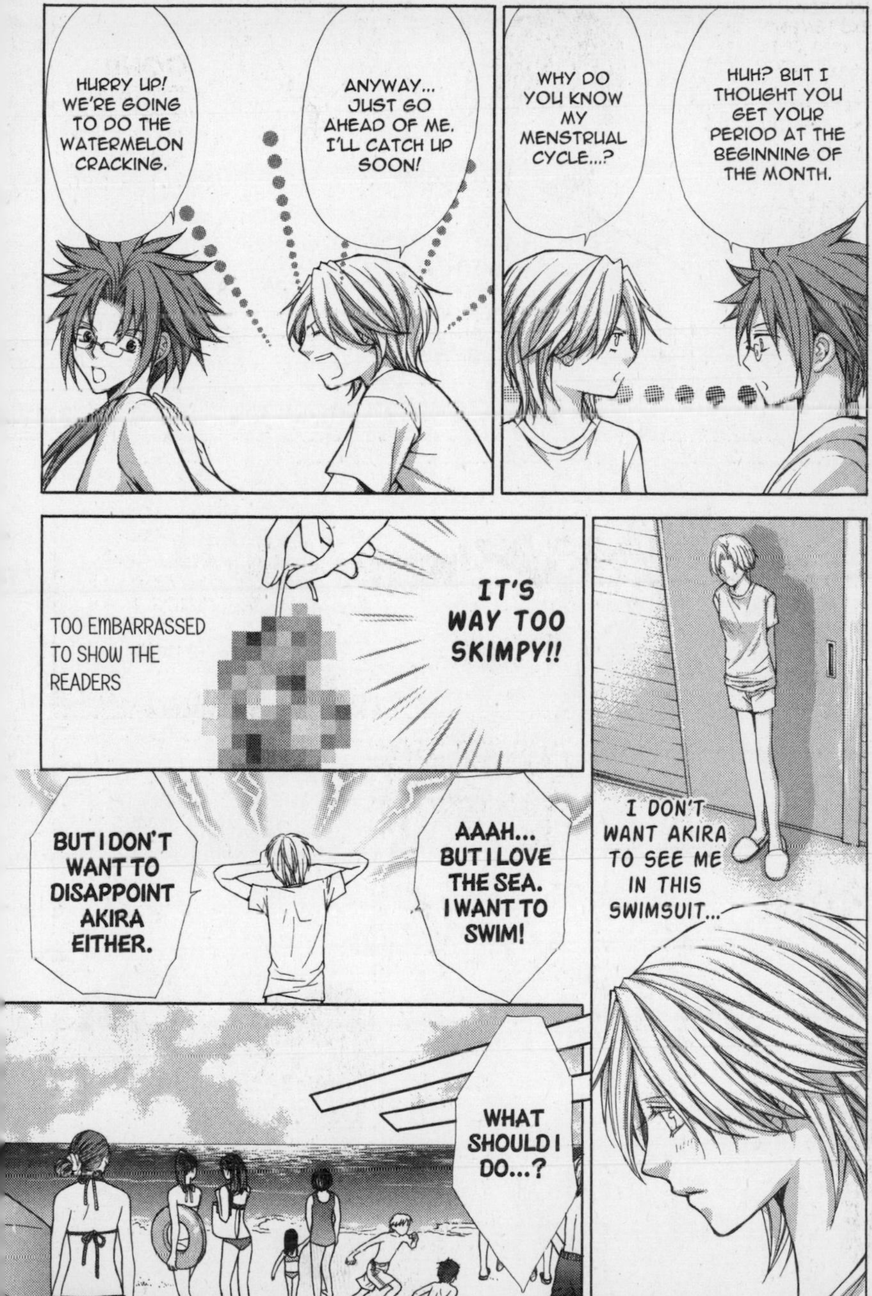
HUH? BUT I THOUGHT YOU GET YOUR PERIOD AT THE BEGINNING OF THE MONTH.
WHY DO YOU KNOW MY MENSTRUAL CYCLE...?
ANYWAY... JUST GO AHEAD OF ME. I'LL CATCH UP SOON!
HURRY UP! WE'RE GOING TO DO THE WATERMELON CRACKING.
I DON'T WANT AKIRA TO SEE ME IN THIS SWIMSUIT...
IT'S WAY TOO SKIMPY!!
TOO EMBARRASSED TO SHOW THE READERS
AAAH... BUT I LOVE THE SEA. I WANT TO SWIM!
BUT I DON'T WANT TO DISAPPOINT AKIRA EITHER.
WHAT SHOULD I DO...?

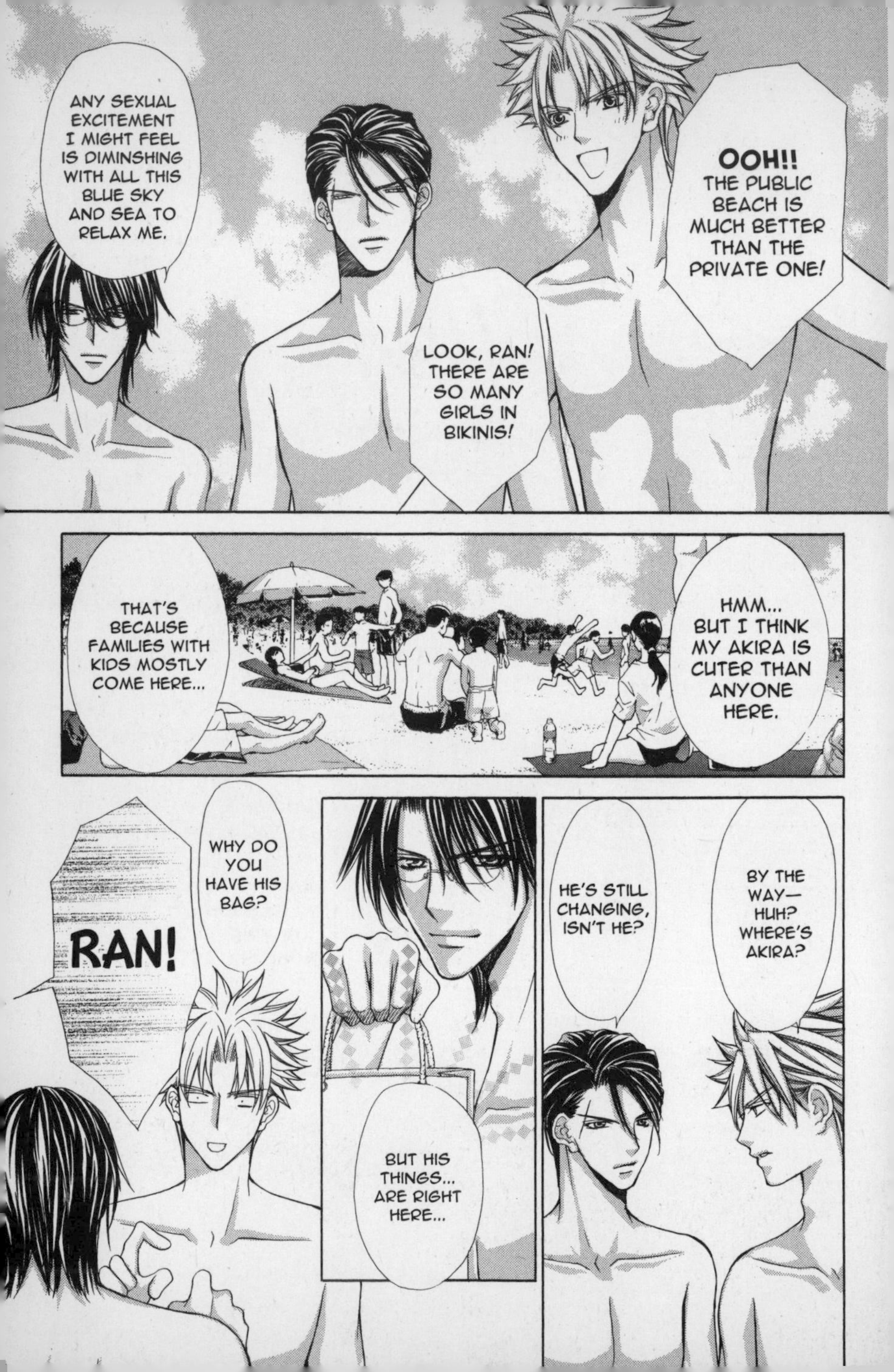
OOH!! THE PUBLIC BEACH IS MUCH BETTER THAN THE PRIVATE ONE!
LOOK, RAN! THERE ARE SO MANY GIRLS IN BIKINIS!
ANY SEXUAL EXCITEMENT I MIGHT FEEL IS DIMINSHING WITH ALL THIS BLUE SKY AND SEA TO RELAX ME.
HMM... BUT I THINK MY AKIRA IS CUTER THAN ANYONE HERE.
THAT'S BECAUSE FAMILIES WITH KIDS MOSTLY COME HERE...
BY THE WAY— HUH? WHERE'S AKIRA?
HE'S STILL CHANGING, ISN'T HE?
BUT HIS THINGS... ARE RIGHT HERE...
WHY DO YOU HAVE HIS BAG?
RAN!

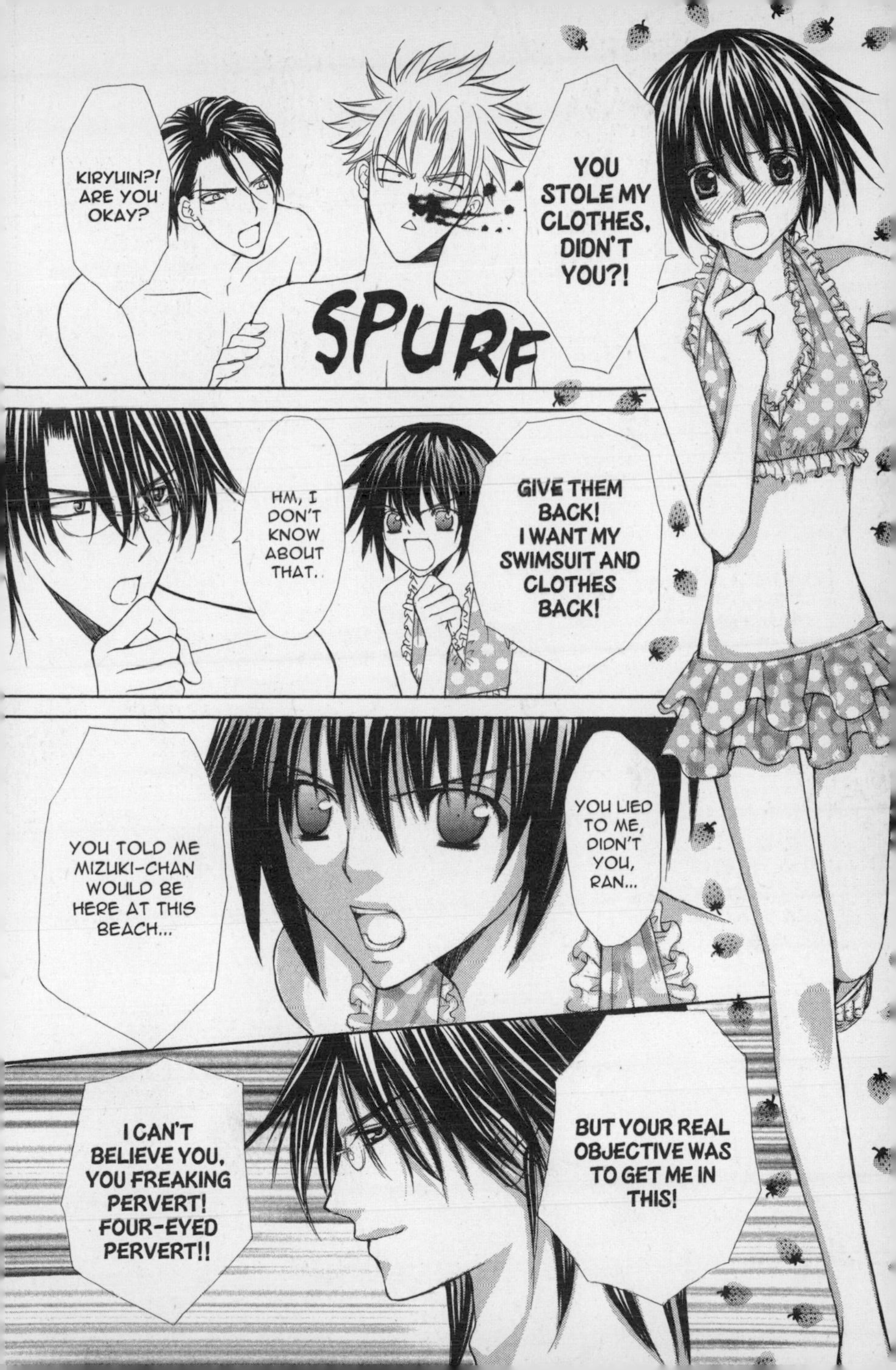
YOU STOLE MY CLOTHES, DIDN'T YOU?!
SPURF
KIRYUIN?! ARE YOU OKAY?
GIVE THEM BACK! I WANT MY SWIMSUIT AND CLOTHES BACK!
HM, I DON'T KNOW ABOUT THAT.
YOU LIED TO ME, DIDN'T YOU, RAN...
YOU TOLD ME MIZUKI-CHAN WOULD BE HERE AT THIS BEACH...
BUT YOUR REAL OBJECTIVE WAS TO GET ME IN THIS!
I CAN'T BELIEVE YOU, YOU FREAKING PERVERT! FOUR-EYED PERVERT!!

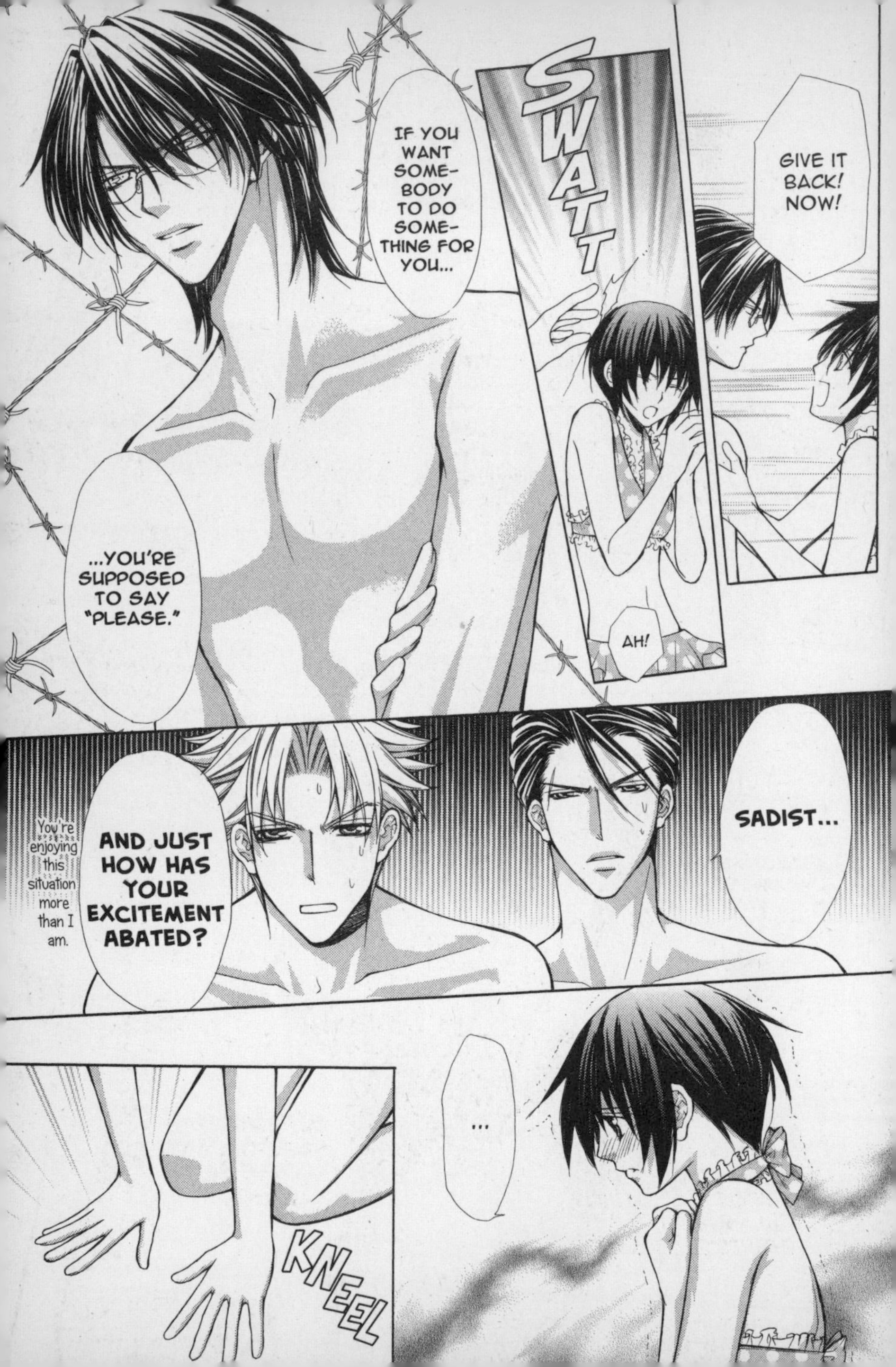
GIVE IT BACK! NOW!
SWATT
AH!
IF YOU WANT SOMEBODY TO DO SOMETHING FOR YOU...
...YOU'RE SUPPOSED TO SAY "PLEASE."
SADIST...
AND JUST HOW HAS YOUR EXCITEMENT ABATED?
You're enjoying this situation more than I am.
...
KNEEL

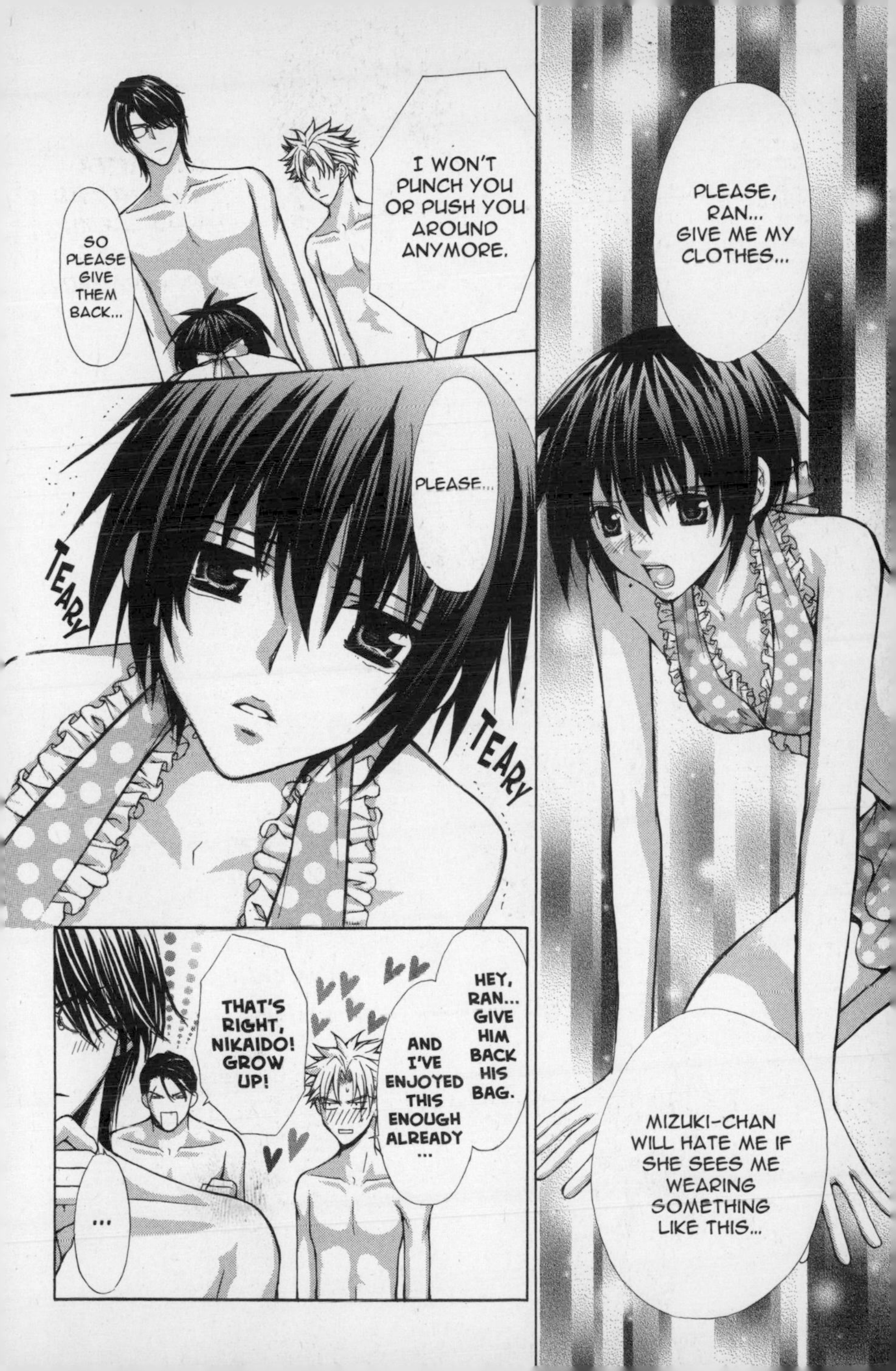
PLEASE, RAN... GIVE ME MY CLOTHES...
MIZUKI-CHAN WILL HATE ME IF SHE SEES ME WEARING SOMETHING LIKE THIS...
I WON'T PUNCH YOU OR PUSH YOU AROUND ANYMORE.
SO PLEASE GIVE THEM BACK...
PLEASE...
TEARY
TEARY
HEY, RAN... GIVE HIM BACK HIS BAG.
AND I'VE ENJOYED THIS ENOUGH ALREADY ...
THAT'S RIGHT, NIKAIDO! GROW UP!
...

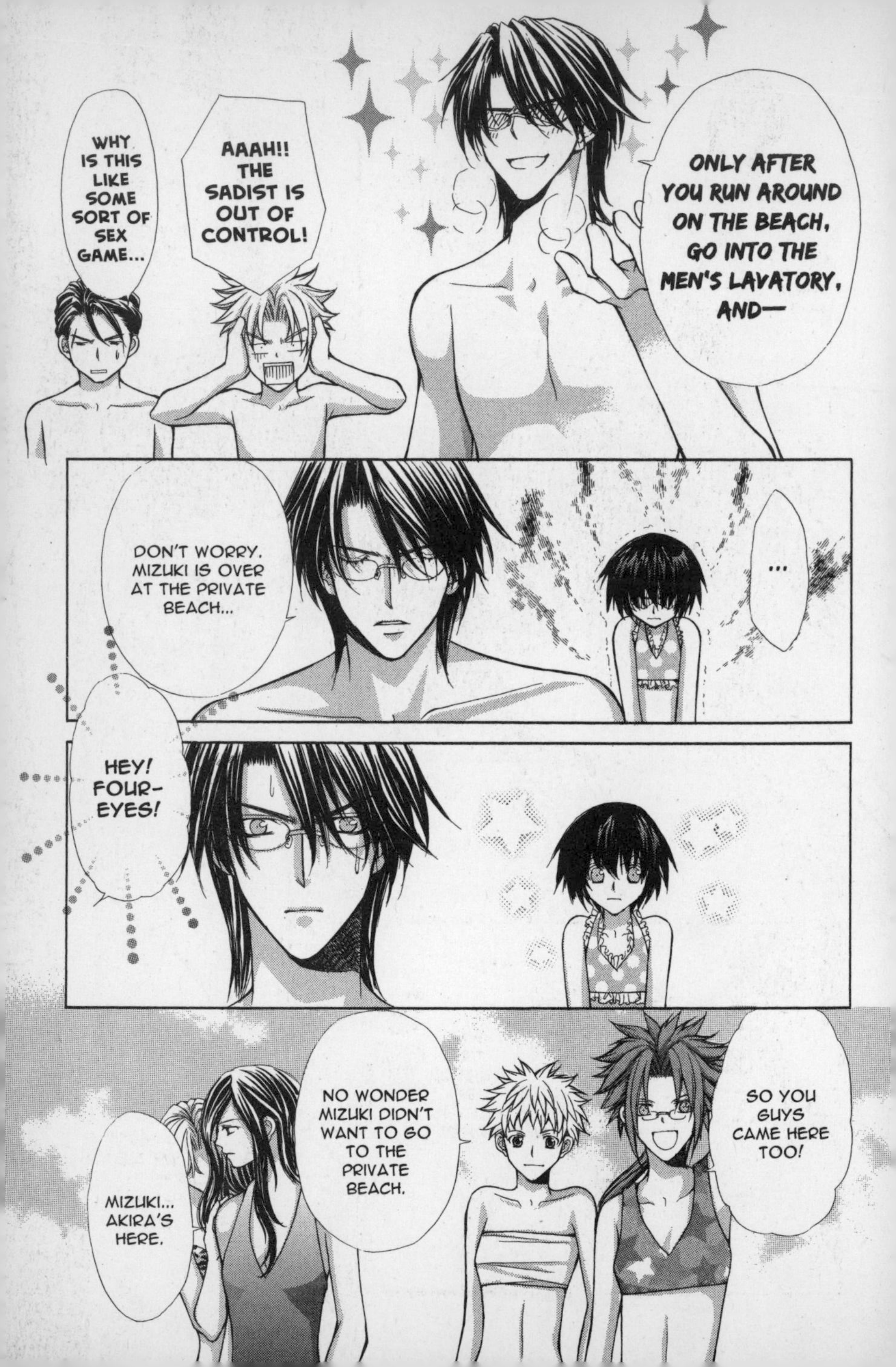

ONLY AFTER YOU RUN AROUND ON THE BEACH, GO INTO THE MEN'S LAVATORY, AND—
AAAH!! THE SADIST IS OUT OF CONTROL!
WHY IS THIS LIKE SOME SORT OF SEX GAME...
...
DON'T WORRY. MIZUKI IS OVER AT THE PRIVATE BEACH...
HEY! FOUR-EYES!
SO YOU GUYS CAME HERE TOO!
NO WONDER MIZUKI DIDN'T WANT TO GO TO THE PRIVATE BEACH.
MIZUKI... AKIRA'S HERE.

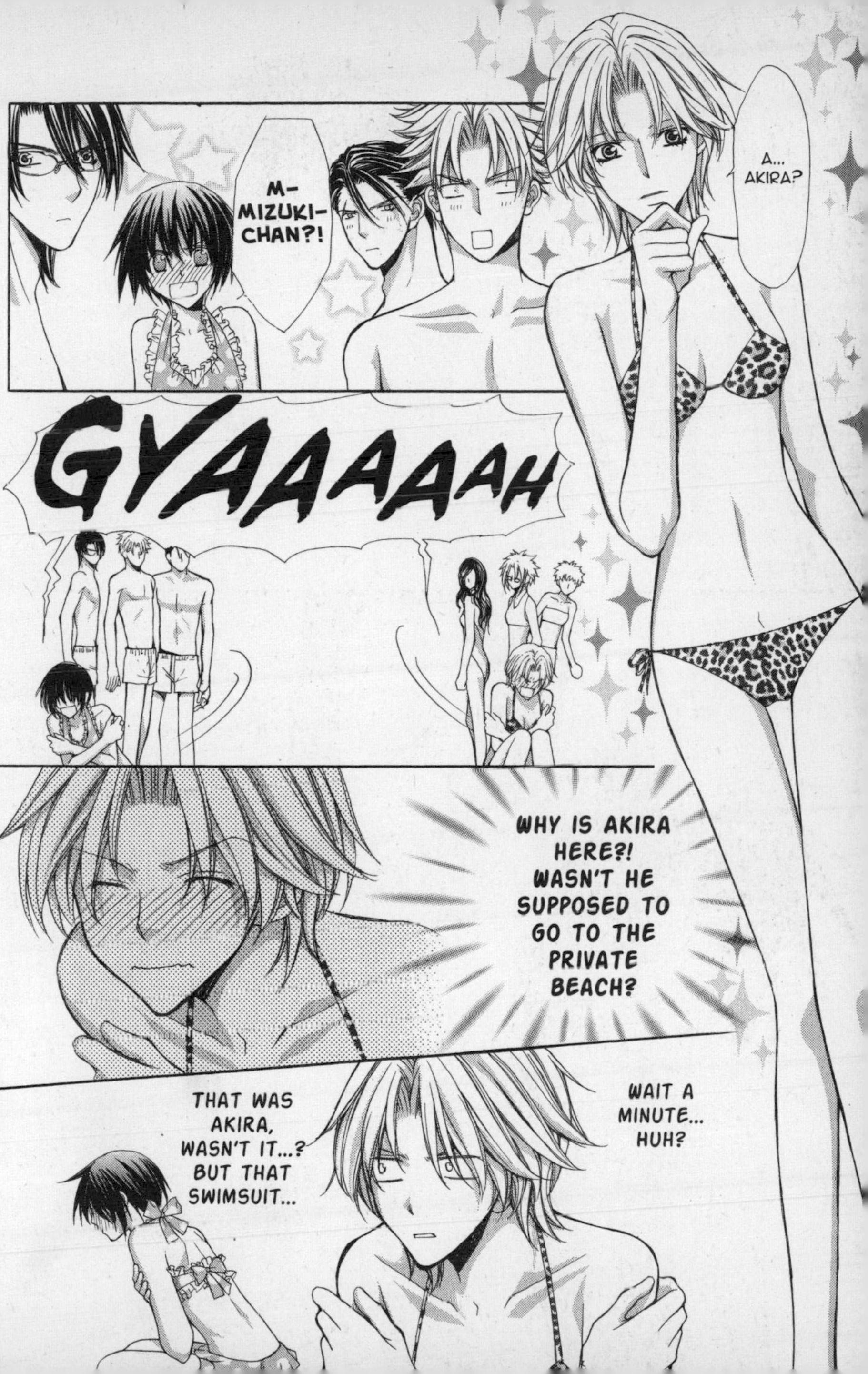
A... AKIRA?
M-MIZUKI-CHAN?!
GYAAAAAH
WHY IS AKIRA HERE?! WASN'T HE SUPPOSED TO GO TO THE PRIVATE BEACH?
WAIT A MINUTE... HUH?
THAT WAS AKIRA, WASN'T IT...? BUT THAT SWIMSUIT...

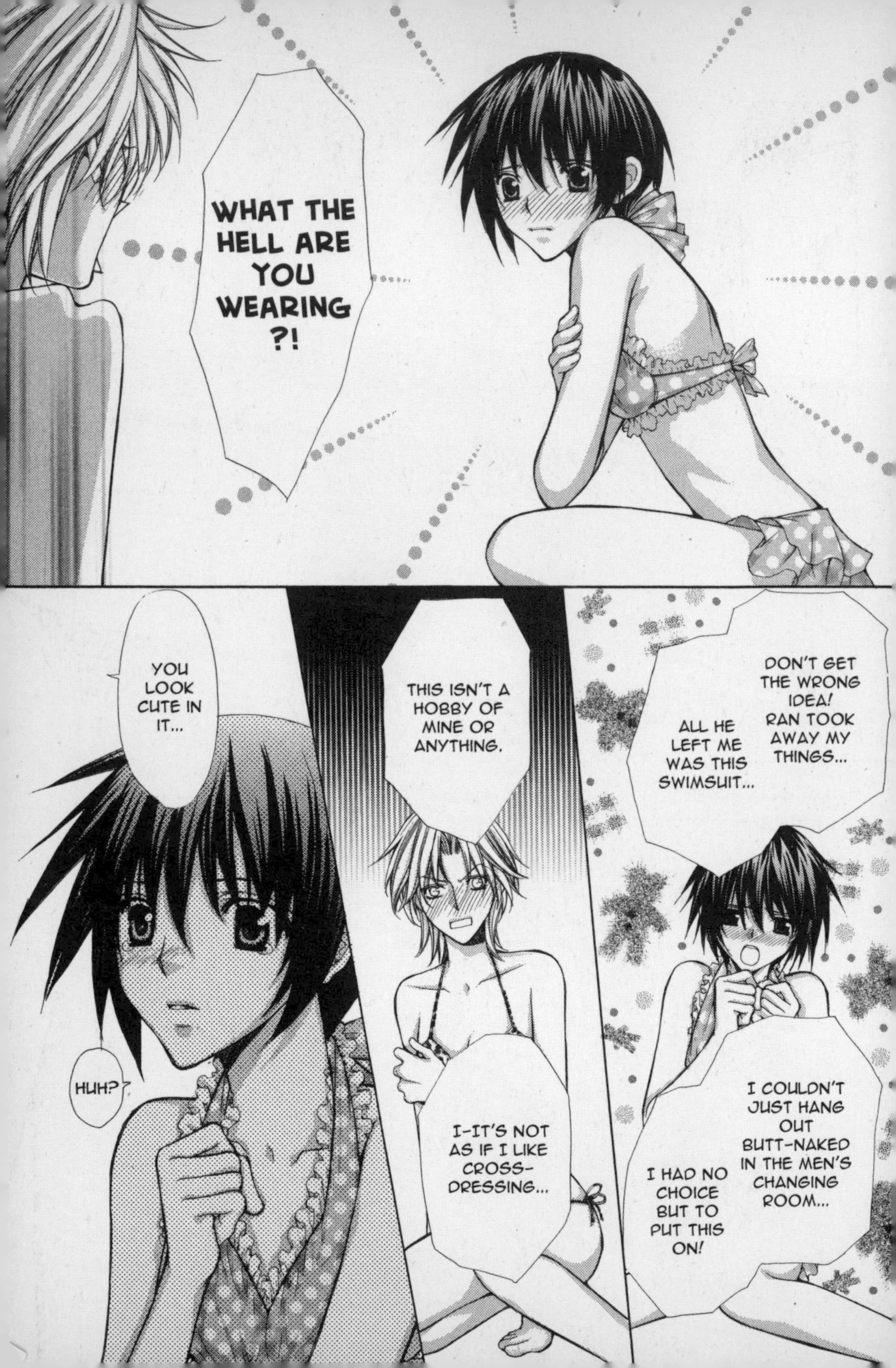
WHAT THE HELL ARE YOU WEARING ?!
DON'T GET THE WRONG IDEA! RAN TOOK AWAY MY THINGS...
ALL HE LEFT ME WAS THIS SWIMSUIT...
I COULDN'T JUST HANG OUT BUTT-NAKED IN THE MEN'S CHANGING ROOM...
I HAD NO CHOICE BUT TO PUT THIS ON!
THIS ISN'T A HOBBY OF MINE OR ANYTHING.
I-IT'S NOT AS IF I LIKE CROSS-DRESSING...
YOU LOOK CUTE IN IT...
HUH?

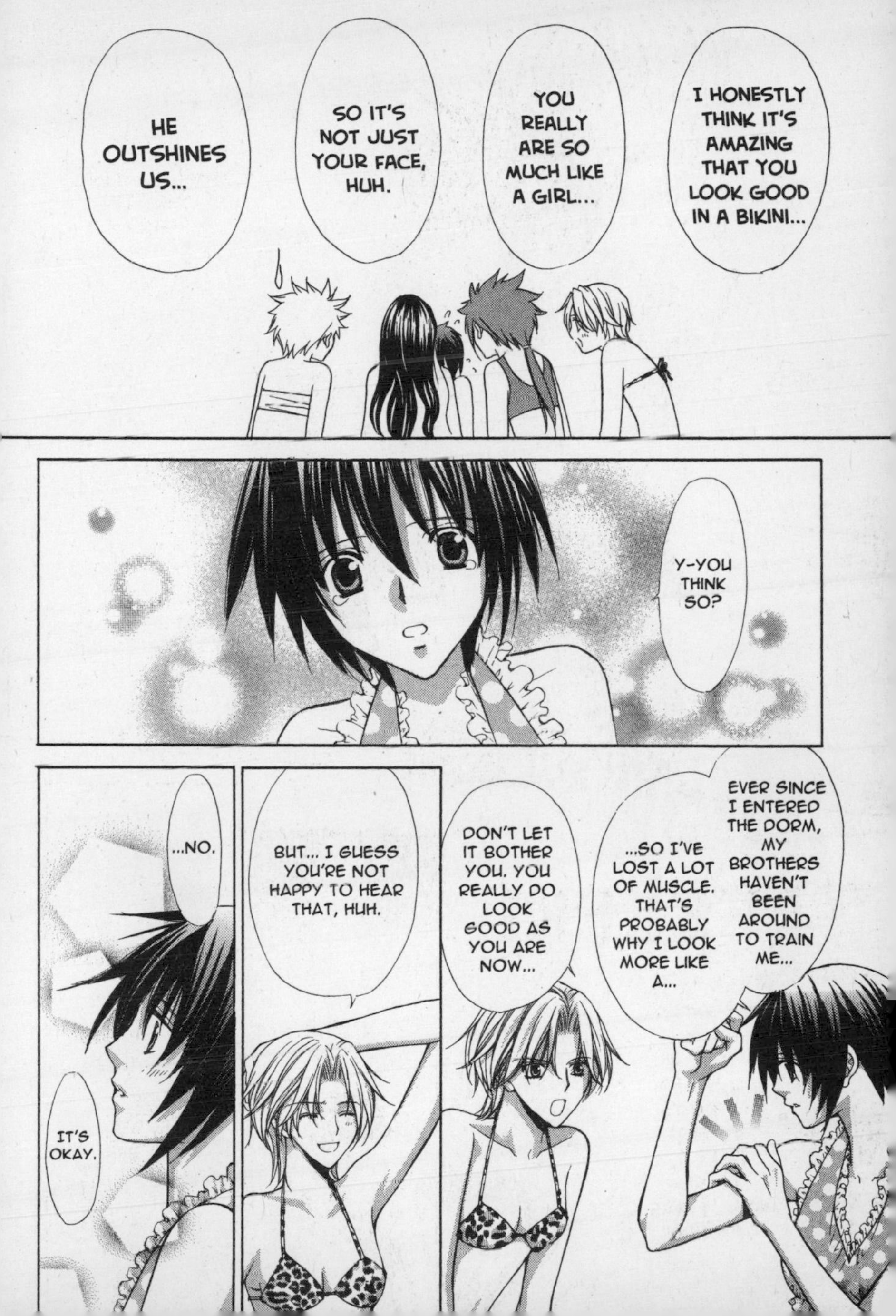
I HONESTLY THINK IT'S AMAZING THAT YOU LOOK GOOD IN A BIKINI...
YOU REALLY ARE SO MUCH LIKE A GIRL...
SO IT'S NOT JUST YOUR FACE, HUH.
HE OUTSHINES US...
Y-YOU THINK SO?
EVER SINCE I ENTERED THE DORM, MY BROTHERS HAVEN'T BEEN AROUND TO TRAIN ME...
...SO I'VE LOST A LOT OF MUSCLE. THAT'S PROBABLY WHY I LOOK MORE LIKE A...
DON'T LET IT BOTHER YOU. YOU REALLY DO LOOK GOOD AS YOU ARE NOW...
BUT... I GUESS YOU'RE NOT HAPPY TO HEAR THAT, HUH.
...NO.
IT'S OKAY.

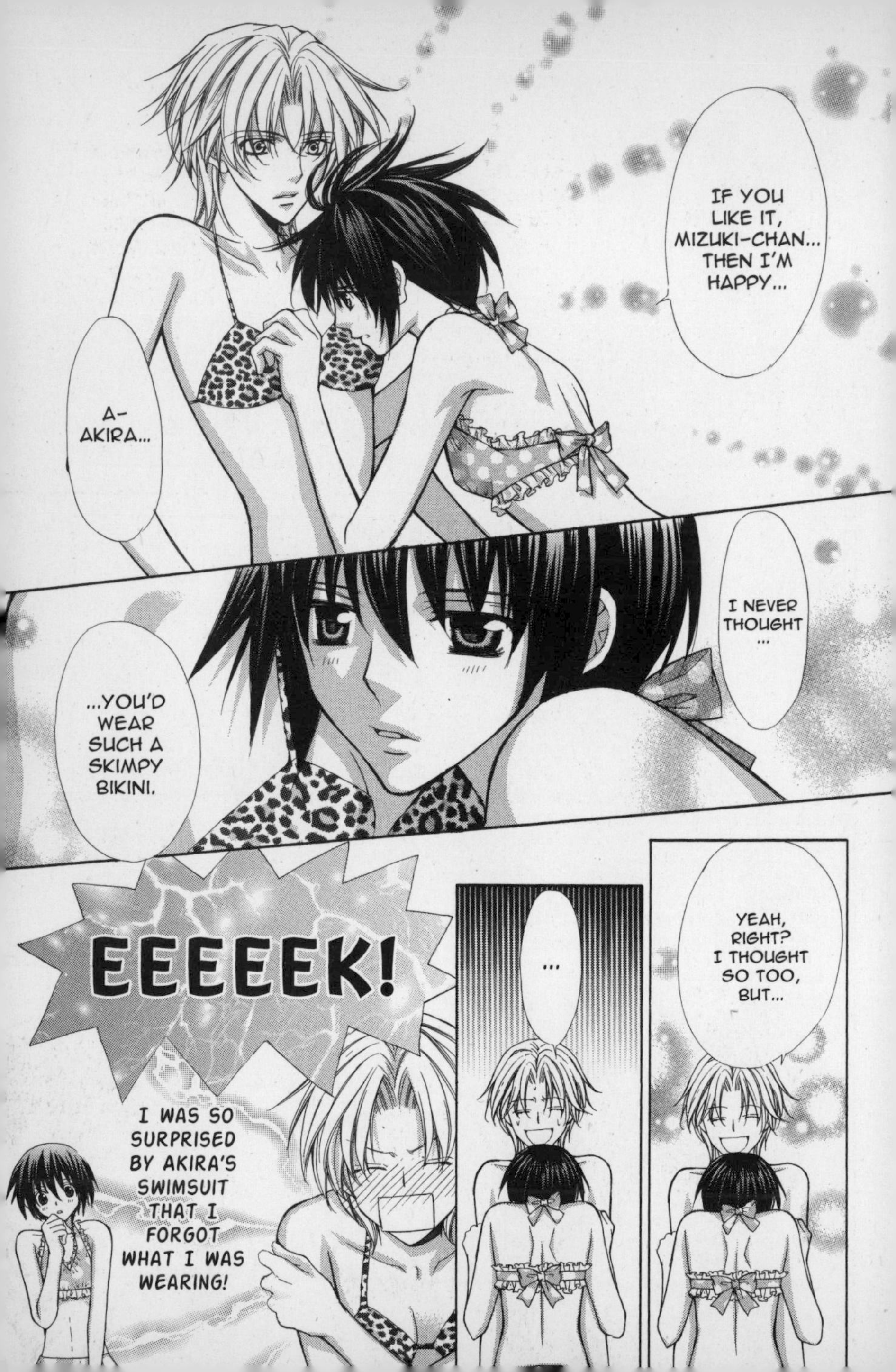

IF YOU LIKE IT, MIZUKI-CHAN... THEN I'M HAPPY...
A- AKIRA...
I NEVER THOUGHT ...
...YOU'D WEAR SUCH A SKIMPY BIKINI.
YEAH, RIGHT? I THOUGHT SO TOO, BUT...
...
EEEEEK!
I WAS SO SURPRISED BY AKIRA'S SWIMSUIT THAT I FORGOT WHAT I WAS WEARING!

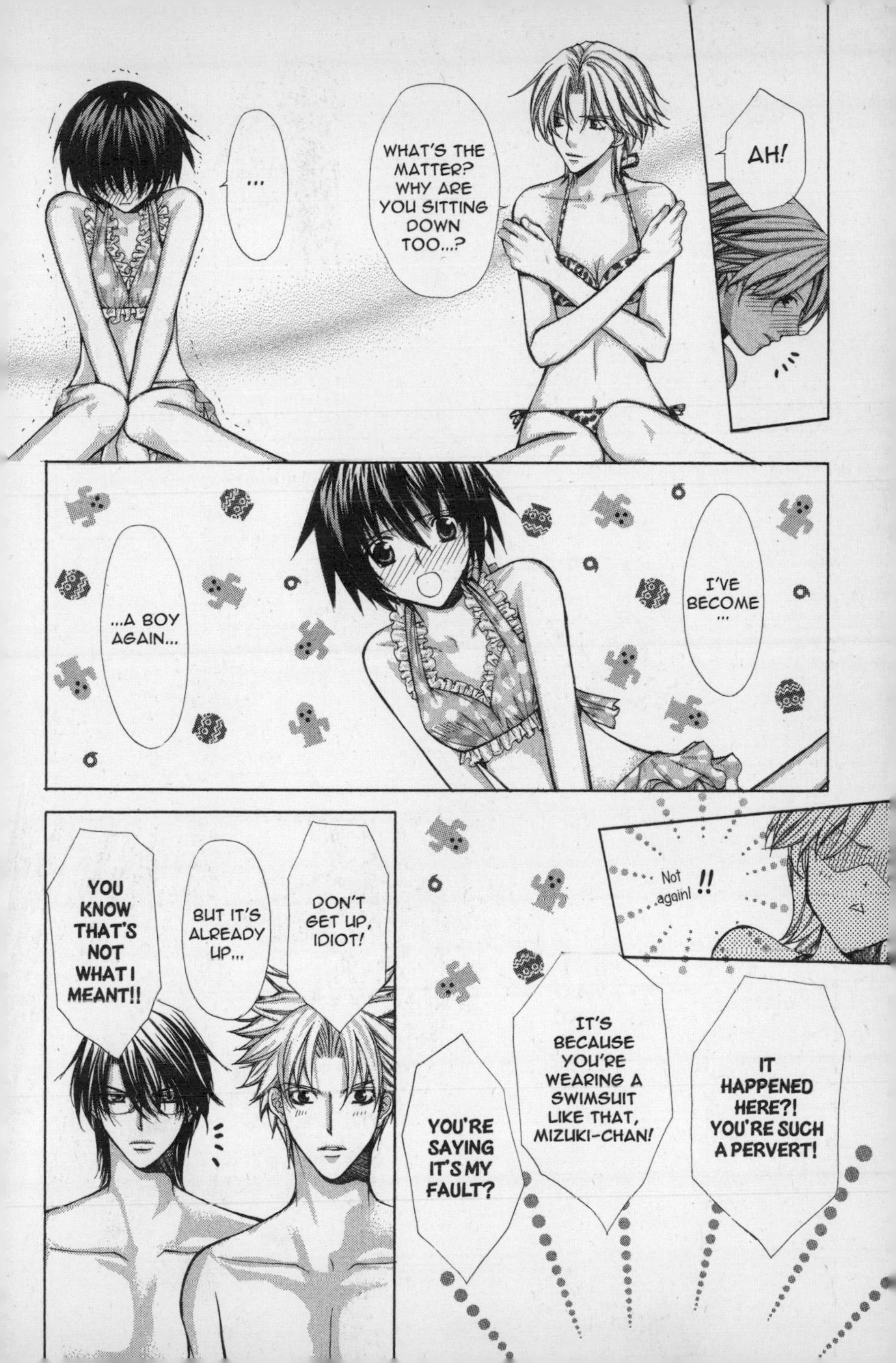
AH!
WHAT'S THE MATTER? WHY ARE YOU SITTING DOWN TOO...?
...
I'VE BECOME...
...A BOY AGAIN...
Not again!!
IT HAPPENED HERE?! YOU'RE SUCH A PERVERT!
IT'S BECAUSE YOU'RE WEARING A SWIMSUIT LIKE THAT, MIZUKI-CHAN!
YOU'RE SAYING IT'S MY FAULT?
DON'T GET UP, IDIOT!
BUT IT'S ALREADY UP...
YOU KNOW THAT'S NOT WHAT I MEANT!!

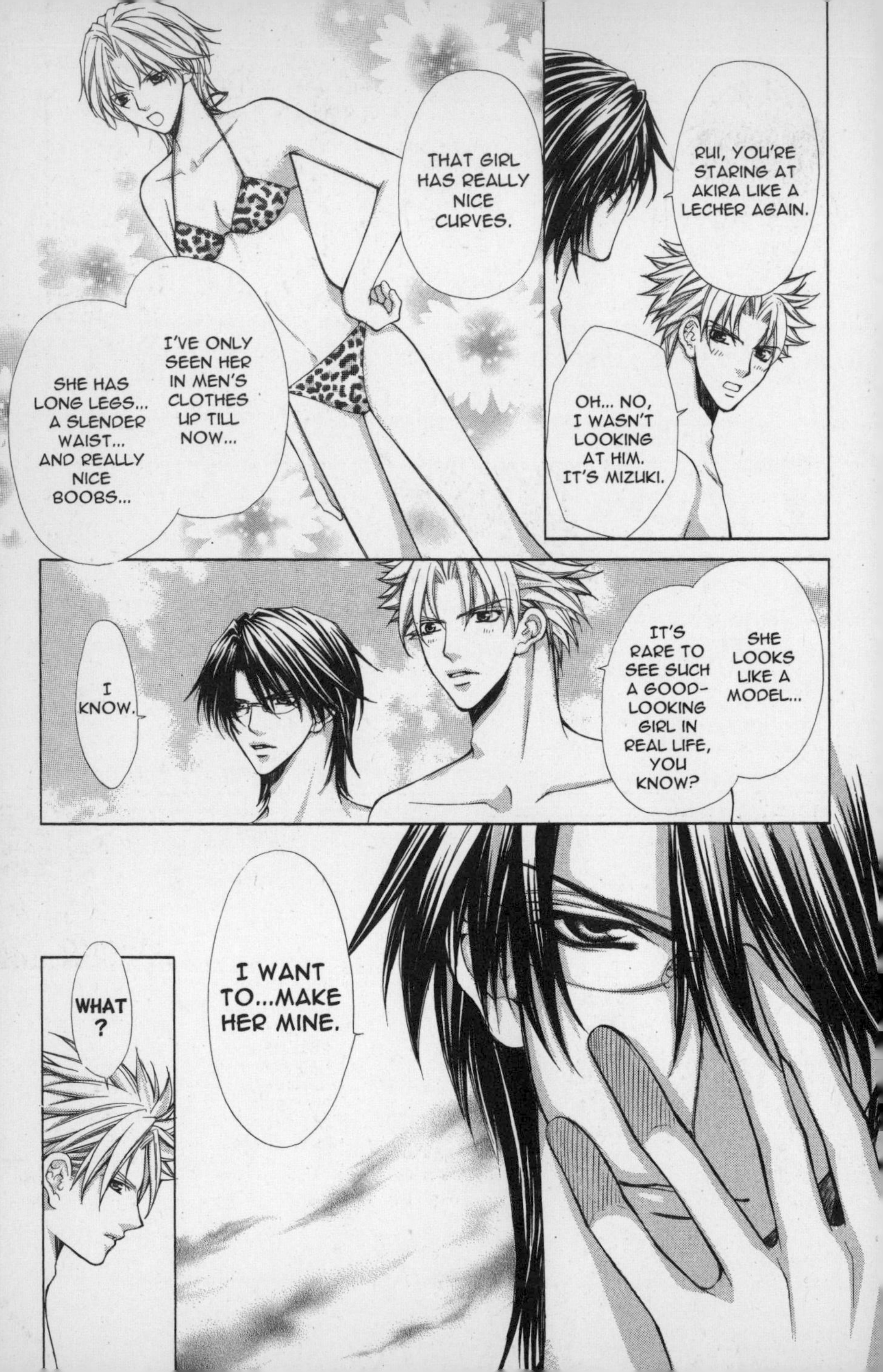
RUI, YOU'RE STARING AT AKIRA LIKE A LECHER AGAIN.
OH... NO, I WASN'T LOOKING AT HIM. IT'S MIZUKI.
THAT GIRL HAS REALLY NICE CURVES.
I'VE ONLY SEEN HER IN MEN'S CLOTHES UP TILL NOW...
SHE HAS LONG LEGS... A SLENDER WAIST... AND REALLY NICE BOOBS...
SHE LOOKS LIKE A MODEL...
IT'S RARE TO SEE SUCH A GOOD-LOOKING GIRL IN REAL LIFE, YOU KNOW?
I KNOW.
I WANT TO...MAKE HER MINE.
WHAT?

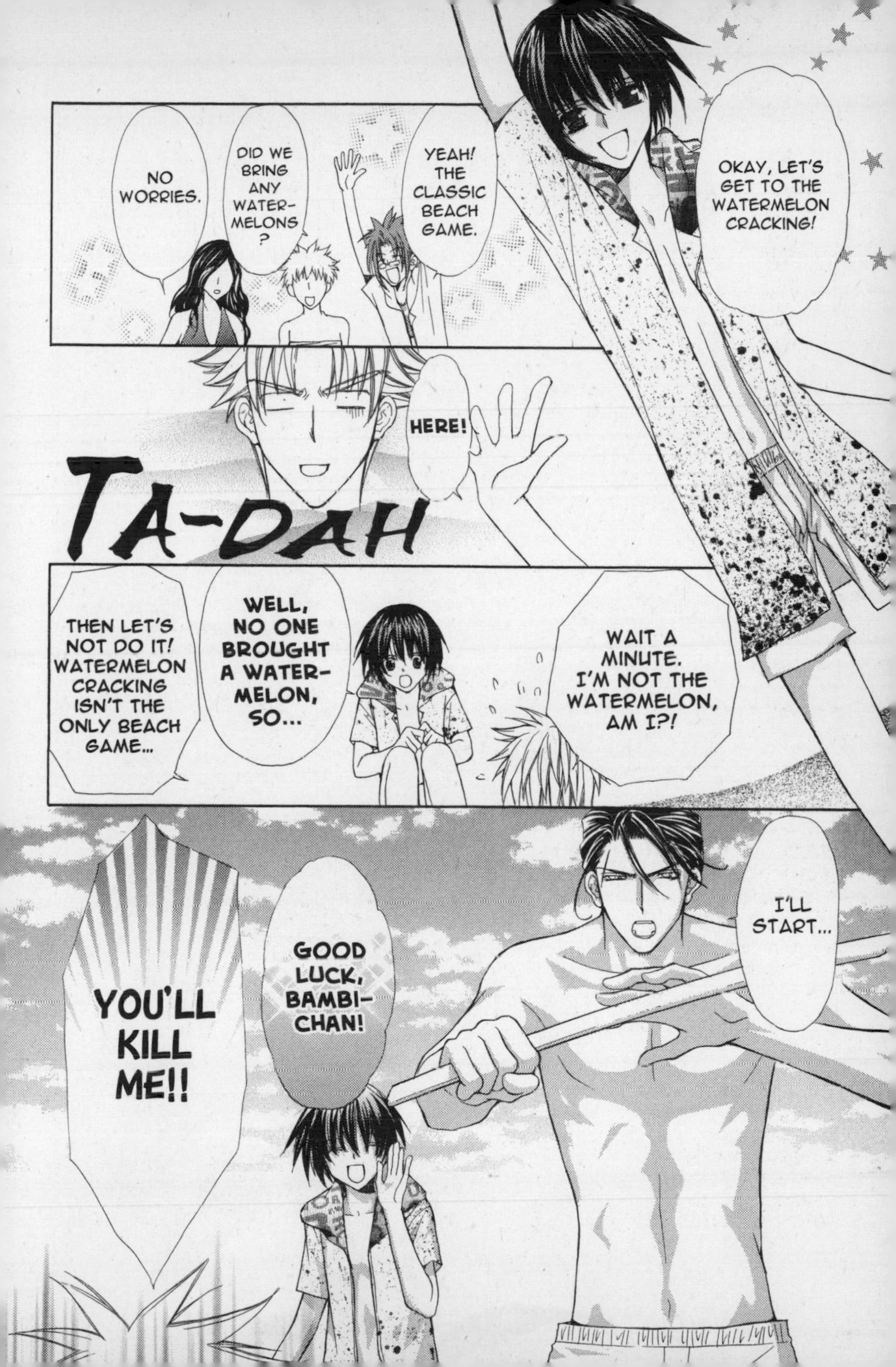
OKAY, LET'S GET TO THE WATERMELON CRACKING!
YEAH! THE CLASSIC BEACH GAME.
DID WE BRING ANY WATER-MELONS?
NO WORRIES.
HERE!
TA-DAH
WAIT A MINUTE. I'M NOT THE WATERMELON, AM I?!
WELL, NO ONE BROUGHT A WATER-MELON, SO...
THEN LET'S NOT DO IT! WATERMELON CRACKING ISN'T THE ONLY BEACH GAME...
I'LL START...
GOOD LUCK, BAMBI-CHAN!
YOU'LL KILL ME!!

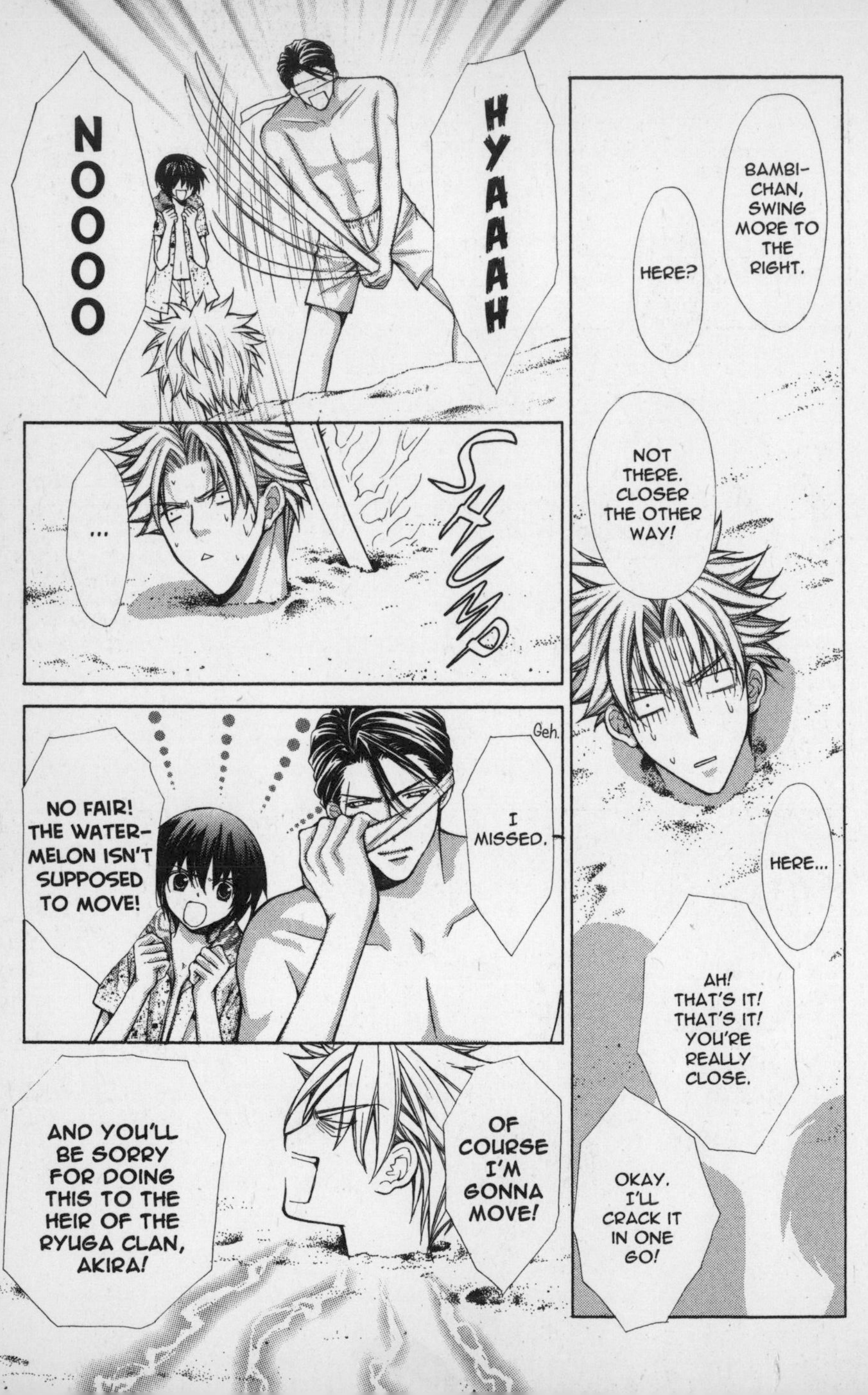
BAMBI-CHAN, SWING MORE TO THE RIGHT.
HERE?
NOT THERE. CLOSER THE OTHER WAY!
HERE...
AH! THAT'S IT! THAT'S IT! YOU'RE REALLY CLOSE.
OKAY. I'LL CRACK IT IN ONE GO!
HYAAAH
NOOOO
SHUMP
...
Geh.
I MISSED.
NO FAIR! THE WATER-MELON ISN'T SUPPOSED TO MOVE!
OF COURSE I'M GONNA MOVE!
AND YOU'LL BE SORRY FOR DOING THIS TO THE HEIR OF THE RYUGA CLAN, AKIRA!

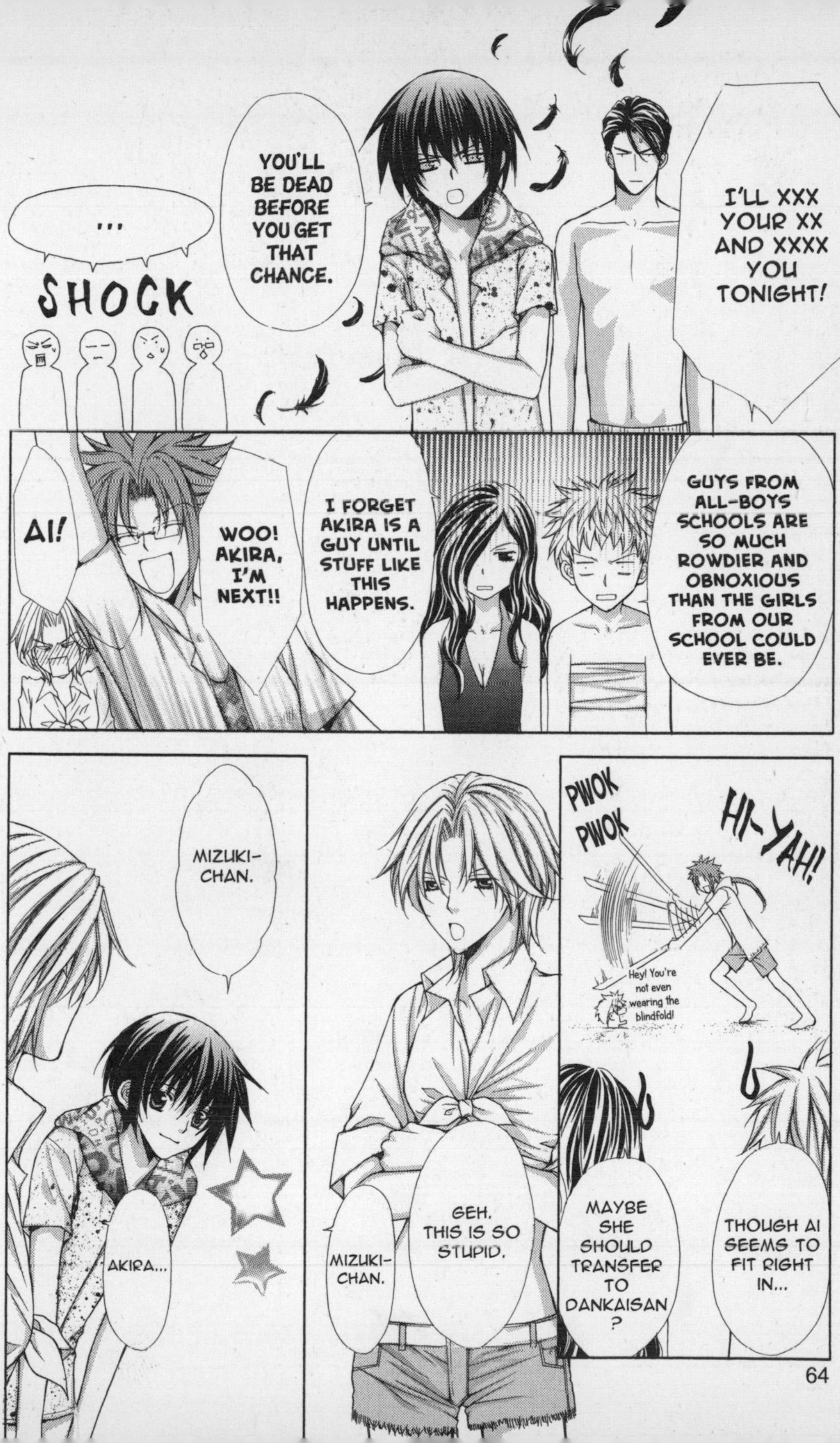
I'LL XXX YOUR XX AND XXXX YOU TONIGHT!
YOU'LL BE DEAD BEFORE YOU GET THAT CHANCE.
...
SHOCK
GUYS FROM ALL-BOYS SCHOOLS ARE SO MUCH ROWDIER AND OBNOXIOUS THAN THE GIRLS FROM OUR SCHOOL COULD EVER BE.
I FORGET AKIRA IS A GUY UNTIL STUFF LIKE THIS HAPPENS.
WOO! AKIRA, I'M NEXT!!
AI!
PWOK PWOK
HI-YAH!
Hey! You're not even wearing the blindfold!
THOUGH AI SEEMS TO FIT RIGHT IN...
MAYBE SHE SHOULD TRANSFER TO DANKAISAN?
GEH. THIS IS SO STUPID.
MIZUKI-CHAN.
MIZUKI-CHAN.
AKIRA...

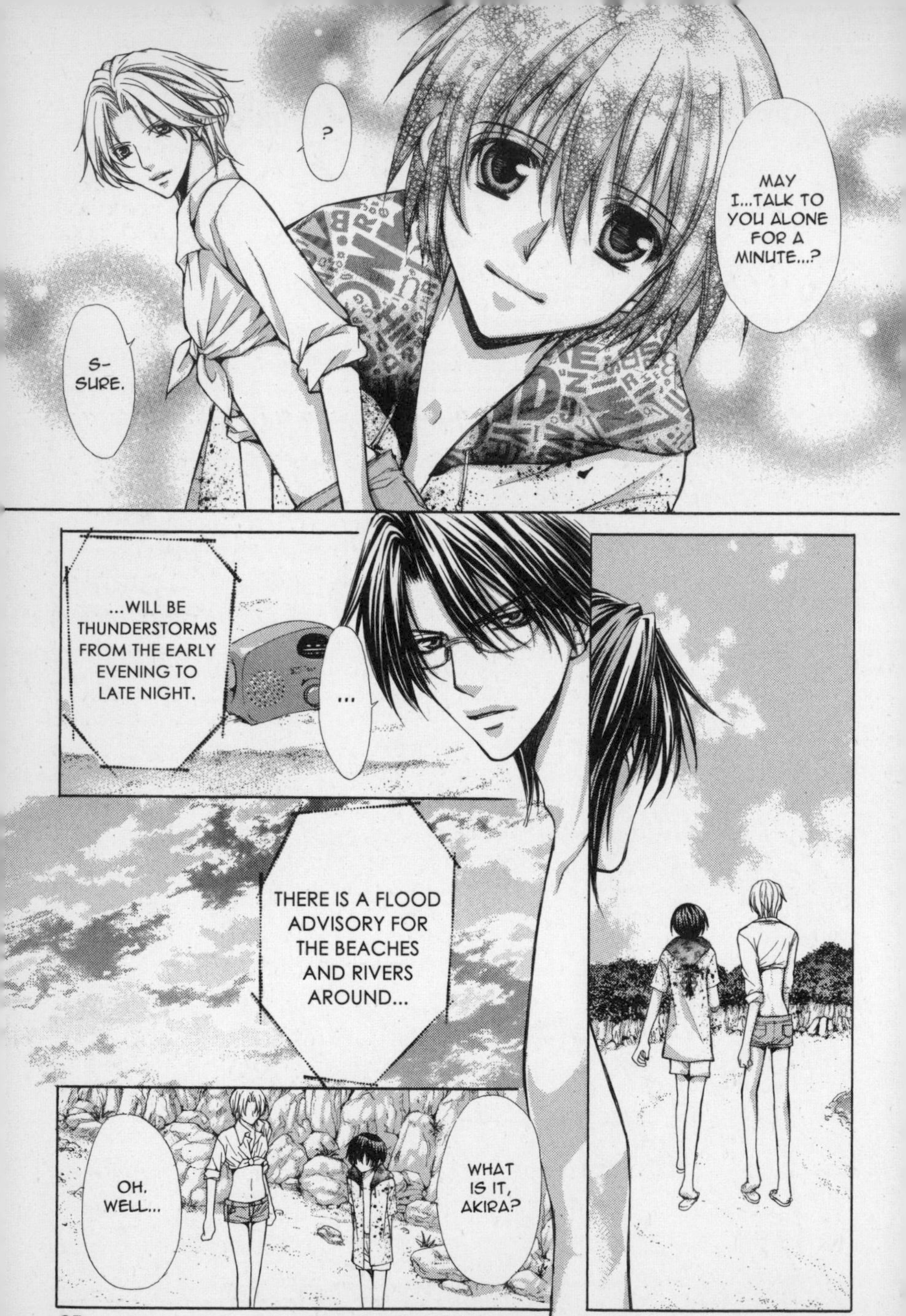
MAY I...TALK TO YOU ALONE FOR A MINUTE...?
?
S-SURE.
...
...WILL BE THUNDERSTORMS FROM THE EARLY EVENING TO LATE NIGHT.
THERE IS A FLOOD ADVISORY FOR THE BEACHES AND RIVERS AROUND...
WHAT IS IT, AKIRA?
OH. WELL...

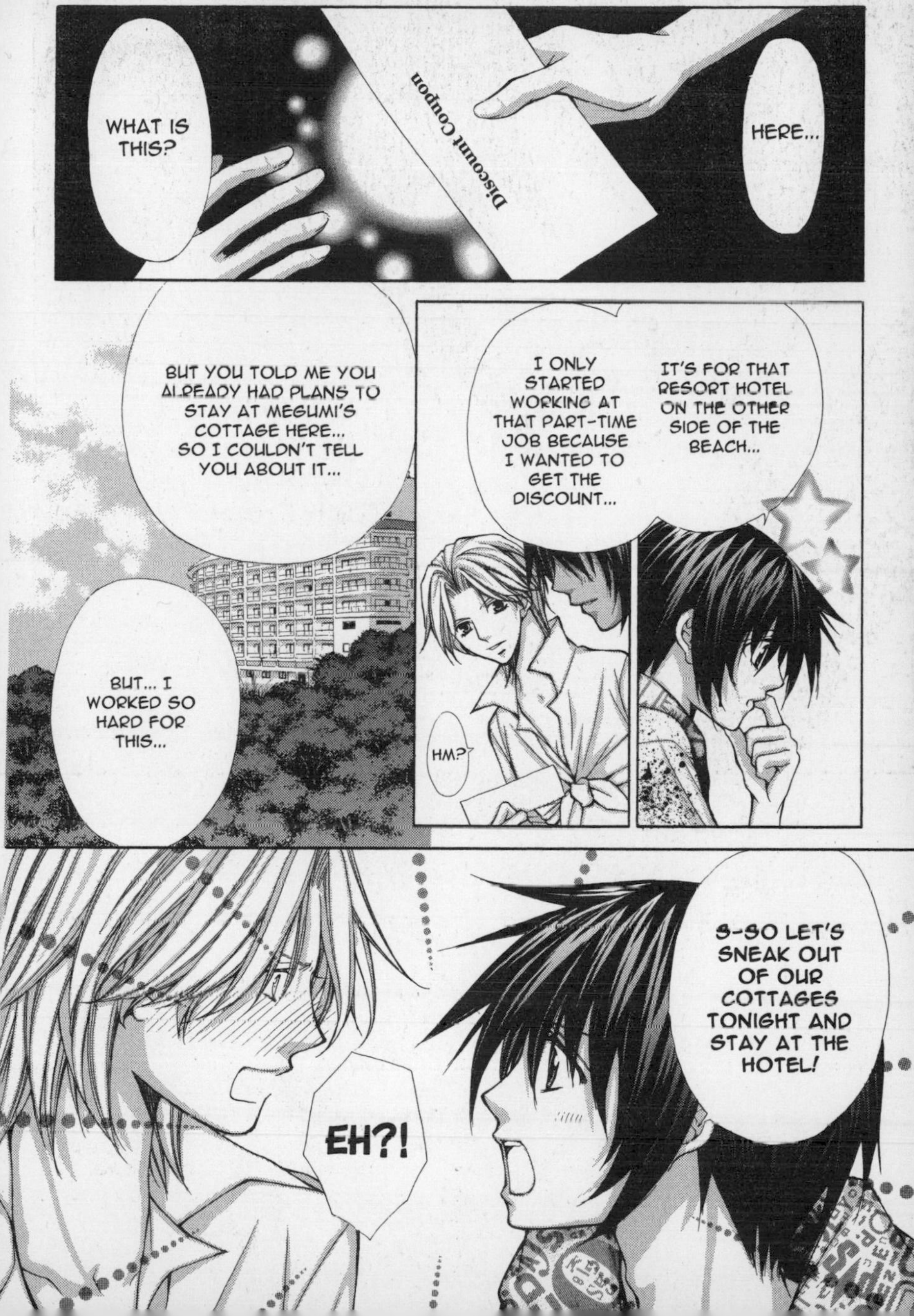
HERE...
Discount Coupon
WHAT IS THIS?
IT'S FOR THAT RESORT HOTEL ON THE OTHER SIDE OF THE BEACH...
I ONLY STARTED WORKING AT THAT PART-TIME JOB BECAUSE I WANTED TO GET THE DISCOUNT...
HM?
BUT YOU TOLD ME YOU ALREADY HAD PLANS TO STAY AT MEGUMI'S COTTAGE HERE... SO I COULDN'T TELL YOU ABOUT IT...
BUT... I WORKED SO HARD FOR THIS...
S-SO LET'S SNEAK OUT OF OUR COTTAGES TONIGHT AND STAY AT THE HOTEL!
EH?!

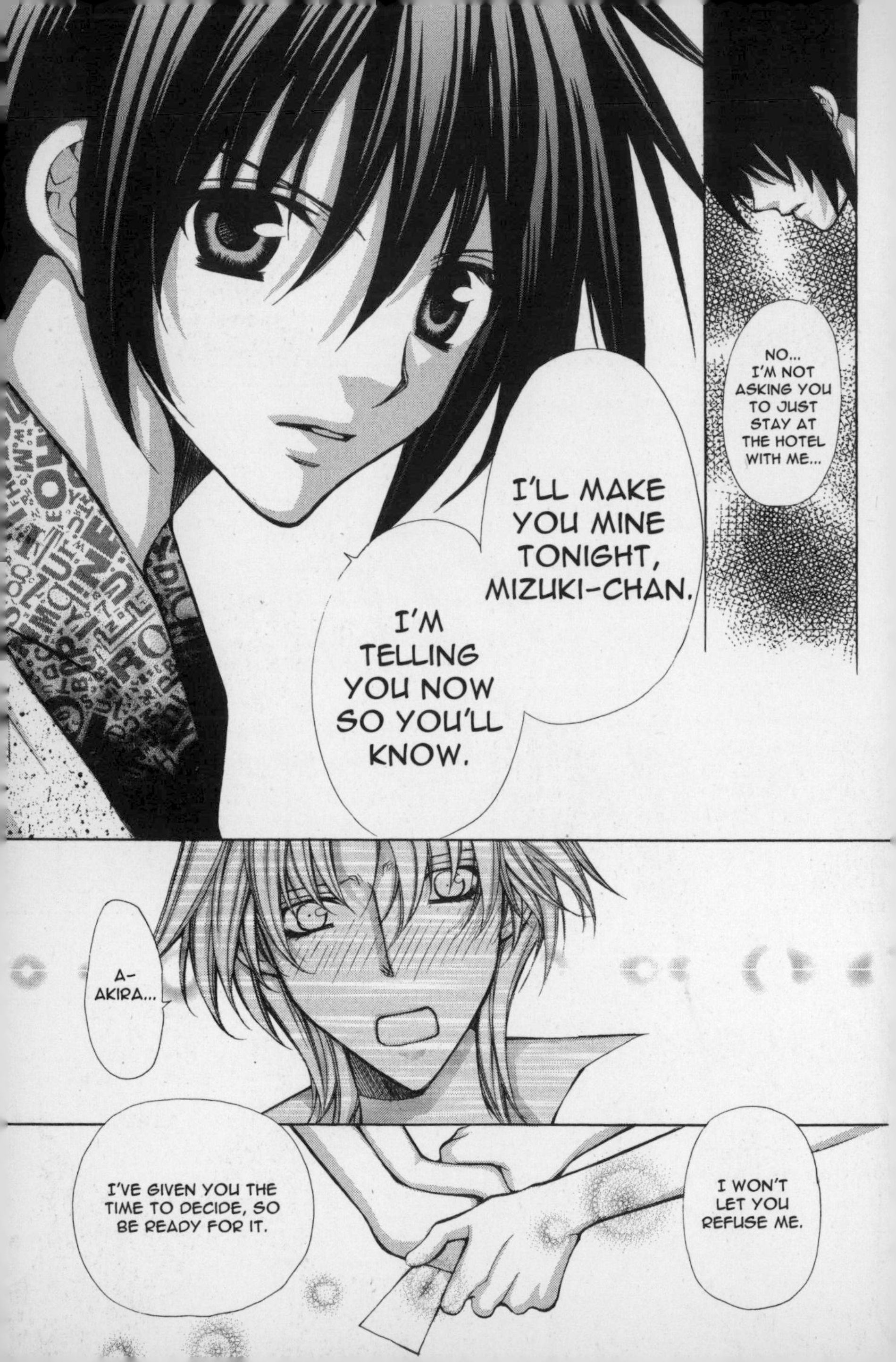
NO... I'M NOT ASKING YOU TO JUST STAY AT THE HOTEL WITH ME...
I'LL MAKE YOU MINE TONIGHT, MIZUKI-CHAN.
I'M TELLING YOU NOW SO YOU'LL KNOW.
A-AKIRA...
I WON'T LET YOU REFUSE ME.
I'VE GIVEN YOU THE TIME TO DECIDE, SO BE READY FOR IT.

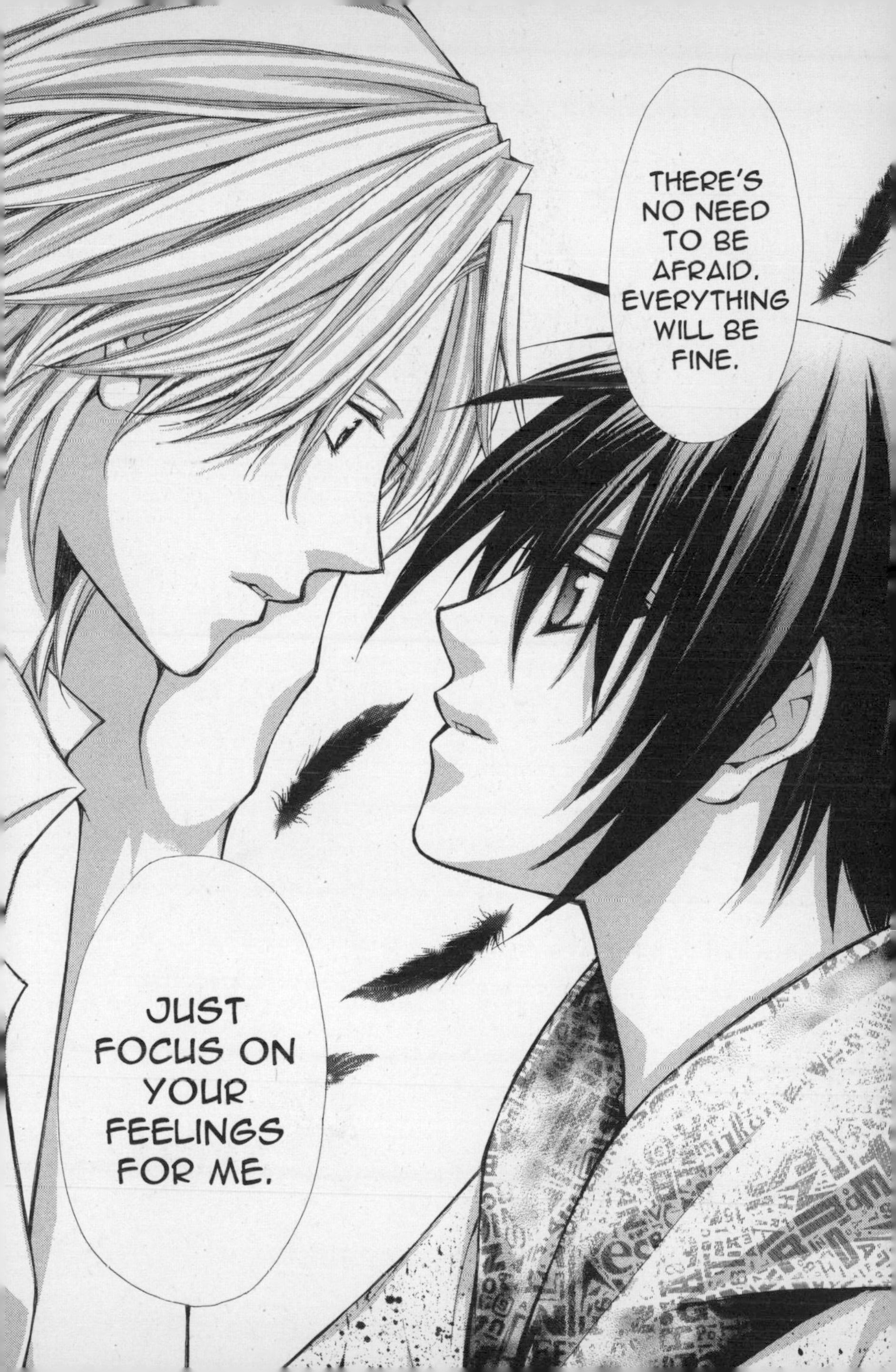
THERE'S NO NEED TO BE AFRAID. EVERYTHING WILL BE FINE.
JUST FOCUS ON YOUR FEELINGS FOR ME.

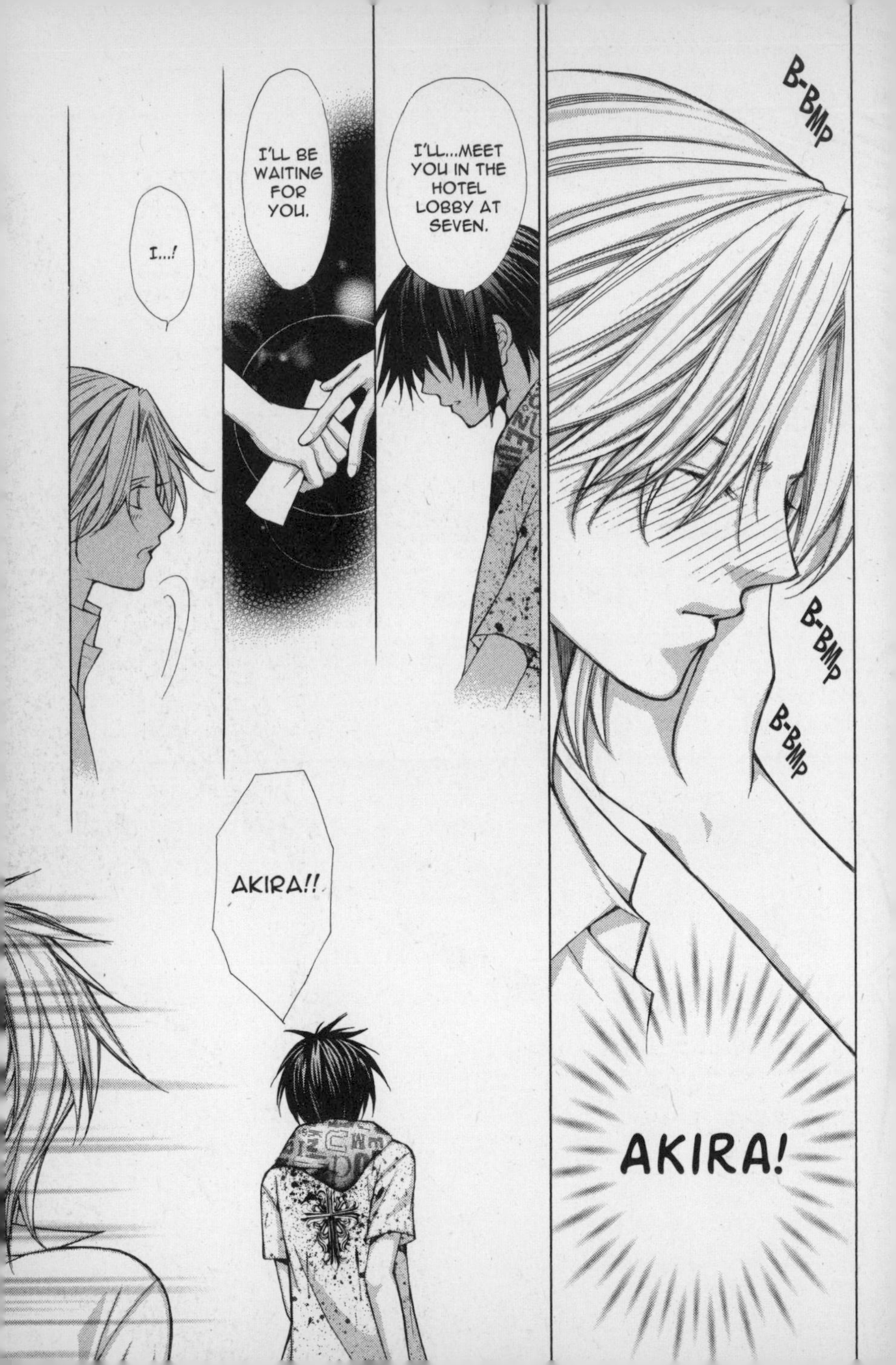
B-BMP
B-BMP
B-BMP
AKIRA!
I'LL...MEET YOU IN THE HOTEL LOBBY AT SEVEN.
I'LL BE WAITING FOR YOU.
I...!
AKIRA!!

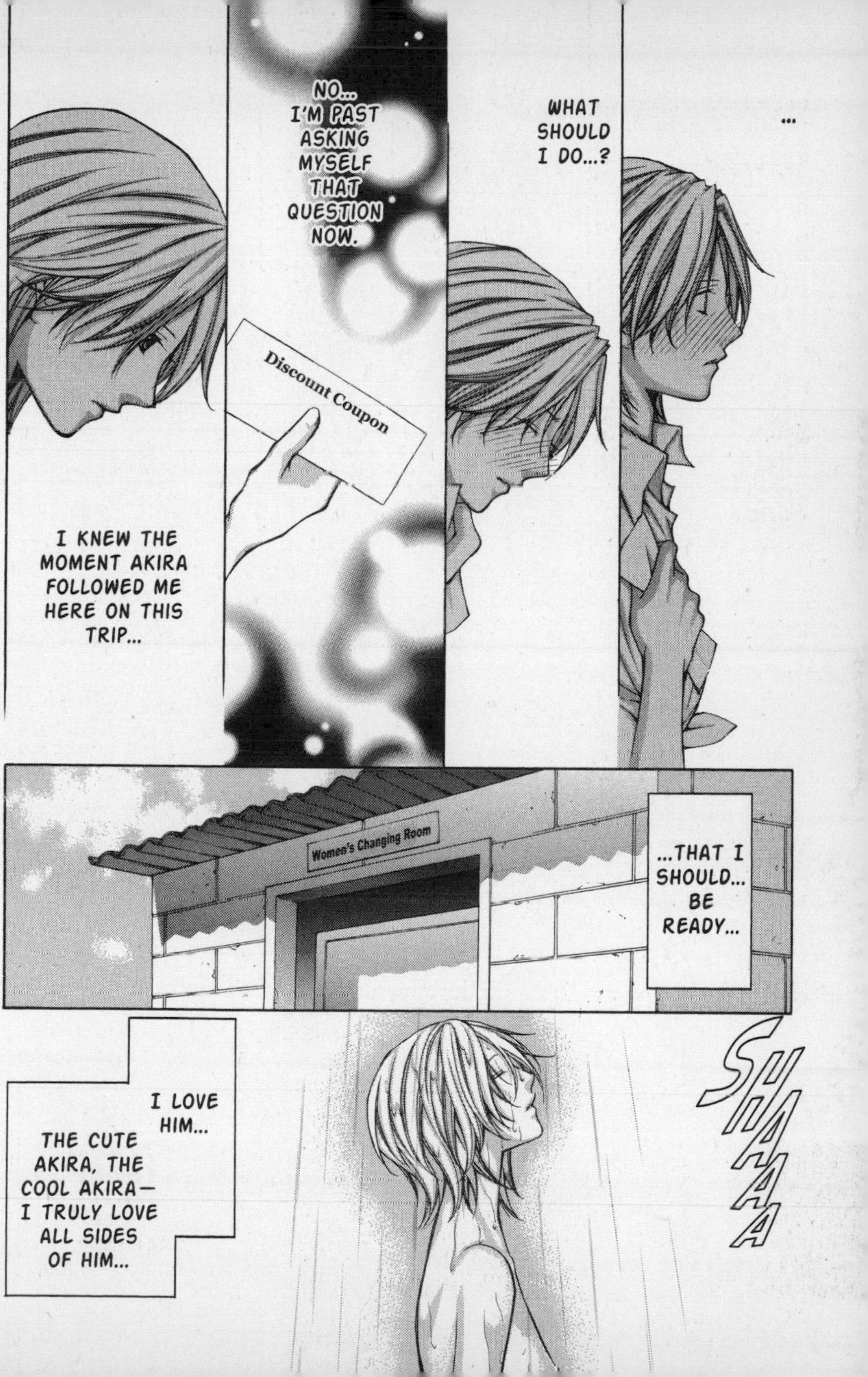
...
WHAT SHOULD I DO...?
NO... I'M PAST ASKING MYSELF THAT QUESTION NOW.
Discount Coupon
I KNEW THE MOMENT AKIRA FOLLOWED ME HERE ON THIS TRIP...
...THAT I SHOULD... BE READY...
Women's Changing Room
SHAAA
I LOVE HIM...
THE CUTE AKIRA, THE COOL AKIRA— I TRULY LOVE ALL SIDES OF HIM...

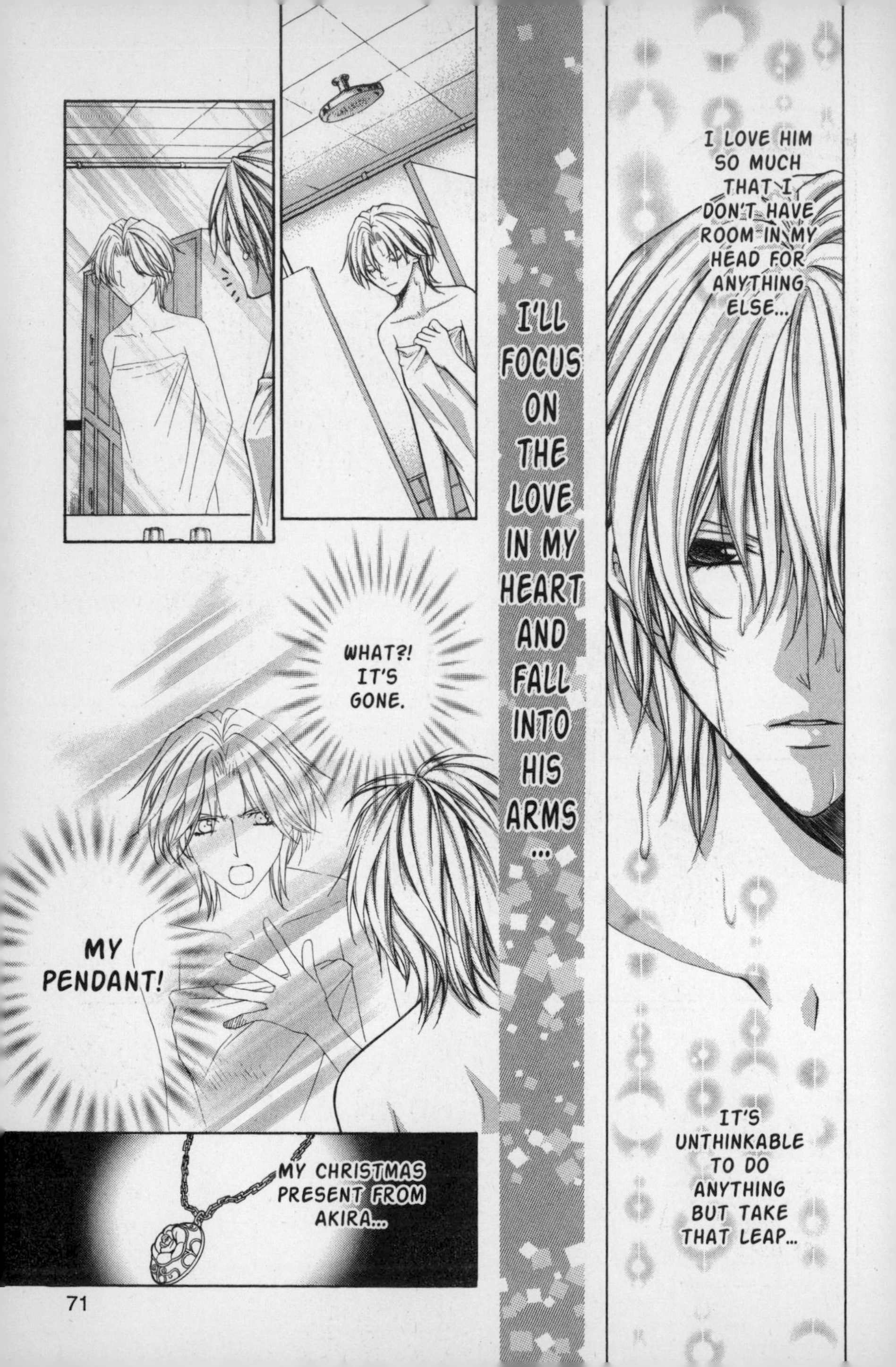
I LOVE HIM SO MUCH THAT I DON'T HAVE ROOM IN MY HEAD FOR ANYTHING ELSE...
IT'S UNTHINKABLE TO DO ANYTHING BUT TAKE THAT LEAP...
I'LL FOCUS ON THE LOVE IN MY HEART AND FALL INTO HIS ARMS...
WHAT?! IT'S GONE.
MY PENDANT!
MY CHRISTMAS PRESENT FROM AKIRA...

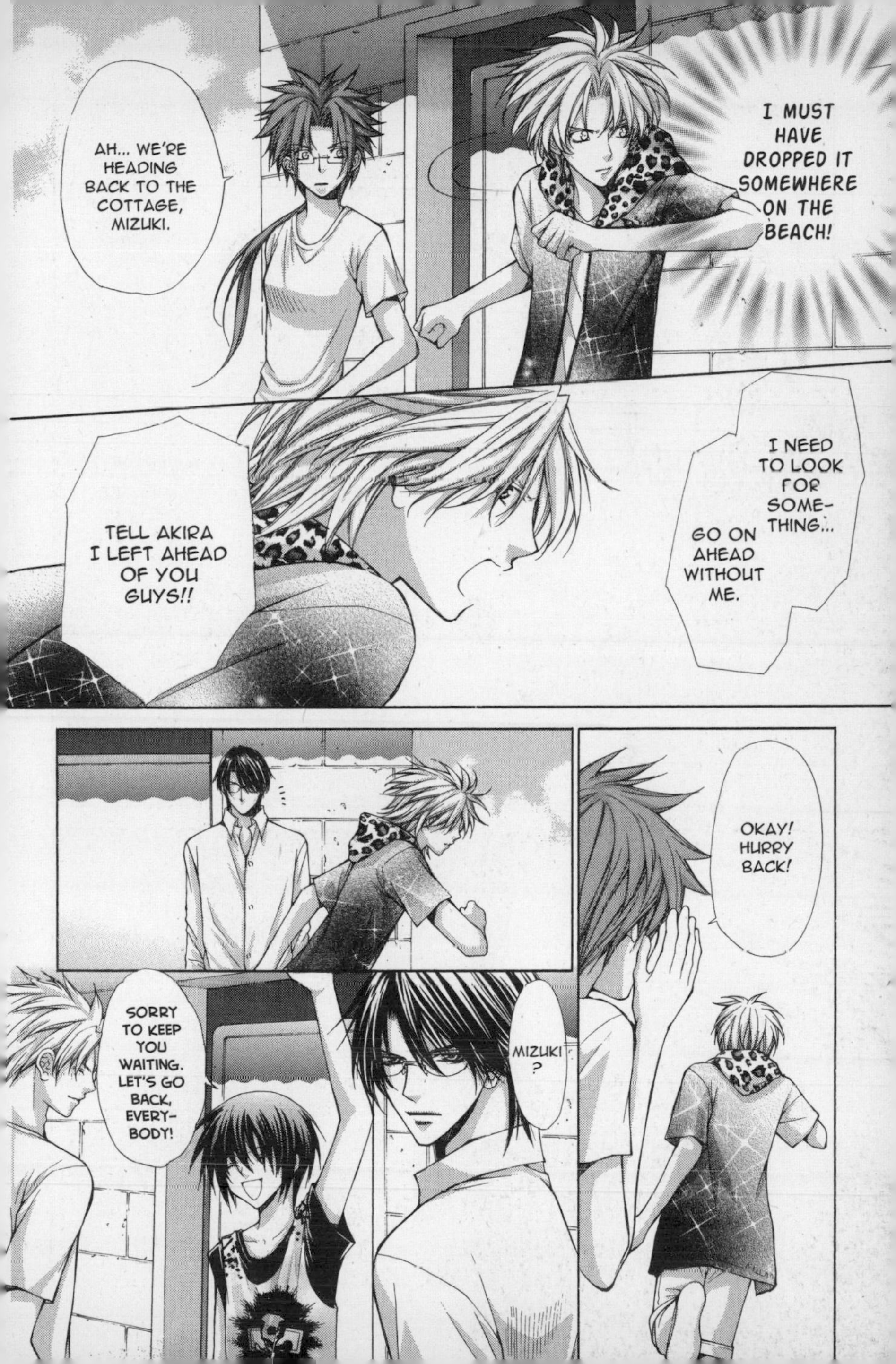
I MUST HAVE DROPPED IT SOMEWHERE ON THE BEACH!
AH... WE'RE HEADING BACK TO THE COTTAGE, MIZUKI.
I NEED TO LOOK FOR SOME-THING...
GO ON AHEAD WITHOUT ME.
TELL AKIRA I LEFT AHEAD OF YOU GUYS!!
OKAY! HURRY BACK!
MIZUKI ?
SORRY TO KEEP YOU WAITING. LET'S GO BACK, EVERY-BODY!

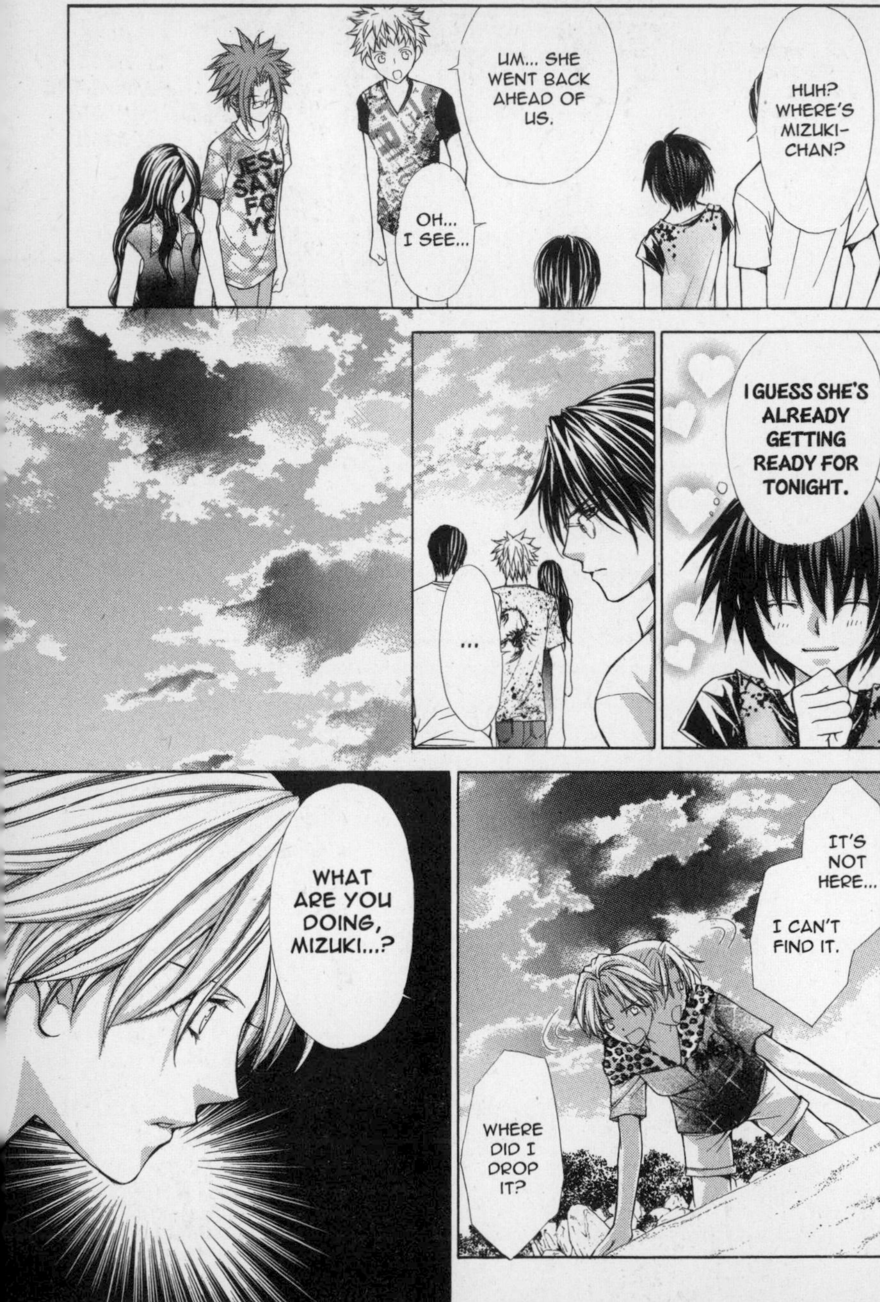
HUH? WHERE'S MIZUKI-CHAN?
UM... SHE WENT BACK AHEAD OF US.
OH... I SEE...
I GUESS SHE'S ALREADY GETTING READY FOR TONIGHT.
...
IT'S NOT HERE...
I CAN'T FIND IT.
WHERE DID I DROP IT?
WHAT ARE YOU DOING, MIZUKI...?

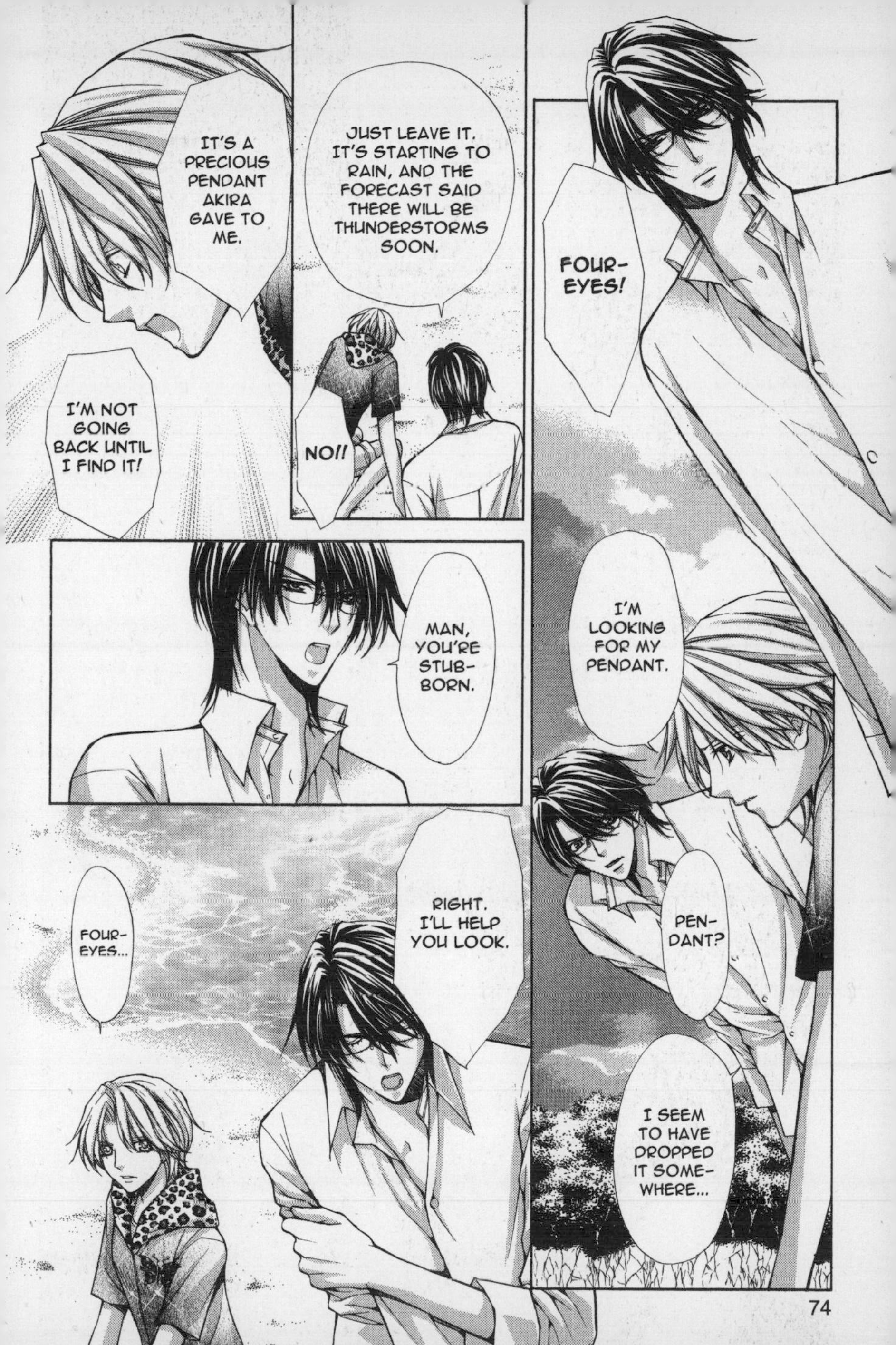
FOUR-EYES!
I'M LOOKING FOR MY PENDANT.
PEN-DANT?
I SEEM TO HAVE DROPPED IT SOME-WHERE...
JUST LEAVE IT. IT'S STARTING TO RAIN, AND THE FORECAST SAID THERE WILL BE THUNDERSTORMS SOON.
NO!!
IT'S A PRECIOUS PENDANT AKIRA GAVE TO ME.
I'M NOT GOING BACK UNTIL I FIND IT!
MAN, YOU'RE STUB-BORN.
RIGHT. I'LL HELP YOU LOOK.
FOUR-EYES...

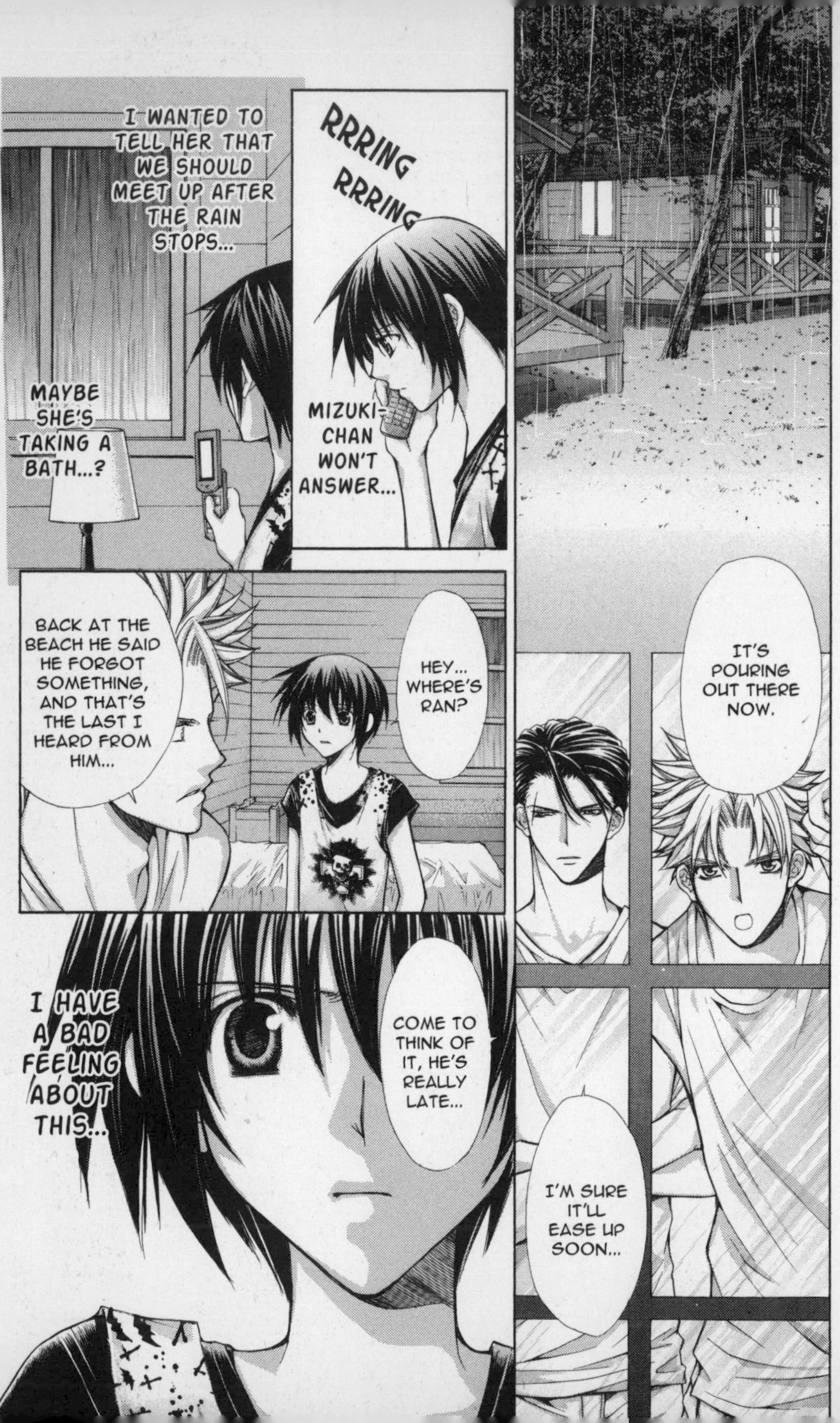
IT'S POURING OUT THERE NOW.
I'M SURE IT'LL EASE UP SOON...
RRRING RRRING
MIZUKI-CHAN WON'T ANSWER...
I WANTED TO TELL HER THAT WE SHOULD MEET UP AFTER THE RAIN STOPS...
MAYBE SHE'S TAKING A BATH...?
HEY... WHERE'S RAN?
BACK AT THE BEACH HE SAID HE FORGOT SOMETHING, AND THAT'S THE LAST I HEARD FROM HIM...
COME TO THINK OF IT, HE'S REALLY LATE...
I HAVE A BAD FEELING ABOUT THIS...

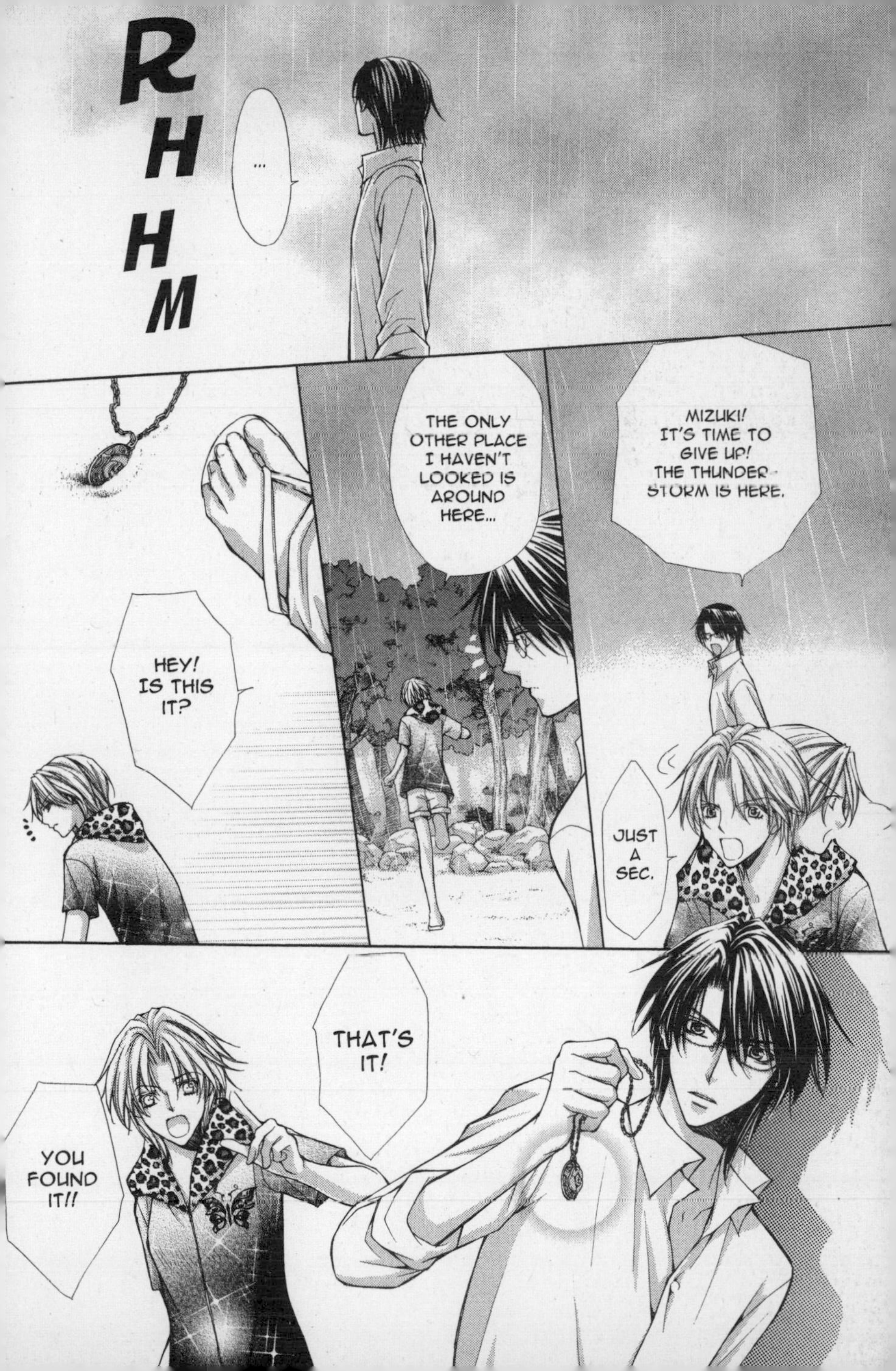
...
RHHM
MIZUKI! IT'S TIME TO GIVE UP! THE THUNDER-STORM IS HERE.
JUST A SEC.
THE ONLY OTHER PLACE I HAVEN'T LOOKED IS AROUND HERE...
HEY! IS THIS IT?
THAT'S IT!
YOU FOUND IT!!

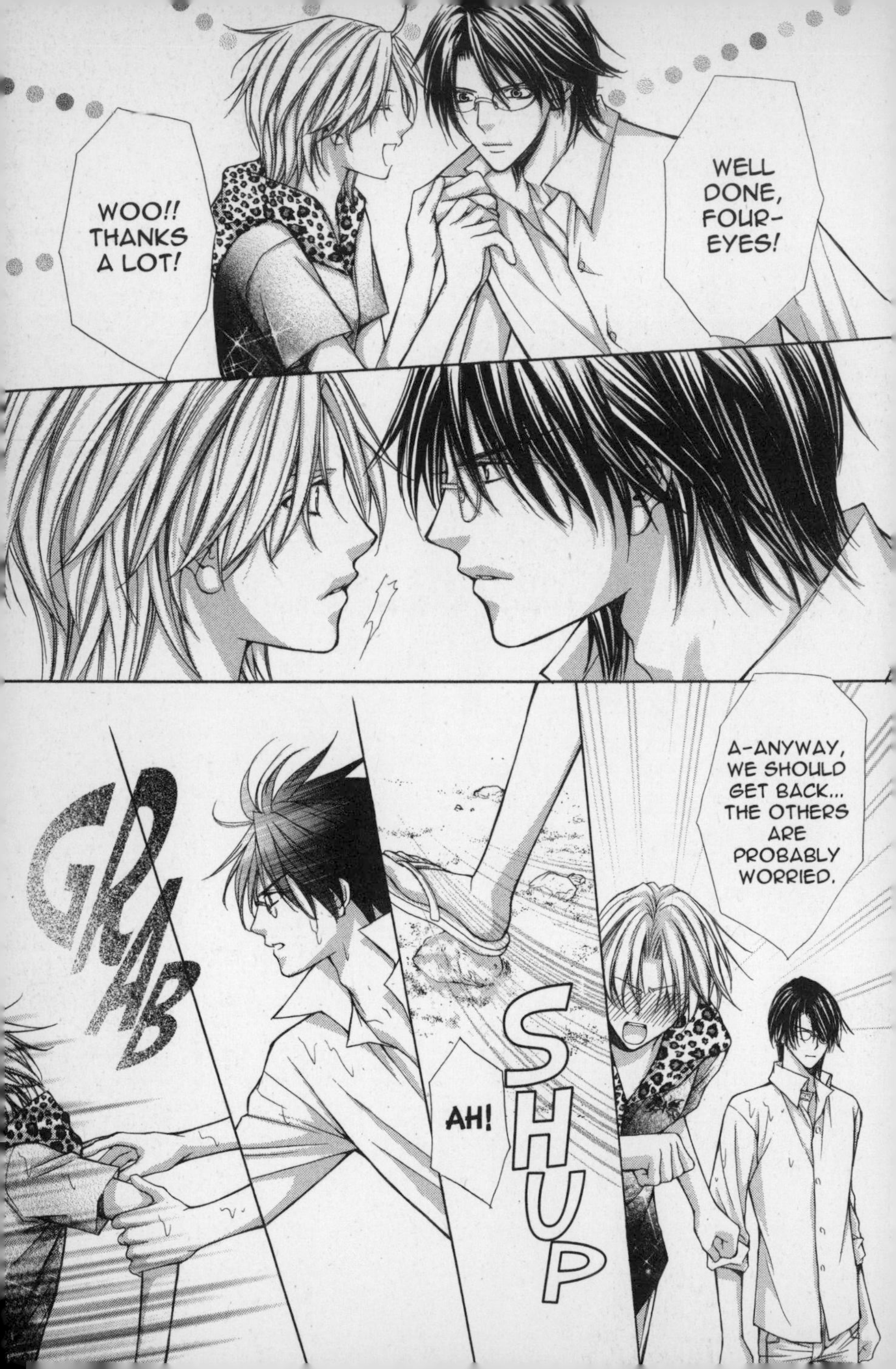
WELL DONE, FOUR-EYES!
WOO!! THANKS A LOT!
A-ANYWAY, WE SHOULD GET BACK... THE OTHERS ARE PROBABLY WORRIED.
SHUP
AH!
GRAB

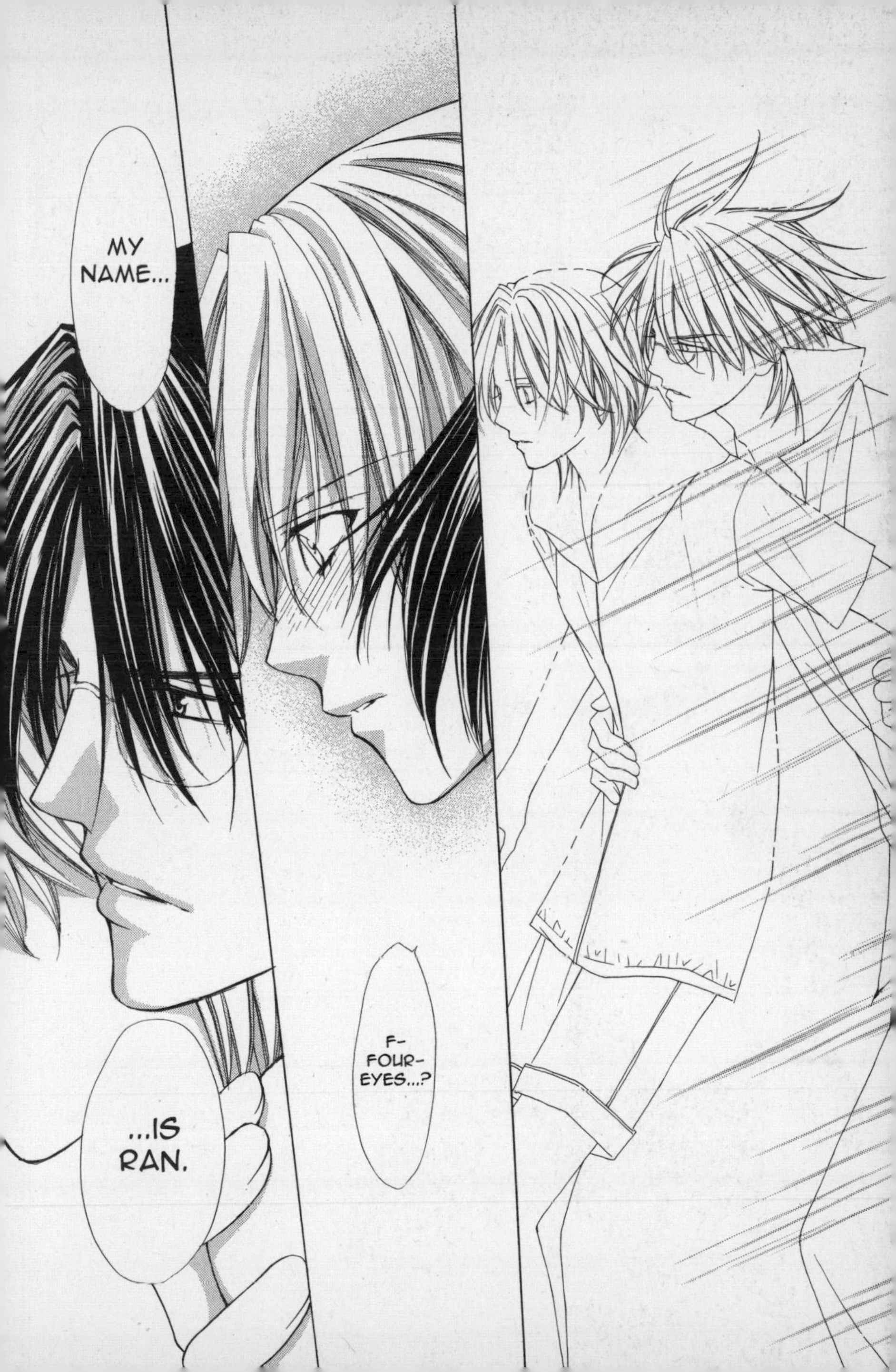
F-FOUR-EYES...?
MY NAME...
...IS RAN.

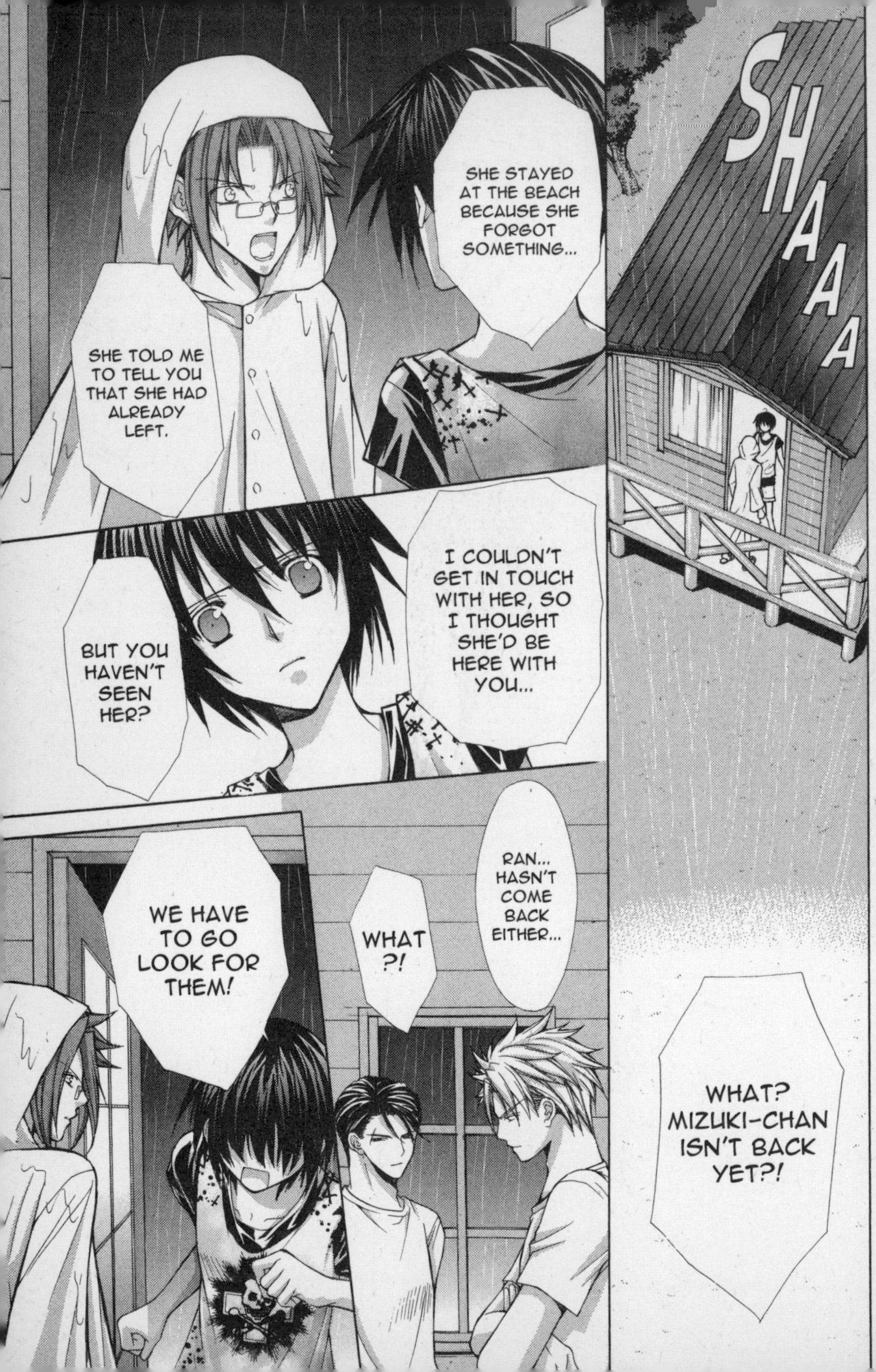
SHAAA
WHAT? MIZUKI-CHAN ISN'T BACK YET?!
SHE STAYED AT THE BEACH BECAUSE SHE FORGOT SOMETHING...
SHE TOLD ME TO TELL YOU THAT SHE HAD ALREADY LEFT.
I COULDN'T GET IN TOUCH WITH HER, SO I THOUGHT SHE'D BE HERE WITH YOU...
BUT YOU HAVEN'T SEEN HER?
RAN... HASN'T COME BACK EITHER...
WHAT?!
WE HAVE TO GO LOOK FOR THEM!

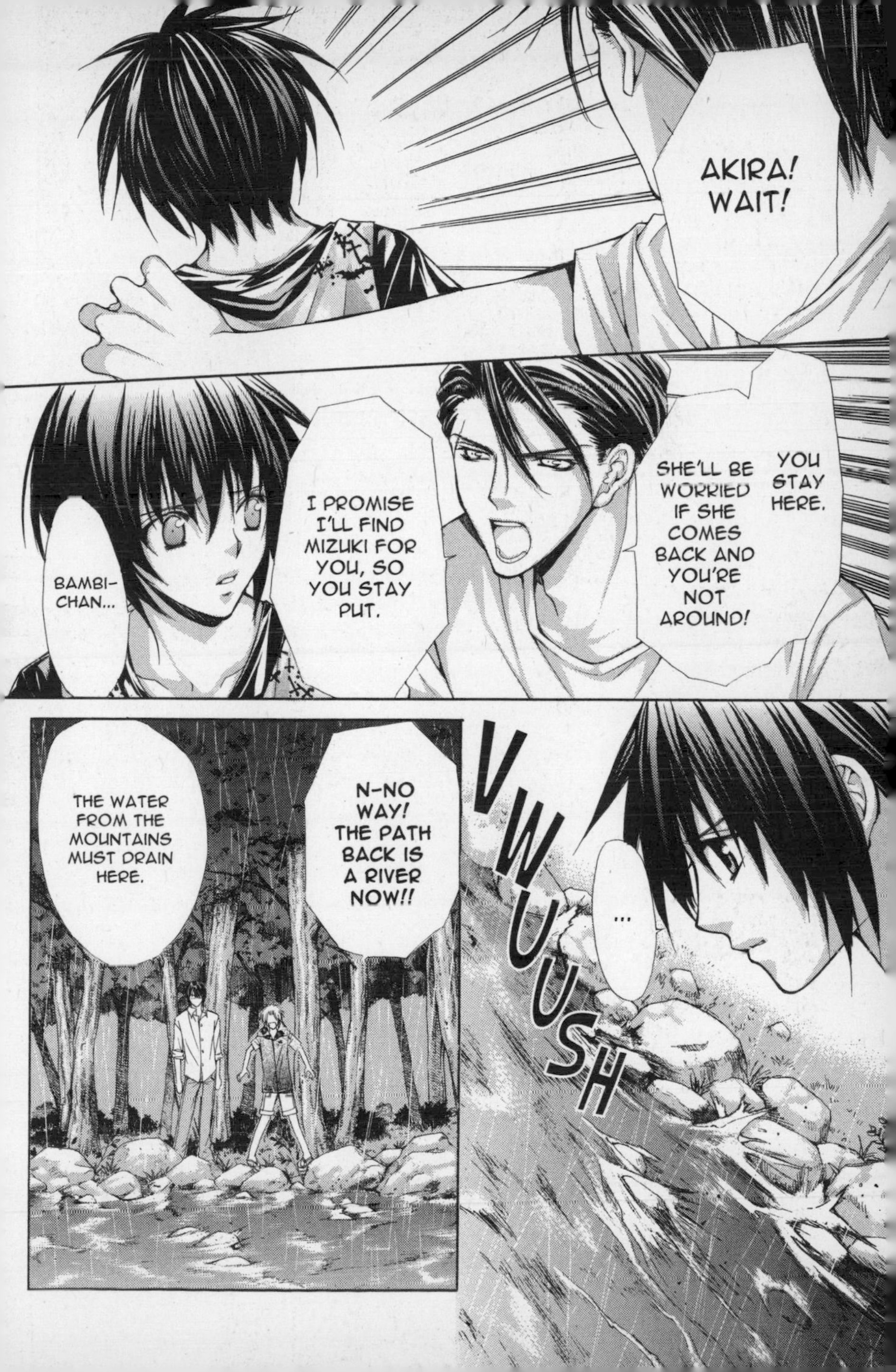
AKIRA! WAIT!
YOU STAY HERE.
SHE'LL BE WORRIED IF SHE COMES BACK AND YOU'RE NOT AROUND!
I PROMISE I'LL FIND MIZUKI FOR YOU, SO YOU STAY PUT.
BAMBI-CHAN...
VWUUSH
...
N-NO WAY! THE PATH BACK IS A RIVER NOW!!
THE WATER FROM THE MOUNTAINS MUST DRAIN HERE.

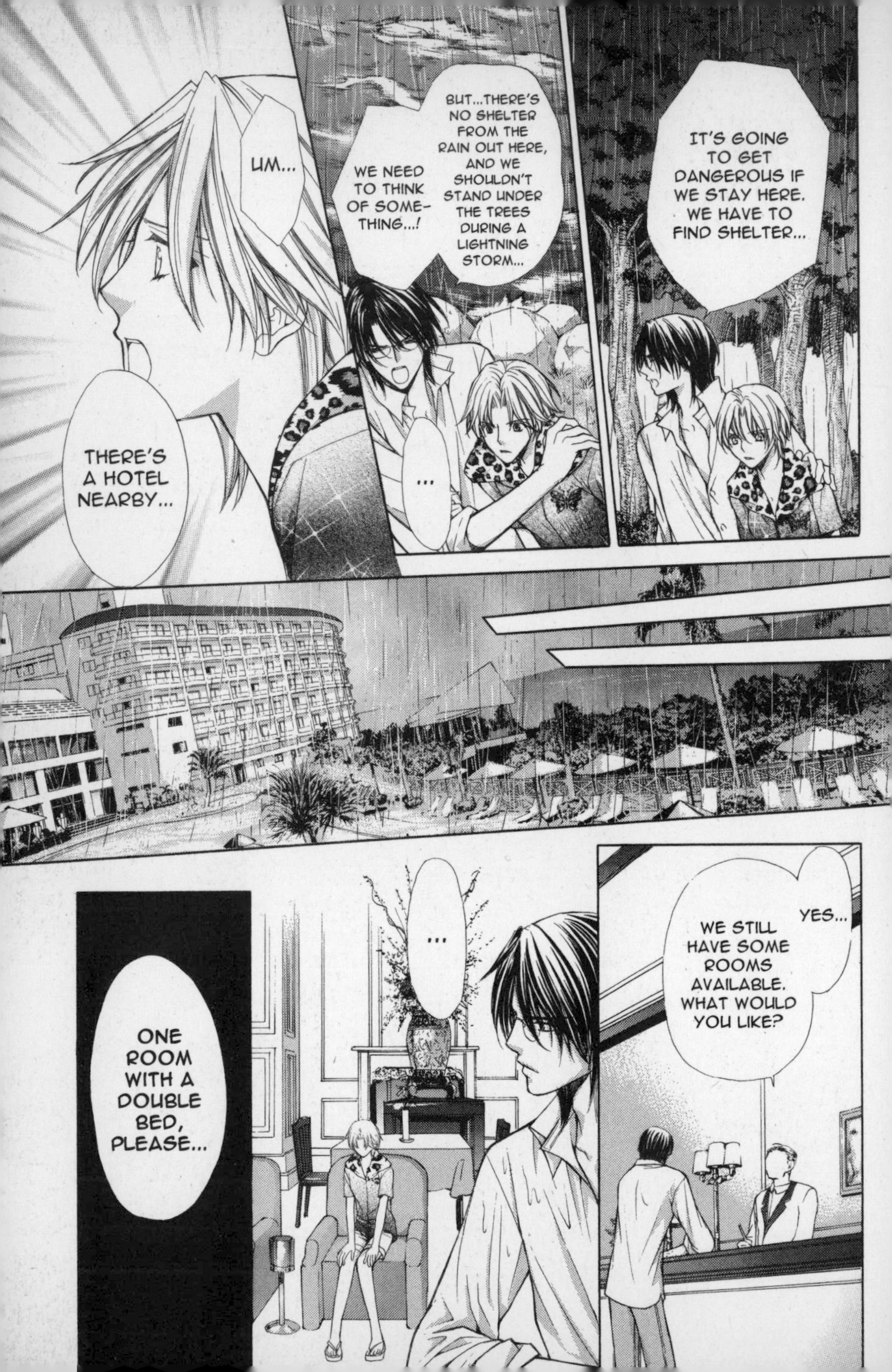
IT'S GOING TO GET DANGEROUS IF WE STAY HERE. WE HAVE TO FIND SHELTER...
BUT...THERE'S NO SHELTER FROM THE RAIN OUT HERE, AND WE SHOULDN'T STAND UNDER THE TREES DURING A LIGHTNING STORM...
WE NEED TO THINK OF SOME-THING...!
...
UM...
THERE'S A HOTEL NEARBY...
YES...
WE STILL HAVE SOME ROOMS AVAILABLE. WHAT WOULD YOU LIKE?
...
ONE ROOM WITH A DOUBLE BED, PLEASE...

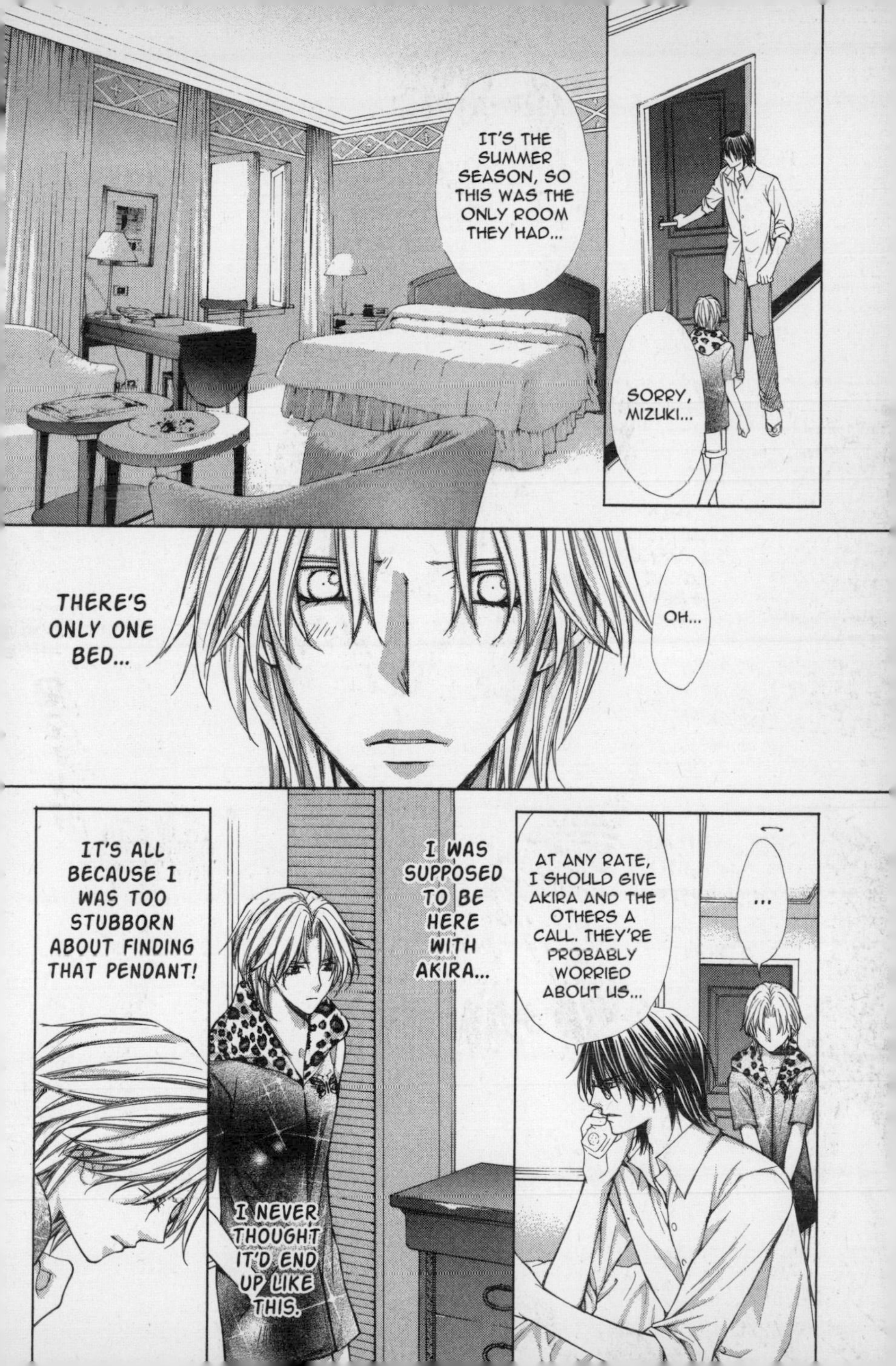
IT'S THE SUMMER SEASON, SO THIS WAS THE ONLY ROOM THEY HAD...
SORRY, MIZUKI...
OH...
THERE'S ONLY ONE BED...
...
AT ANY RATE, I SHOULD GIVE AKIRA AND THE OTHERS A CALL. THEY'RE PROBABLY WORRIED ABOUT US...
I WAS SUPPOSED TO BE HERE WITH AKIRA...
IT'S ALL BECAUSE I WAS TOO STUBBORN ABOUT FINDING THAT PENDANT!
I NEVER THOUGHT IT'D END UP LIKE THIS.

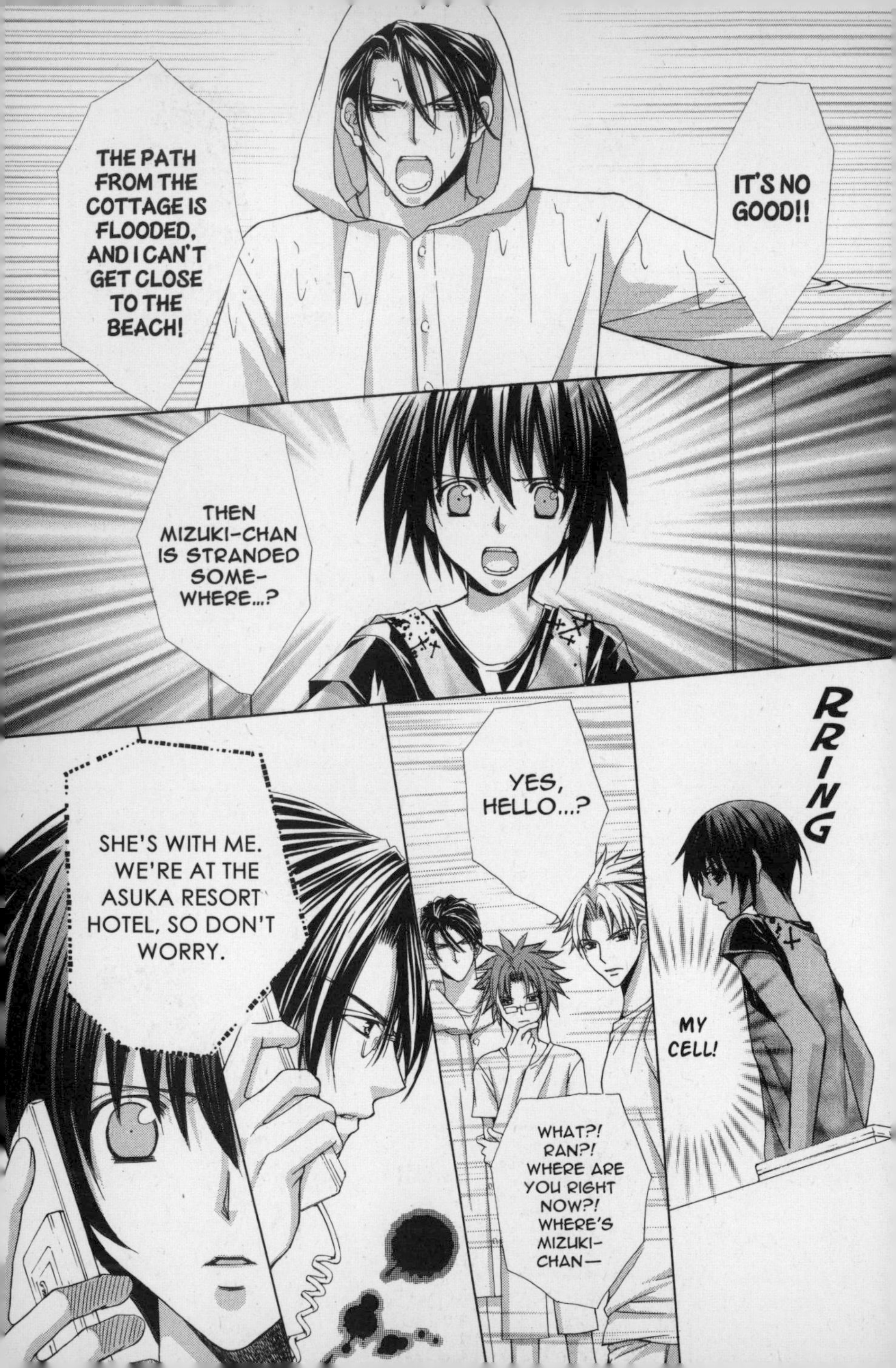
IT'S NO GOOD!!
THE PATH FROM THE COTTAGE IS FLOODED, AND I CAN'T GET CLOSE TO THE BEACH!
THEN MIZUKI-CHAN IS STRANDED SOME-WHERE...?
RRING
MY CELL!
YES, HELLO...?
WHAT?! RAN?! WHERE ARE YOU RIGHT NOW?! WHERE'S MIZUKI-CHAN—
SHE'S WITH ME. WE'RE AT THE ASUKA RESORT HOTEL, SO DON'T WORRY.

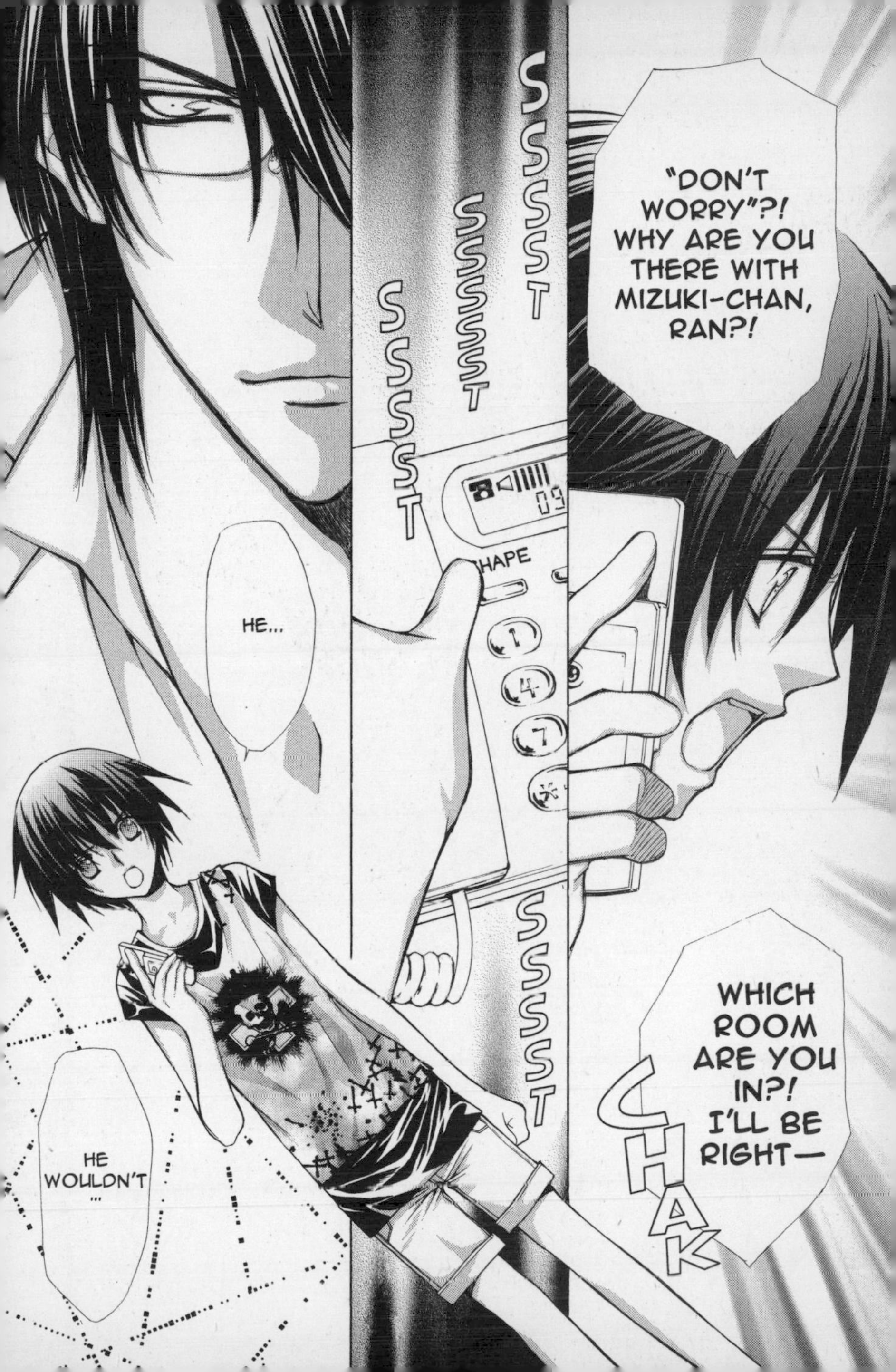
"DON'T WORRY"?! WHY ARE YOU THERE WITH MIZUKI-CHAN, RAN?!
WHICH ROOM ARE YOU IN?! I'LL BE RIGHT—
CHAK
SSSSST
SSSSSST
SSSSSST
SSSSSST
SHAPE
HE...
HE WOULDN'T ...

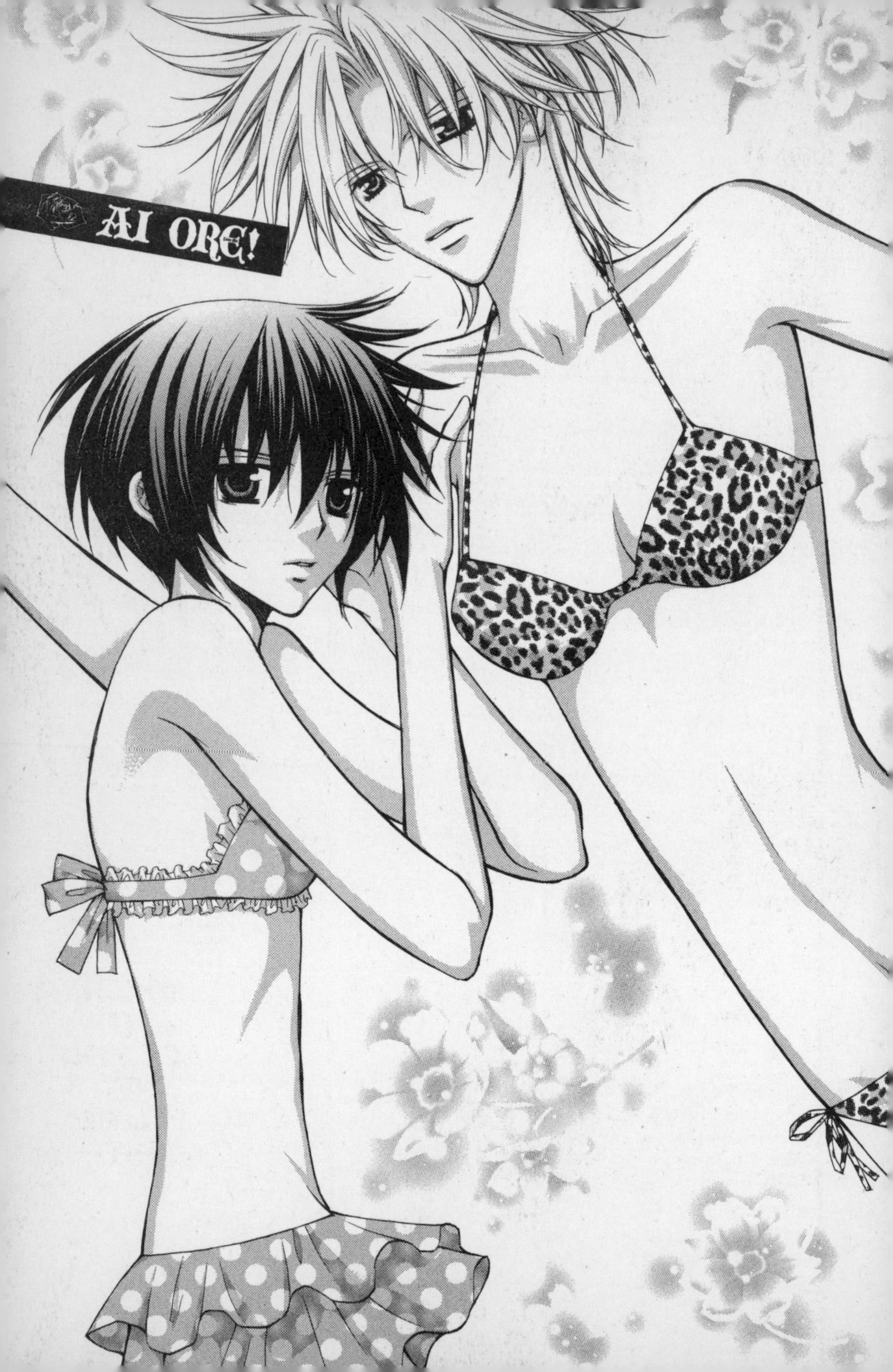
AI ORE!

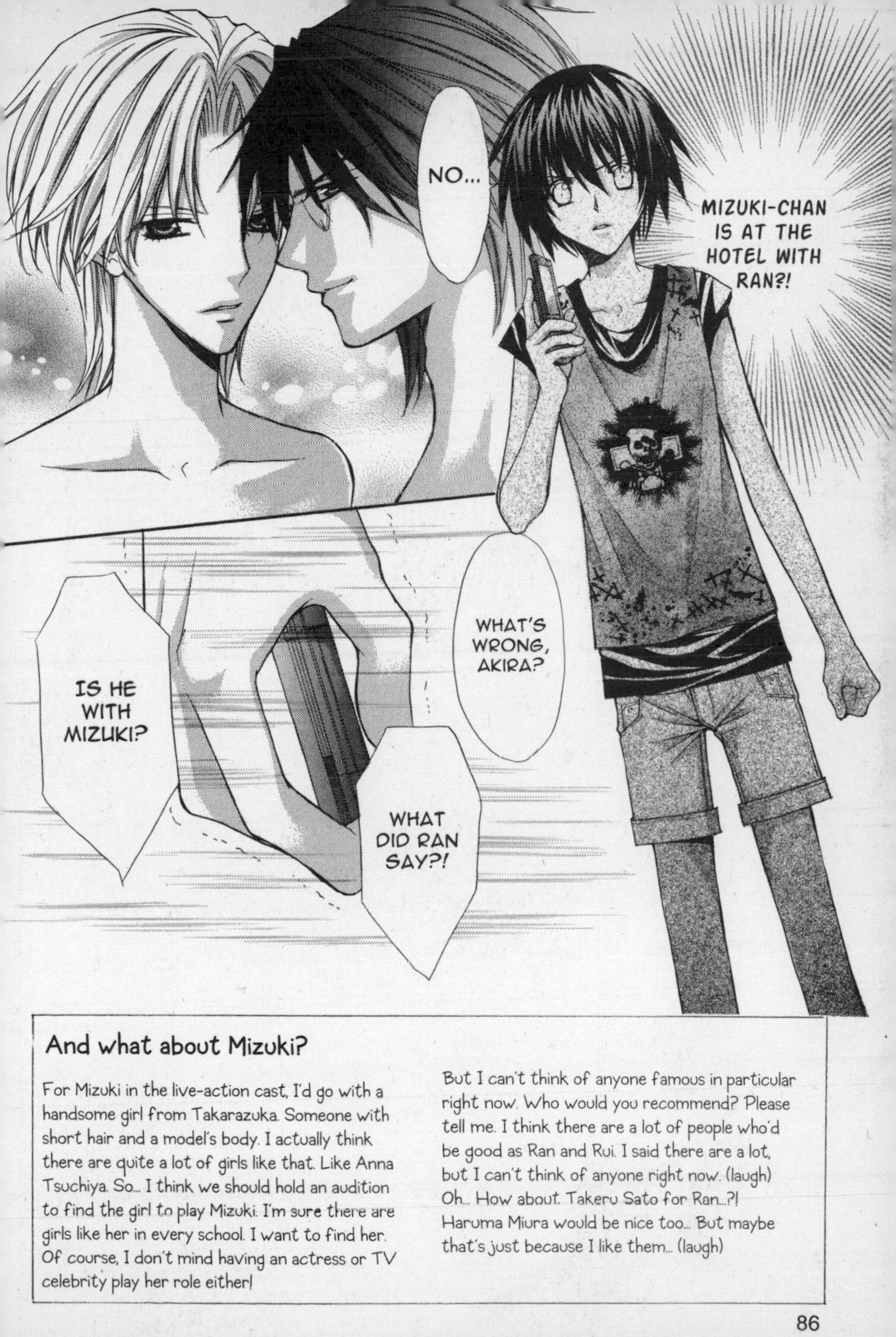
MIZUKI-CHAN IS AT THE HOTEL WITH RAN?!
NO...
WHAT'S WRONG, AKIRA?
WHAT DID RAN SAY?!
IS HE WITH MIZUKI?

And what about Mizuki?

For Mizuki in the live-action cast, I'd go with a handsome girl from Takarazuka. Someone with short hair and a model's body. I actually think there are quite a lot of girls like that. Like Anna Tsuchiya. So... I think we should hold an audition to find the girl to play Mizuki. I'm sure there are girls like her in every school. I want to find her. Of course, I don't mind having an actress or TV celebrity play her role either! But I can't think of anyone famous in particular right now. Who would you recommend? Please tell me. I think there are a lot of people who'd be good as Ran and Rui. I said there are a lot, but I can't think of anyone right now. (laugh) Oh... How about Takeru Sato for Ran...?! Haruma Miura would be nice too... But maybe that's just because I like them... (laugh)

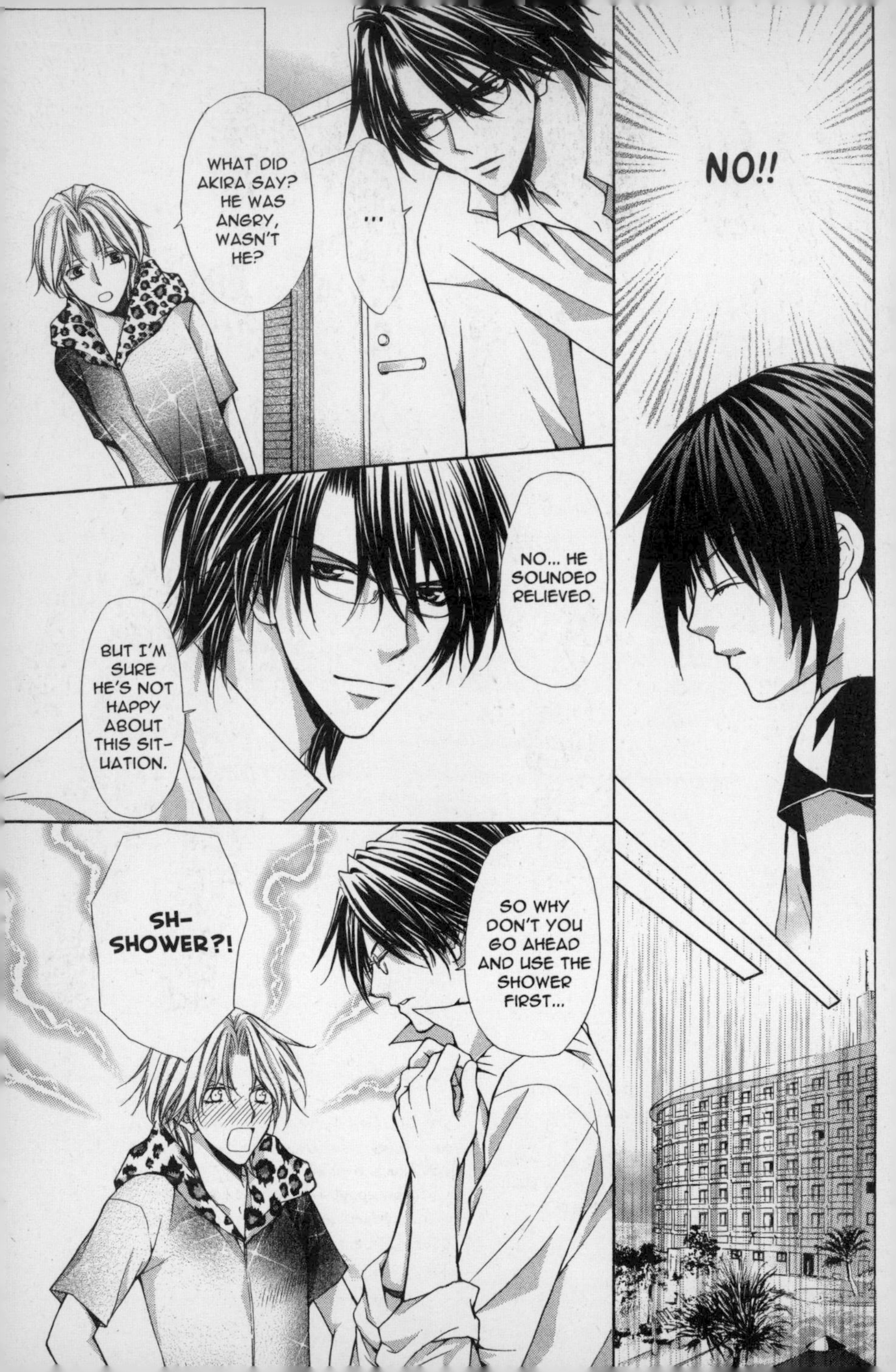
NO!!
WHAT DID AKIRA SAY? HE WAS ANGRY, WASN'T HE?
...
NO... HE SOUNDED RELIEVED.
BUT I'M SURE HE'S NOT HAPPY ABOUT THIS SIT-UATION.
SO WHY DON'T YOU GO AHEAD AND USE THE SHOWER FIRST...
SH-SHOWER?!

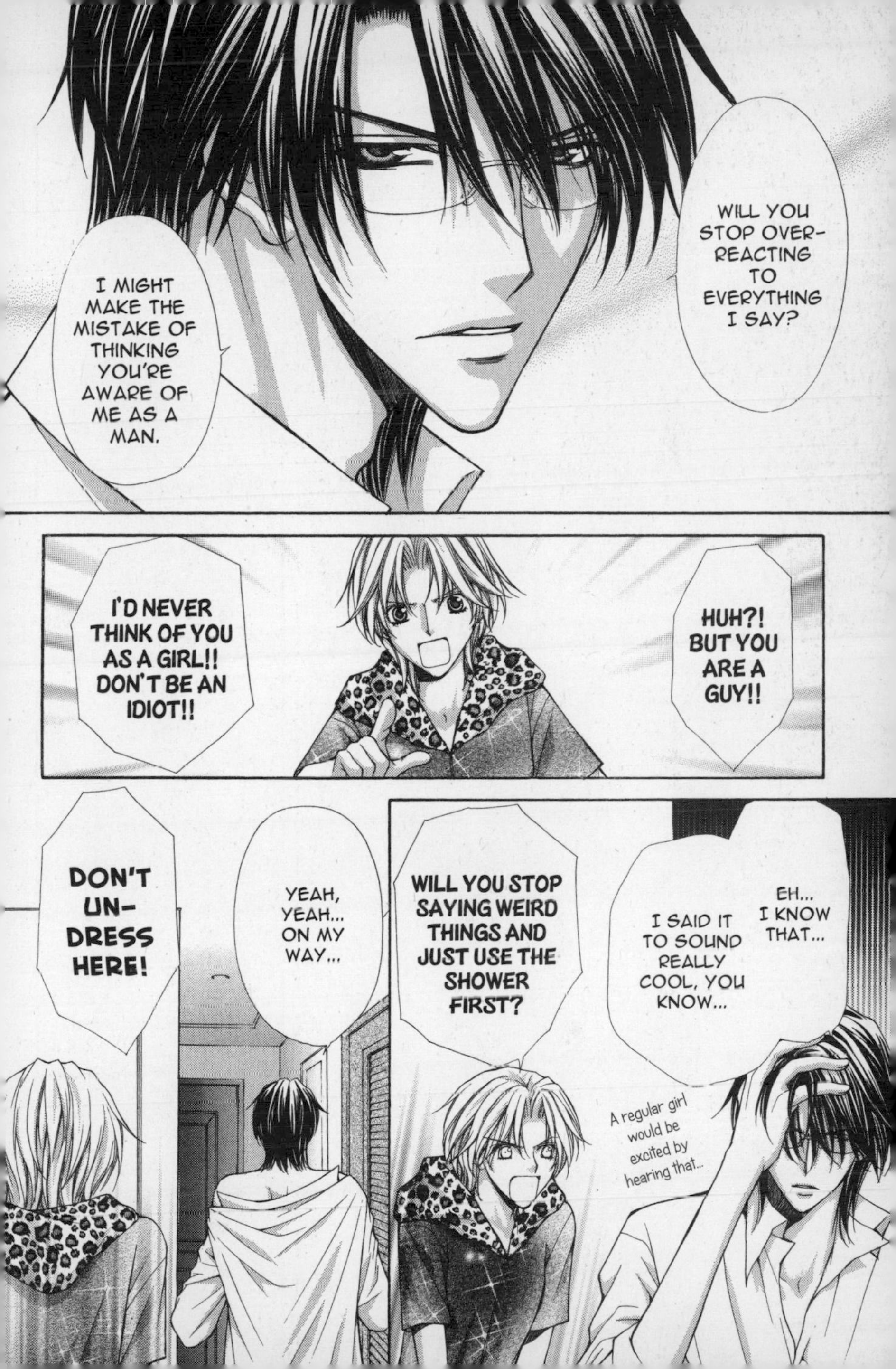
WILL YOU STOP OVER-REACTING TO EVERYTHING I SAY?
I MIGHT MAKE THE MISTAKE OF THINKING YOU'RE AWARE OF ME AS A MAN.
HUH?! BUT YOU ARE A GUY!!
I'D NEVER THINK OF YOU AS A GIRL!! DON'T BE AN IDIOT!!
EH... I KNOW THAT...
I SAID IT TO SOUND REALLY COOL, YOU KNOW...
A regular girl would be excited by hearing that...
WILL YOU STOP SAYING WEIRD THINGS AND JUST USE THE SHOWER FIRST?
YEAH, YEAH... ON MY WAY...
DON'T UN-DRESS HERE!

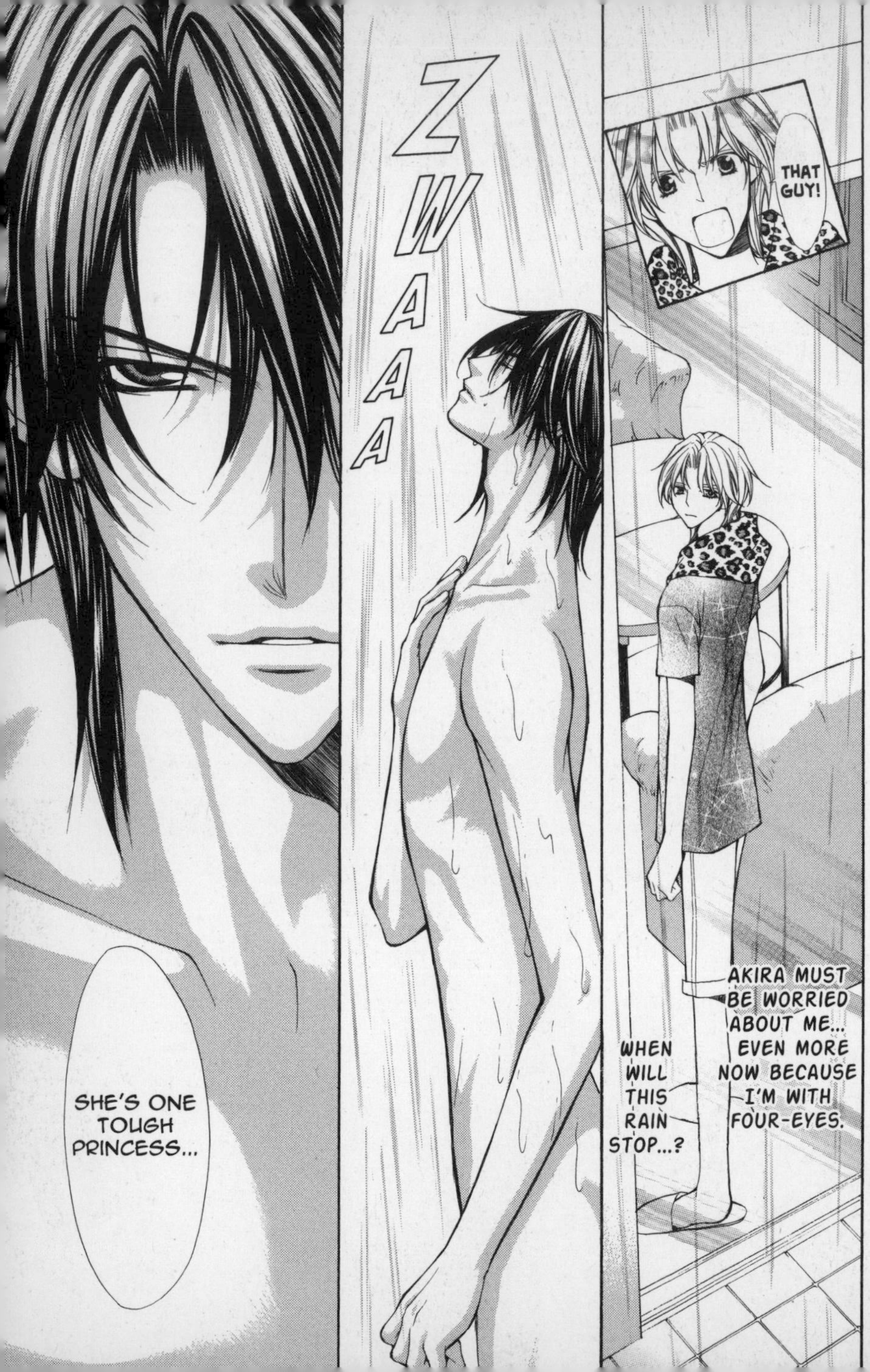
THAT GUY!
AKIRA MUST BE WORRIED ABOUT ME... EVEN MORE NOW BECAUSE I'M WITH FOUR-EYES.
WHEN WILL THIS RAIN STOP...?
ZWAAAA
SHE'S ONE TOUGH PRINCESS...

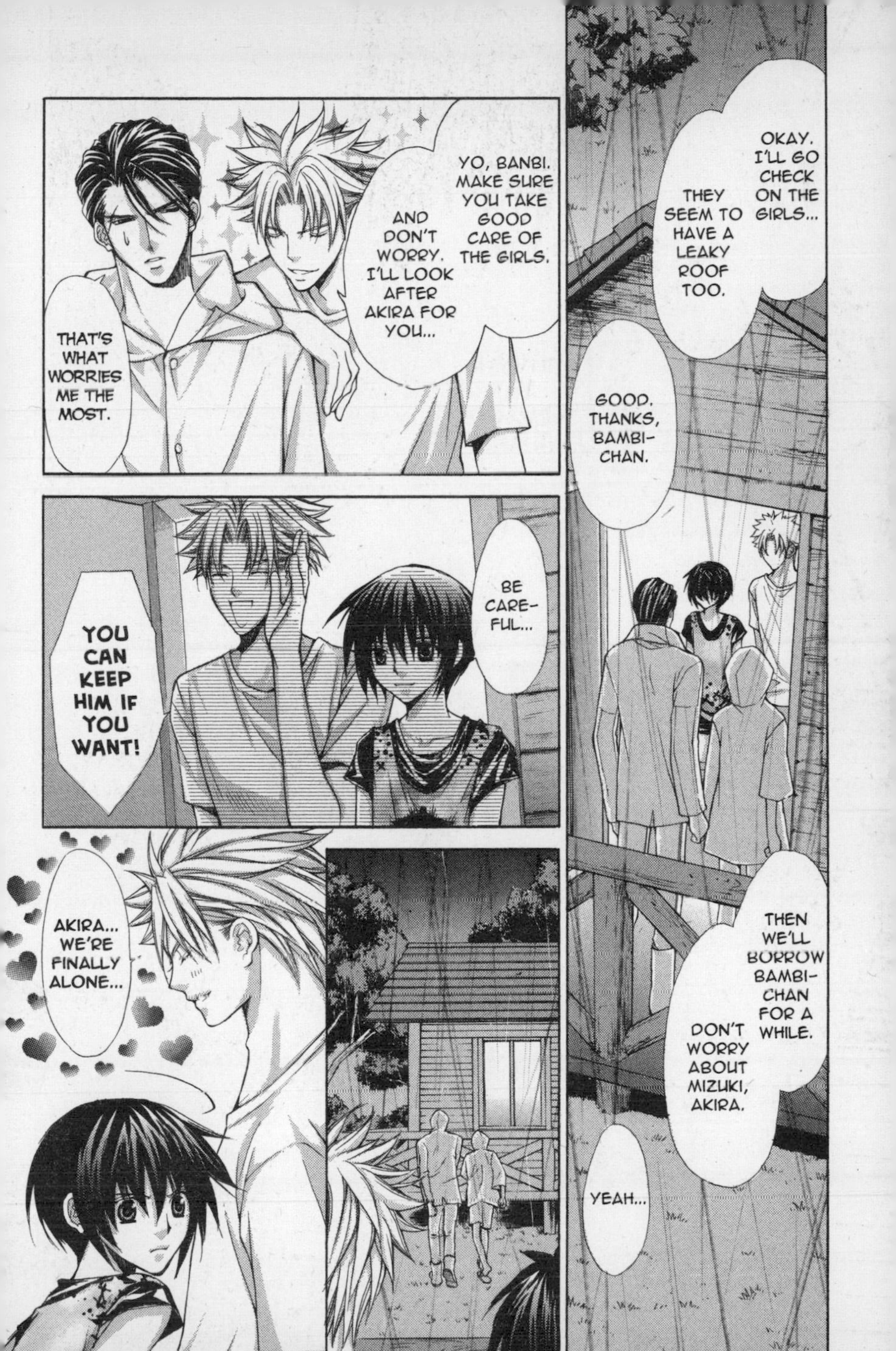
OKAY. I'LL GO CHECK ON THE GIRLS...
THEY SEEM TO HAVE A LEAKY ROOF TOO.
GOOD. THANKS, BAMBI-CHAN.
THEN WE'LL BORROW BAMBI-CHAN FOR A WHILE.
DON'T WORRY ABOUT MIZUKI, AKIRA.
YEAH...
YO, BANBI. MAKE SURE YOU TAKE GOOD CARE OF THE GIRLS.
AND DON'T WORRY. I'LL LOOK AFTER AKIRA FOR YOU...
THAT'S WHAT WORRIES ME THE MOST.
BE CARE-FUL...
YOU CAN KEEP HIM IF YOU WANT!
AKIRA... WE'RE FINALLY ALONE...

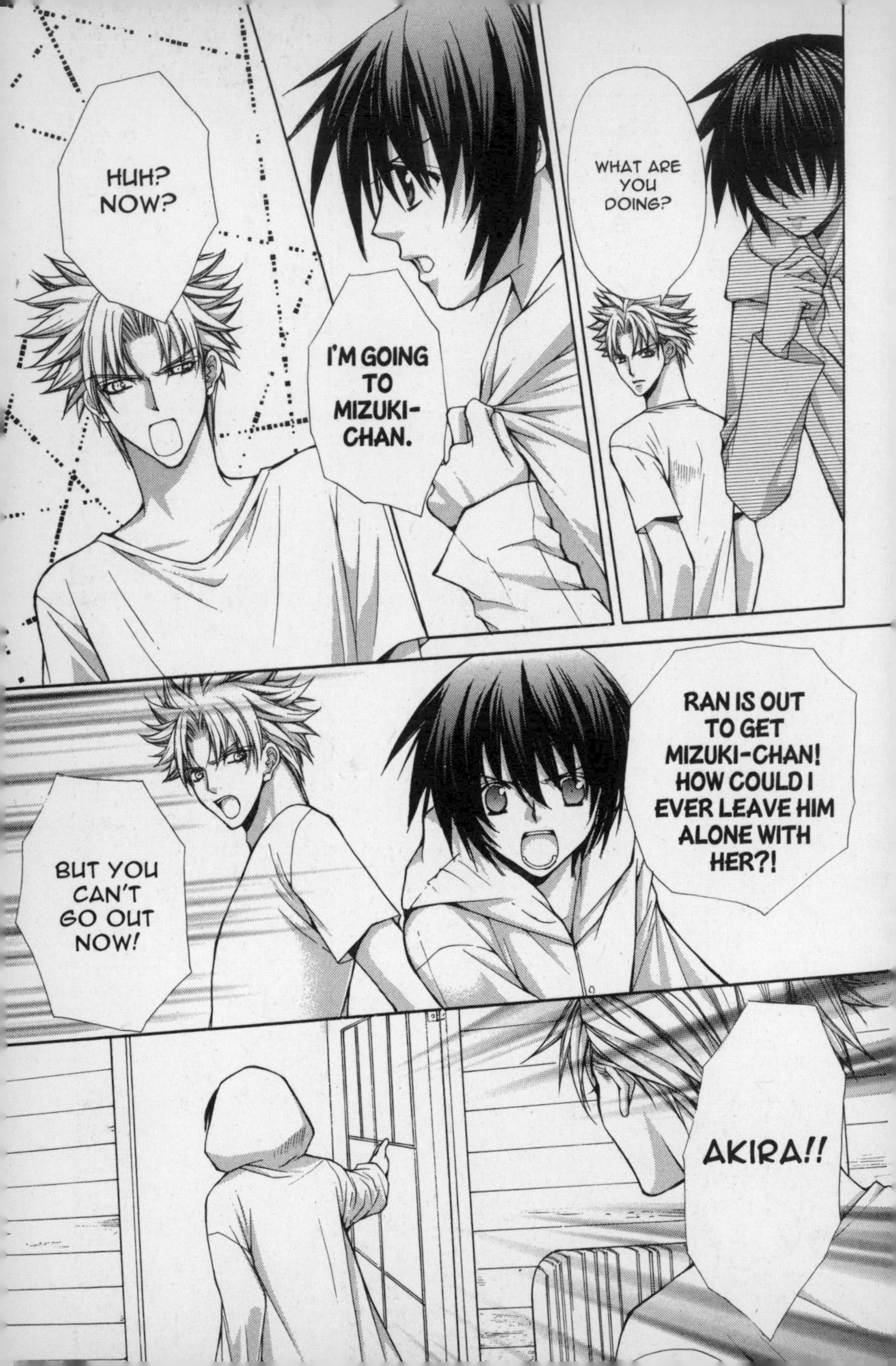
WHAT ARE YOU DOING?
I'M GOING TO MIZUKI-CHAN.
HUH? NOW?
RAN IS OUT TO GET MIZUKI-CHAN! HOW COULD I EVER LEAVE HIM ALONE WITH HER?!
BUT YOU CAN'T GO OUT NOW!
AKIRA!!

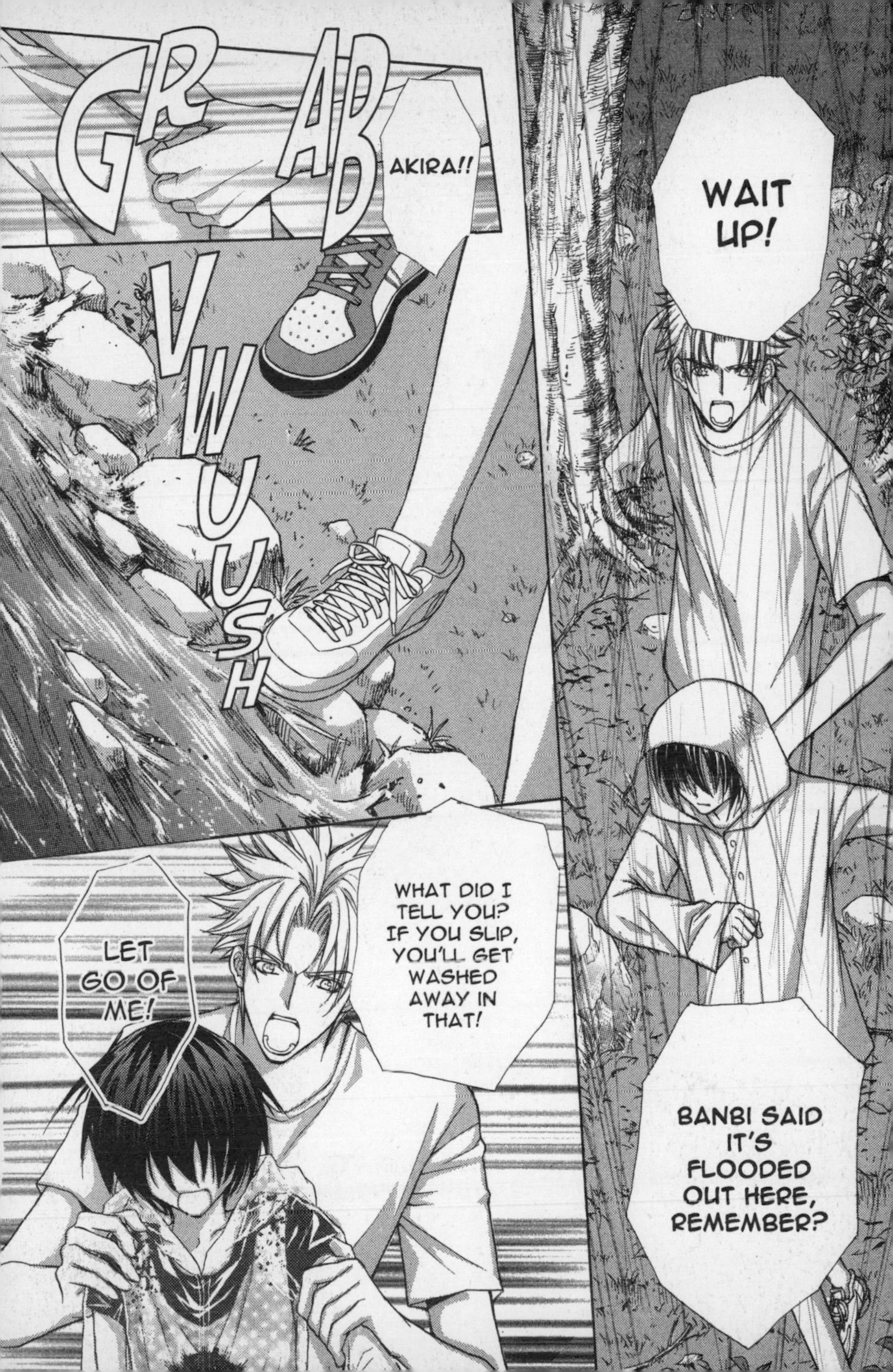
WAIT UP!
BANBI SAID IT'S FLOODED OUT HERE, REMEMBER?
GRAB
AKIRA!!
VWUUSH
WHAT DID I TELL YOU? IF YOU SLIP, YOU'LL GET WASHED AWAY IN THAT!
LET GO OF ME!

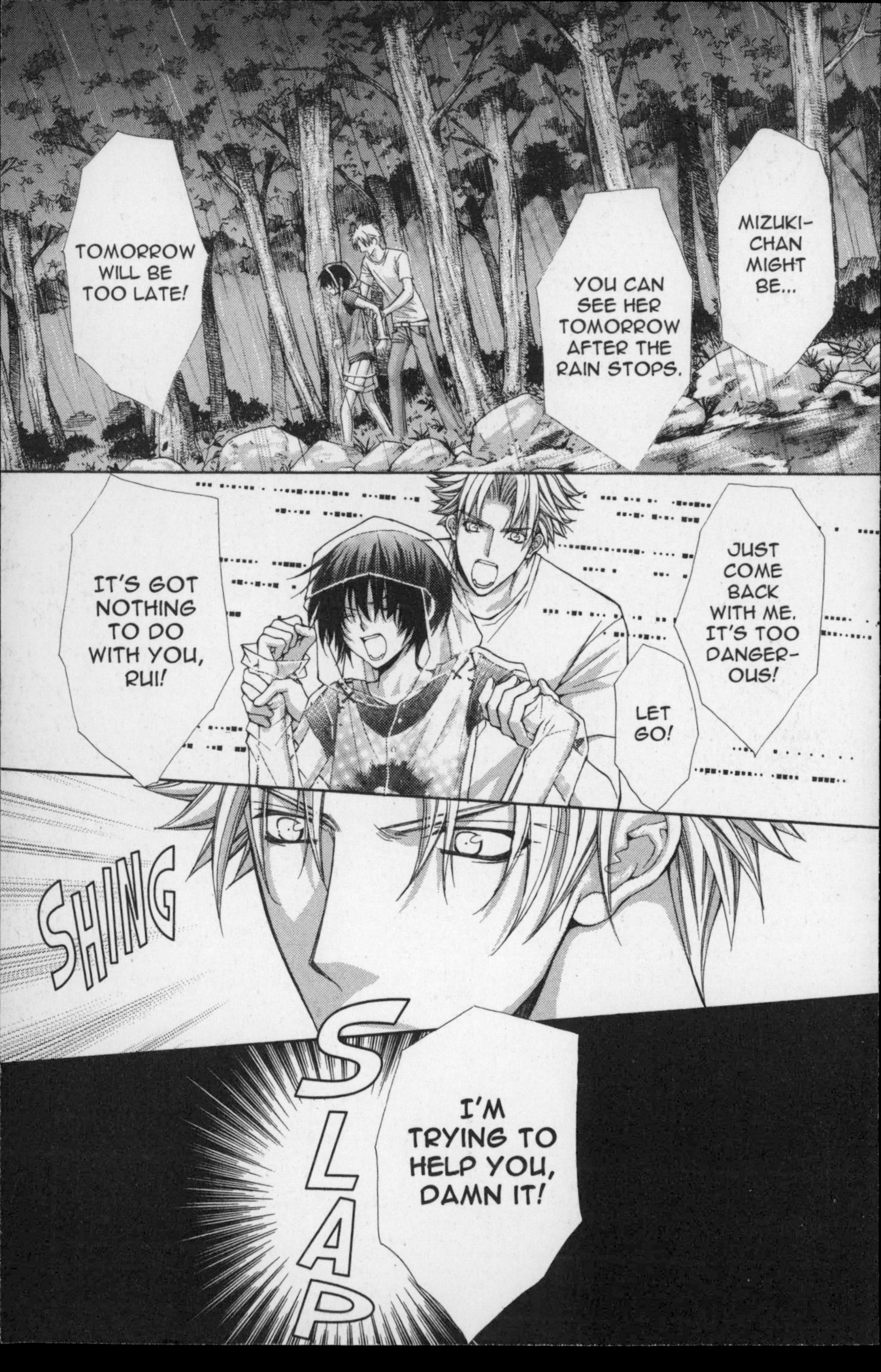
MIZUKI-CHAN MIGHT BE...
YOU CAN SEE HER TOMORROW AFTER THE RAIN STOPS.
TOMORROW WILL BE TOO LATE!
JUST COME BACK WITH ME. IT'S TOO DANGER-OUS!
LET GO!
IT'S GOT NOTHING TO DO WITH YOU, RUI!
SHING
SLAP
I'M TRYING TO HELP YOU, DAMN IT!

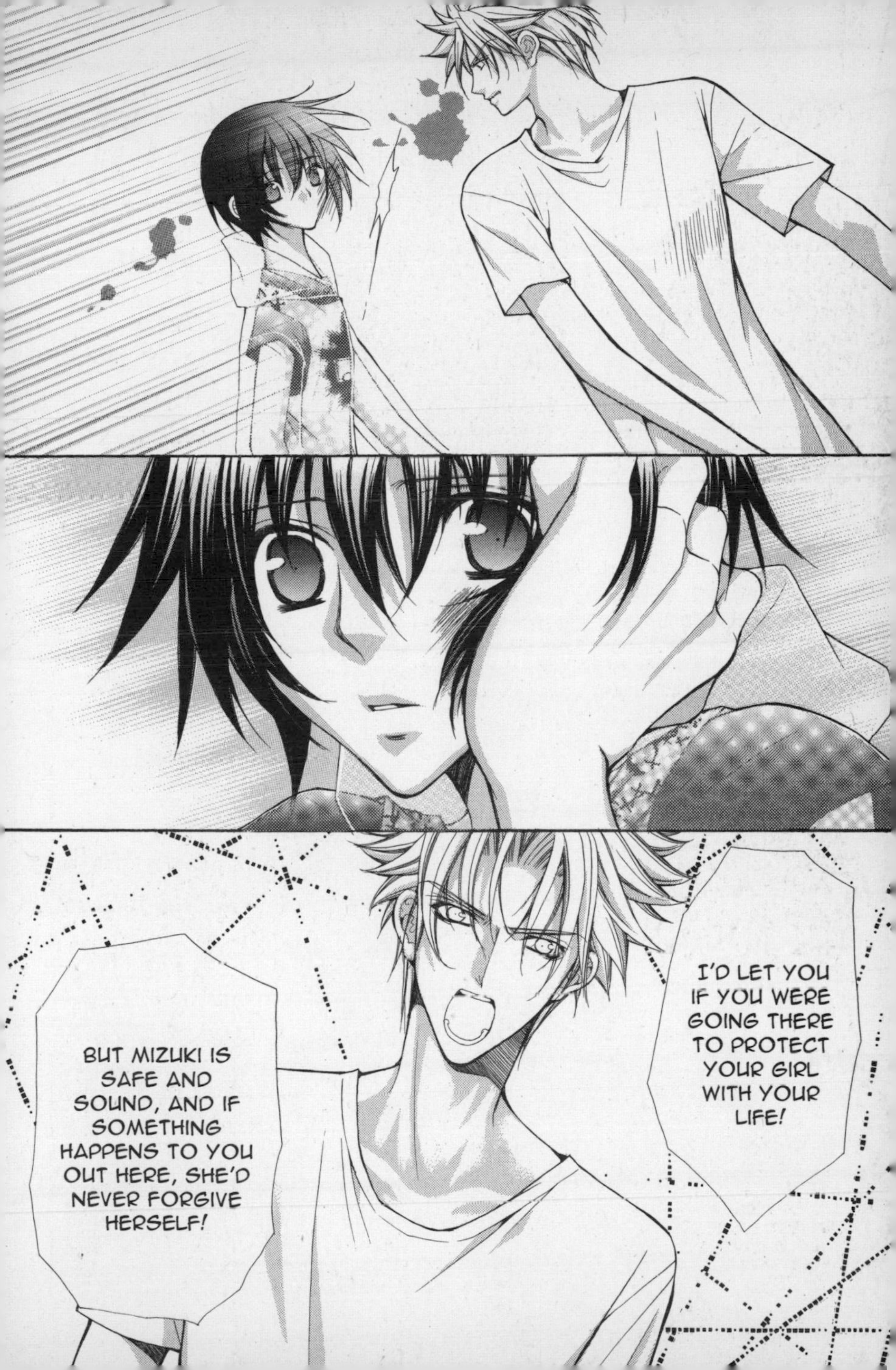
I'D LET YOU IF YOU WERE GOING THERE TO PROTECT YOUR GIRL WITH YOUR LIFE!
BUT MIZUKI IS SAFE AND SOUND, AND IF SOMETHING HAPPENS TO YOU OUT HERE, SHE'D NEVER FORGIVE HERSELF!

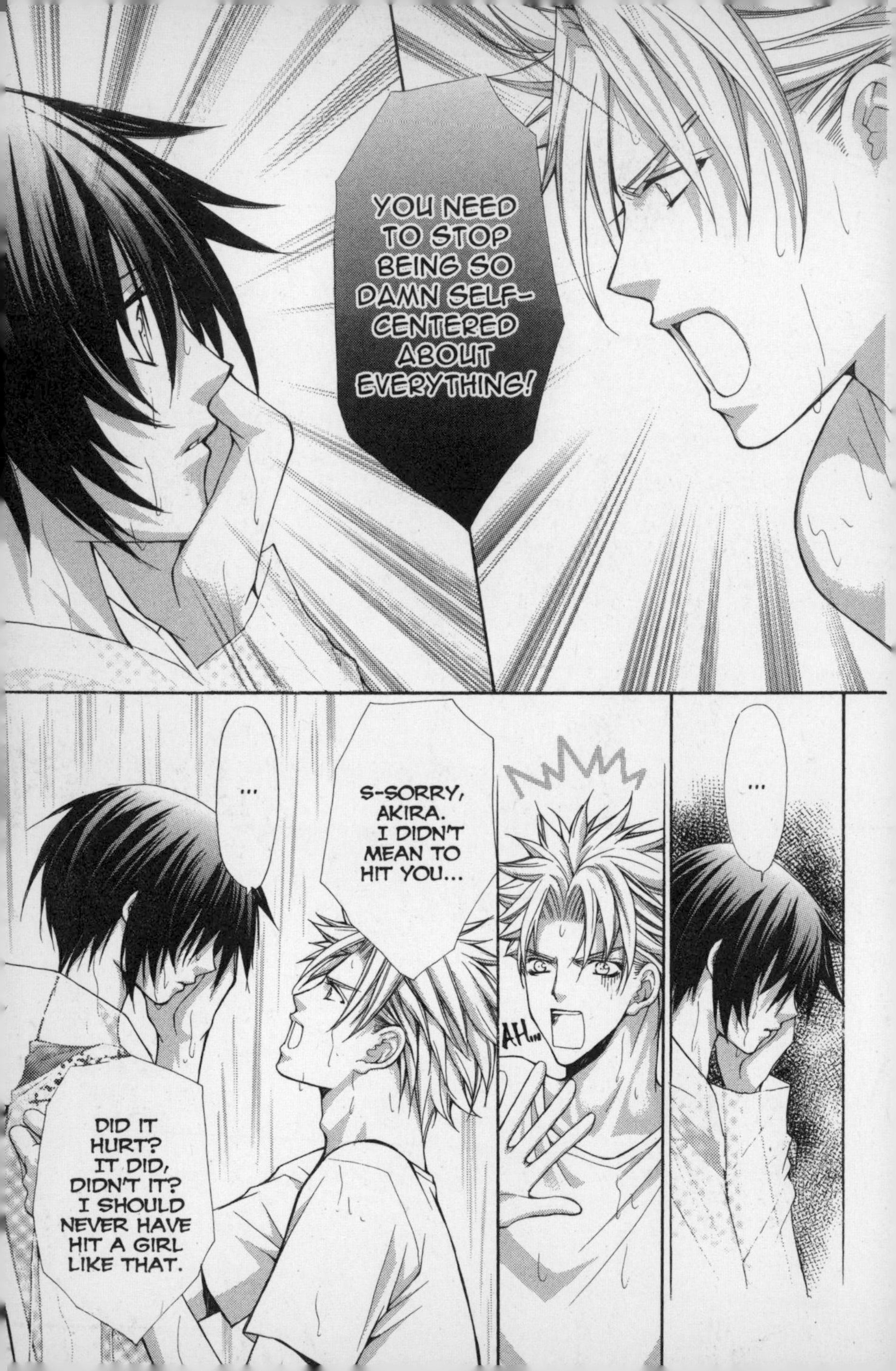
YOU NEED TO STOP BEING SO DAMN SELF-CENTERED ABOUT EVERYTHING!
...
AH...
S-SORRY, AKIRA. I DIDN'T MEAN TO HIT YOU...
...
DID IT HURT? IT DID, DIDN'T IT? I SHOULD NEVER HAVE HIT A GIRL LIKE THAT.

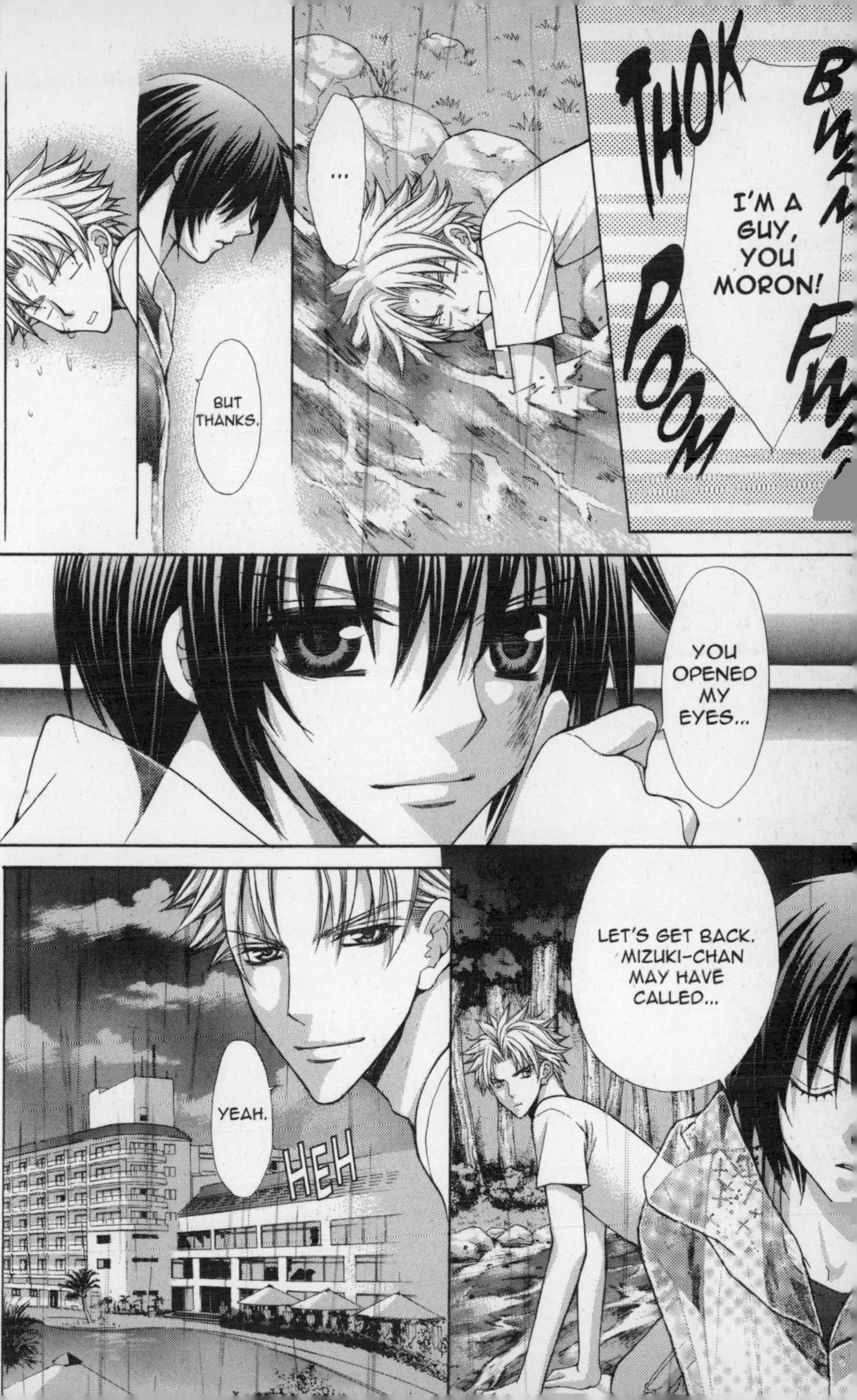
THOK
I'M A GUY, YOU MORON!
POOOM
...
BUT THANKS.
YOU OPENED MY EYES...
LET'S GET BACK. MIZUKI-CHAN MAY HAVE CALLED...
YEAH.
HEH

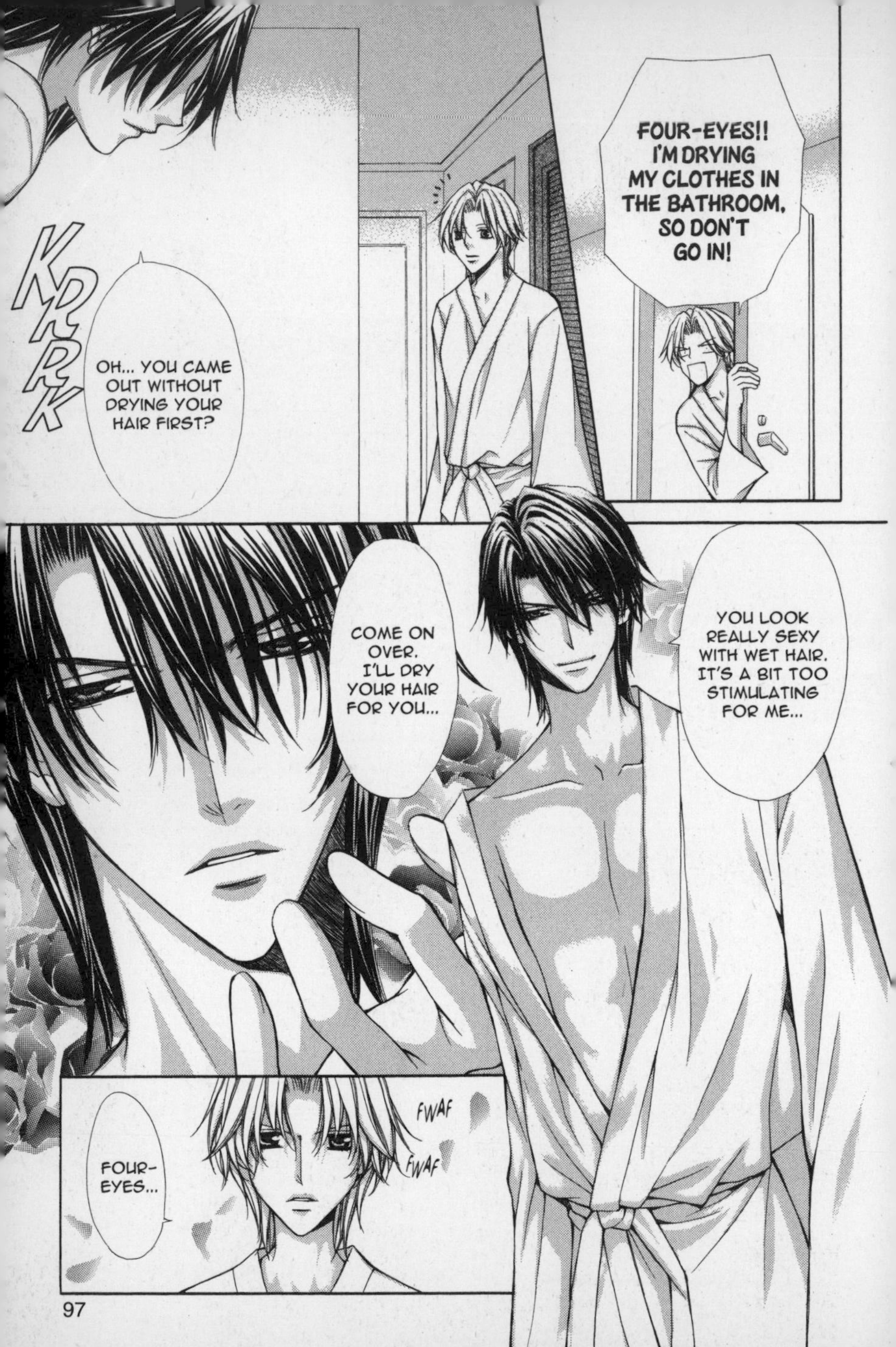

FOUR-EYES!! I'M DRYING MY CLOTHES IN THE BATHROOM, SO DON'T GO IN!
KRRK
OH... YOU CAME OUT WITHOUT DRYING YOUR HAIR FIRST?
YOU LOOK REALLY SEXY WITH WET HAIR. IT'S A BIT TOO STIMULATING FOR ME...
COME ON OVER. I'LL DRY YOUR HAIR FOR YOU...
FWAF
FWAF
FOUR-EYES...

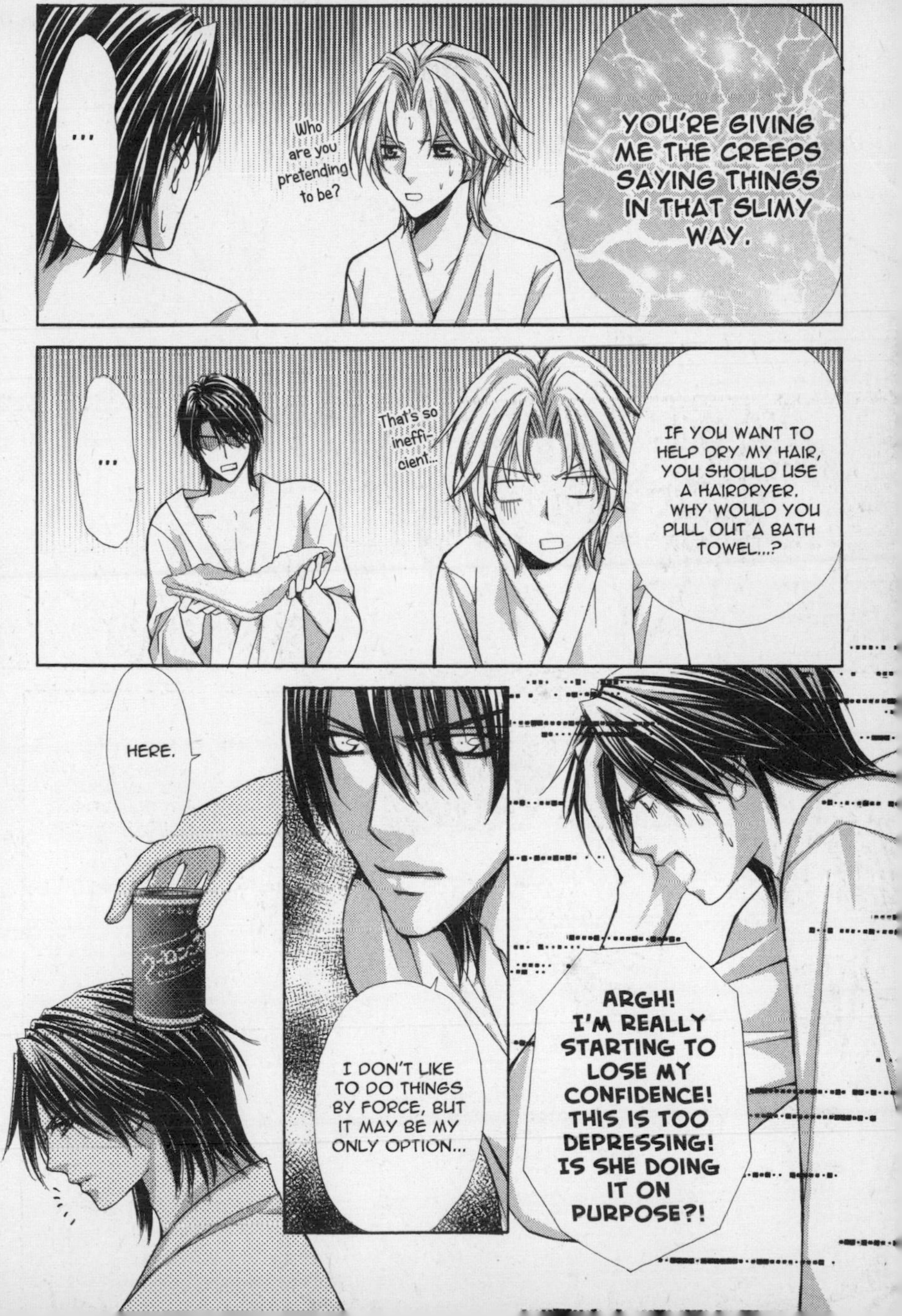
YOU'RE GIVING ME THE CREEPS SAYING THINGS IN THAT SLIMY WAY.
Who are you pretending to be?
...
IF YOU WANT TO HELP DRY MY HAIR, YOU SHOULD USE A HAIRDRYER. WHY WOULD YOU PULL OUT A BATH TOWEL...?
That's so ineffi-cient...
...
ARGH! I'M REALLY STARTING TO LOSE MY CONFIDENCE! THIS IS TOO DEPRESSING! IS SHE DOING IT ON PURPOSE?!
I DON'T LIKE TO DO THINGS BY FORCE, BUT IT MAY BE MY ONLY OPTION...
HERE.

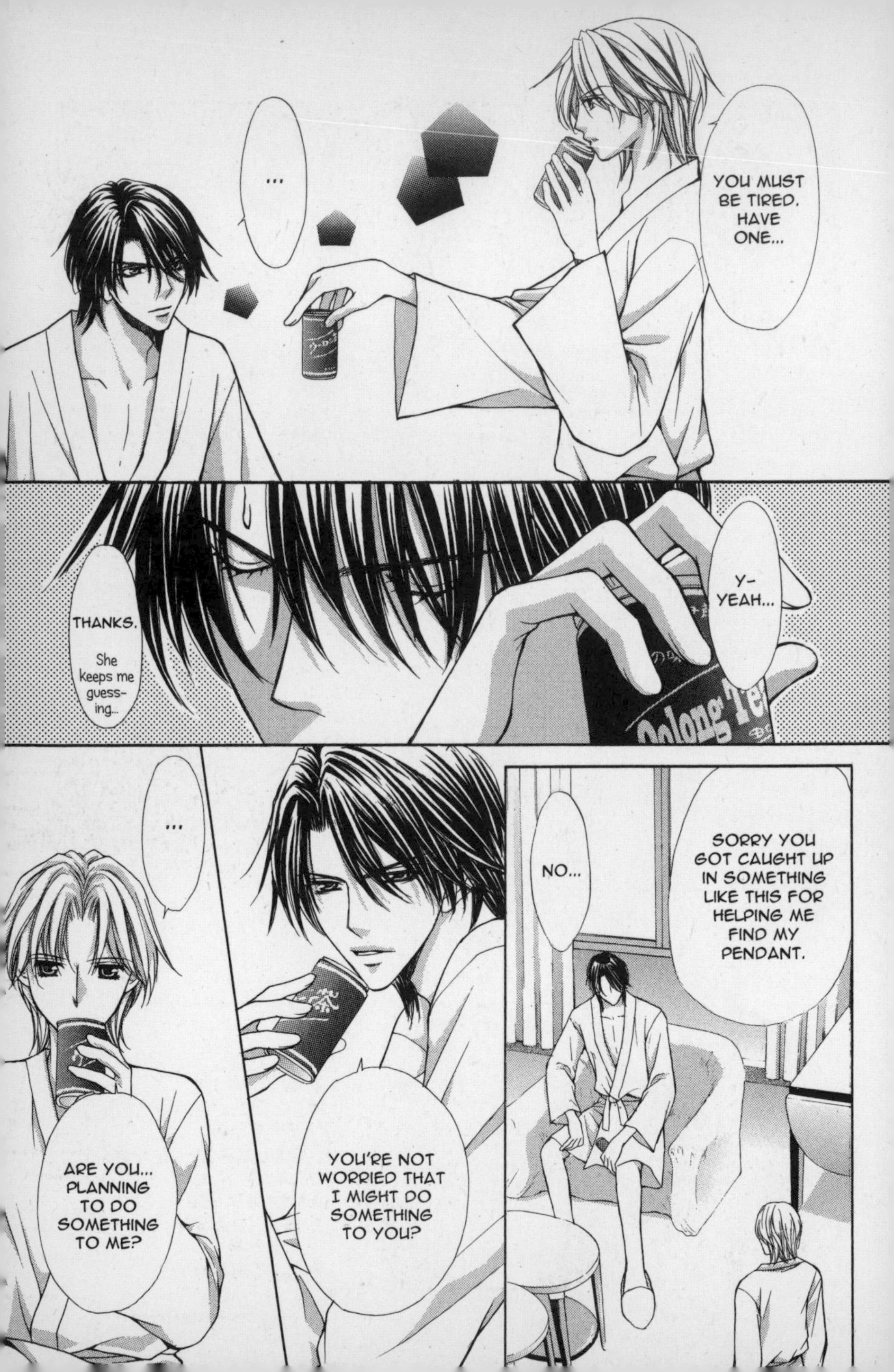

YOU MUST BE TIRED. HAVE ONE...
...
Y- YEAH...
THANKS.
She keeps me guessing...
SORRY YOU GOT CAUGHT UP IN SOMETHING LIKE THIS FOR HELPING ME FIND MY PENDANT.
NO...
YOU'RE NOT WORRIED THAT I MIGHT DO SOMETHING TO YOU?
...
ARE YOU... PLANNING TO DO SOMETHING TO ME?

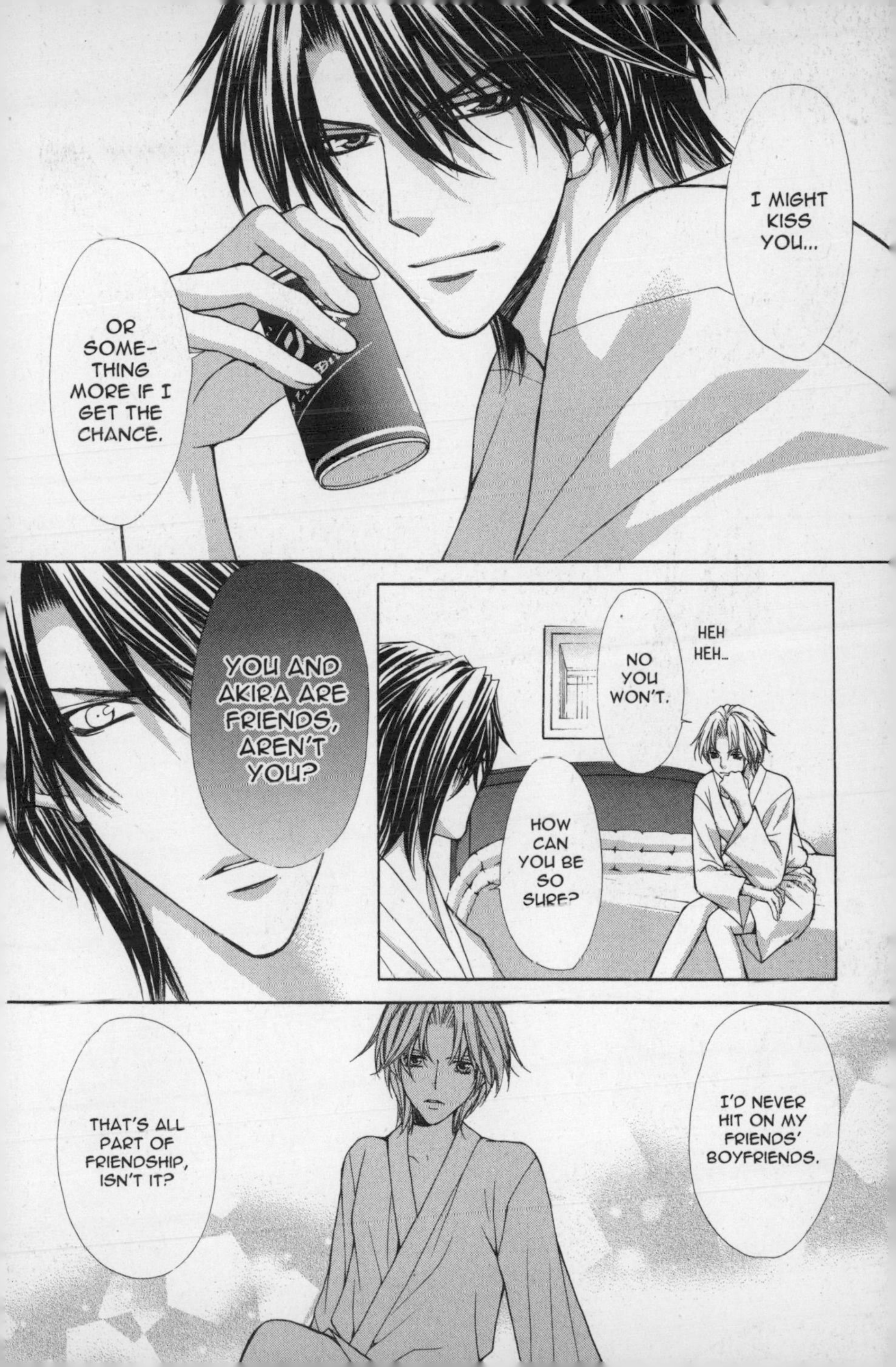
I MIGHT KISS YOU...
OR SOME-THING MORE IF I GET THE CHANCE.
HEH HEH...
NO YOU WON'T.
HOW CAN YOU BE SO SURE?
YOU AND AKIRA ARE FRIENDS, AREN'T YOU?
I'D NEVER HIT ON MY FRIENDS' BOYFRIENDS.
THAT'S ALL PART OF FRIENDSHIP, ISN'T IT?

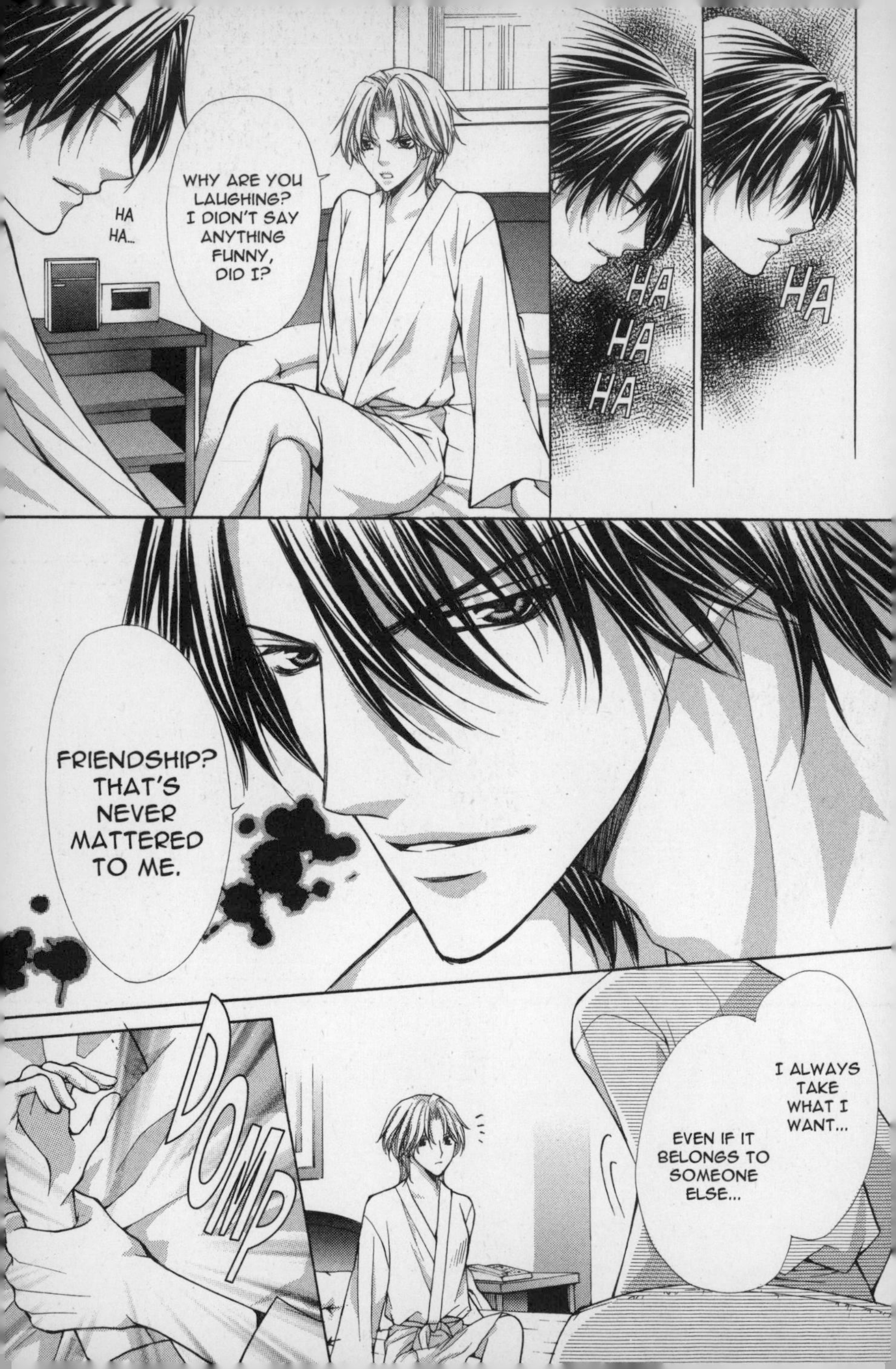
HA
HA HA HA
WHY ARE YOU LAUGHING? I DIDN'T SAY ANYTHING FUNNY, DID I?
HA HA...
FRIENDSHIP? THAT'S NEVER MATTERED TO ME.
I ALWAYS TAKE WHAT I WANT...
EVEN IF IT BELONGS TO SOMEONE ELSE...
DOMP

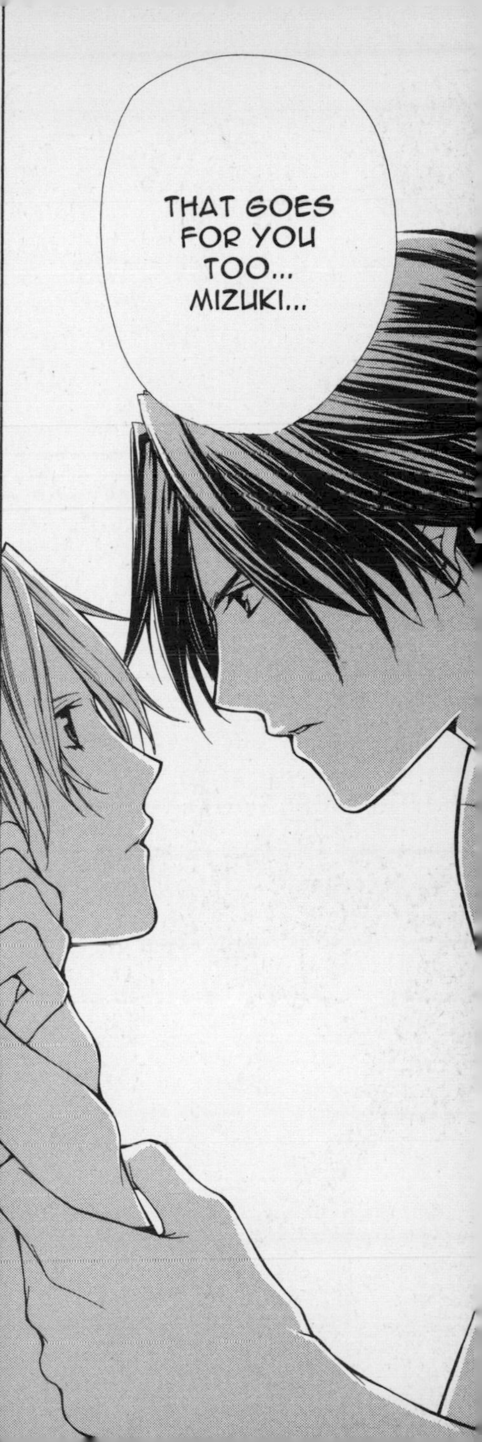
THAT GOES FOR YOU TOO... MIZUKI...

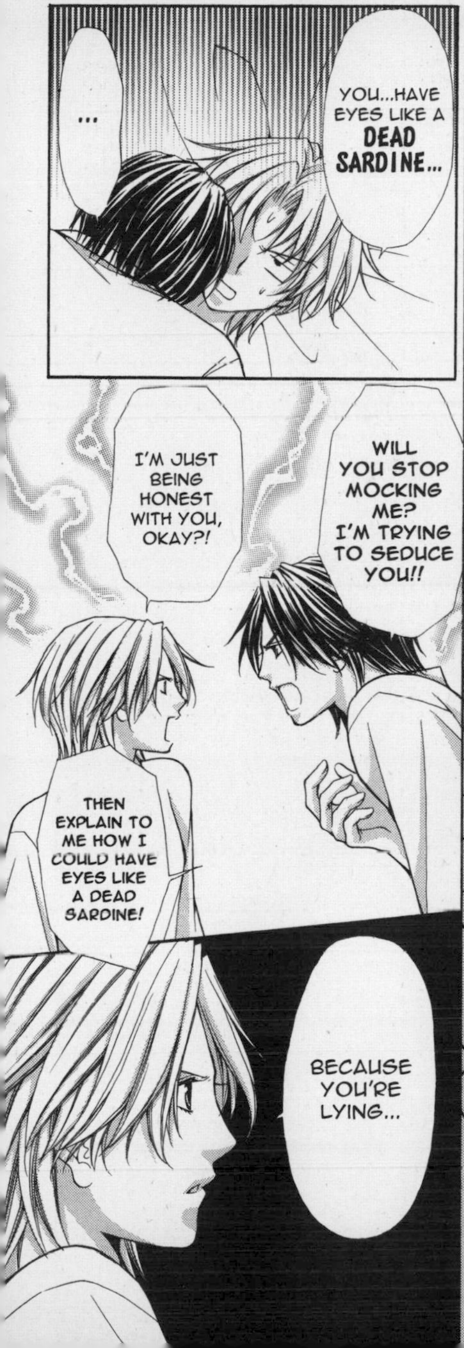
YOU...HAVE EYES LIKE A DEAD SARDINE...
...
WILL YOU STOP MOCKING ME? I'M TRYING TO SEDUCE YOU!!
I'M JUST BEING HONEST WITH YOU, OKAY?!
THEN EXPLAIN TO ME HOW I COULD HAVE EYES LIKE A DEAD SARDINE!
BECAUSE YOU'RE LYING...

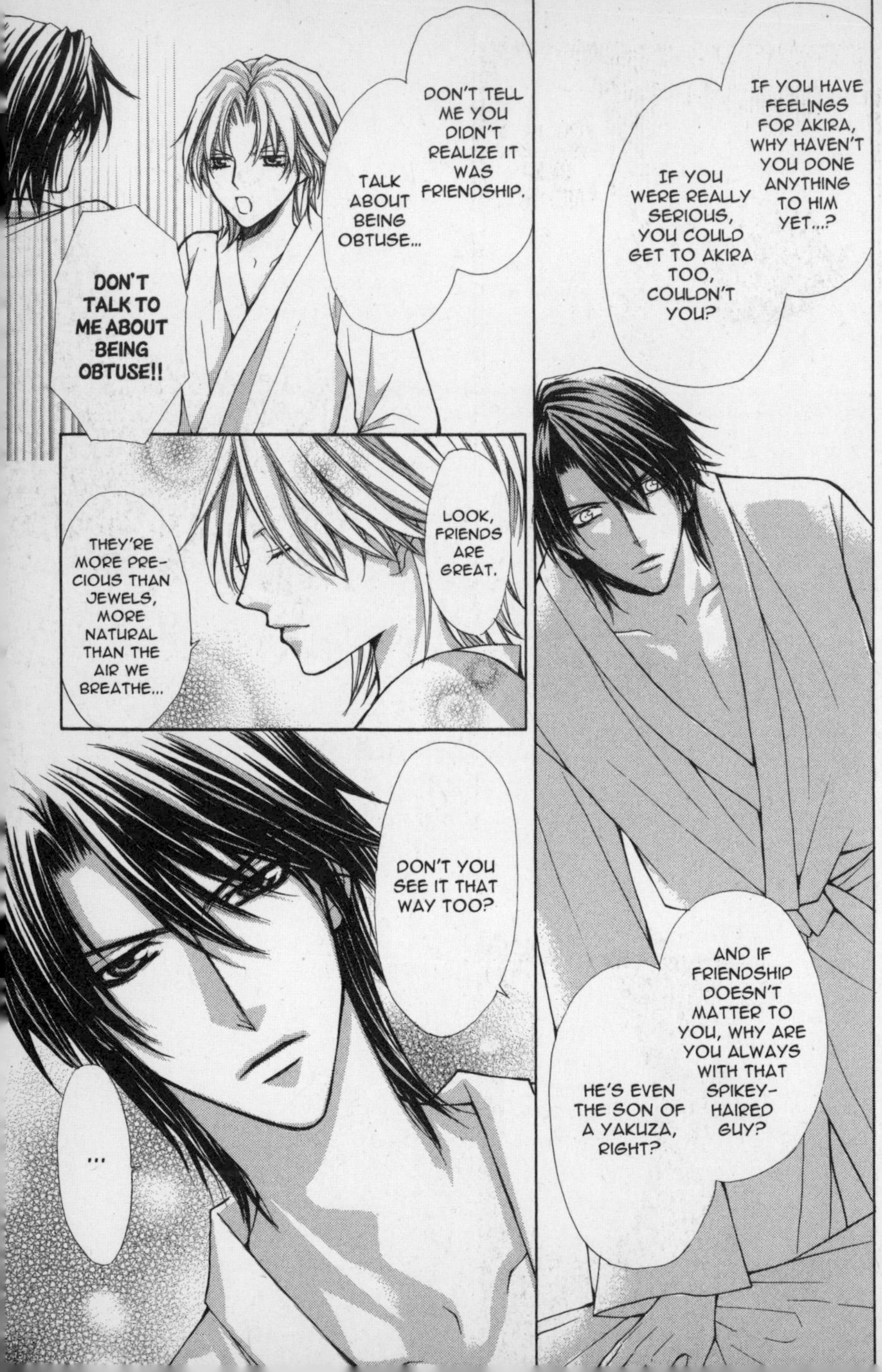
IF YOU HAVE FEELINGS FOR AKIRA, WHY HAVEN'T YOU DONE ANYTHING TO HIM YET...?
IF YOU WERE REALLY SERIOUS, YOU COULD GET TO AKIRA TOO, COULDN'T YOU?
AND IF FRIENDSHIP DOESN'T MATTER TO YOU, WHY ARE YOU ALWAYS WITH THAT SPIKEY-HAIRED GUY?
HE'S EVEN THE SON OF A YAKUZA, RIGHT?
DON'T TELL ME YOU DIDN'T REALIZE IT WAS FRIENDSHIP.
TALK ABOUT BEING OBTUSE...
DON'T TALK TO ME ABOUT BEING OBTUSE!!
LOOK, FRIENDS ARE GREAT.
THEY'RE MORE PRECIOUS THAN JEWELS, MORE NATURAL THAN THE AIR WE BREATHE...
DON'T YOU SEE IT THAT WAY TOO?
...

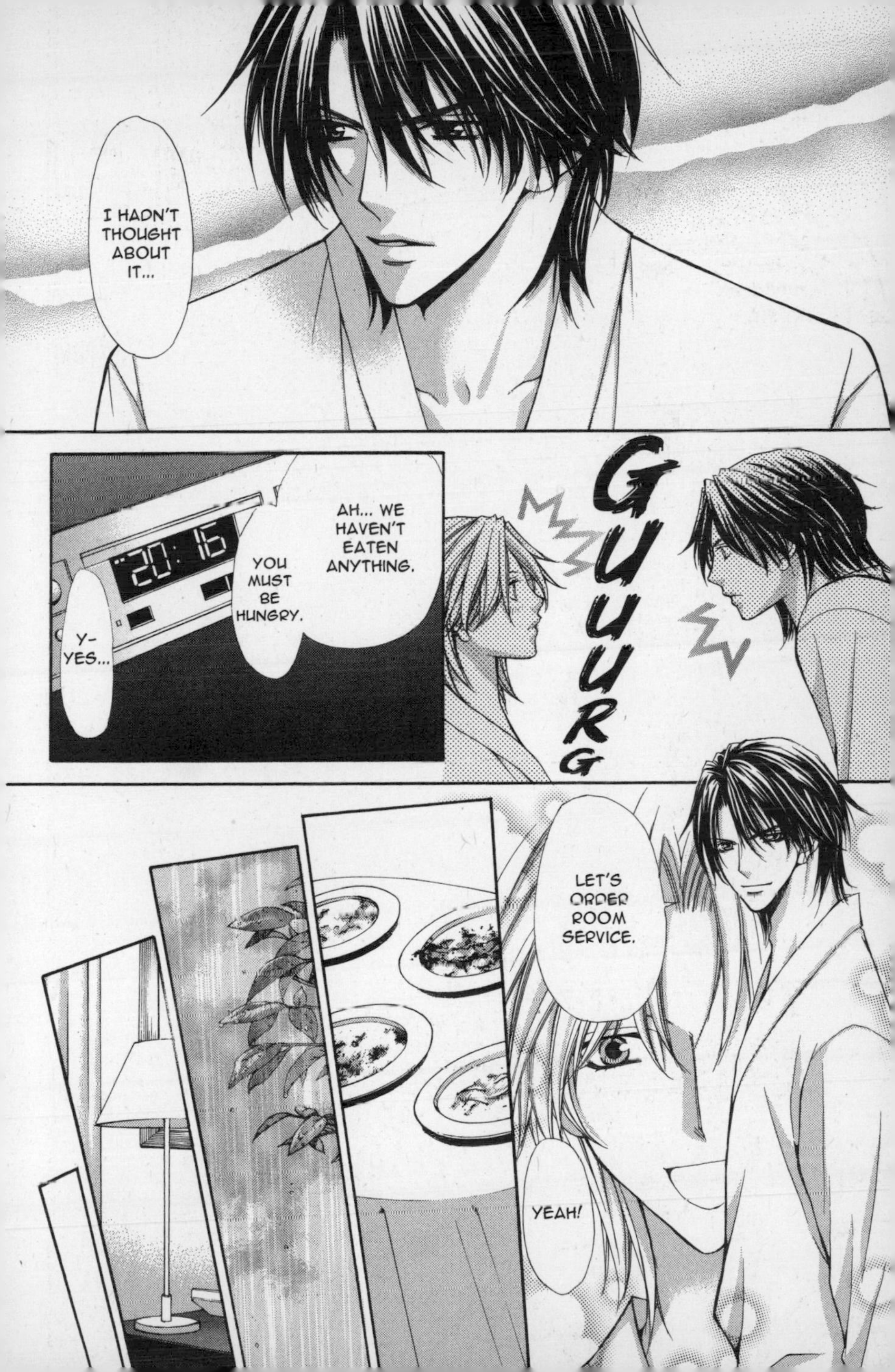
I HADN'T THOUGHT ABOUT IT...
GUUURG
AH... WE HAVEN'T EATEN ANYTHING.
YOU MUST BE HUNGRY.
20:16
Y-YES...
LET'S ORDER ROOM SERVICE.
YEAH!

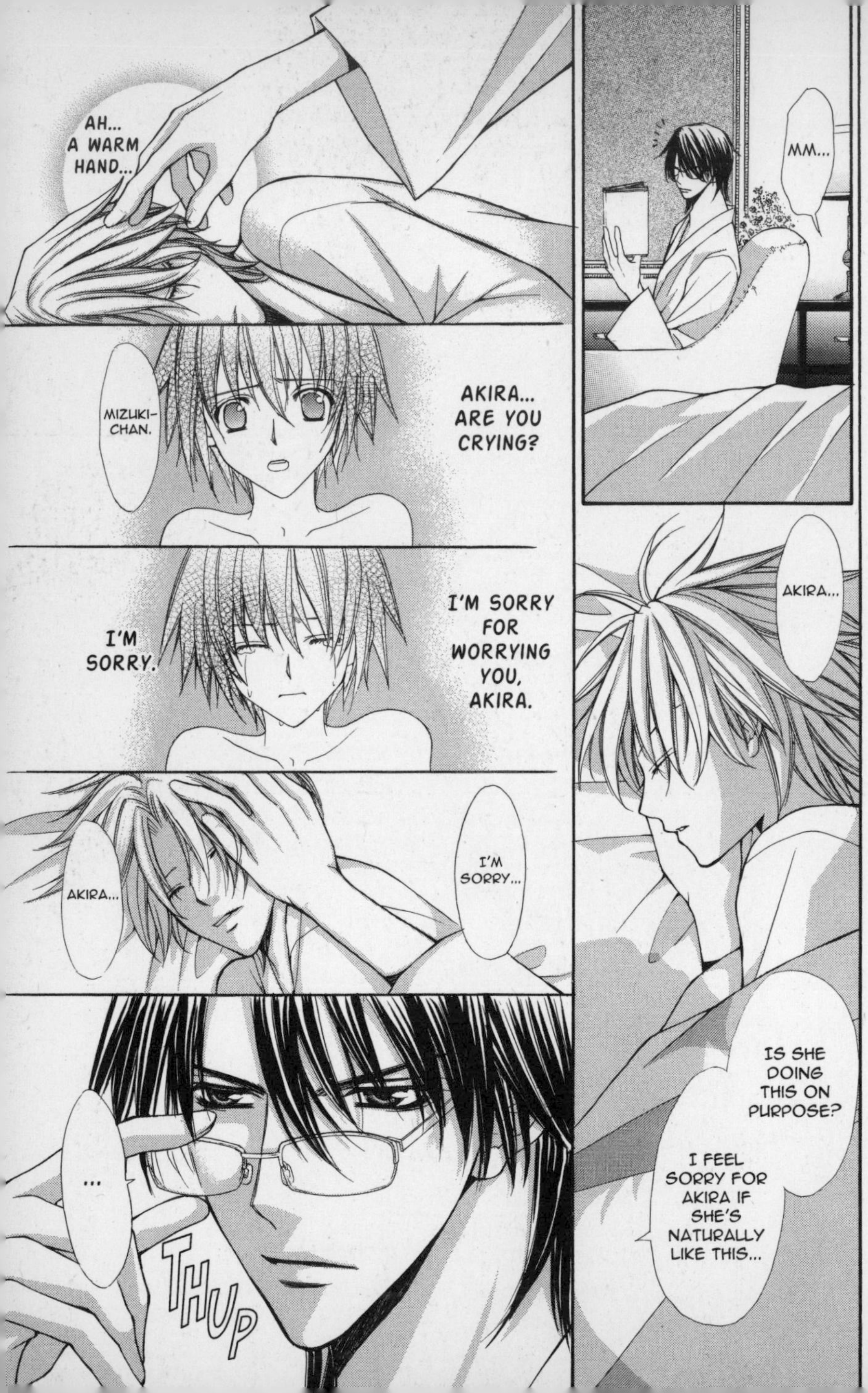
MM...
AH... A WARM HAND...
AKIRA... ARE YOU CRYING?
MIZUKI-CHAN.
I'M SORRY FOR WORRYING YOU, AKIRA.
I'M SORRY.
I'M SORRY...
AKIRA...
...
THUP
AKIRA...
IS SHE DOING THIS ON PURPOSE?
I FEEL SORRY FOR AKIRA IF SHE'S NATURALLY LIKE THIS...

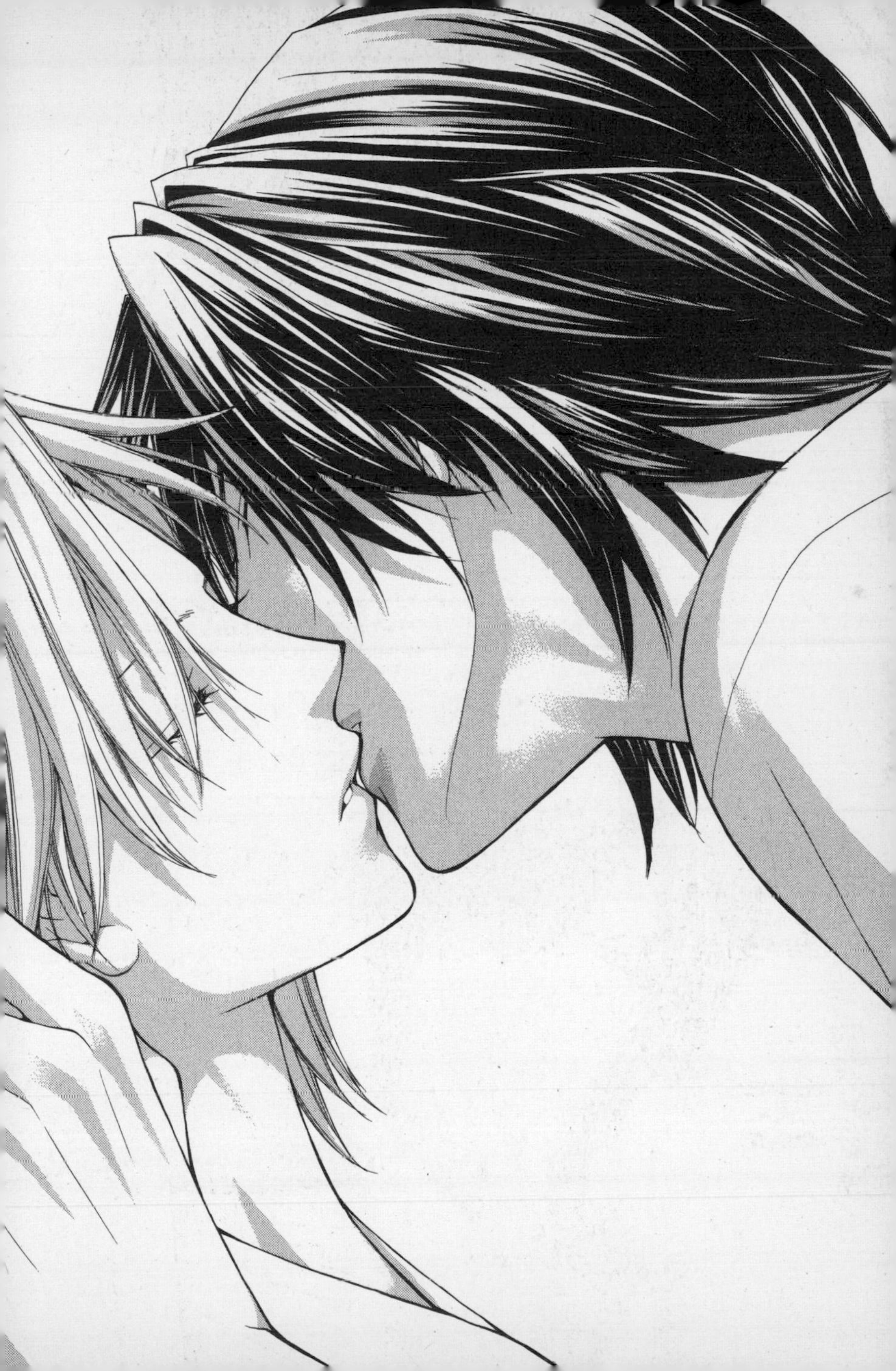

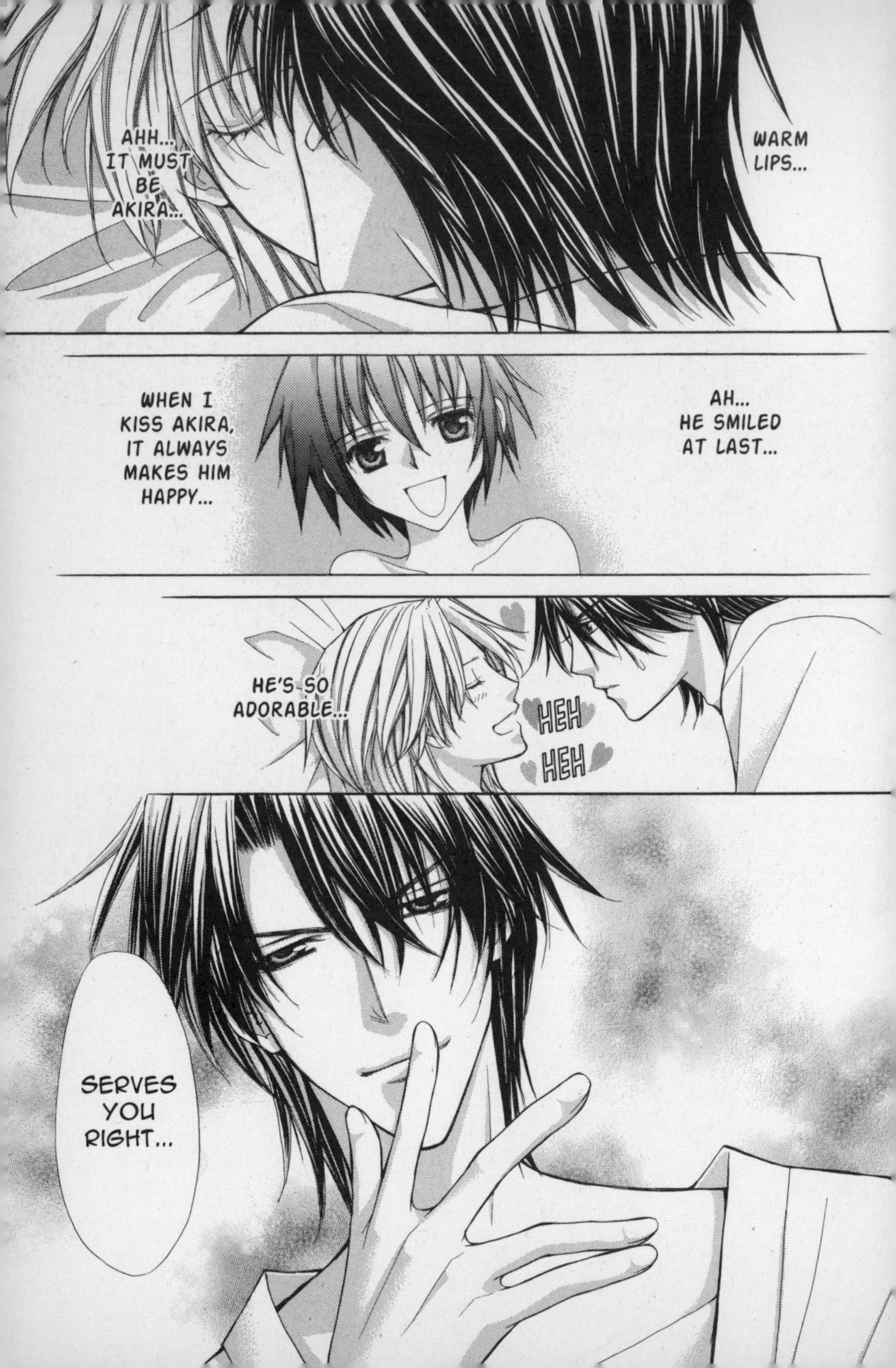
WARM LIPS...
AHH... IT MUST BE AKIRA...
AH... HE SMILED AT LAST...
WHEN I KISS AKIRA, IT ALWAYS MAKES HIM HAPPY...
HEH HEH
HE'S SO ADORABLE...
SERVES YOU RIGHT...

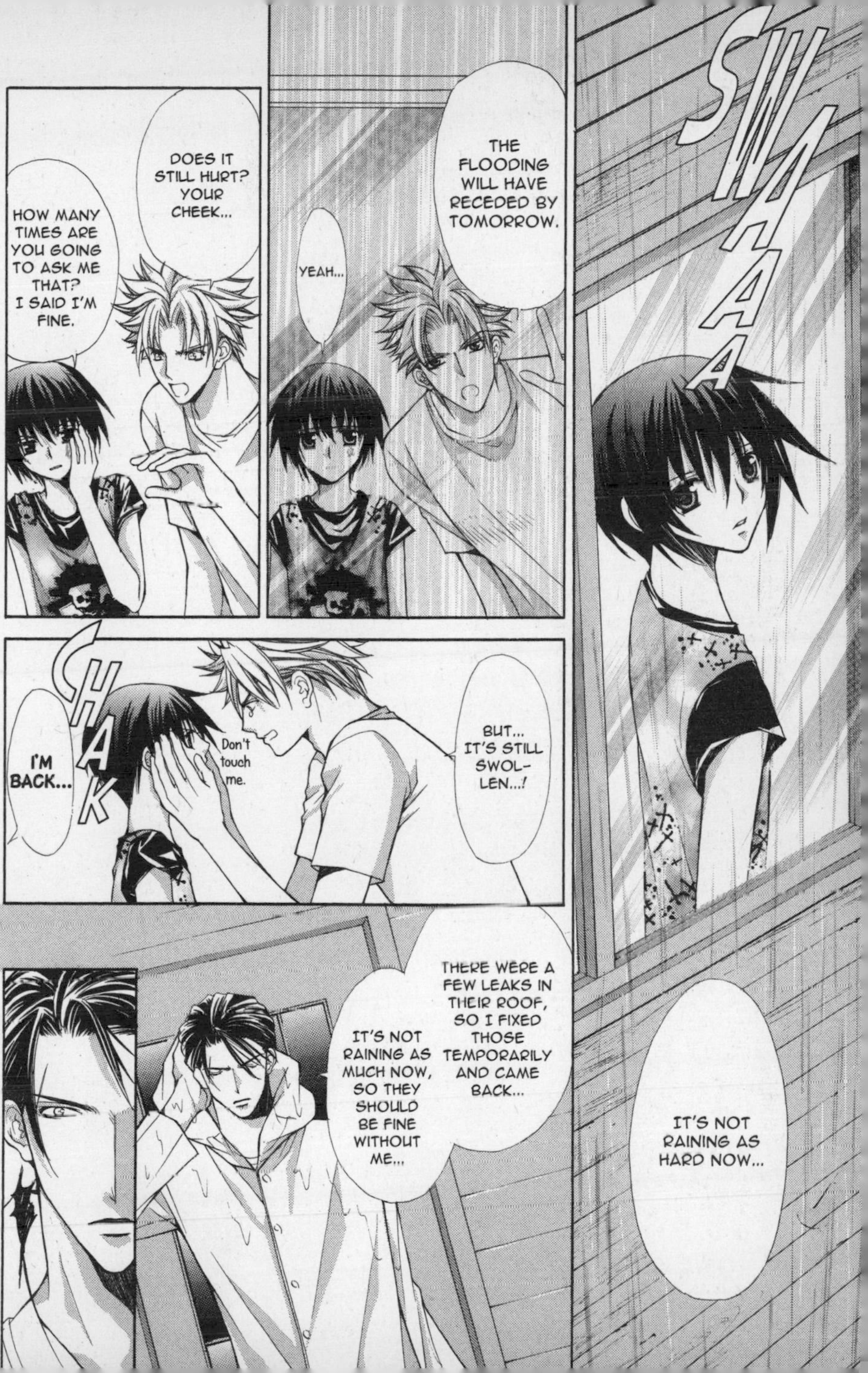
SWAAAA
IT'S NOT RAINING AS HARD NOW...
THE FLOODING WILL HAVE RECEDED BY TOMORROW.
YEAH...
DOES IT STILL HURT? YOUR CHEEK...
HOW MANY TIMES ARE YOU GOING TO ASK ME THAT? I SAID I'M FINE.
BUT... IT'S STILL SWOL-LEN...!
Don't touch me.
SHAK
I'M BACK...
THERE WERE A FEW LEAKS IN THEIR ROOF, SO I FIXED THOSE TEMPORARILY AND CAME BACK...
IT'S NOT RAINING AS MUCH NOW, SO THEY SHOULD BE FINE WITHOUT ME...

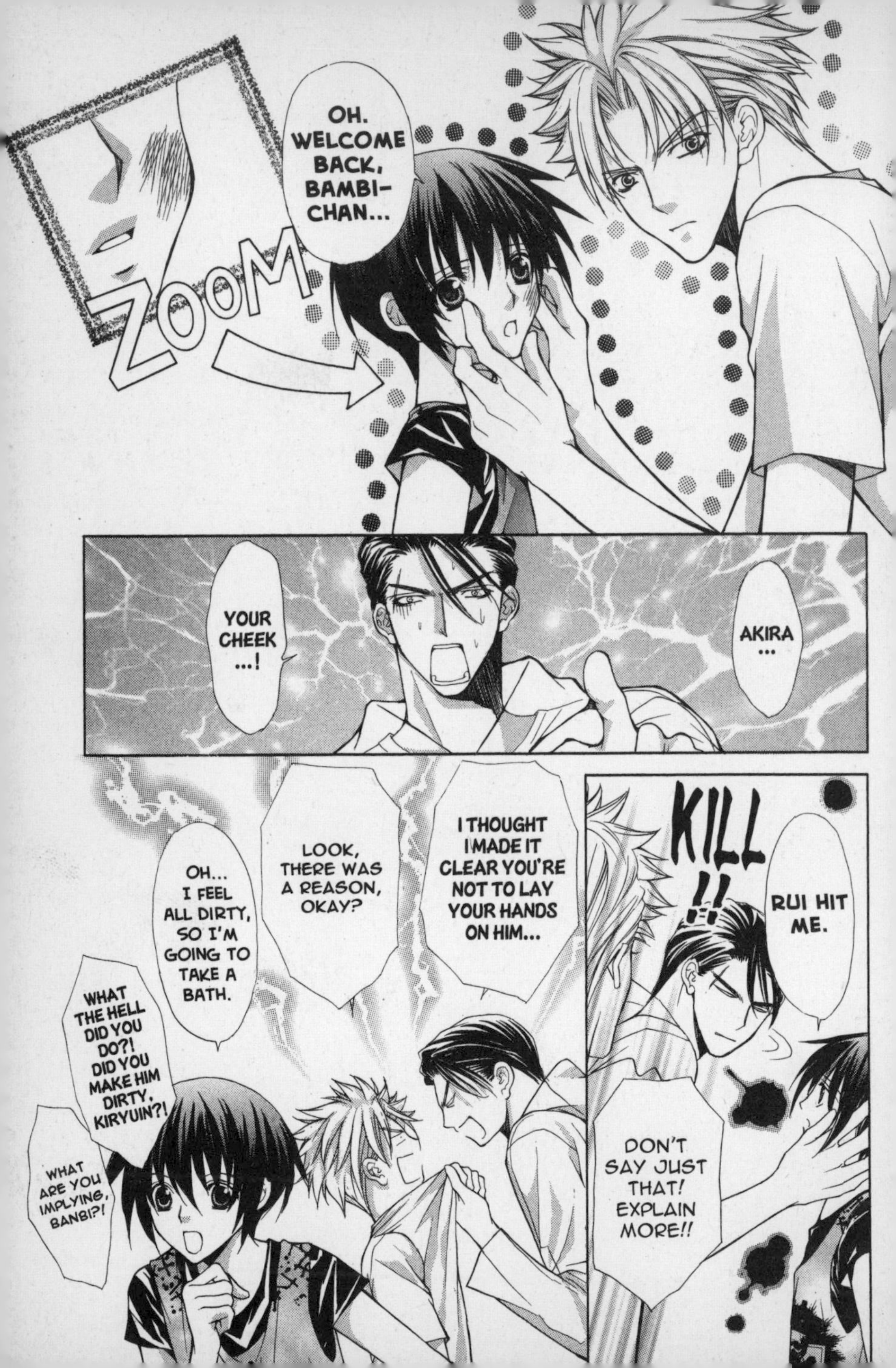
OH. WELCOME BACK, BAMBI-CHAN...
ZOOM
AKIRA ...
YOUR CHEEK ...!
KILL!!
RUI HIT ME.
DON'T SAY JUST THAT! EXPLAIN MORE!!
I THOUGHT I MADE IT CLEAR YOU'RE NOT TO LAY YOUR HANDS ON HIM...
LOOK, THERE WAS A REASON, OKAY?
OH... I FEEL ALL DIRTY, SO I'M GOING TO TAKE A BATH.
WHAT THE HELL DID YOU DO?! DID YOU MAKE HIM DIRTY, KIRYUIN?!
WHAT ARE YOU IMPLYING, BANBI?!

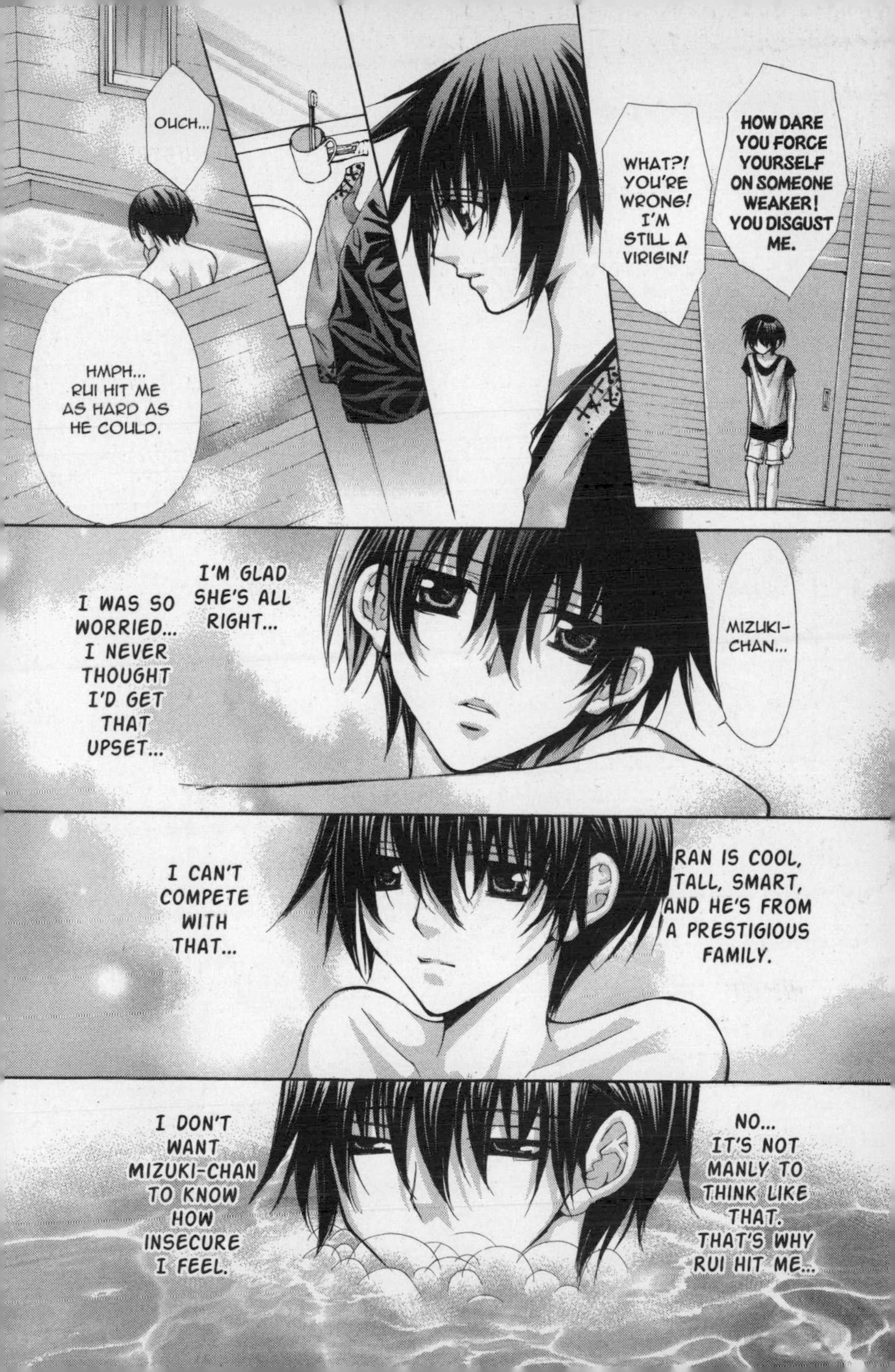
HOW DARE YOU FORCE YOURSELF ON SOMEONE WEAKER! YOU DISGUST ME.
WHAT?! YOU'RE WRONG! I'M STILL A VIRIGIN!
OUCH...
HMPH... RUI HIT ME AS HARD AS HE COULD.
MIZUKI-CHAN...
I'M GLAD SHE'S ALL RIGHT...
I WAS SO WORRIED... I NEVER THOUGHT I'D GET THAT UPSET...
RAN IS COOL, TALL, SMART, AND HE'S FROM A PRESTIGIOUS FAMILY.
I CAN'T COMPETE WITH THAT...
NO... IT'S NOT MANLY TO THINK LIKE THAT. THAT'S WHY RUI HIT ME...
I DON'T WANT MIZUKI-CHAN TO KNOW HOW INSECURE I FEEL.

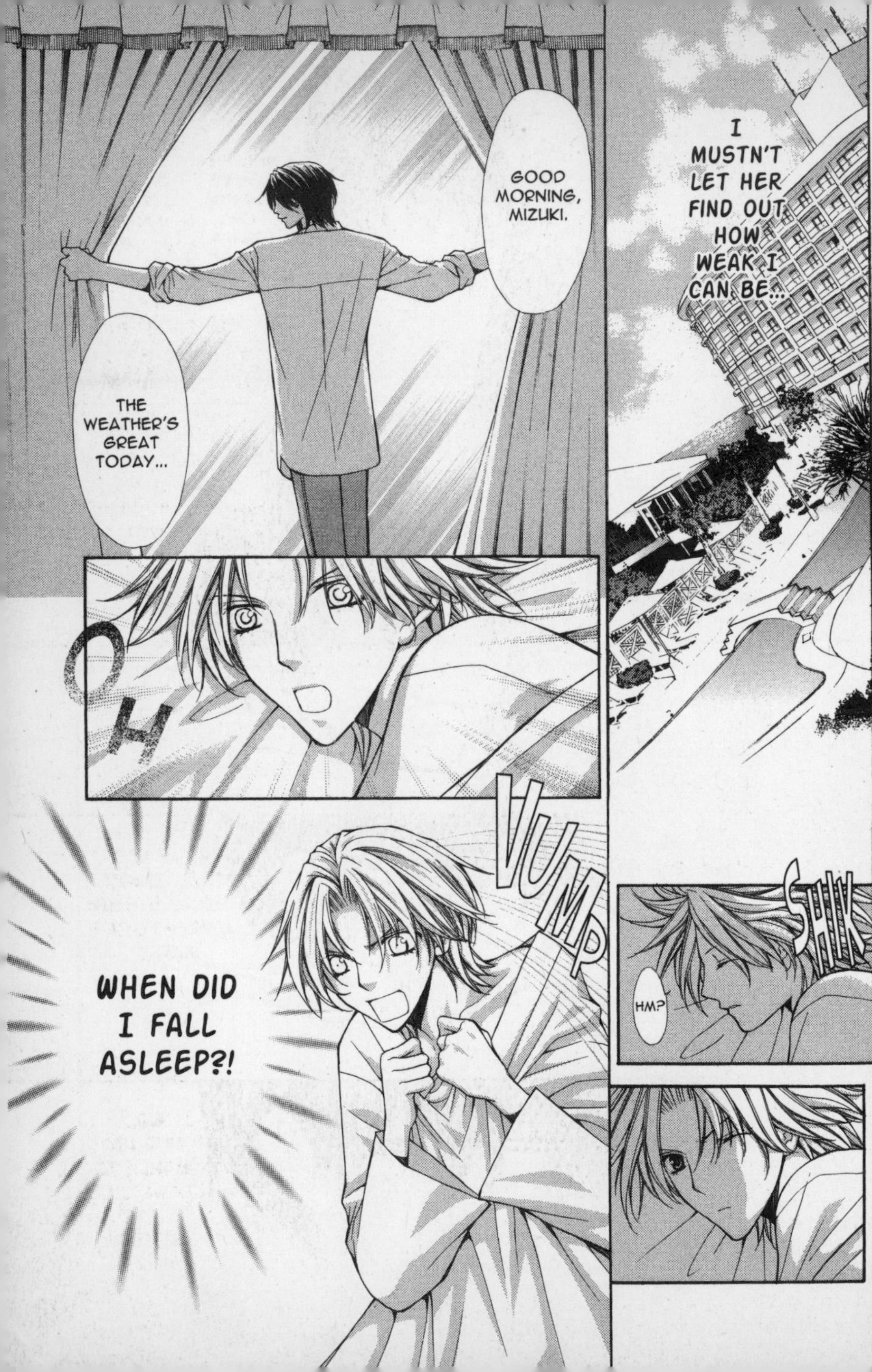
I MUSTN'T LET HER FIND OUT HOW WEAK I CAN BE...
GOOD MORNING, MIZUKI.
THE WEATHER'S GREAT TODAY...
OH
VUMP
WHEN DID I FALL ASLEEP?!
SHK
HM?

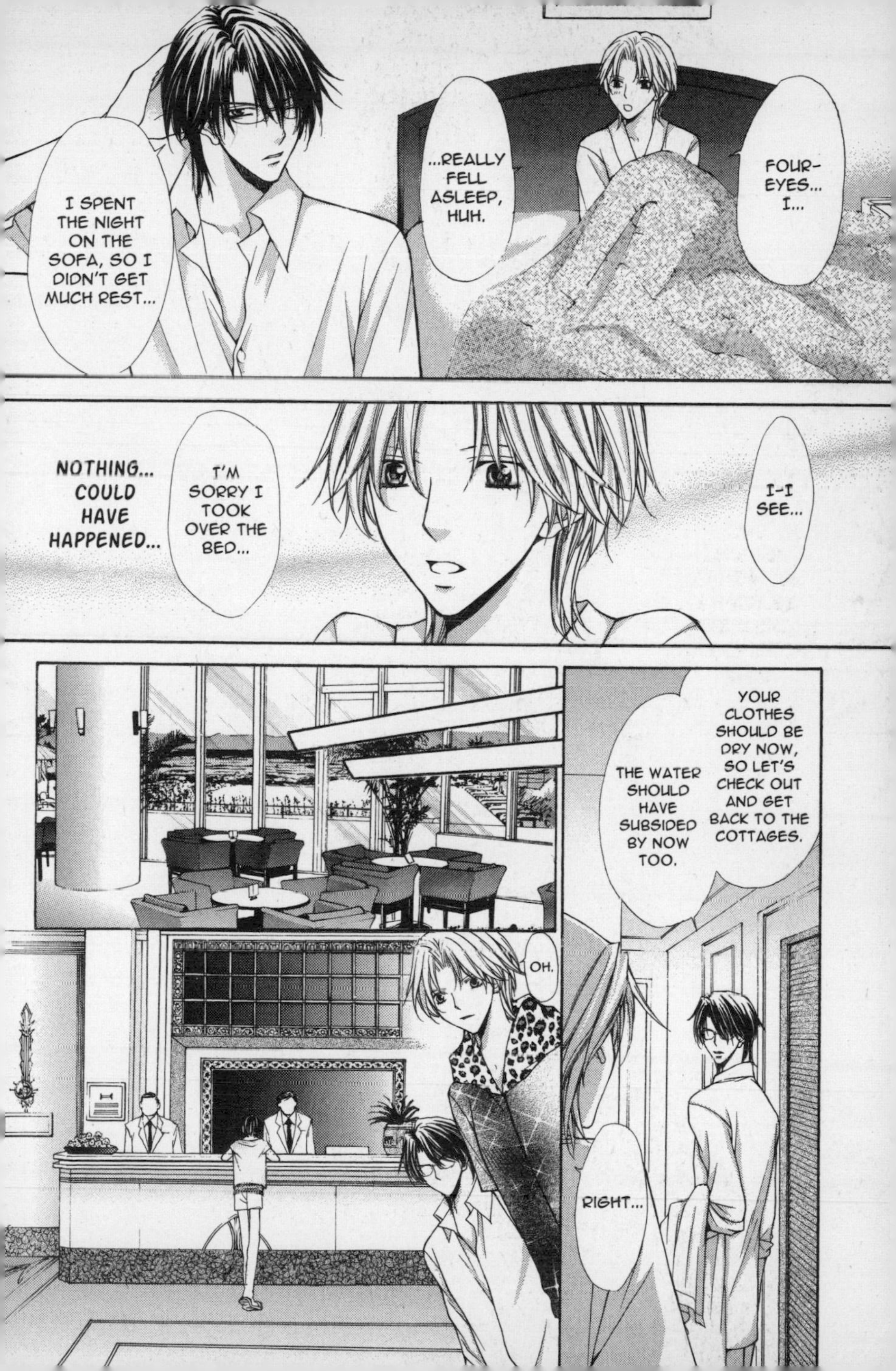
FOUR-EYES... I...
...REALLY FELL ASLEEP, HUH.
I SPENT THE NIGHT ON THE SOFA, SO I DIDN'T GET MUCH REST...
I-I SEE...
I'M SORRY I TOOK OVER THE BED...
NOTHING... COULD HAVE HAPPENED...
YOUR CLOTHES SHOULD BE DRY NOW, SO LET'S CHECK OUT AND GET BACK TO THE COTTAGES.
THE WATER SHOULD HAVE SUBSIDED BY NOW TOO.
RIGHT...
OH.

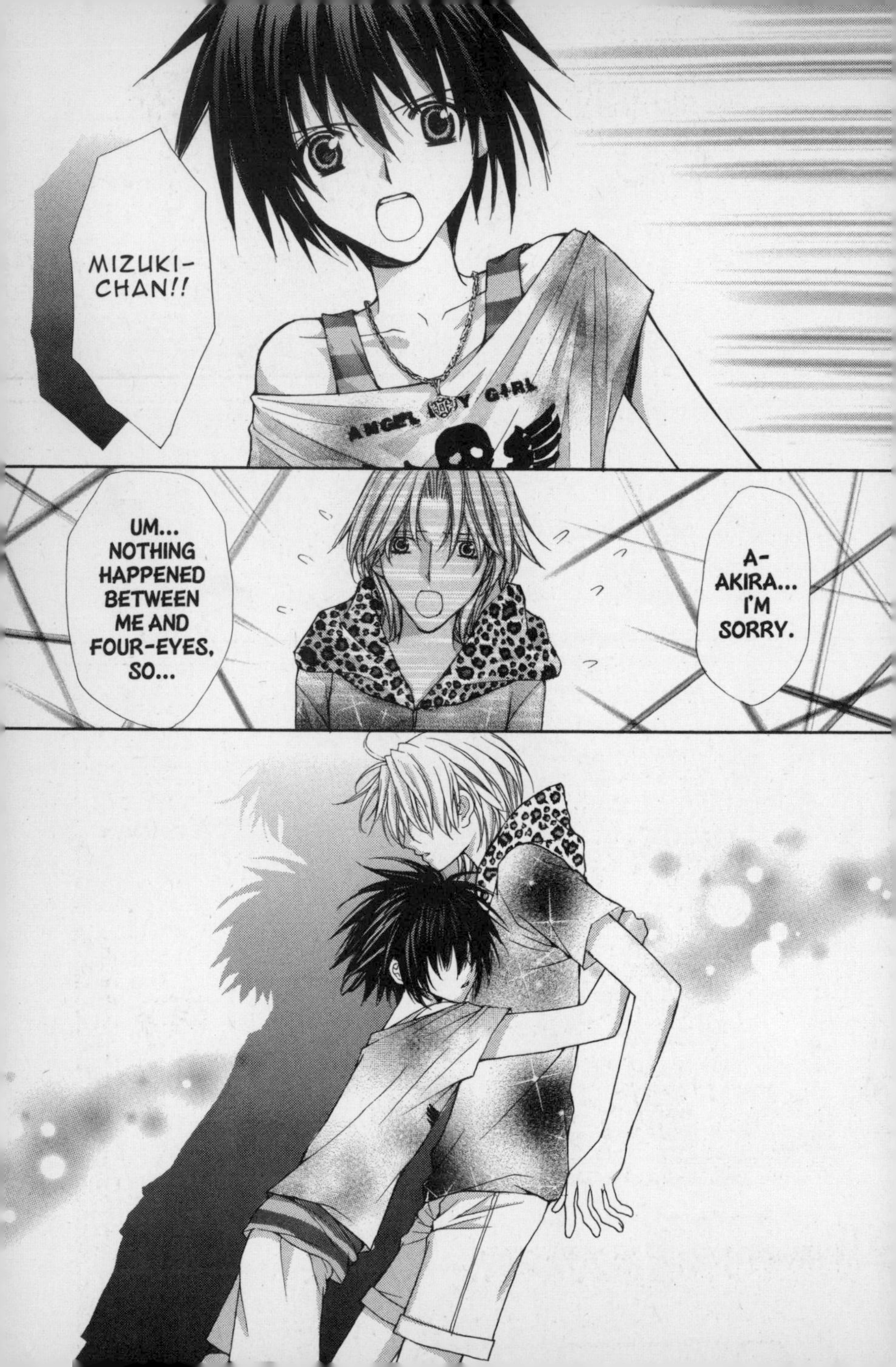
MIZUKI-CHAN!!
A-AKIRA... I'M SORRY.
UM... NOTHING HAPPENED BETWEEN ME AND FOUR-EYES, SO...

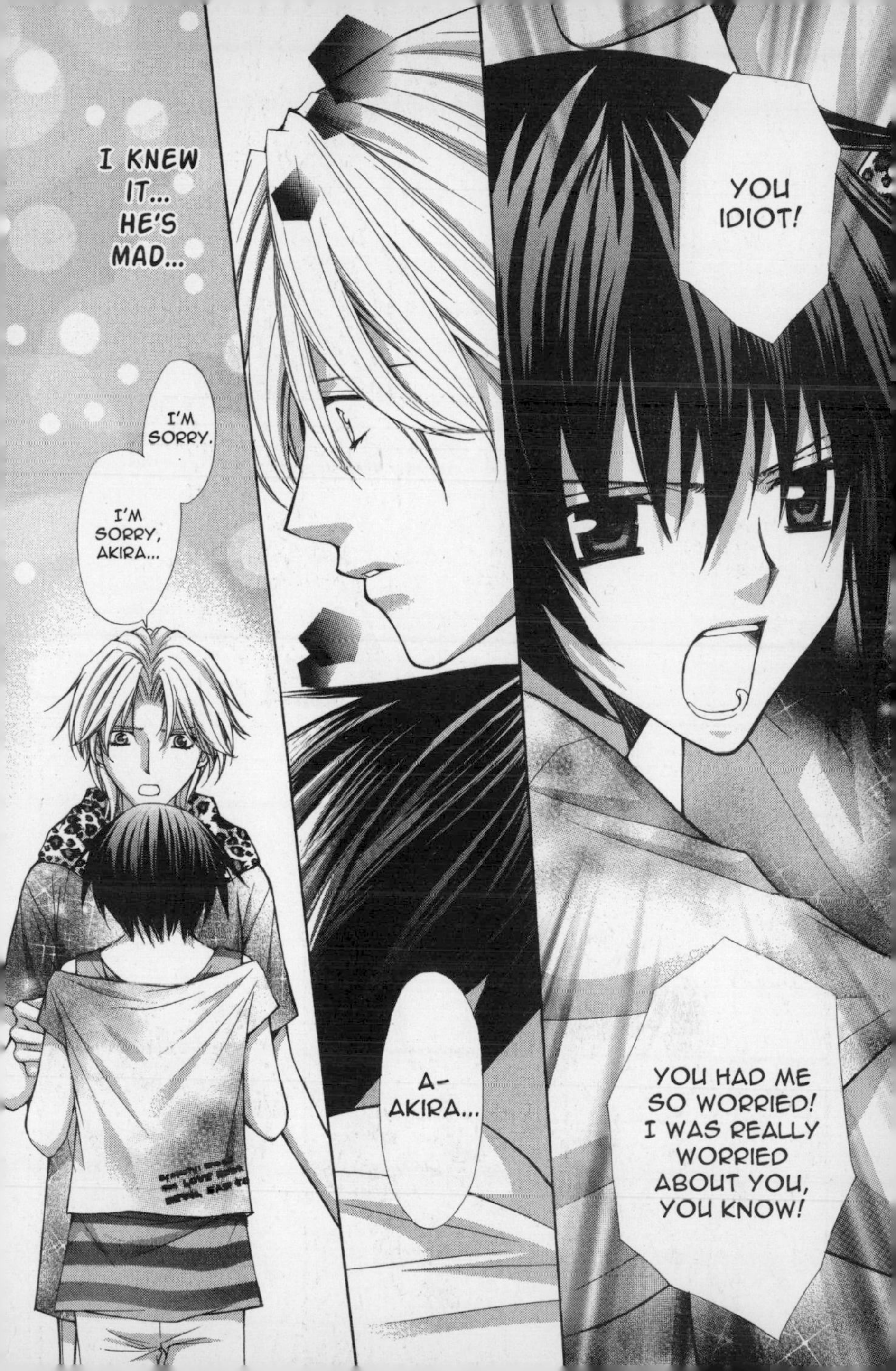
YOU IDIOT!
YOU HAD ME SO WORRIED! I WAS REALLY WORRIED ABOUT YOU, YOU KNOW!
A- AKIRA...
I KNEW IT... HE'S MAD...
I'M SORRY.
I'M SORRY, AKIRA...

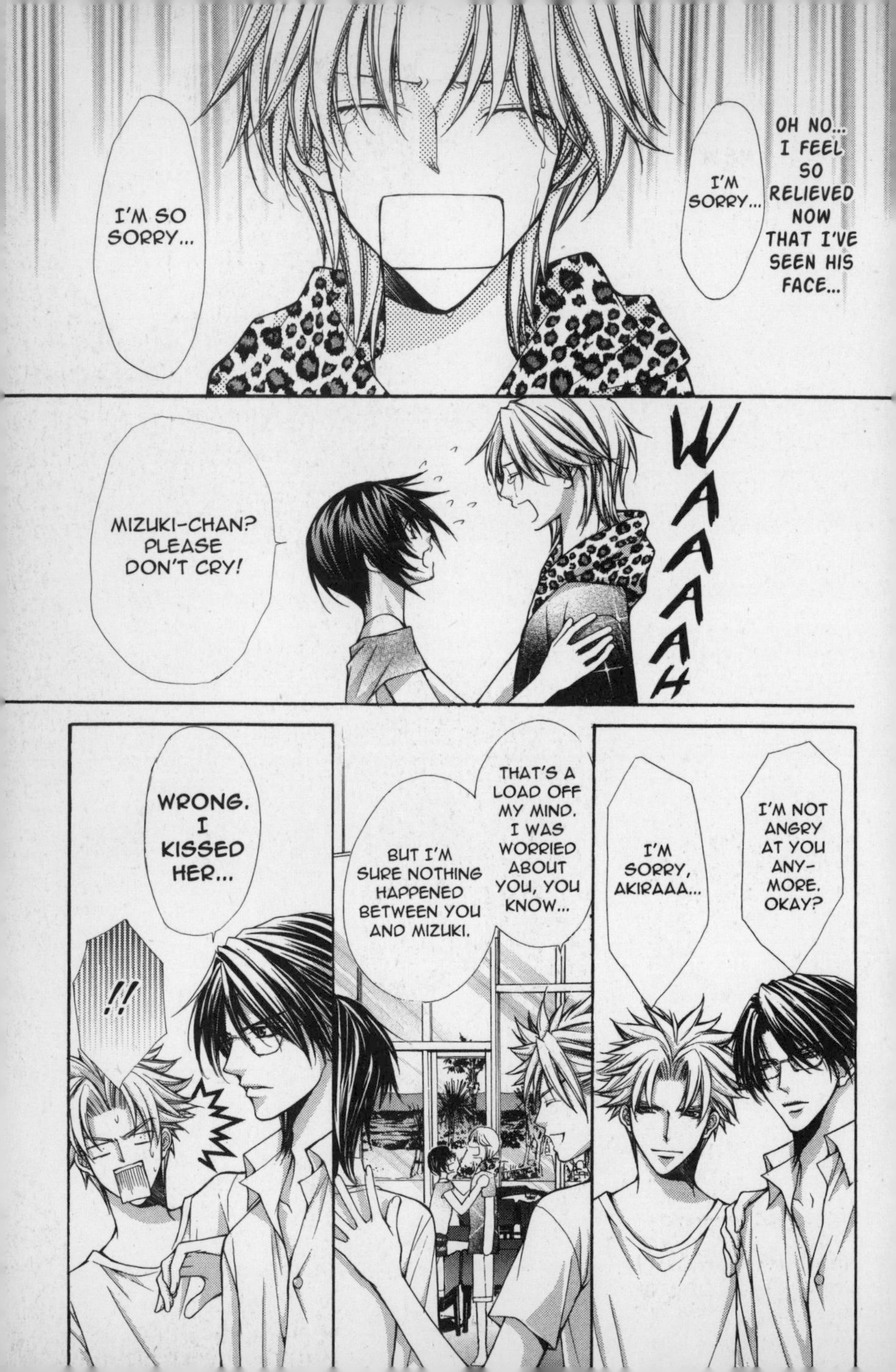
OH NO... I FEEL SO RELIEVED NOW THAT I'VE SEEN HIS FACE...
I'M SORRY...
I'M SO SORRY...
WAAAAAH
MIZUKI-CHAN? PLEASE DON'T CRY!
I'M NOT ANGRY AT YOU ANY-MORE. OKAY?
I'M SORRY, AKIRAAA...
THAT'S A LOAD OFF MY MIND. I WAS WORRIED ABOUT YOU, YOU KNOW...
BUT I'M SURE NOTHING HAPPENED BETWEEN YOU AND MIZUKI.
WRONG. I KISSED HER...
!!

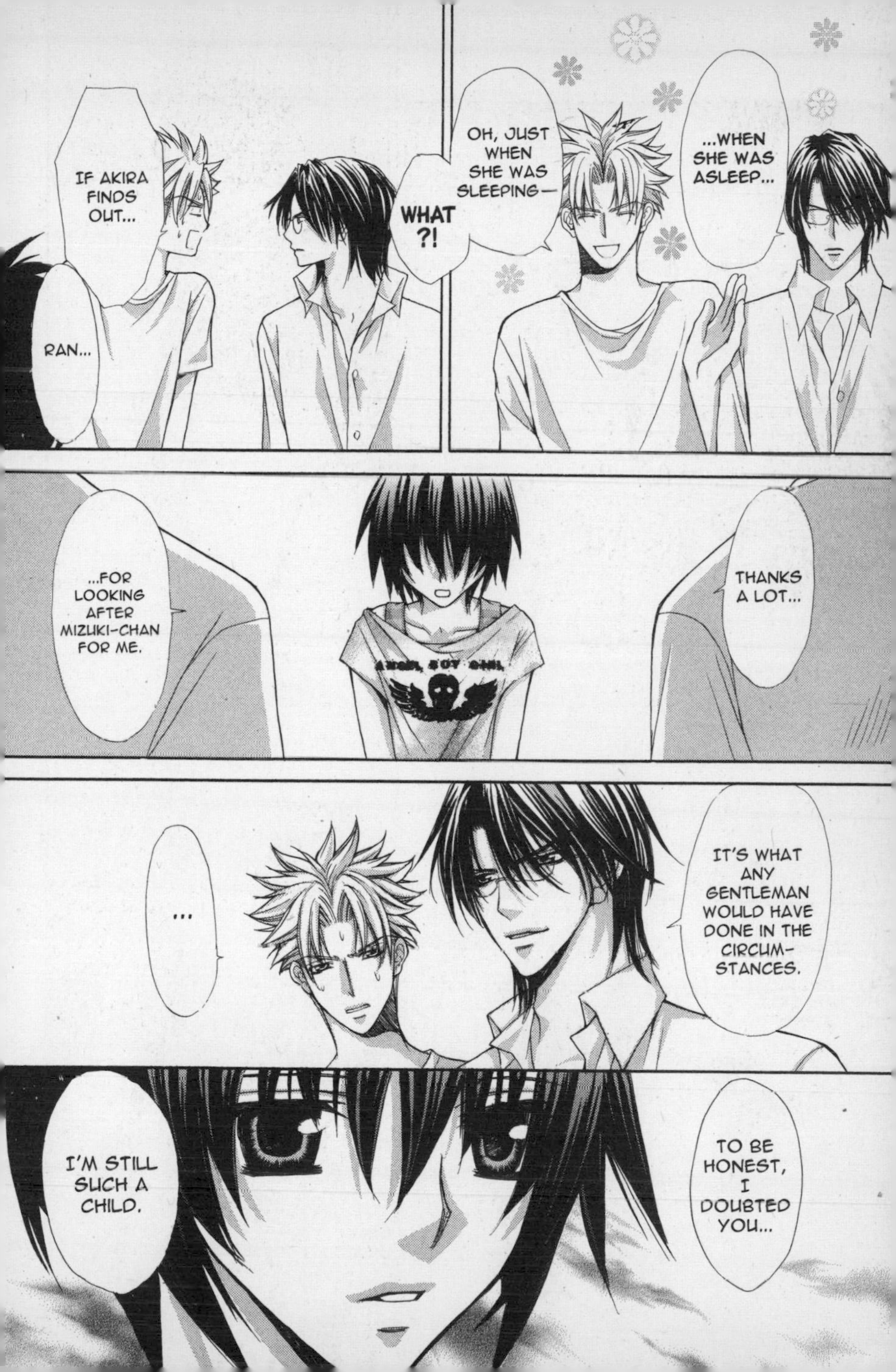
...WHEN SHE WAS ASLEEP...
OH, JUST WHEN SHE WAS SLEEPING—
WHAT ?!
IF AKIRA FINDS OUT...
RAN...
THANKS A LOT...
...FOR LOOKING AFTER MIZUKI-CHAN FOR ME.
IT'S WHAT ANY GENTLEMAN WOULD HAVE DONE IN THE CIRCUM-STANCES.
...
TO BE HONEST, I DOUBTED YOU...
I'M STILL SUCH A CHILD.

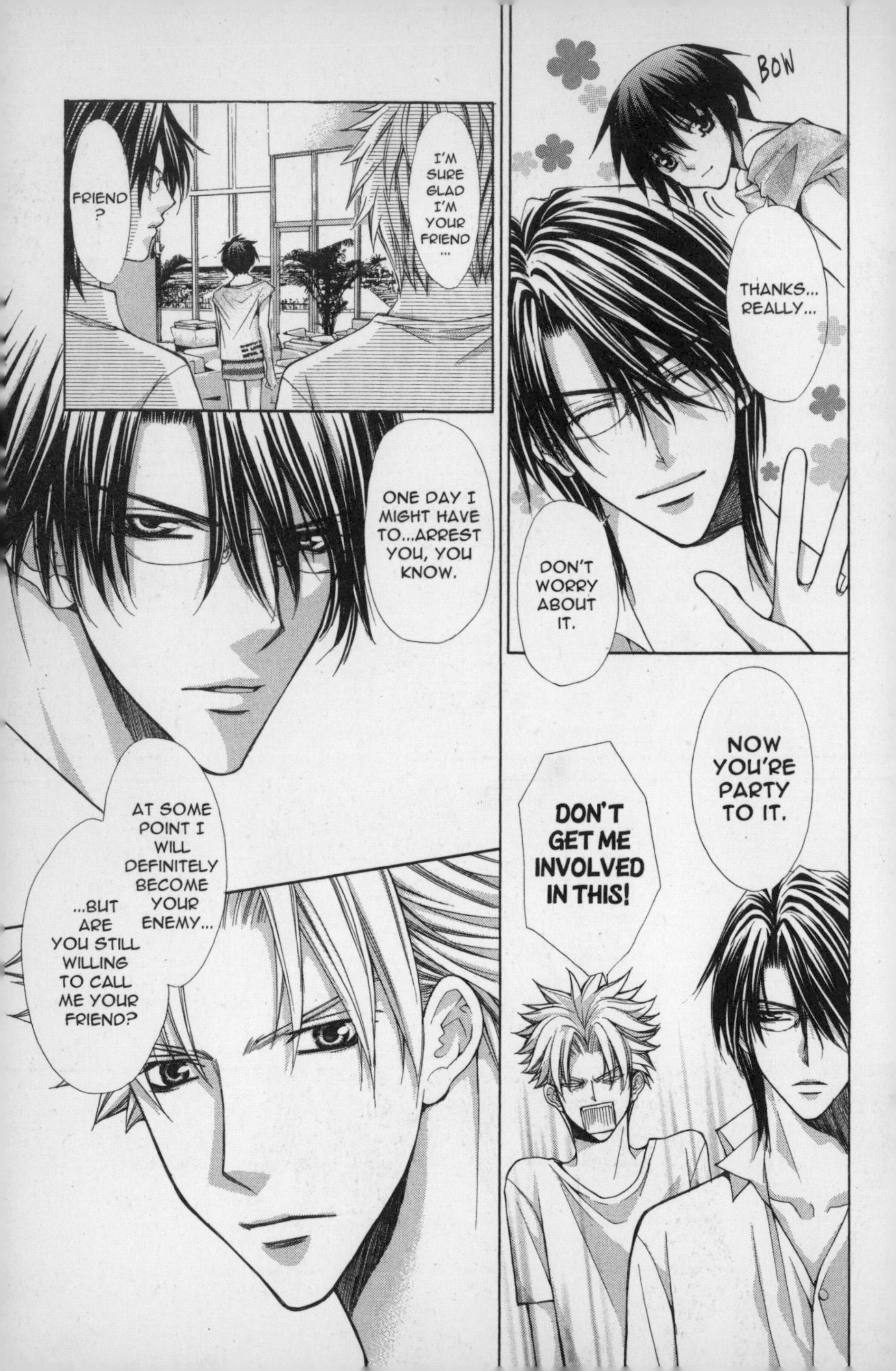
BOW
THANKS... REALLY...
DON'T WORRY ABOUT IT.
NOW YOU'RE PARTY TO IT.
DON'T GET ME INVOLVED IN THIS!
I'M SURE GLAD I'M YOUR FRIEND...
FRIEND?
ONE DAY I MIGHT HAVE TO...ARREST YOU, YOU KNOW.
AT SOME POINT I WILL DEFINITELY BECOME YOUR ENEMY...
...BUT ARE YOU STILL WILLING TO CALL ME YOUR FRIEND?

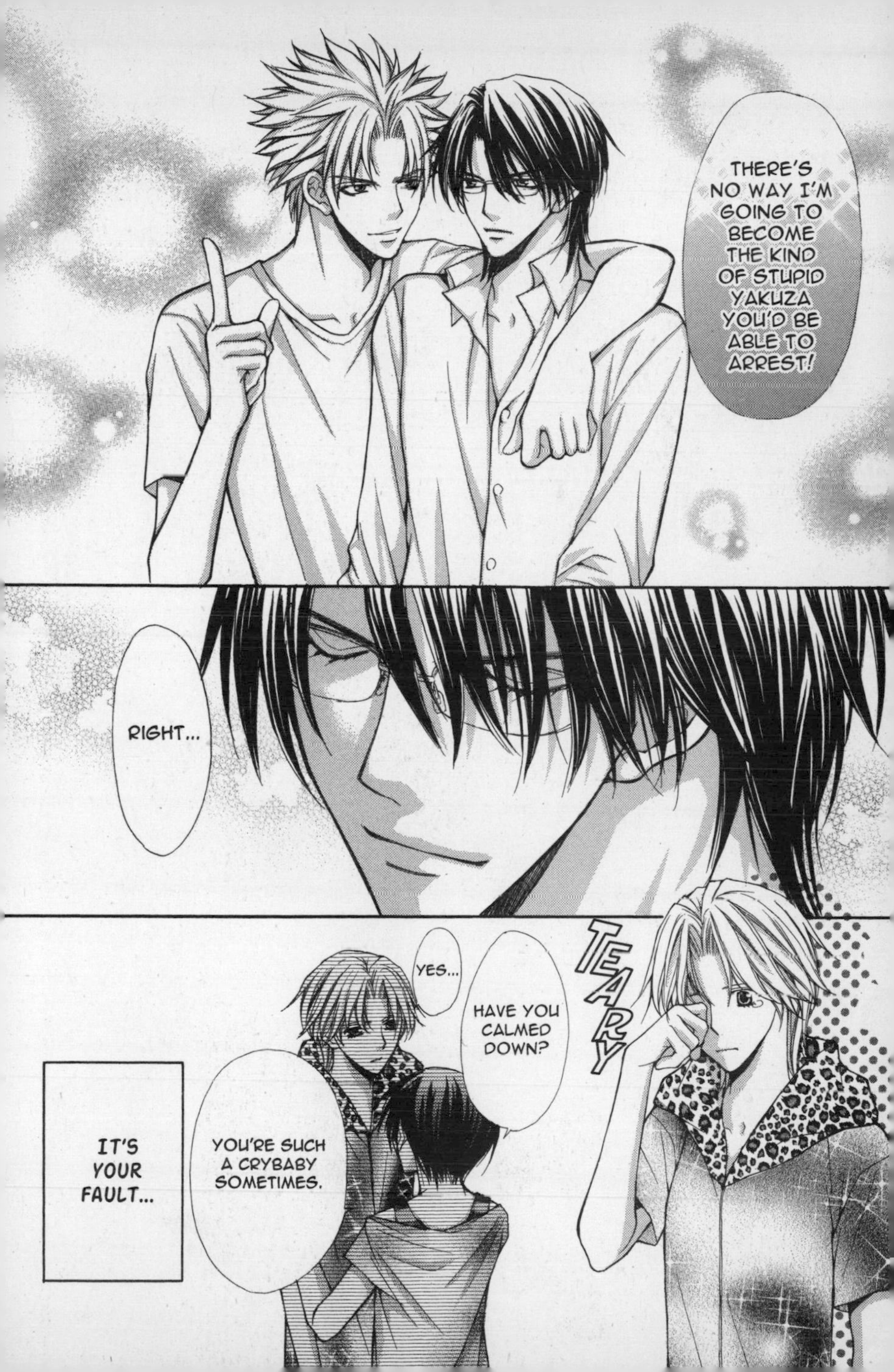
THERE'S NO WAY I'M GOING TO BECOME THE KIND OF STUPID YAKUZA YOU'D BE ABLE TO ARREST!
RIGHT...
TEARY
HAVE YOU CALMED DOWN?
YES...
YOU'RE SUCH A CRYBABY SOMETIMES.
IT'S YOUR FAULT...

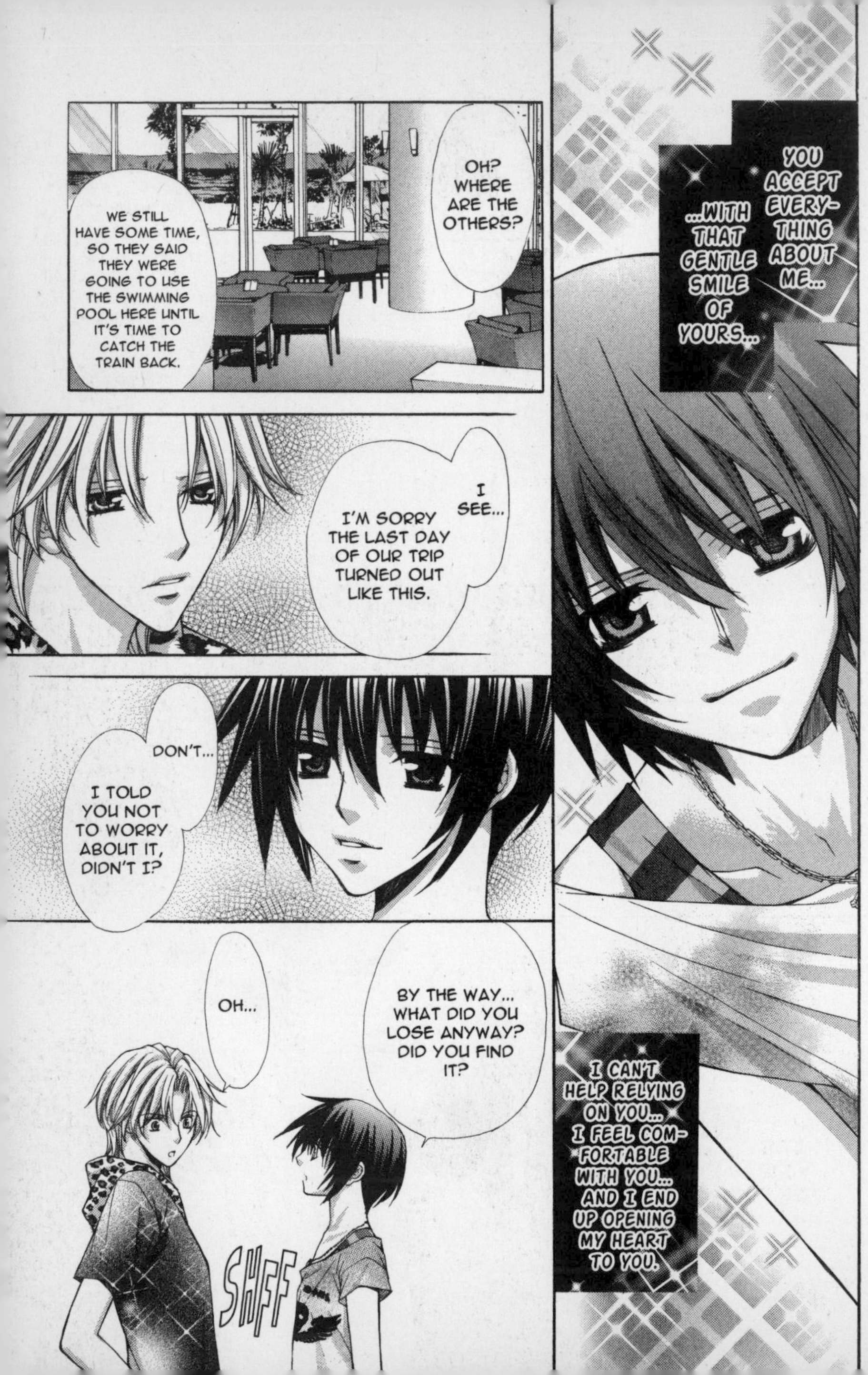
YOU ACCEPT EVERYTHING ABOUT ME...
...WITH THAT GENTLE SMILE OF YOURS...
I CAN'T HELP RELYING ON YOU... I FEEL COMFORTABLE WITH YOU... AND I END UP OPENING MY HEART TO YOU.
OH? WHERE ARE THE OTHERS?
WE STILL HAVE SOME TIME, SO THEY SAID THEY WERE GOING TO USE THE SWIMMING POOL HERE UNTIL IT'S TIME TO CATCH THE TRAIN BACK.
I SEE...
I'M SORRY THE LAST DAY OF OUR TRIP TURNED OUT LIKE THIS.
DON'T...
I TOLD YOU NOT TO WORRY ABOUT IT, DIDN'T I?
BY THE WAY... WHAT DID YOU LOSE ANYWAY? DID YOU FIND IT?
OH...
SHFF

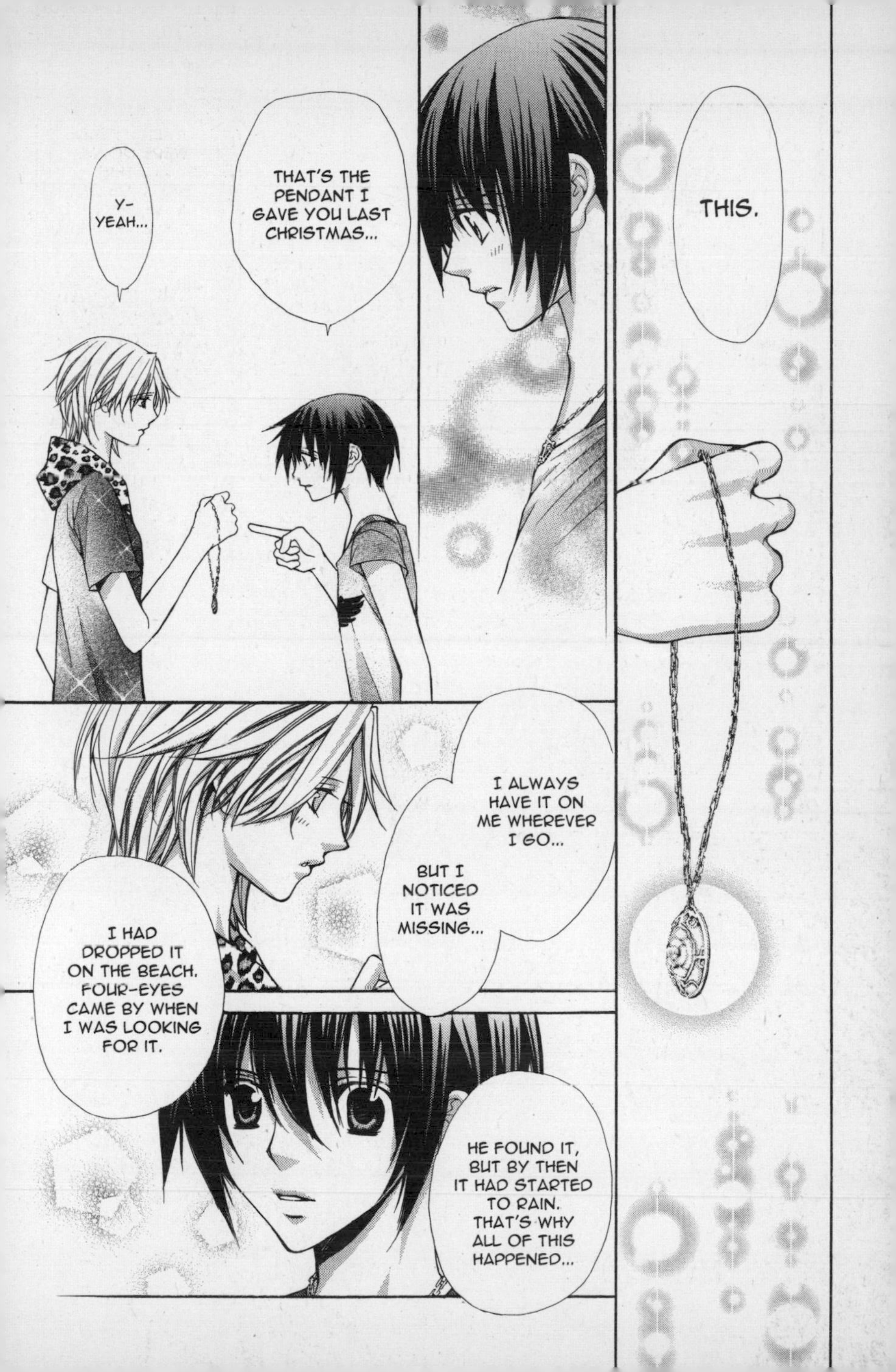
THIS.
THAT'S THE PENDANT I GAVE YOU LAST CHRISTMAS...
Y-YEAH...
I ALWAYS HAVE IT ON ME WHEREVER I GO...
BUT I NOTICED IT WAS MISSING...
I HAD DROPPED IT ON THE BEACH. FOUR-EYES CAME BY WHEN I WAS LOOKING FOR IT.
HE FOUND IT, BUT BY THEN IT HAD STARTED TO RAIN. THAT'S WHY ALL OF THIS HAPPENED...

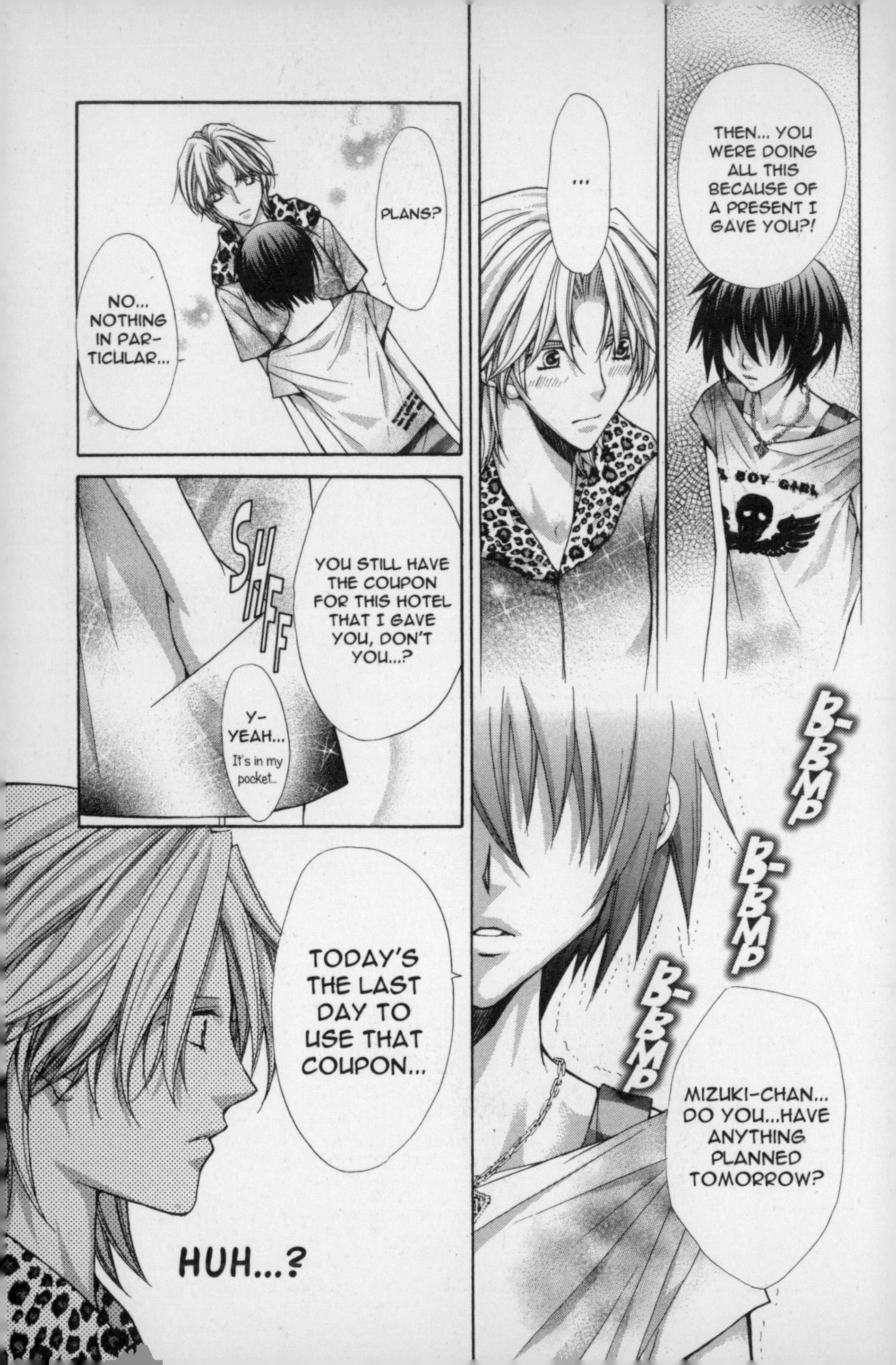
THEN... YOU WERE DOING ALL THIS BECAUSE OF A PRESENT I GAVE YOU?!
...
B-BMP
B-BMP
B-BMP
MIZUKI-CHAN... DO YOU...HAVE ANYTHING PLANNED TOMORROW?
PLANS?
NO... NOTHING IN PAR-TICULAR...
YOU STILL HAVE THE COUPON FOR THIS HOTEL THAT I GAVE YOU, DON'T YOU...?
SHUFF
Y-YEAH... It's in my pocket...
TODAY'S THE LAST DAY TO USE THAT COUPON...
HUH...?

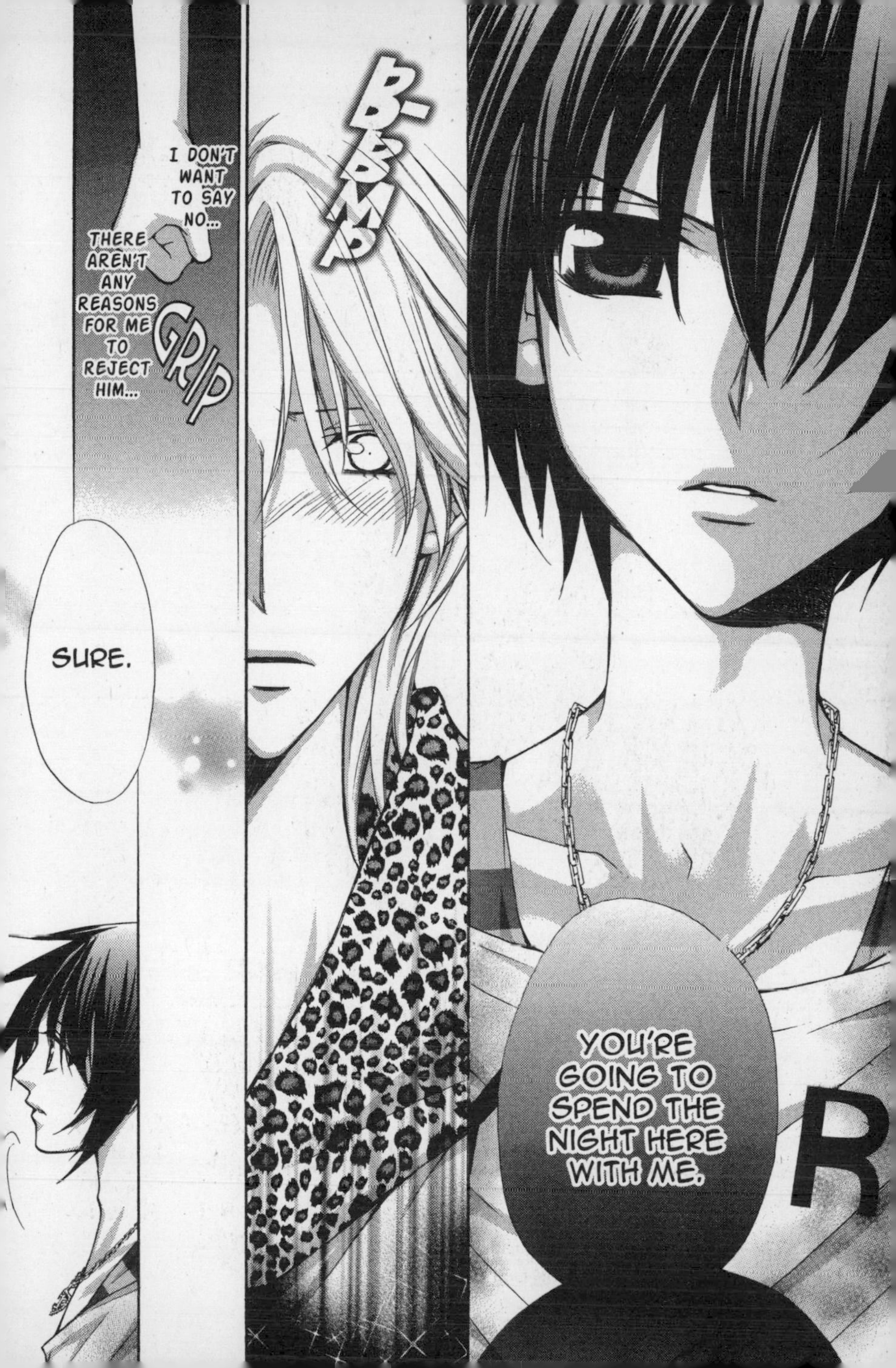
YOU'RE GOING TO SPEND THE NIGHT HERE WITH ME.
R
B-BDUMP
I DON'T WANT TO SAY NO...
THERE AREN'T ANY REASONS FOR ME TO REJECT HIM...
GRIP
SURE.

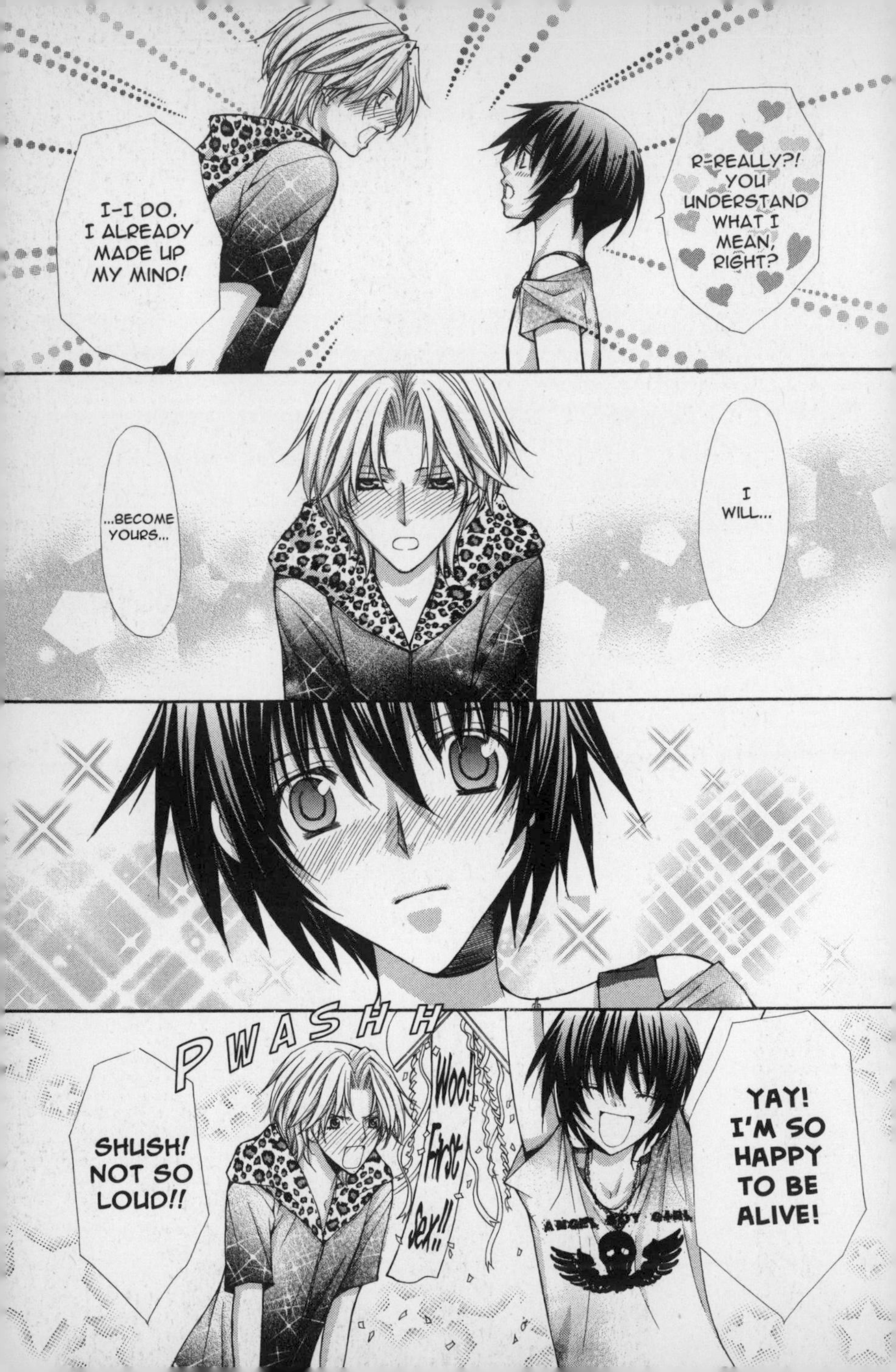
R-REALLY?! YOU UNDERSTAND WHAT I MEAN, RIGHT?
I-I DO. I ALREADY MADE UP MY MIND!
I WILL...
...BECOME YOURS...
YAY! I'M SO HAPPY TO BE ALIVE!
Woo! First Sex!!
PWASHH
SHUSH! NOT SO LOUD!!

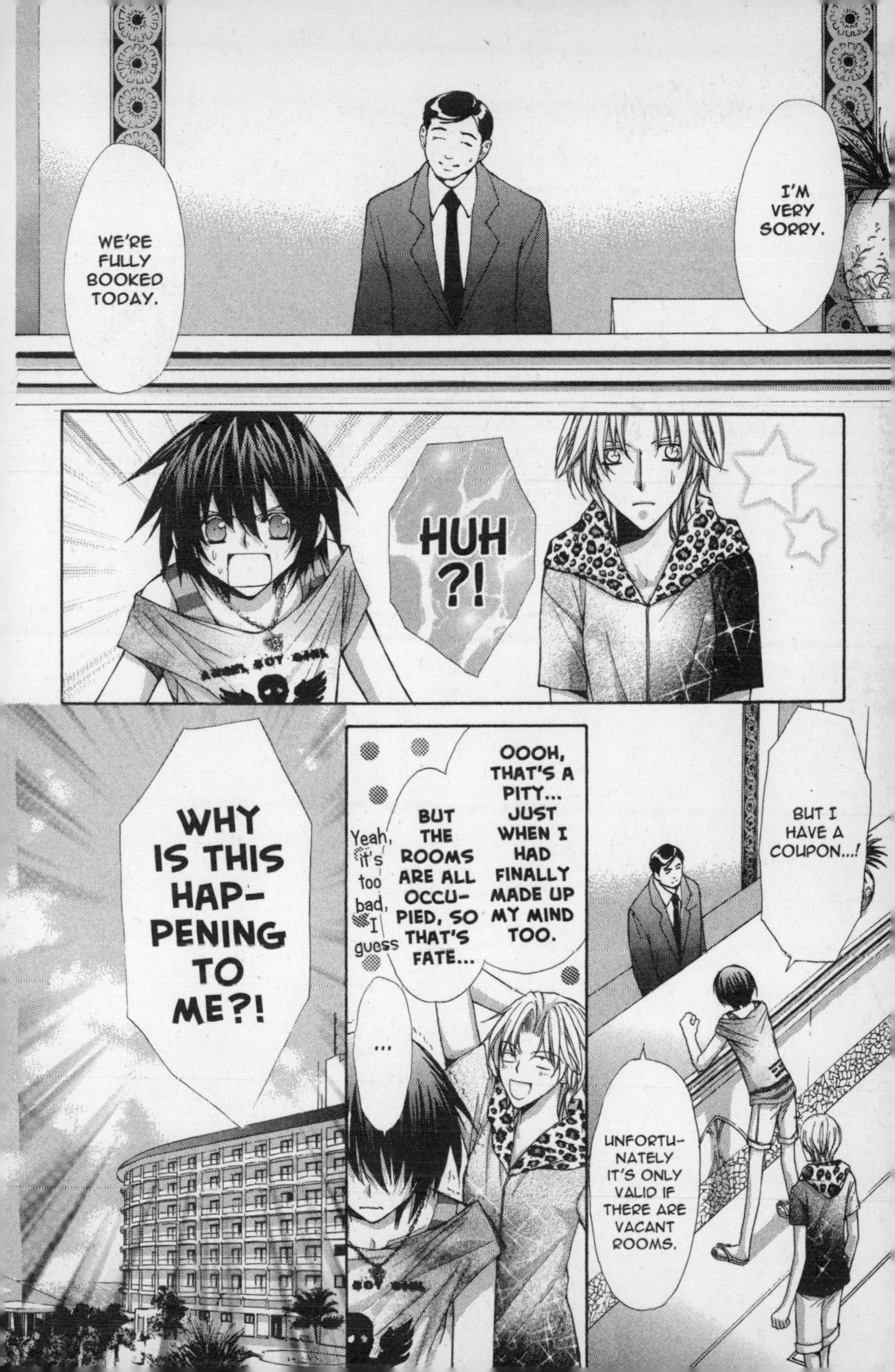
I'M VERY SORRY.
WE'RE FULLY BOOKED TODAY.
HUH?!
BUT I HAVE A COUPON...!
UNFORTU-NATELY IT'S ONLY VALID IF THERE ARE VACANT ROOMS.
OOOH, THAT'S A PITY... JUST WHEN I HAD FINALLY MADE UP MY MIND TOO.
BUT THE ROOMS ARE ALL OCCU-PIED, SO THAT'S FATE...
Yeah, it's too bad, I guess
...
WHY IS THIS HAP-PENING TO ME?!

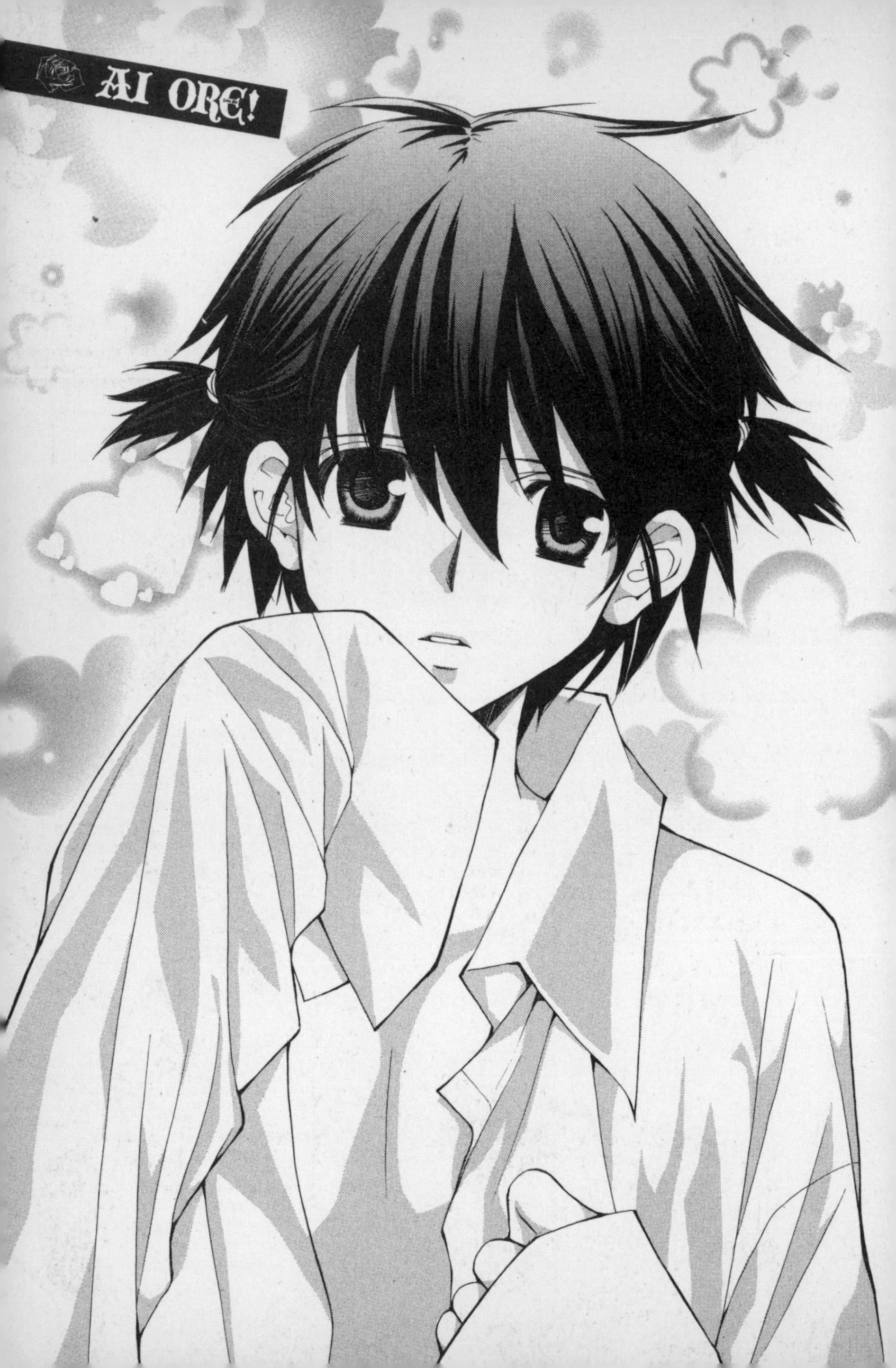
AI ORE!

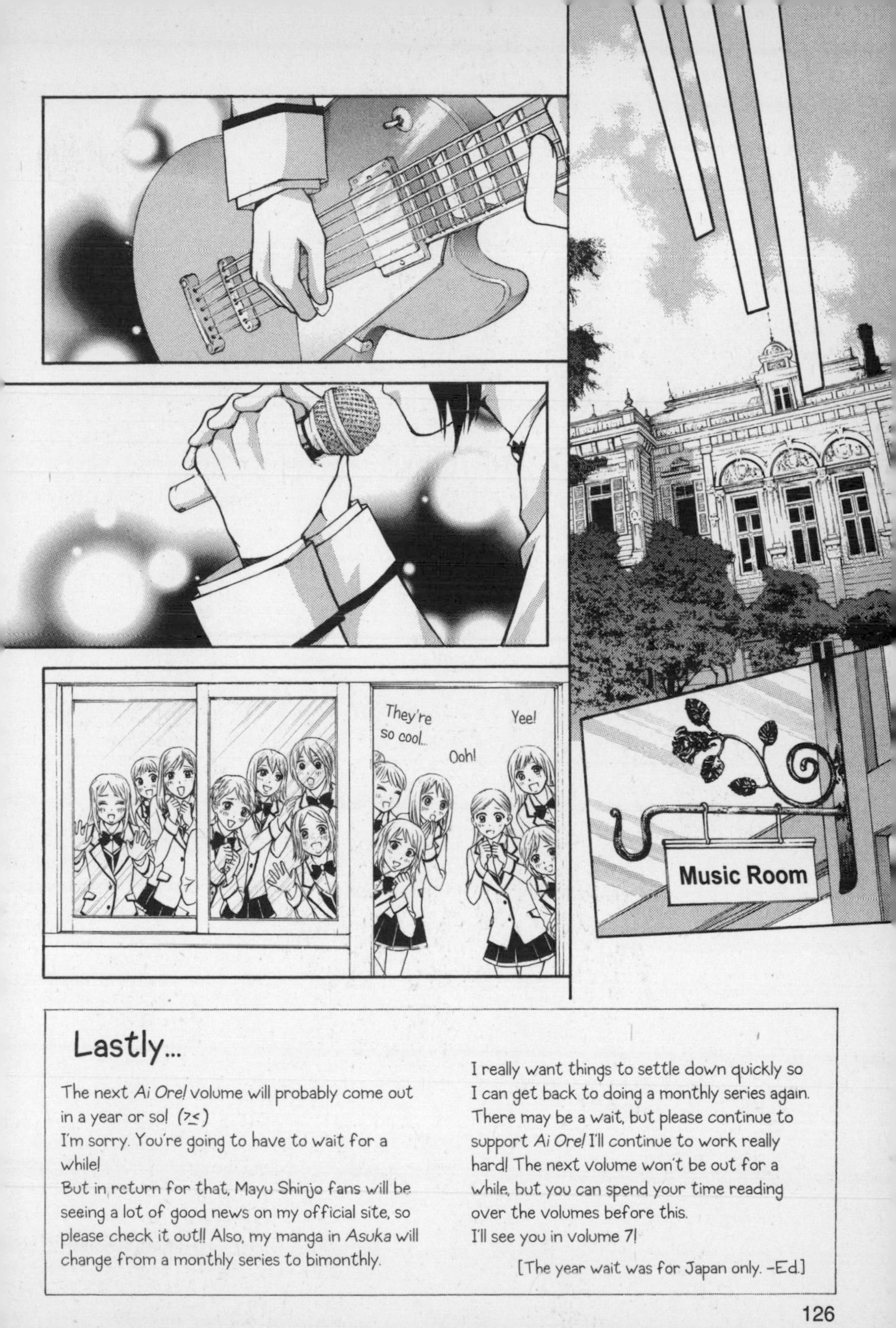
Music Room
Yee!
They're so cool...
Ooh!

Lastly...

The next *Ai Ore!* volume will probably come out in a year or so! (>_<)
I'm sorry. You're going to have to wait for a while!
But in return for that, Mayu Shinjo fans will be seeing a lot of good news on my official site, so please check it out!! Also, my manga in *Asuka* will change from a monthly series to bimonthly.
I really want things to settle down quickly so I can get back to doing a monthly series again. There may be a wait, but please continue to support *Ai Ore!* I'll continue to work really hard! The next volume won't be out for a while, but you can spend your time reading over the volumes before this.
I'll see you in volume 7!

[The year wait was for Japan only. –Ed.]

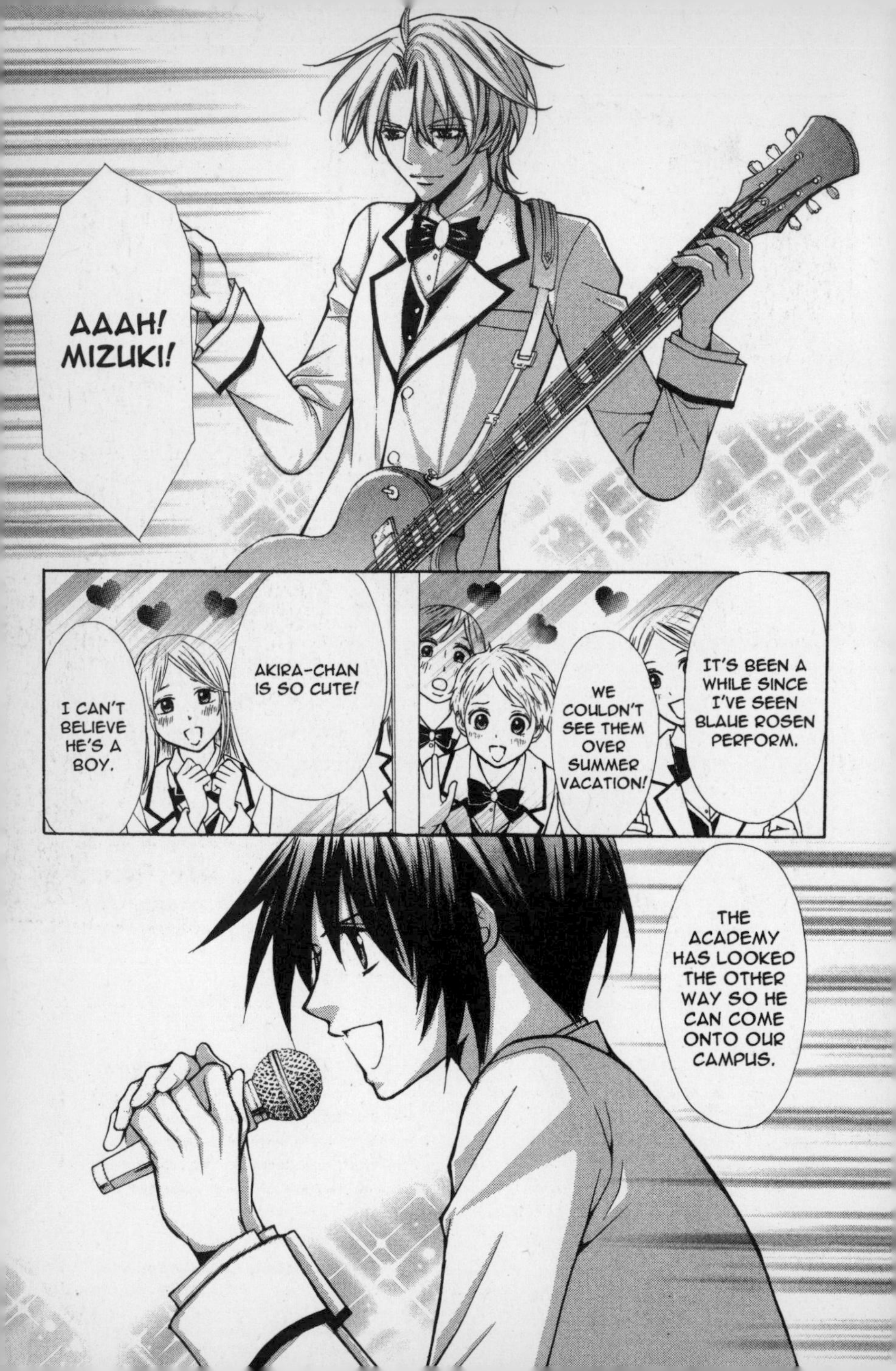
AAAH! MIZUKI!
IT'S BEEN A WHILE SINCE I'VE SEEN BLAUE ROSEN PERFORM.
WE COULDN'T SEE THEM OVER SUMMER VACATION!
AKIRA-CHAN IS SO CUTE!
I CAN'T BELIEVE HE'S A BOY.
THE ACADEMY HAS LOOKED THE OTHER WAY SO HE CAN COME ONTO OUR CAMPUS.

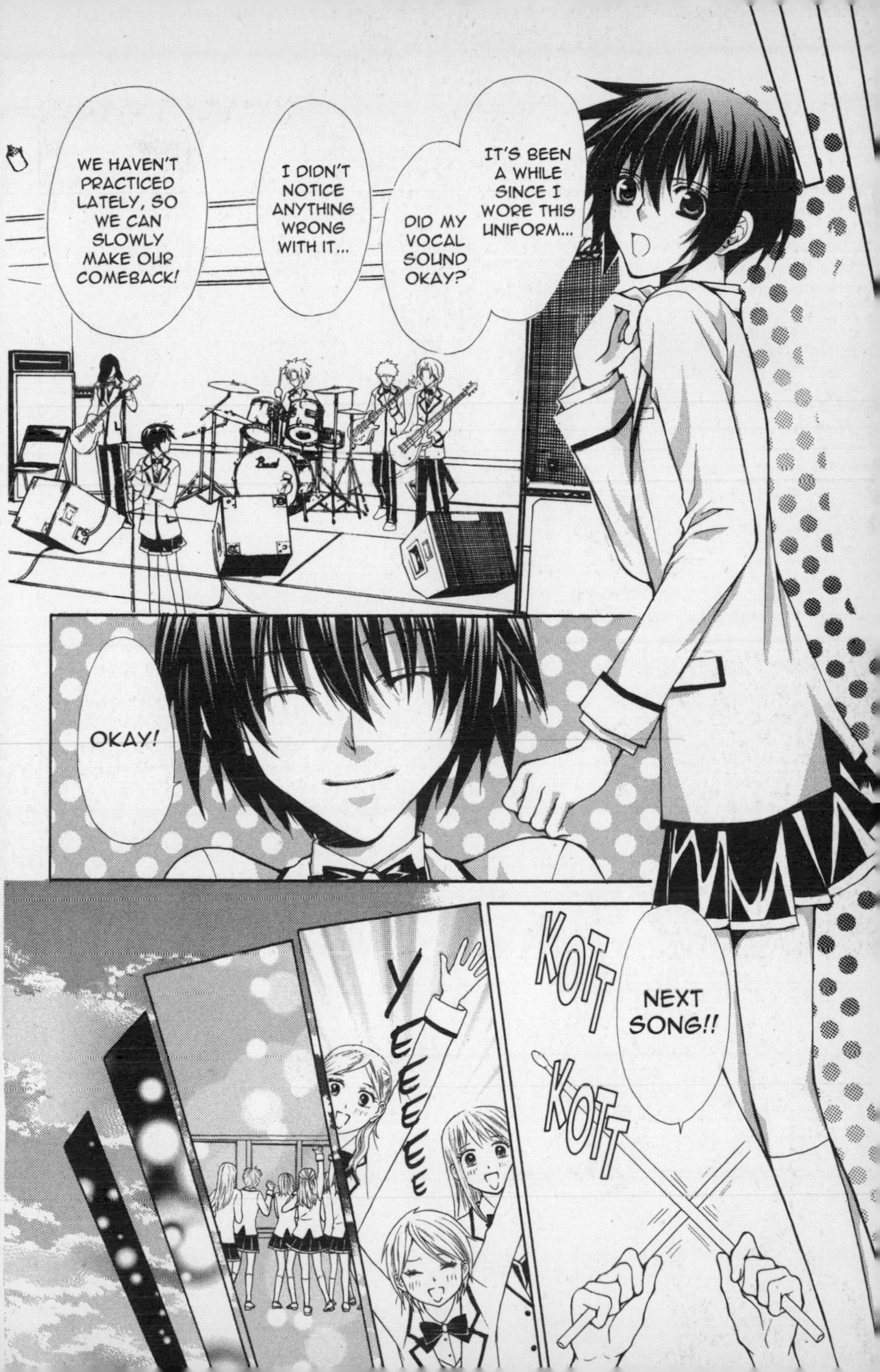
IT'S BEEN A WHILE SINCE I WORE THIS UNIFORM...
DID MY VOCAL SOUND OKAY?
I DIDN'T NOTICE ANYTHING WRONG WITH IT...
WE HAVEN'T PRACTICED LATELY, SO WE CAN SLOWLY MAKE OUR COMEBACK!
OKAY!
NEXT SONG!!
KOTT
KOTT
YEEEEEE

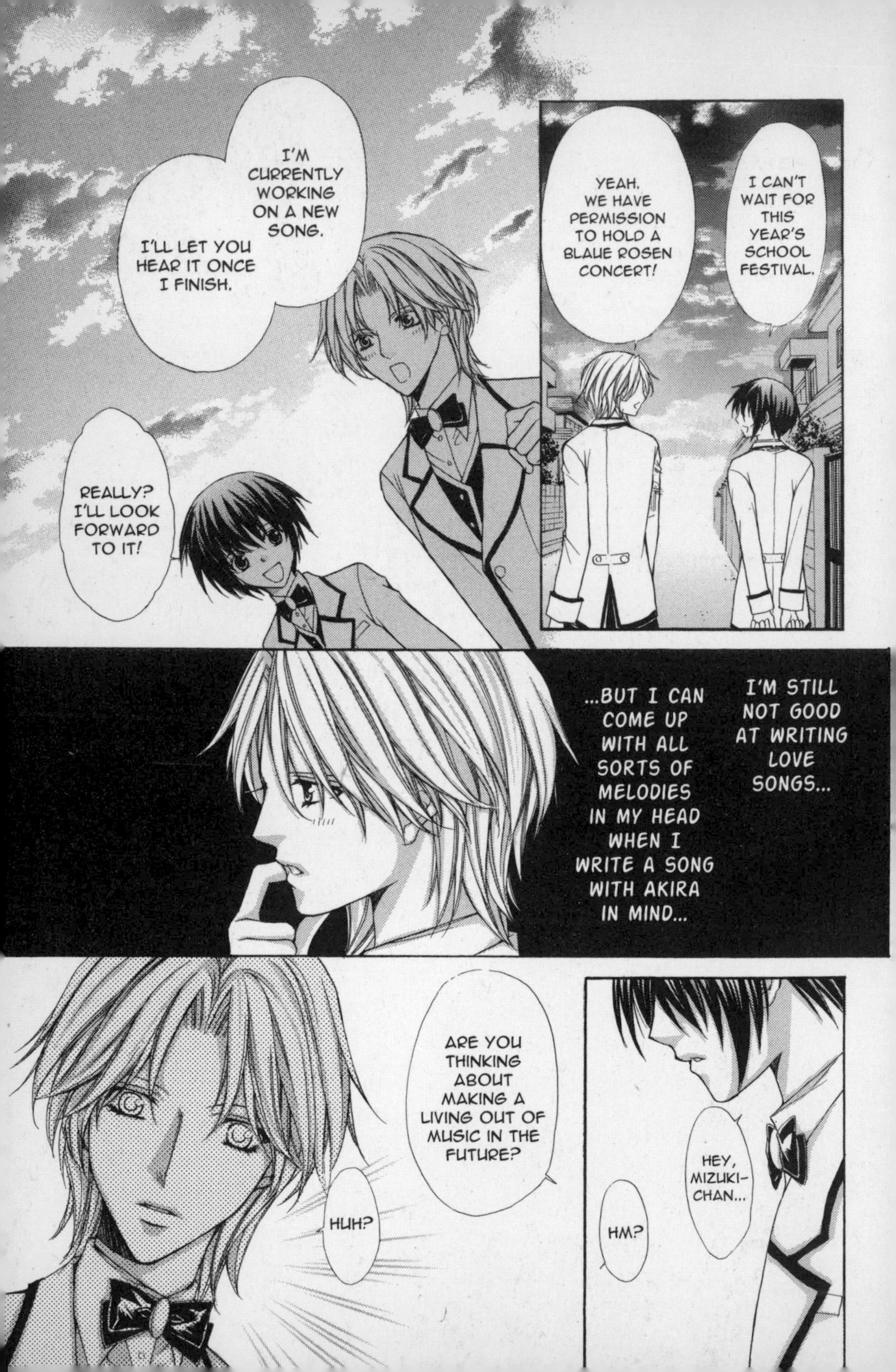
I CAN'T WAIT FOR THIS YEAR'S SCHOOL FESTIVAL.
YEAH. WE HAVE PERMISSION TO HOLD A BLAUE ROSEN CONCERT!
I'M CURRENTLY WORKING ON A NEW SONG.
I'LL LET YOU HEAR IT ONCE I FINISH.
REALLY? I'LL LOOK FORWARD TO IT!
I'M STILL NOT GOOD AT WRITING LOVE SONGS...
...BUT I CAN COME UP WITH ALL SORTS OF MELODIES IN MY HEAD WHEN I WRITE A SONG WITH AKIRA IN MIND...
HEY, MIZUKI-CHAN...
HM?
ARE YOU THINKING ABOUT MAKING A LIVING OUT OF MUSIC IN THE FUTURE?
HUH?

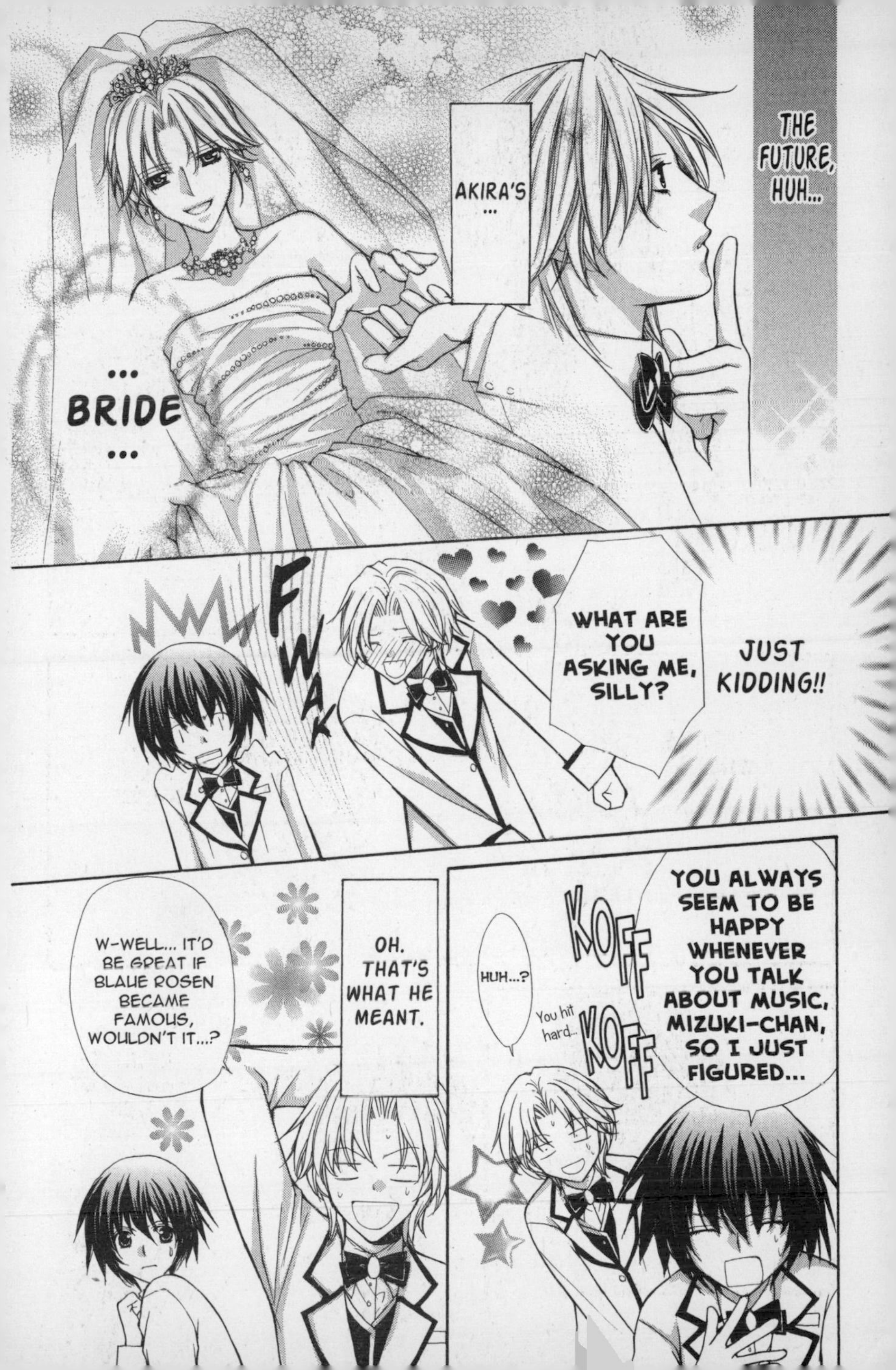
THE FUTURE, HUH...
AKIRA'S ...
... BRIDE ...
JUST KIDDING!!
WHAT ARE YOU ASKING ME, SILLY?
FWAK
YOU ALWAYS SEEM TO BE HAPPY WHENEVER YOU TALK ABOUT MUSIC, MIZUKI-CHAN, SO I JUST FIGURED...
KOFF
KOFF
HUH...?
You hit hard...
OH. THAT'S WHAT HE MEANT.
W-WELL... IT'D BE GREAT IF BLAUE ROSEN BECAME FAMOUS, WOULDN'T IT...?

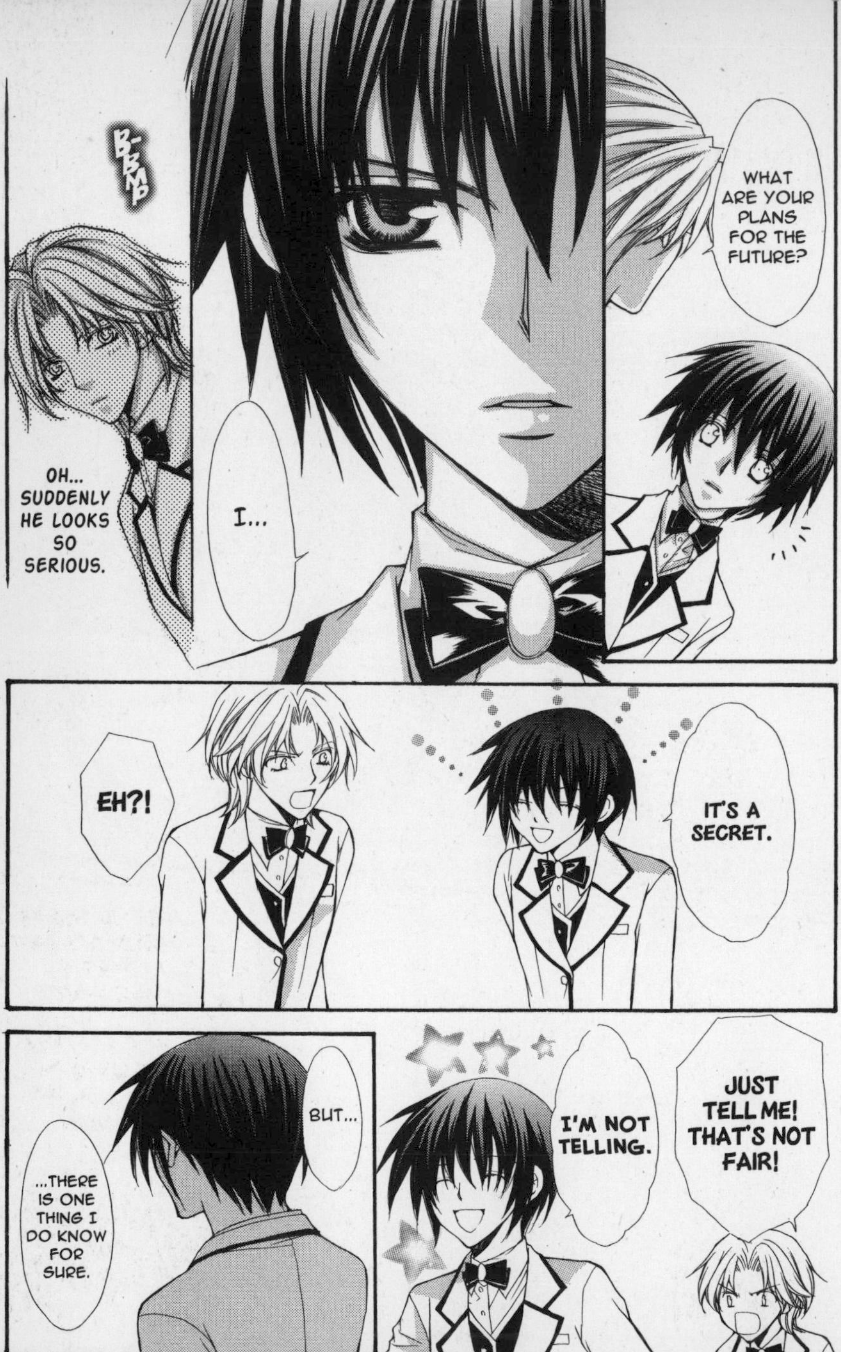
WHAT ARE YOUR PLANS FOR THE FUTURE?
I...
B-BMP
OH... SUDDENLY HE LOOKS SO SERIOUS.
IT'S A SECRET.
EH?!
JUST TELL ME! THAT'S NOT FAIR!
I'M NOT TELLING.
BUT...
...THERE IS ONE THING I DO KNOW FOR SURE.

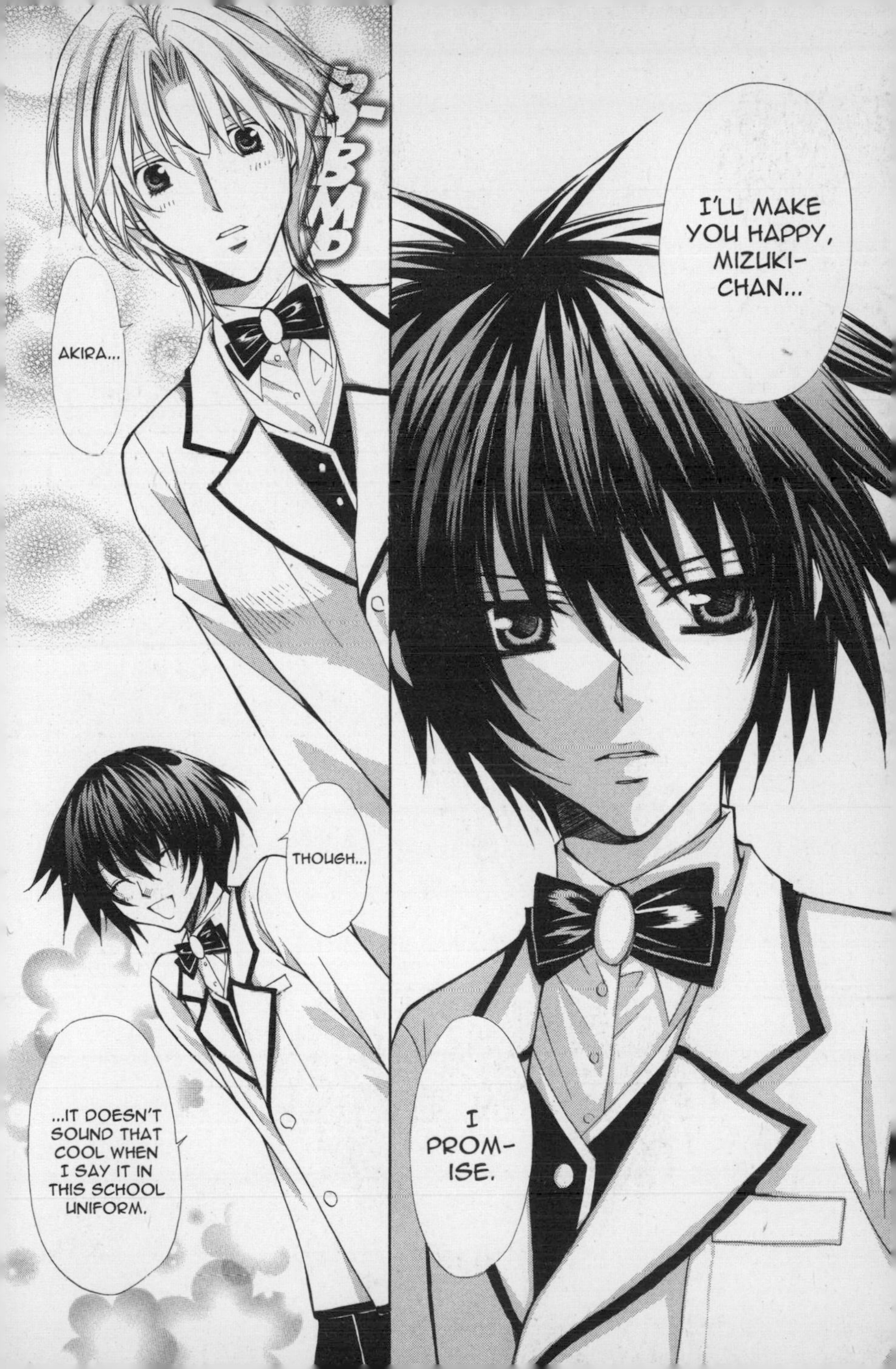
I'LL MAKE YOU HAPPY, MIZUKI-CHAN...
I PROM-ISE.
AKIRA...
THOUGH...
...IT DOESN'T SOUND THAT COOL WHEN I SAY IT IN THIS SCHOOL UNIFORM.

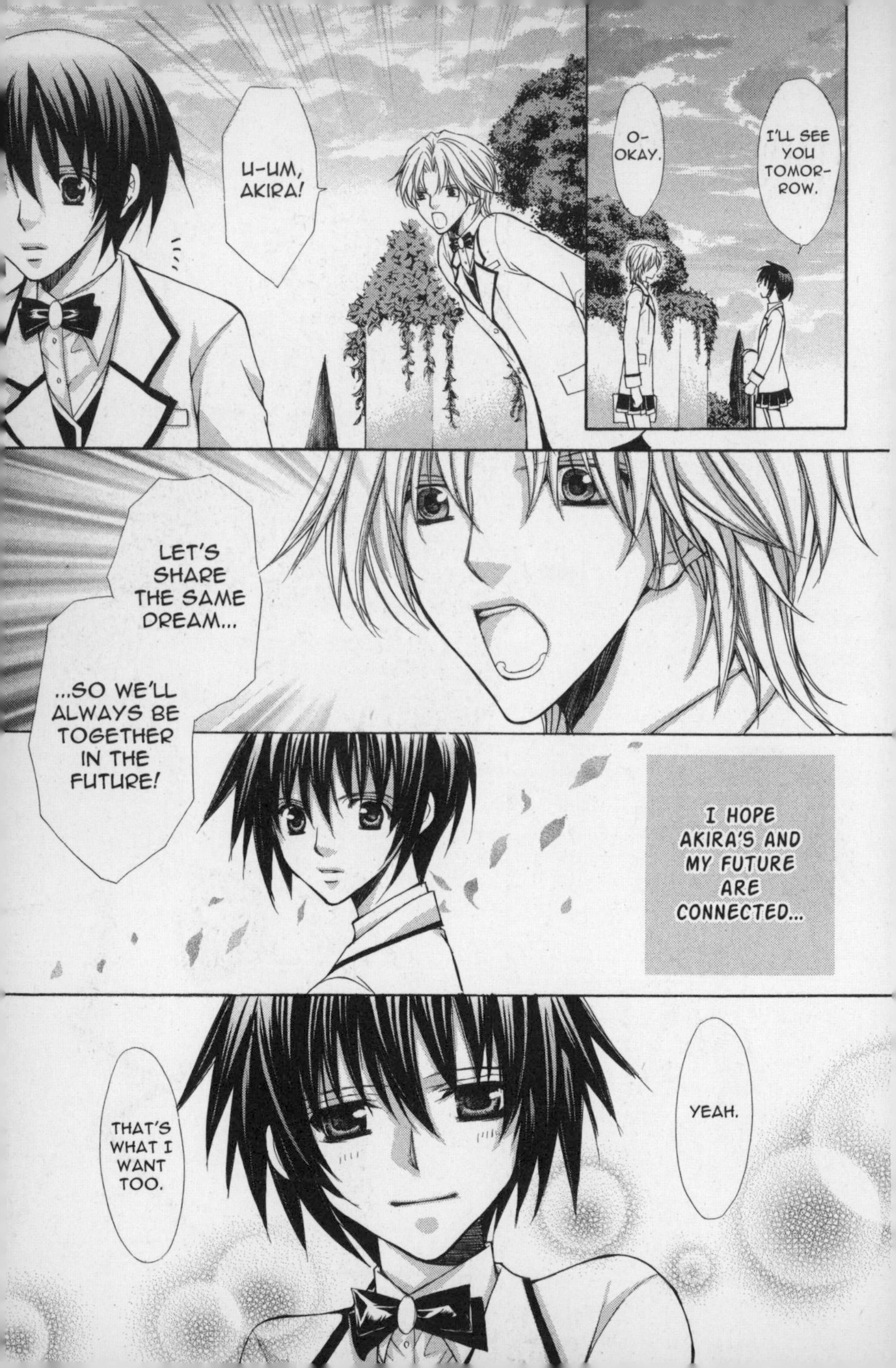
I'LL SEE YOU TOMORROW.
O-OKAY.
U-UM, AKIRA!
LET'S SHARE THE SAME DREAM...
...SO WE'LL ALWAYS BE TOGETHER IN THE FUTURE!
I HOPE AKIRA'S AND MY FUTURE ARE CONNECTED...
YEAH.
THAT'S WHAT I WANT TOO.

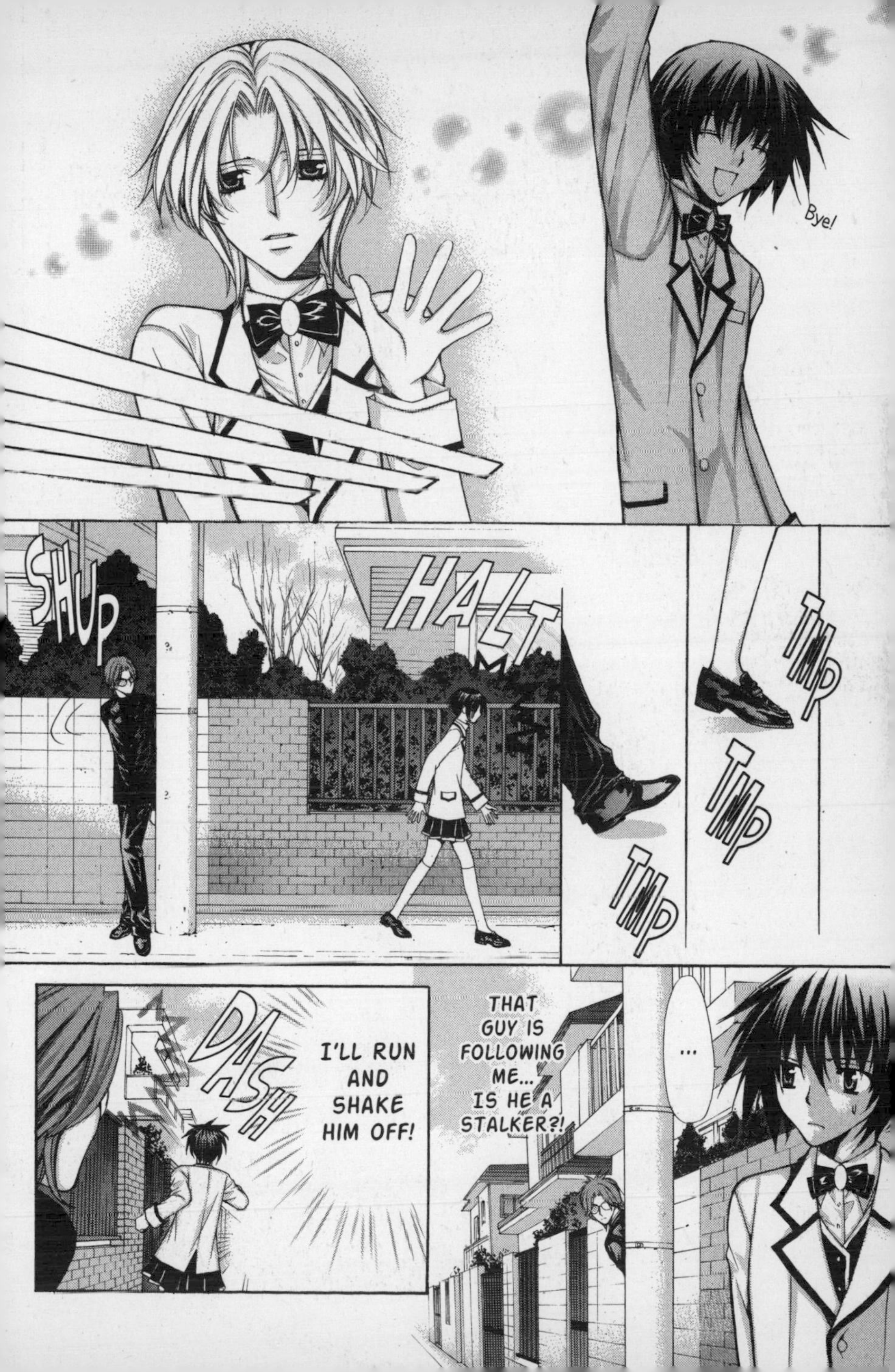
Bye!
TMP
TMP
TMP
HALT
SHUP
...
THAT GUY IS FOLLOWING ME... IS HE A STALKER?!
I'LL RUN AND SHAKE HIM OFF!
DASH

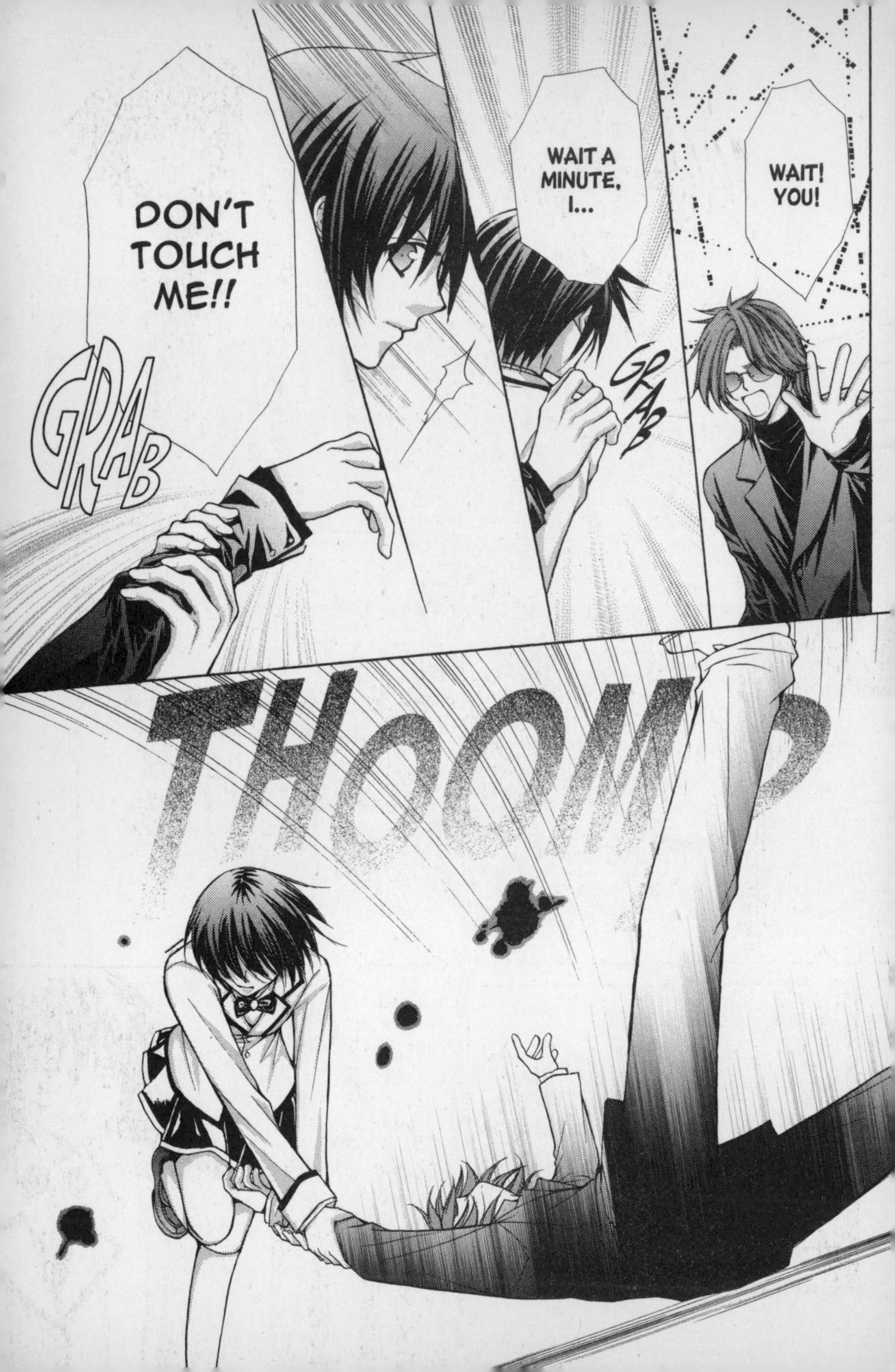
WAIT! YOU!
WAIT A MINUTE, I...
GRAB
DON'T TOUCH ME!!
GRAB
THOOMP

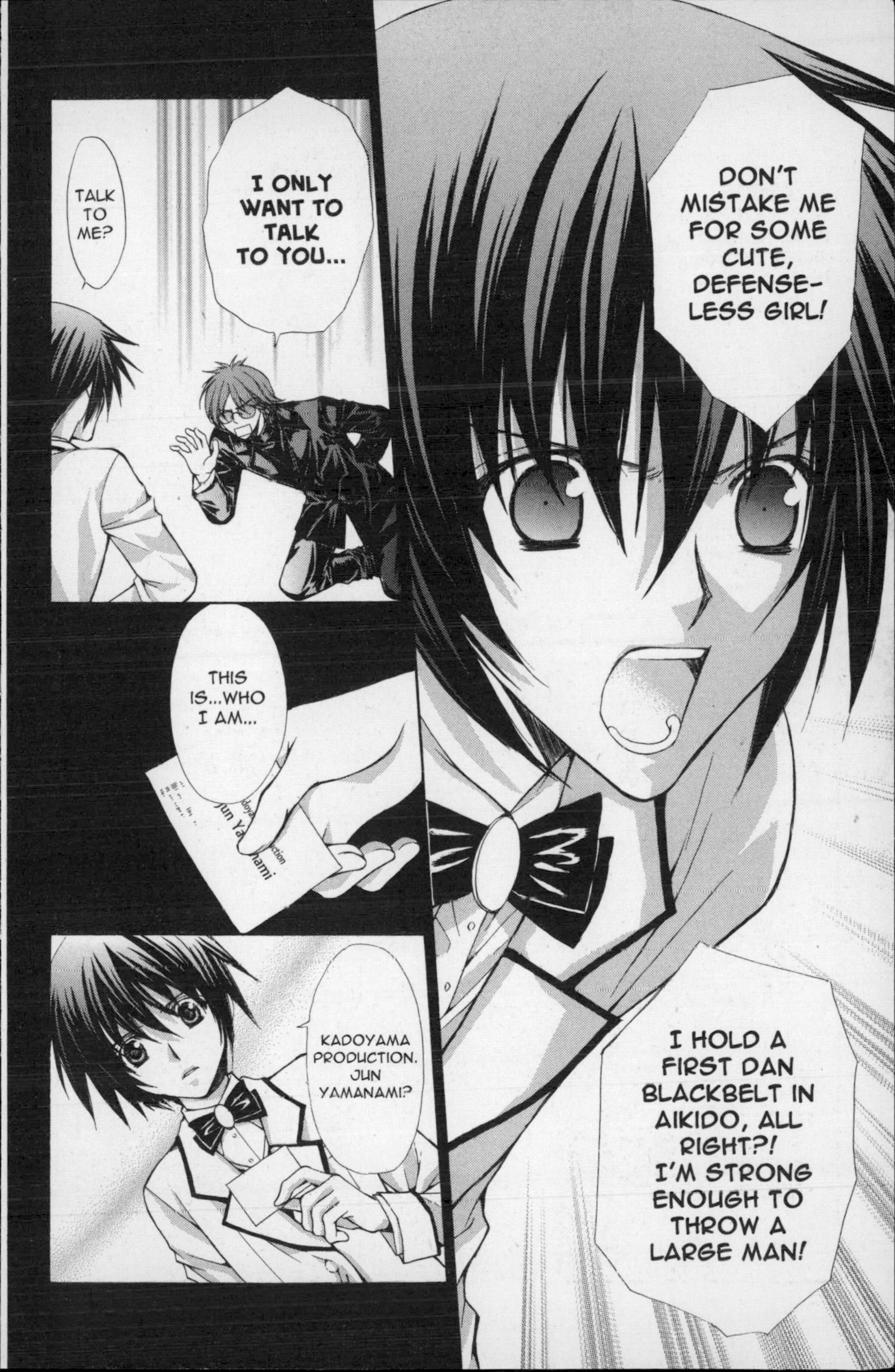
DON'T MISTAKE ME FOR SOME CUTE, DEFENSE-LESS GIRL!
I HOLD A FIRST DAN BLACKBELT IN AIKIDO, ALL RIGHT?! I'M STRONG ENOUGH TO THROW A LARGE MAN!
I ONLY WANT TO TALK TO YOU...
TALK TO ME?
THIS IS...WHO I AM...
KADOYAMA PRODUCTION. JUN YAMANAMI?

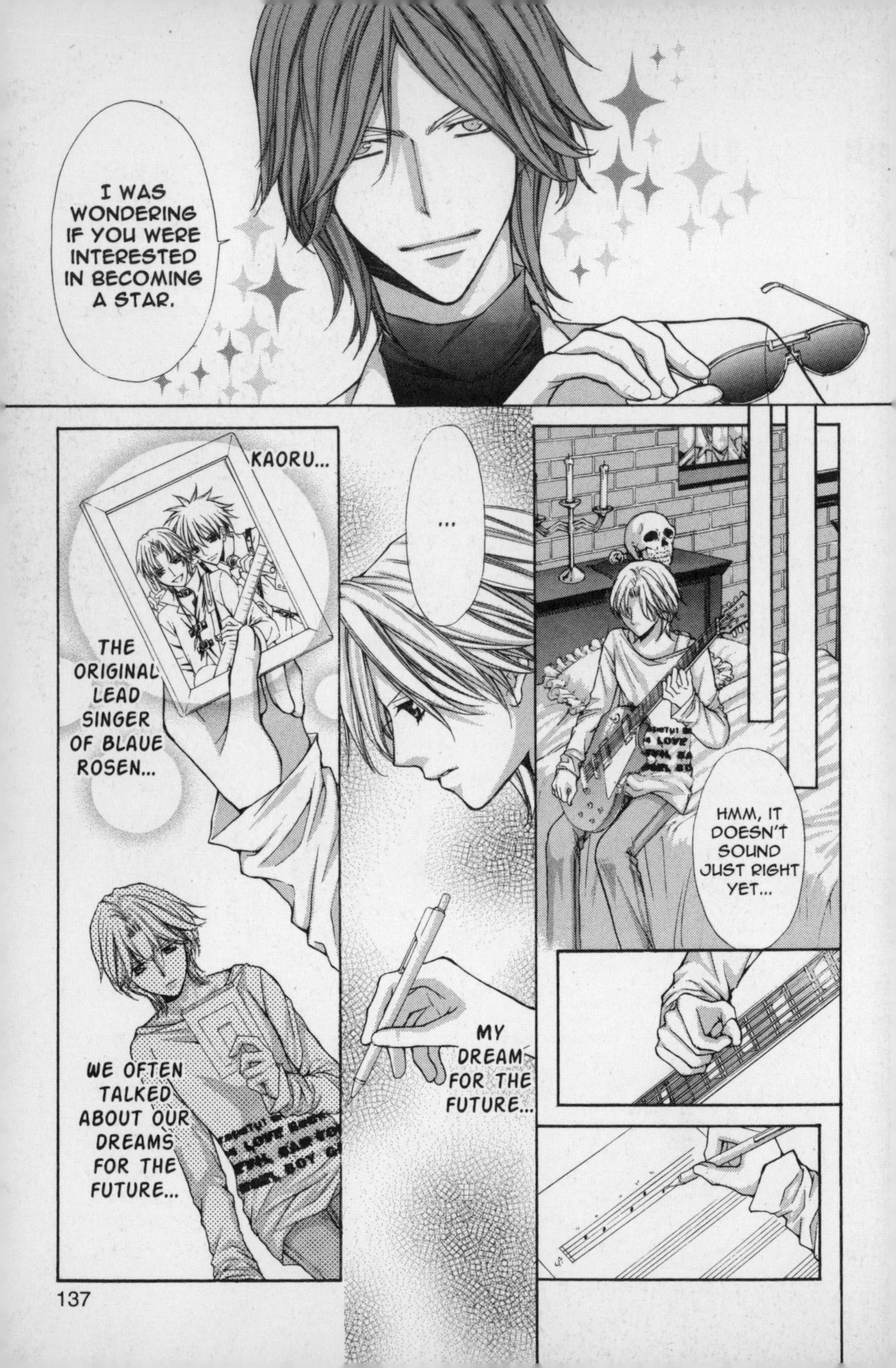
I WAS WONDERING IF YOU WERE INTERESTED IN BECOMING A STAR.
HMM, IT DOESN'T SOUND JUST RIGHT YET...
...
MY DREAM FOR THE FUTURE...
KAORU...
THE ORIGINAL LEAD SINGER OF BLAUE ROSEN...
WE OFTEN TALKED ABOUT OUR DREAMS FOR THE FUTURE...

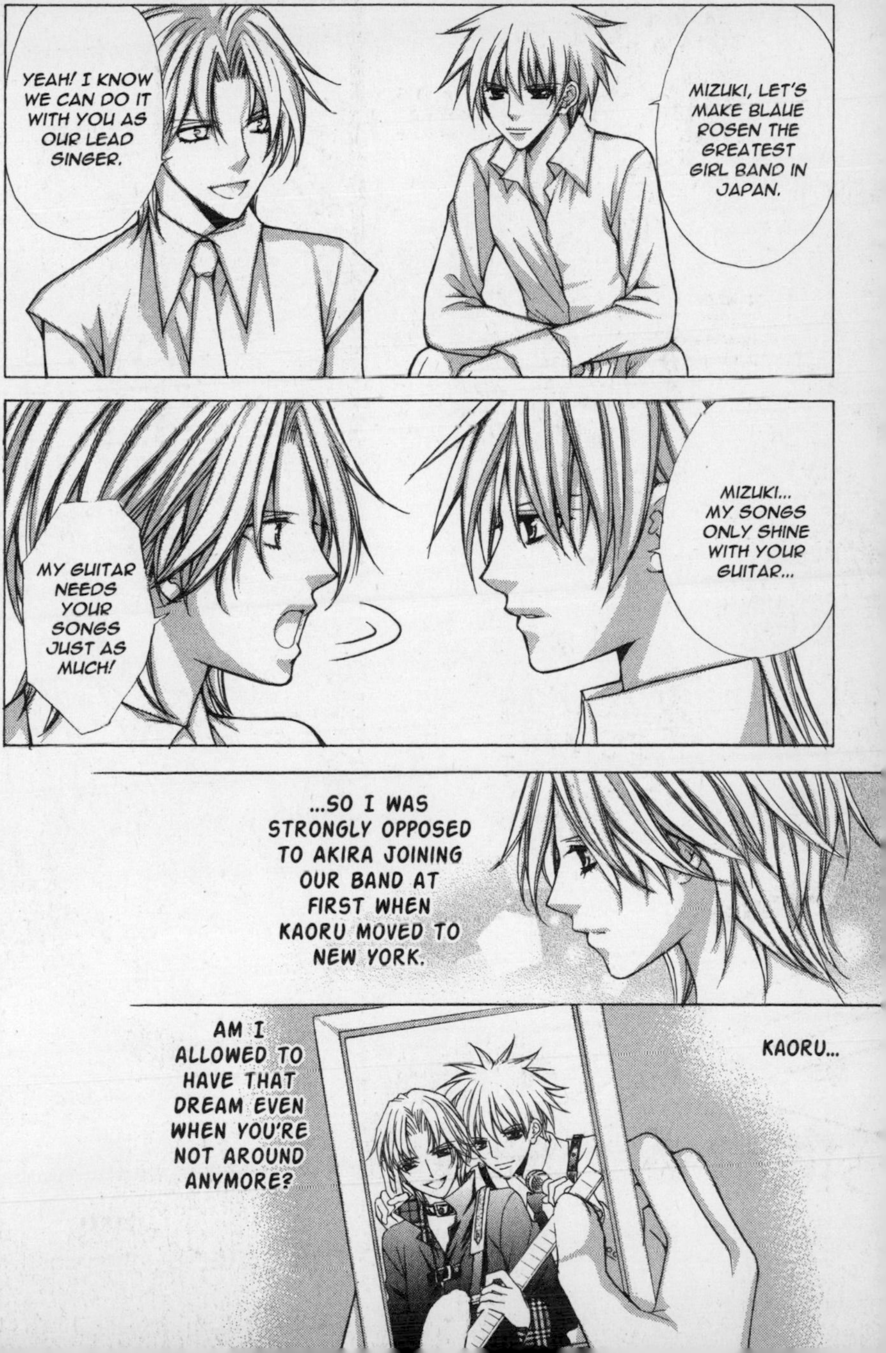
MIZUKI, LET'S MAKE BLAUE ROSEN THE GREATEST GIRL BAND IN JAPAN.
YEAH! I KNOW WE CAN DO IT WITH YOU AS OUR LEAD SINGER.
MIZUKI... MY SONGS ONLY SHINE WITH YOUR GUITAR...
MY GUITAR NEEDS YOUR SONGS JUST AS MUCH!
...SO I WAS STRONGLY OPPOSED TO AKIRA JOINING OUR BAND AT FIRST WHEN KAORU MOVED TO NEW YORK.
KAORU...
AM I ALLOWED TO HAVE THAT DREAM EVEN WHEN YOU'RE NOT AROUND ANYMORE?

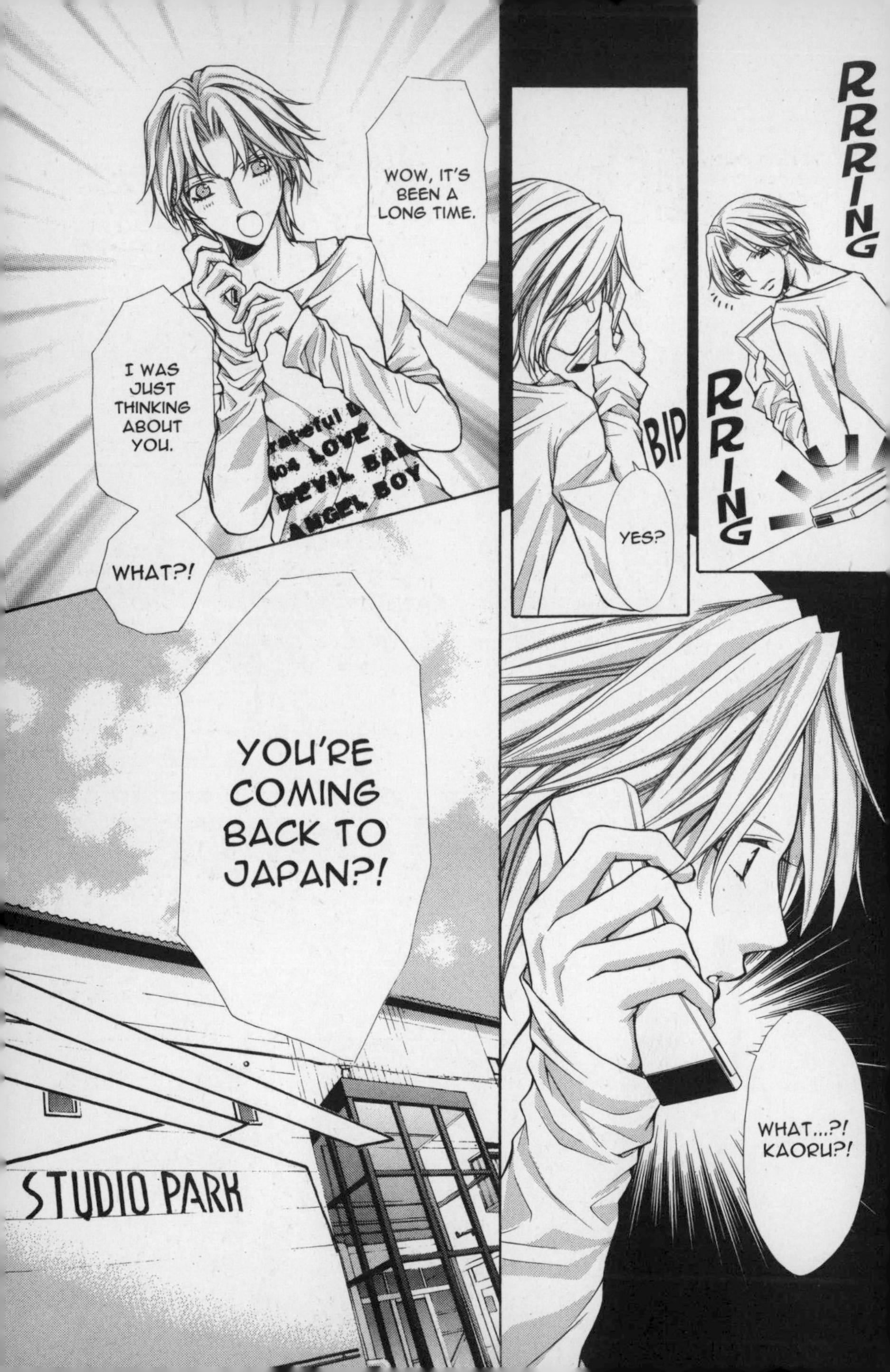
RRRING
RRRING
BIP
YES?
WHAT...?! KAORU?!
WOW, IT'S BEEN A LONG TIME.
I WAS JUST THINKING ABOUT YOU.
WHAT?!
YOU'RE COMING BACK TO JAPAN?!
STUDIO PARK

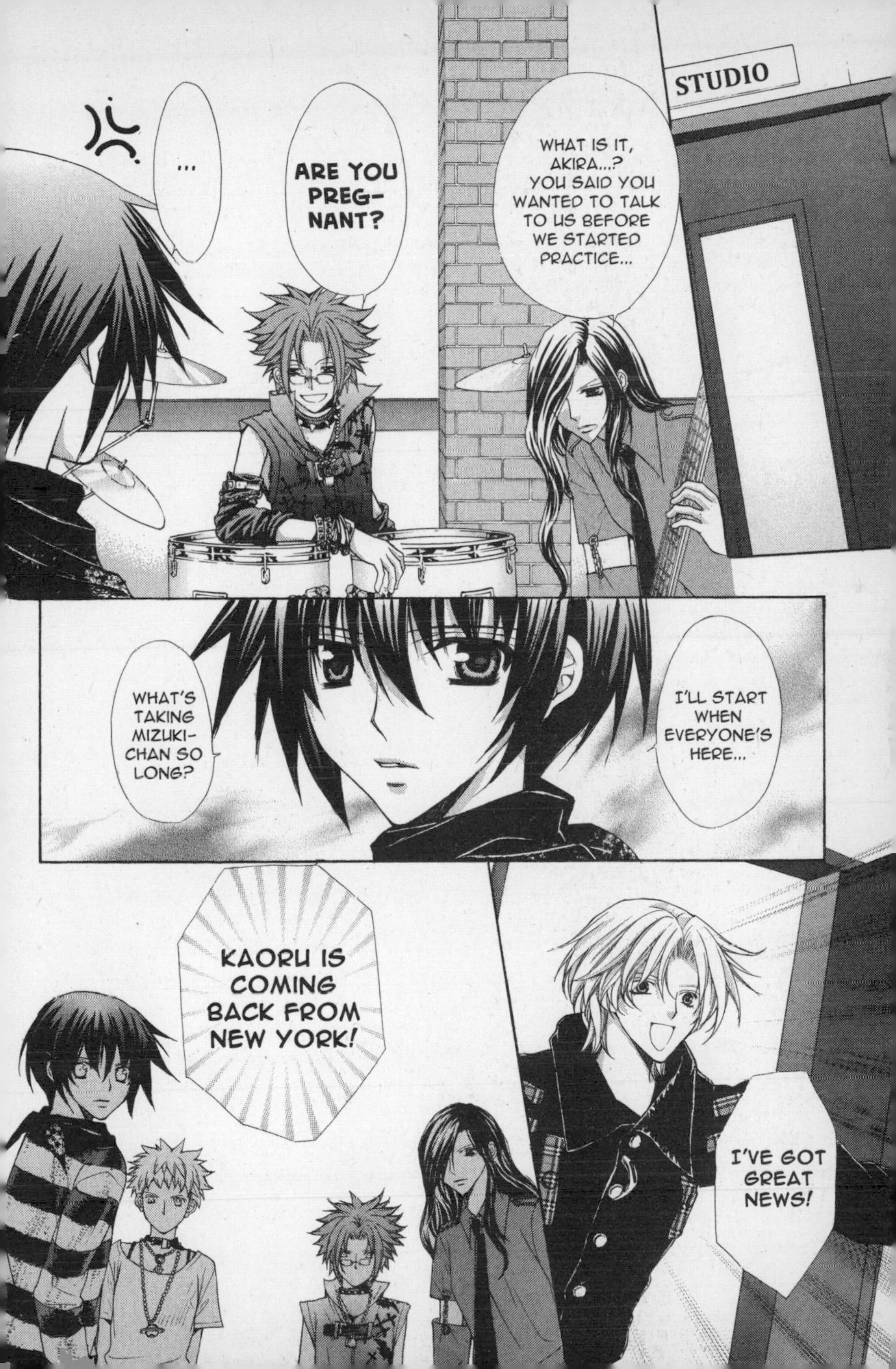
STUDIO
WHAT IS IT, AKIRA...? YOU SAID YOU WANTED TO TALK TO US BEFORE WE STARTED PRACTICE...
ARE YOU PREG-NANT?
...
I'LL START WHEN EVERYONE'S HERE...
WHAT'S TAKING MIZUKI-CHAN SO LONG?
I'VE GOT GREAT NEWS!
KAORU IS COMING BACK FROM NEW YORK!

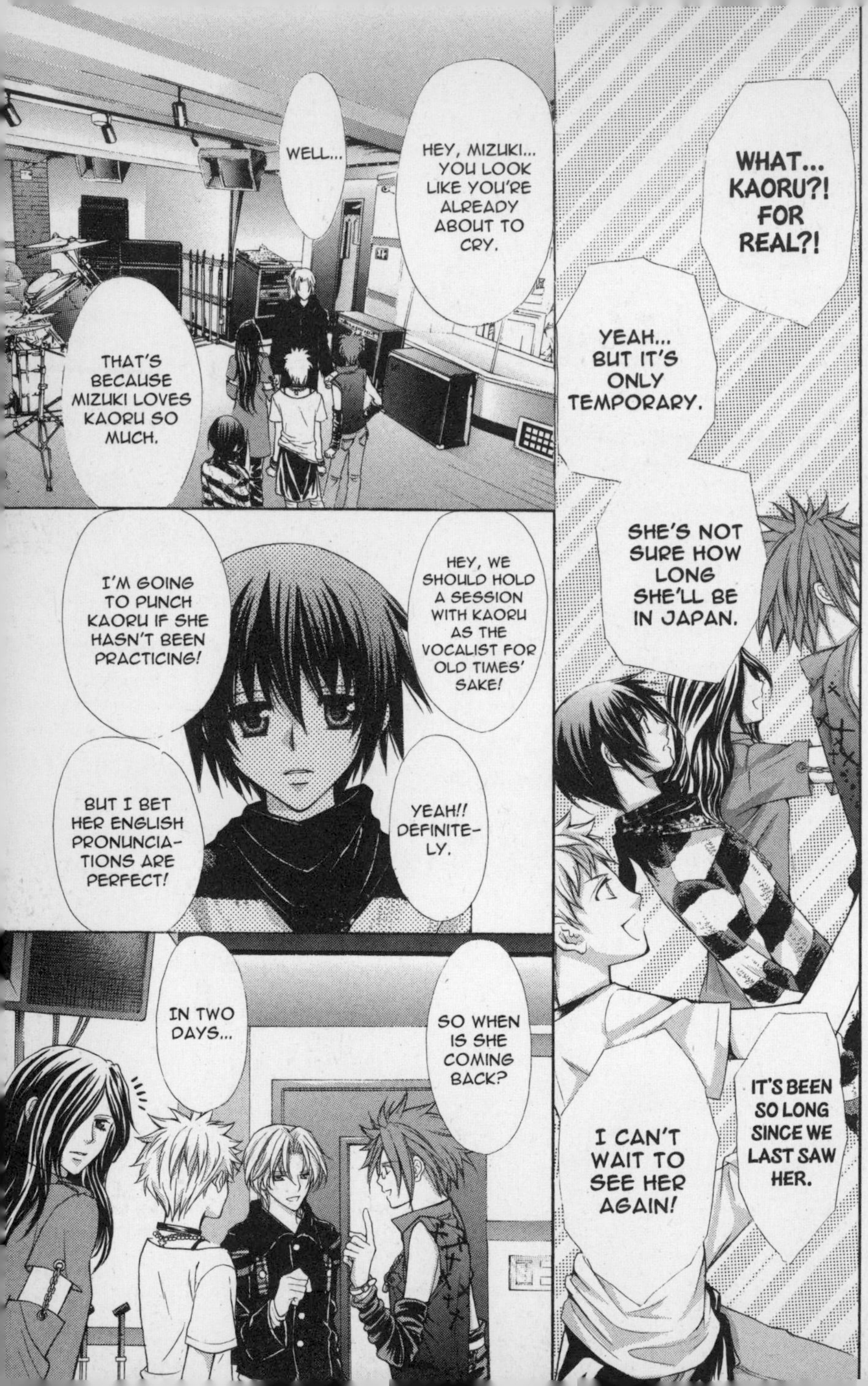
WHAT... KAORU?! FOR REAL?!
YEAH... BUT IT'S ONLY TEMPORARY.
SHE'S NOT SURE HOW LONG SHE'LL BE IN JAPAN.
IT'S BEEN SO LONG SINCE WE LAST SAW HER.
I CAN'T WAIT TO SEE HER AGAIN!
HEY, MIZUKI... YOU LOOK LIKE YOU'RE ALREADY ABOUT TO CRY.
WELL...
THAT'S BECAUSE MIZUKI LOVES KAORU SO MUCH.
HEY, WE SHOULD HOLD A SESSION WITH KAORU AS THE VOCALIST FOR OLD TIMES' SAKE!
I'M GOING TO PUNCH KAORU IF SHE HASN'T BEEN PRACTICING!
YEAH!! DEFINITE-LY.
BUT I BET HER ENGLISH PRONUNCIA-TIONS ARE PERFECT!
SO WHEN IS SHE COMING BACK?
IN TWO DAYS...

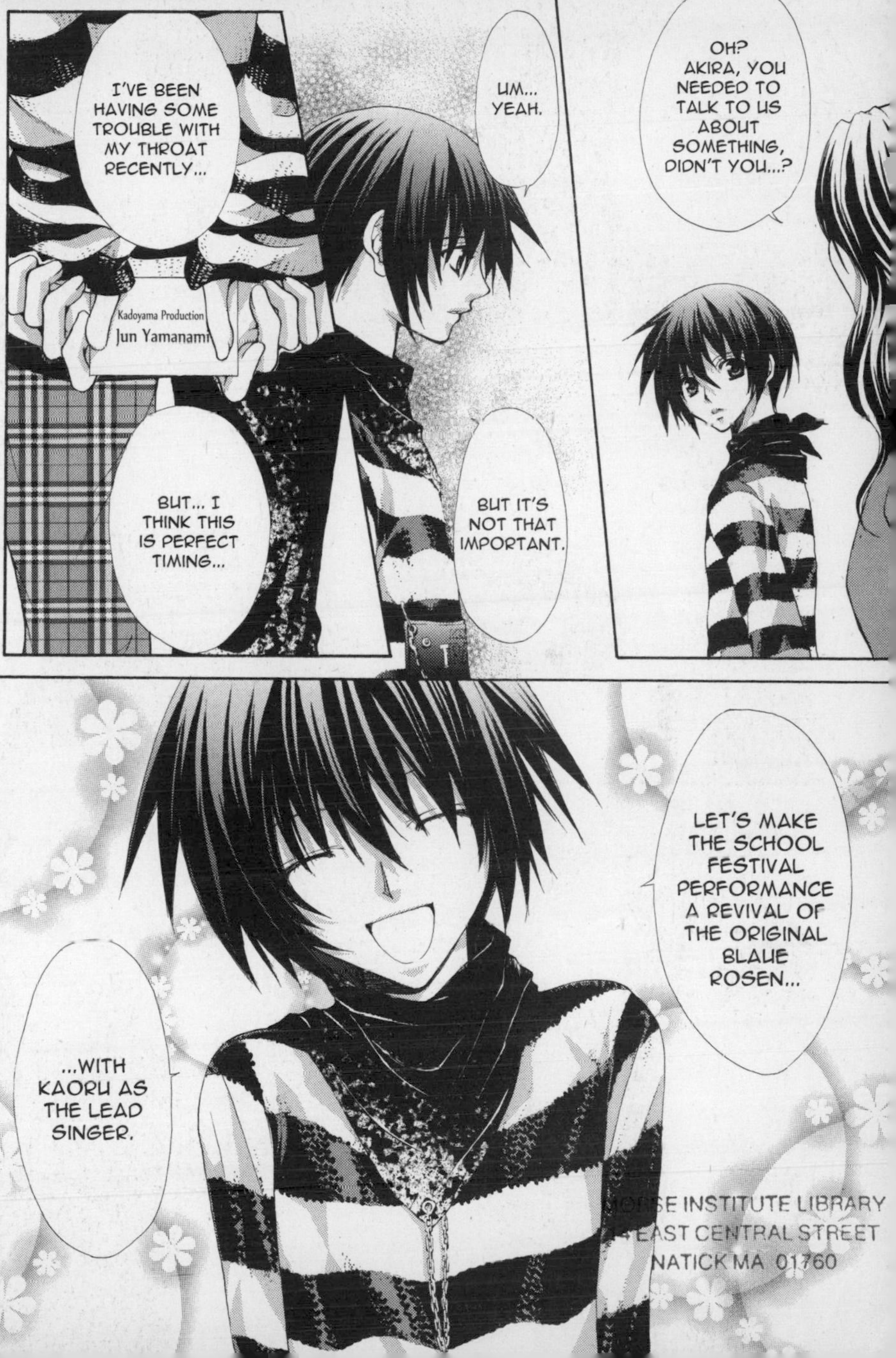
OH? AKIRA, YOU NEEDED TO TALK TO US ABOUT SOMETHING, DIDN'T YOU...?
UM... YEAH.
BUT IT'S NOT THAT IMPORTANT.
I'VE BEEN HAVING SOME TROUBLE WITH MY THROAT RECENTLY...
Kadoyama Production
Jun Yamanami
BUT... I THINK THIS IS PERFECT TIMING...
LET'S MAKE THE SCHOOL FESTIVAL PERFORMANCE A REVIVAL OF THE ORIGINAL BLAUE ROSEN...
...WITH KAORU AS THE LEAD SINGER.

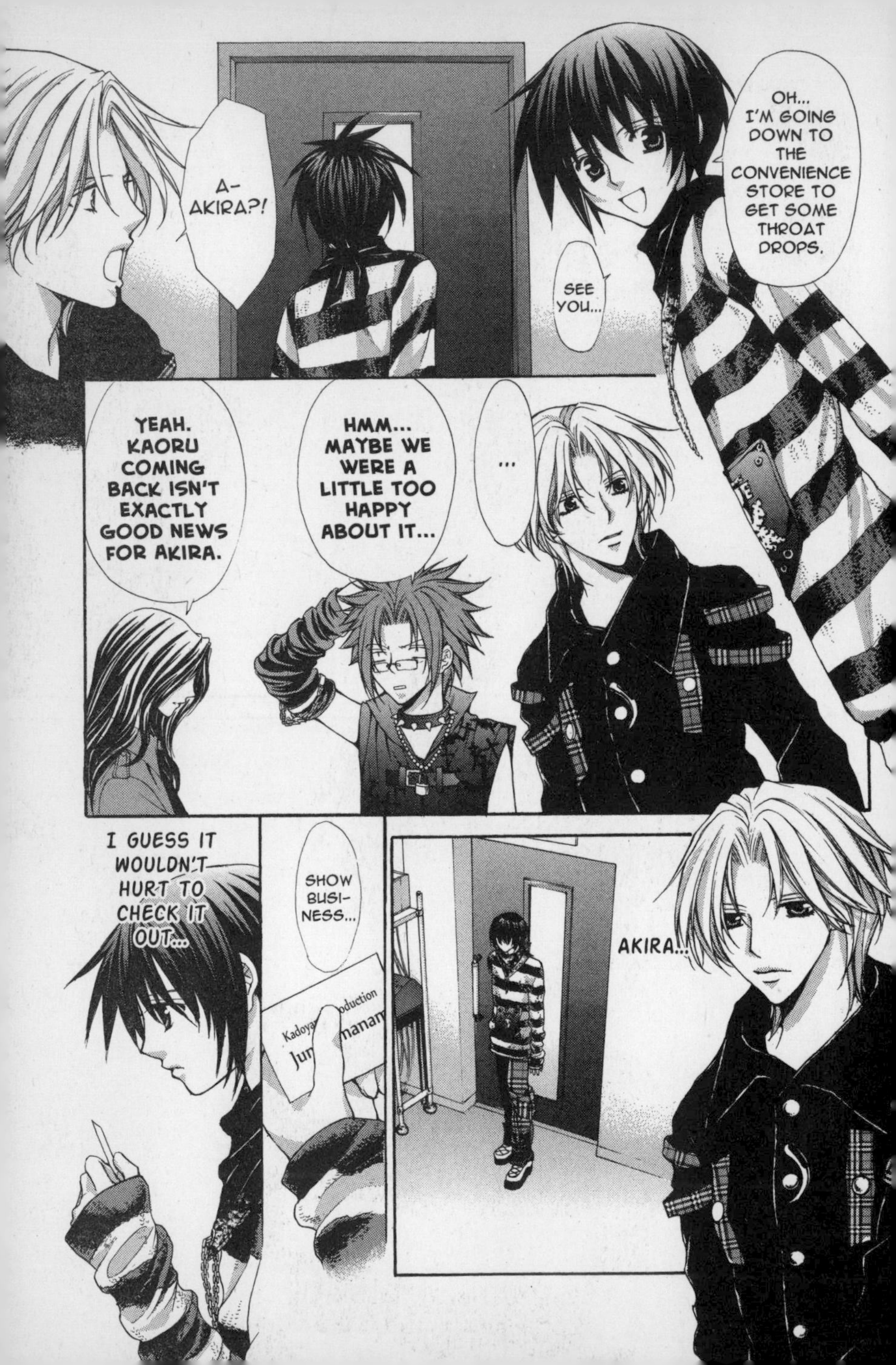
OH... I'M GOING DOWN TO THE CONVENIENCE STORE TO GET SOME THROAT DROPS.
SEE YOU...
A- AKIRA?!
...
HMM... MAYBE WE WERE A LITTLE TOO HAPPY ABOUT IT...
YEAH. KAORU COMING BACK ISN'T EXACTLY GOOD NEWS FOR AKIRA.
AKIRA...
SHOW BUSI- NESS...
I GUESS IT WOULDN'T HURT TO CHECK IT OUT...

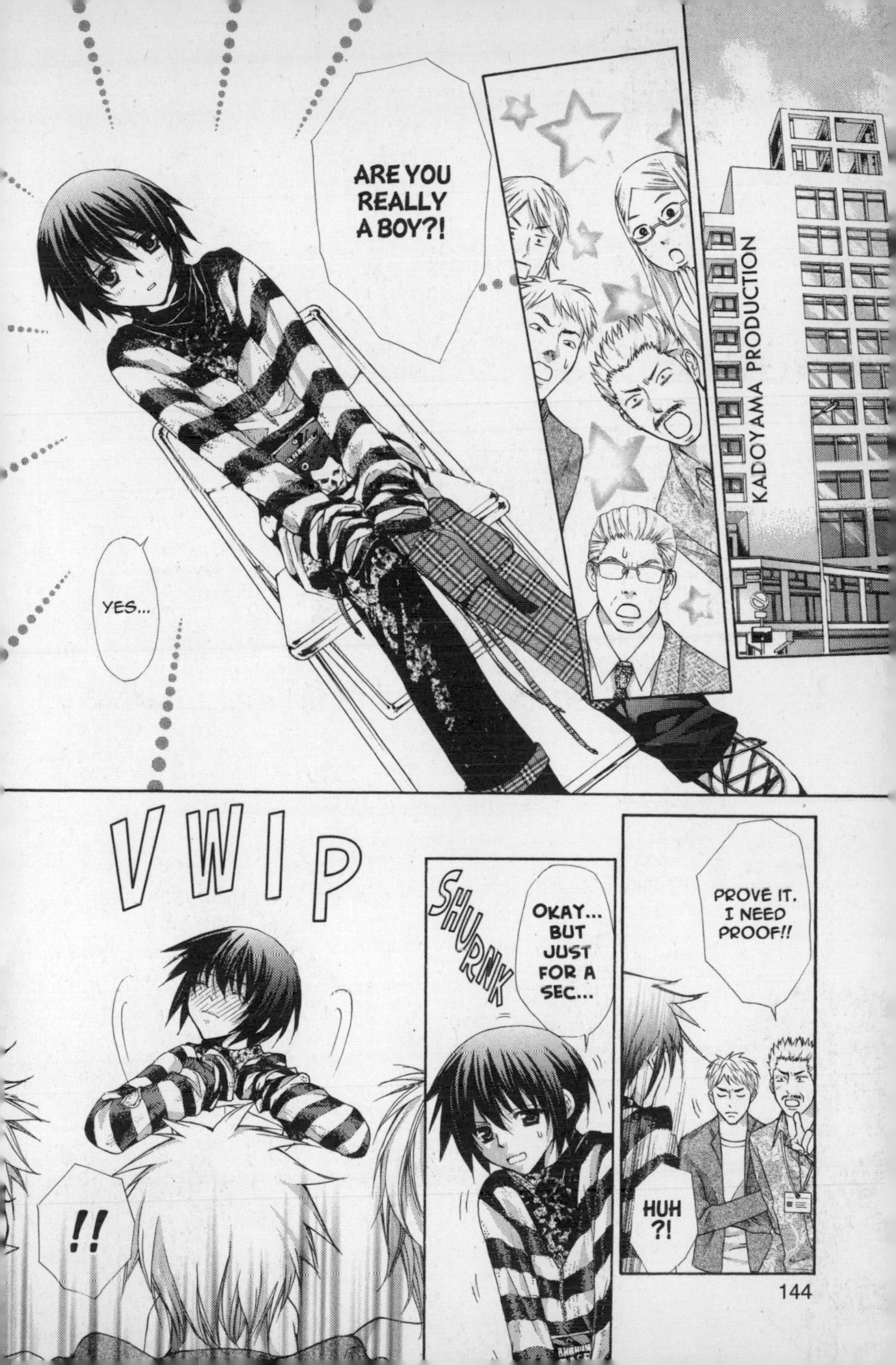
KADOYAMA PRODUCTION
ARE YOU REALLY A BOY?!
YES...
PROVE IT. I NEED PROOF!!
HUH ?!
SHURNK
OKAY... BUT JUST FOR A SEC...
VWIP
!!

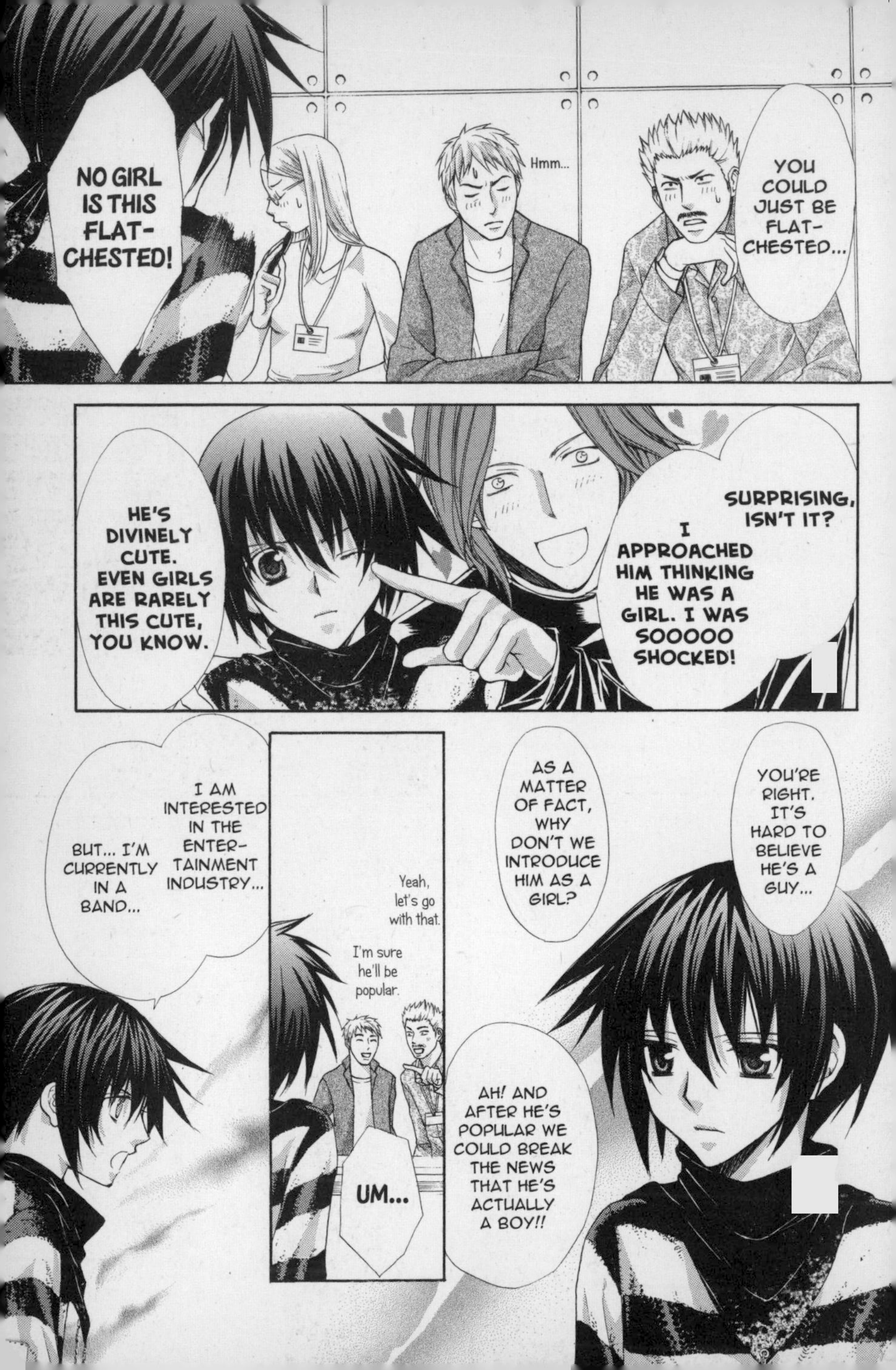
YOU COULD JUST BE FLAT-CHESTED...
Hmm...
NO GIRL IS THIS FLAT-CHESTED!
SURPRISING, ISN'T IT?
I APPROACHED HIM THINKING HE WAS A GIRL. I WAS SOOOOO SHOCKED!
HE'S DIVINELY CUTE. EVEN GIRLS ARE RARELY THIS CUTE, YOU KNOW.
YOU'RE RIGHT. IT'S HARD TO BELIEVE HE'S A GUY...
AS A MATTER OF FACT, WHY DON'T WE INTRODUCE HIM AS A GIRL?
AH! AND AFTER HE'S POPULAR WE COULD BREAK THE NEWS THAT HE'S ACTUALLY A BOY!!
Yeah, let's go with that.
I'm sure he'll be popular.
UM...
I AM INTERESTED IN THE ENTERTAINMENT INDUSTRY...
BUT... I'M CURRENTLY IN A BAND...

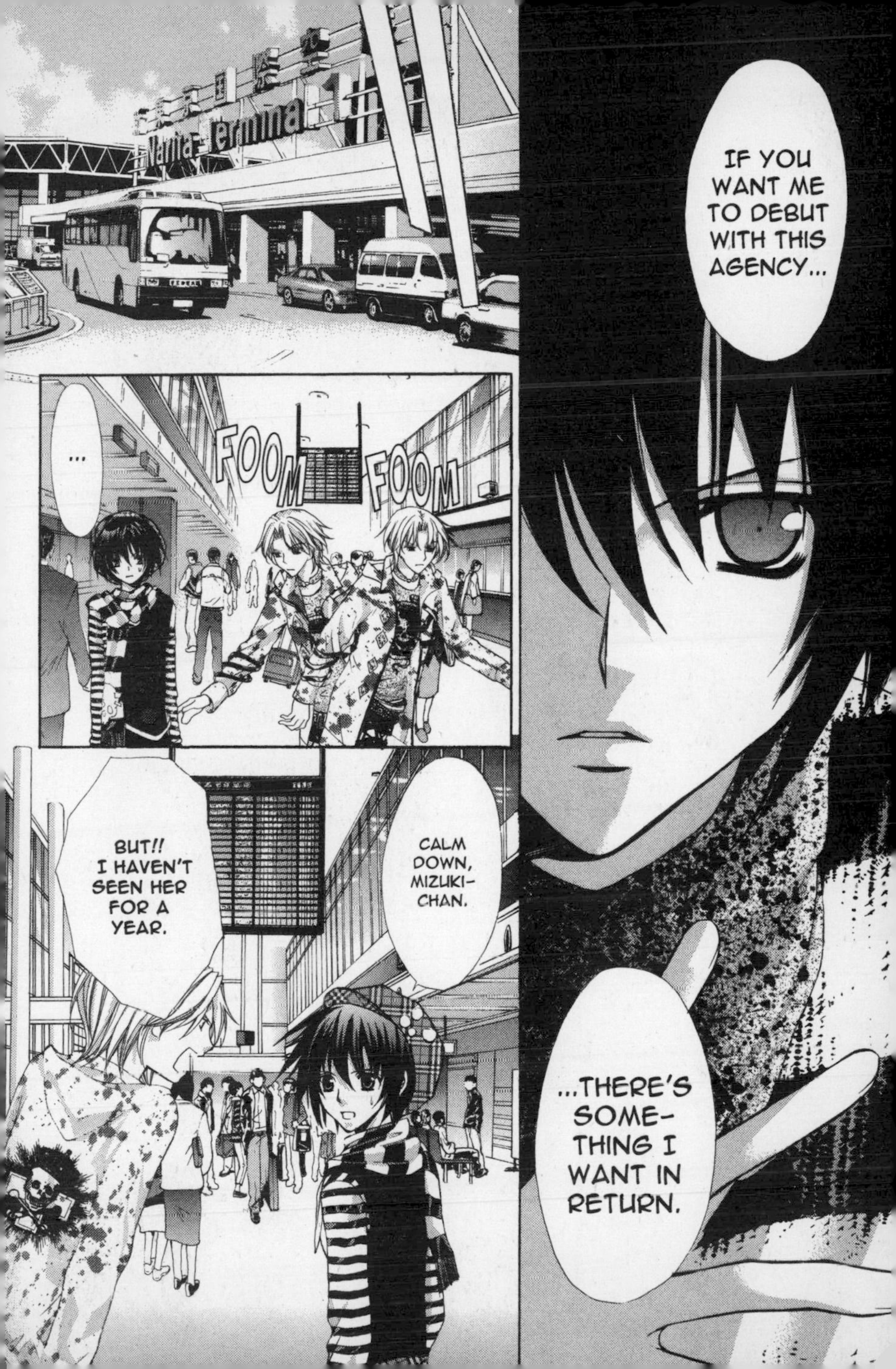
IF YOU WANT ME TO DEBUT WITH THIS AGENCY...
...THERE'S SOME-THING I WANT IN RETURN.
...
FOOM
FOOM
CALM DOWN, MIZUKI-CHAN.
BUT!! I HAVEN'T SEEN HER FOR A YEAR.

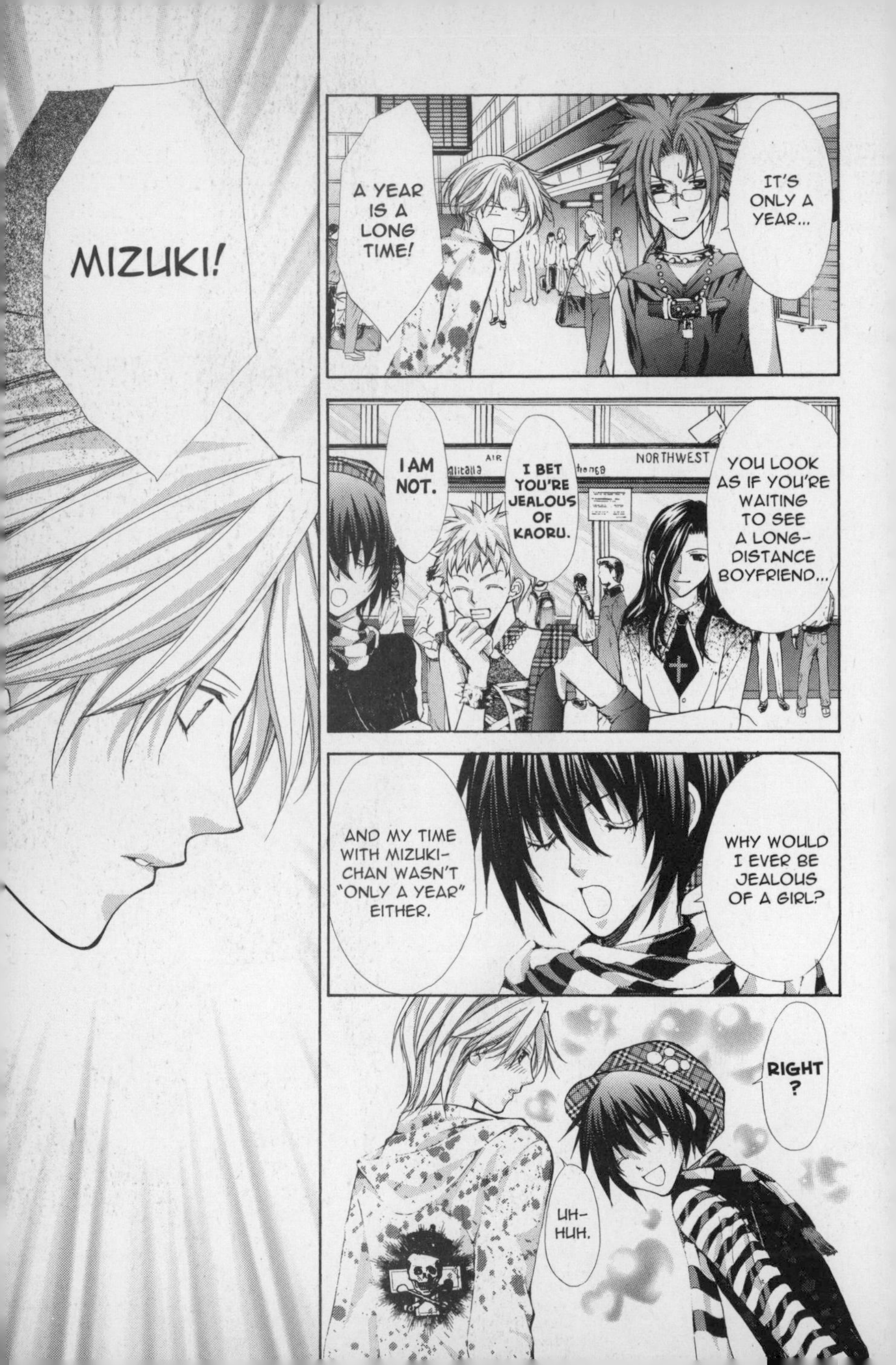
IT'S ONLY A YEAR...
A YEAR IS A LONG TIME!
YOU LOOK AS IF YOU'RE WAITING TO SEE A LONG-DISTANCE BOYFRIEND...
NORTHWEST
I BET YOU'RE JEALOUS OF KAORU.
I AM NOT.
WHY WOULD I EVER BE JEALOUS OF A GIRL?
AND MY TIME WITH MIZUKI-CHAN WASN'T "ONLY A YEAR" EITHER.
RIGHT?
UH-HUH.
MIZUKI!

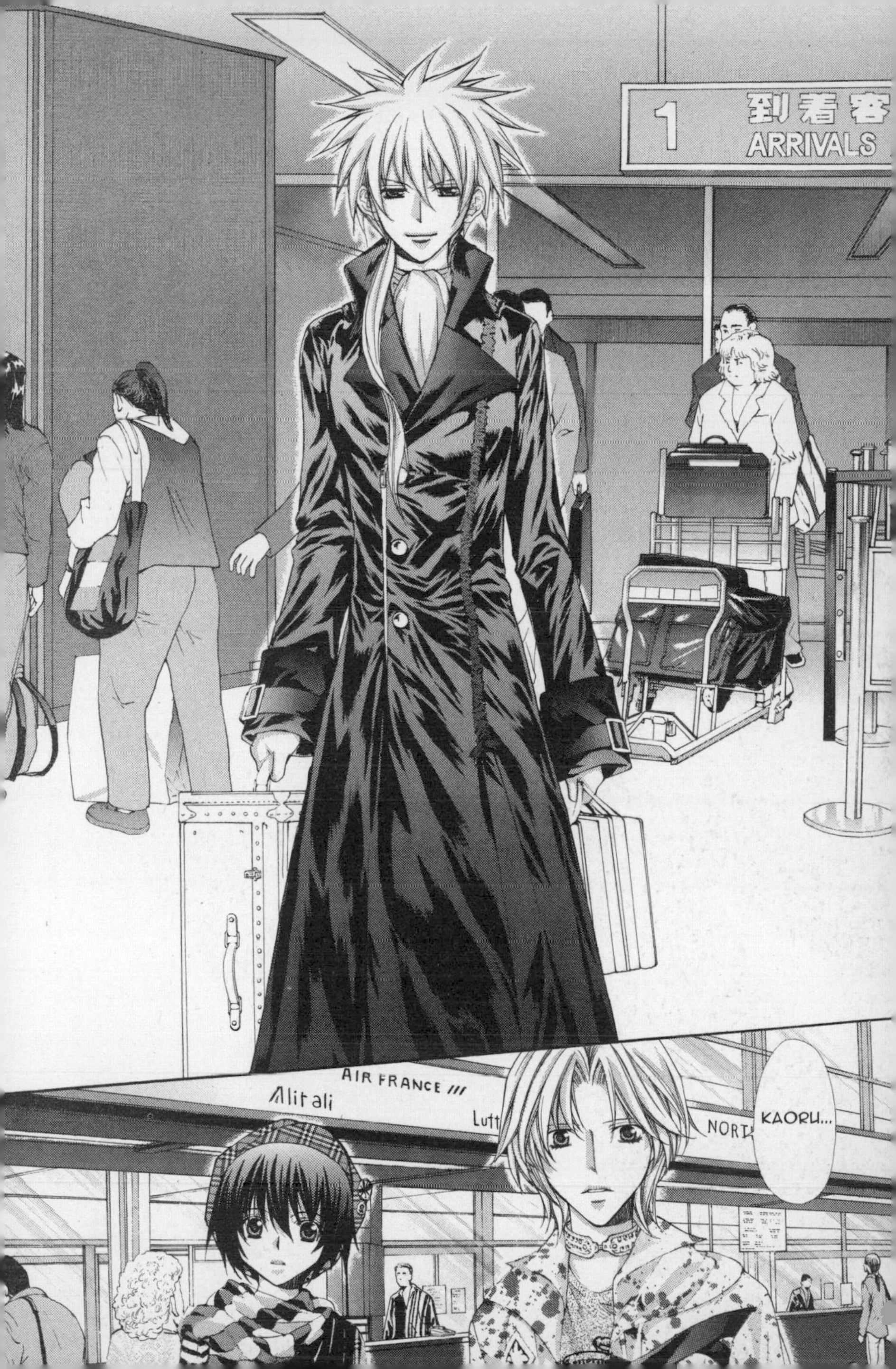
1
到着客
ARRIVALS
KAORU...
AIR FRANCE ///
NORT
Lutt
Alitali

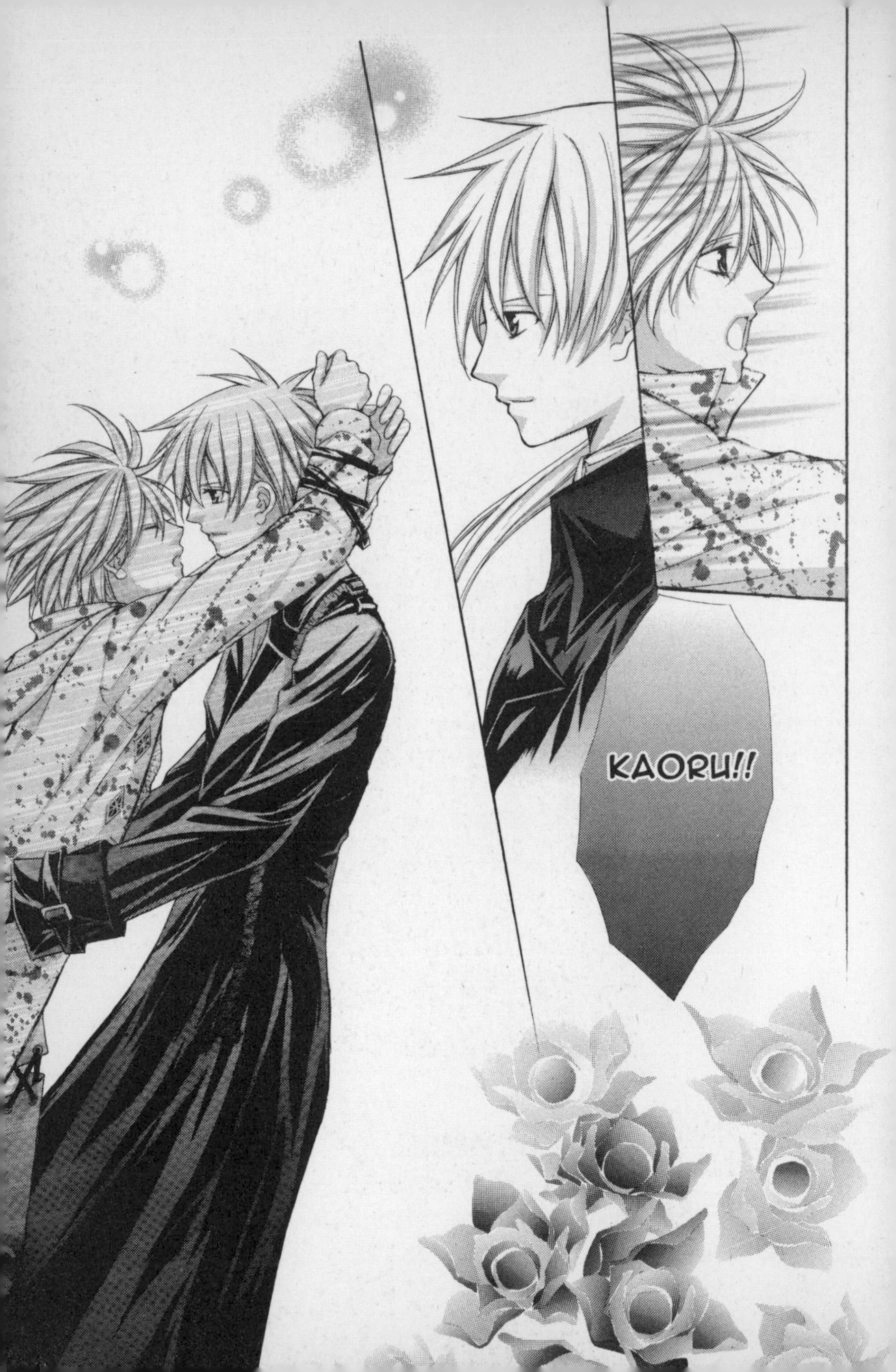
KAORU!!

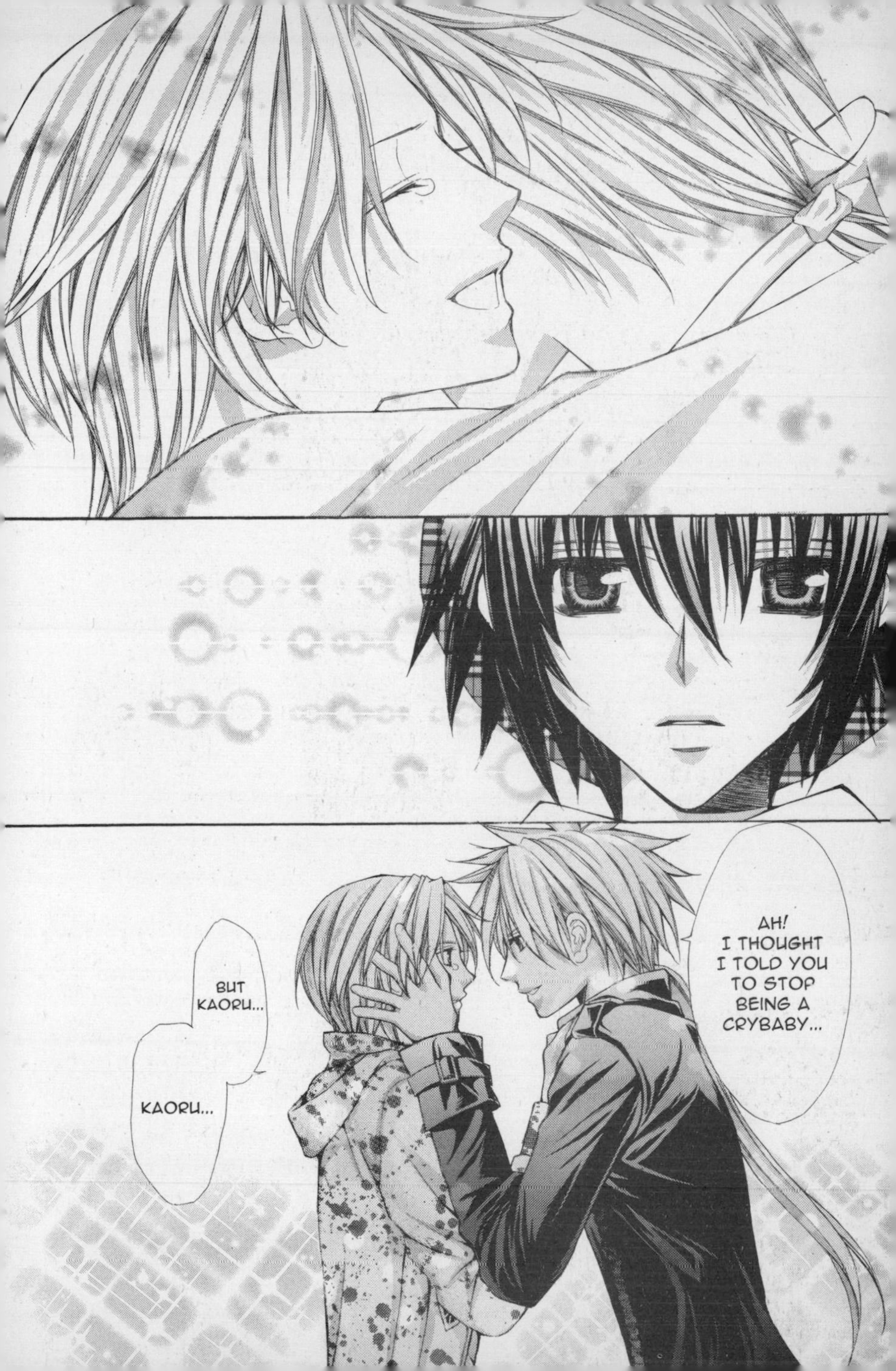
AH! I THOUGHT I TOLD YOU TO STOP BEING A CRYBABY...
BUT KAORU...
KAORU...

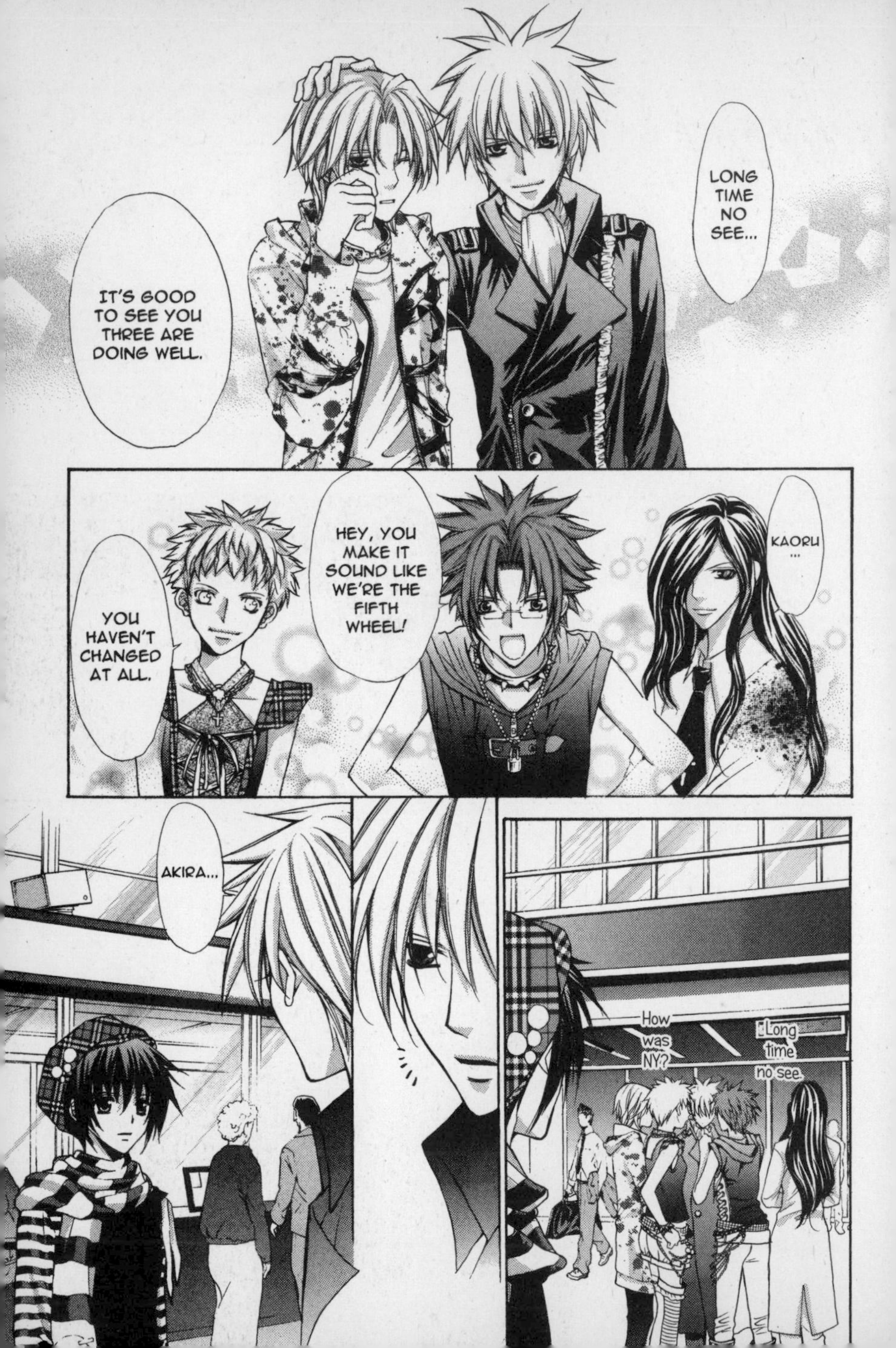
LONG TIME NO SEE...
IT'S GOOD TO SEE YOU THREE ARE DOING WELL.
KAORU ...
HEY, YOU MAKE IT SOUND LIKE WE'RE THE FIFTH WHEEL!
YOU HAVEN'T CHANGED AT ALL.
Long time no see.
How was NY?
AKIRA...

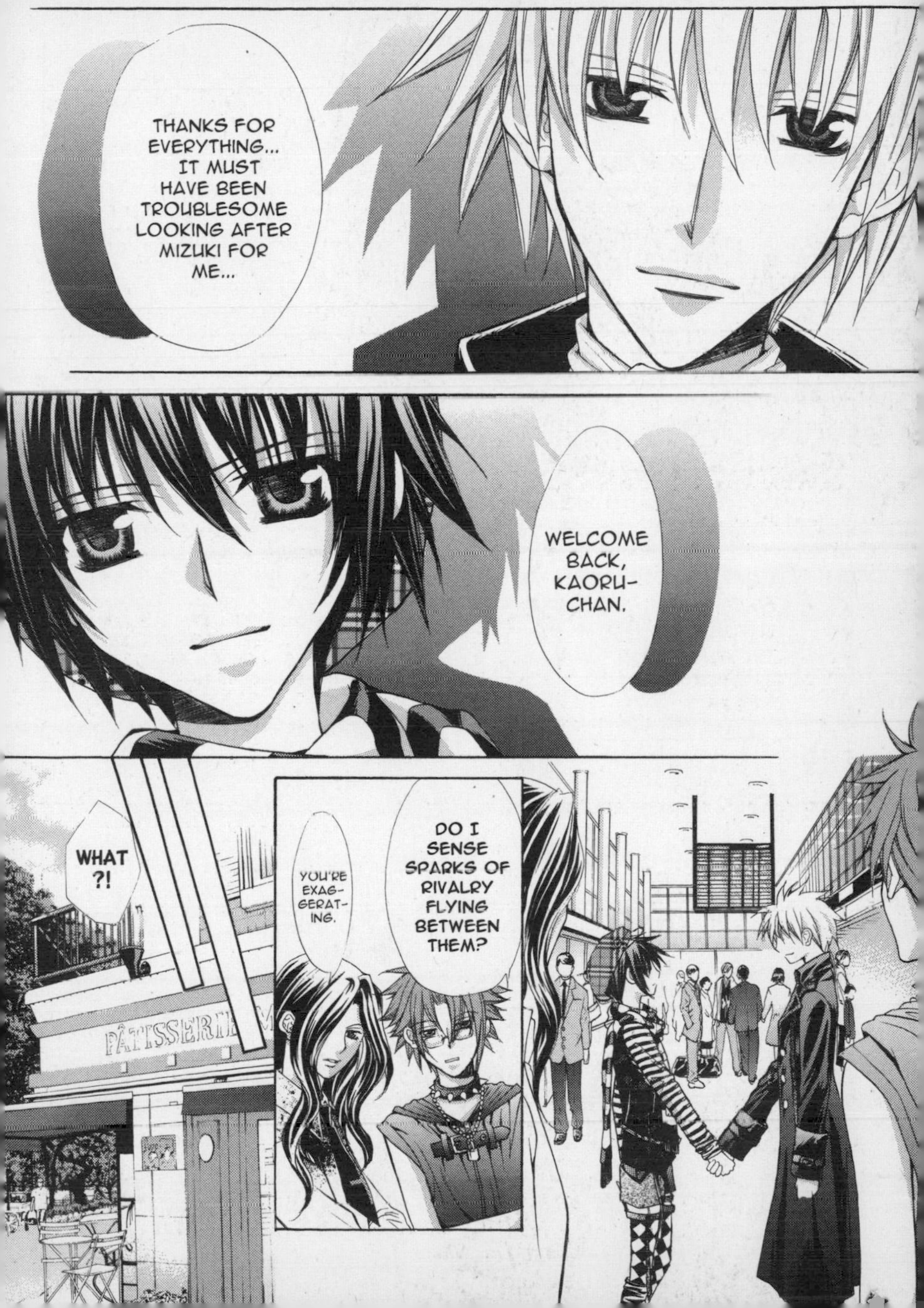
THANKS FOR EVERYTHING... IT MUST HAVE BEEN TROUBLESOME LOOKING AFTER MIZUKI FOR ME...
WELCOME BACK, KAORU-CHAN.
DO I SENSE SPARKS OF RIVALRY FLYING BETWEEN THEM?
YOU'RE EXAG-GERAT-ING.
WHAT ?!
PÂTISSERIE

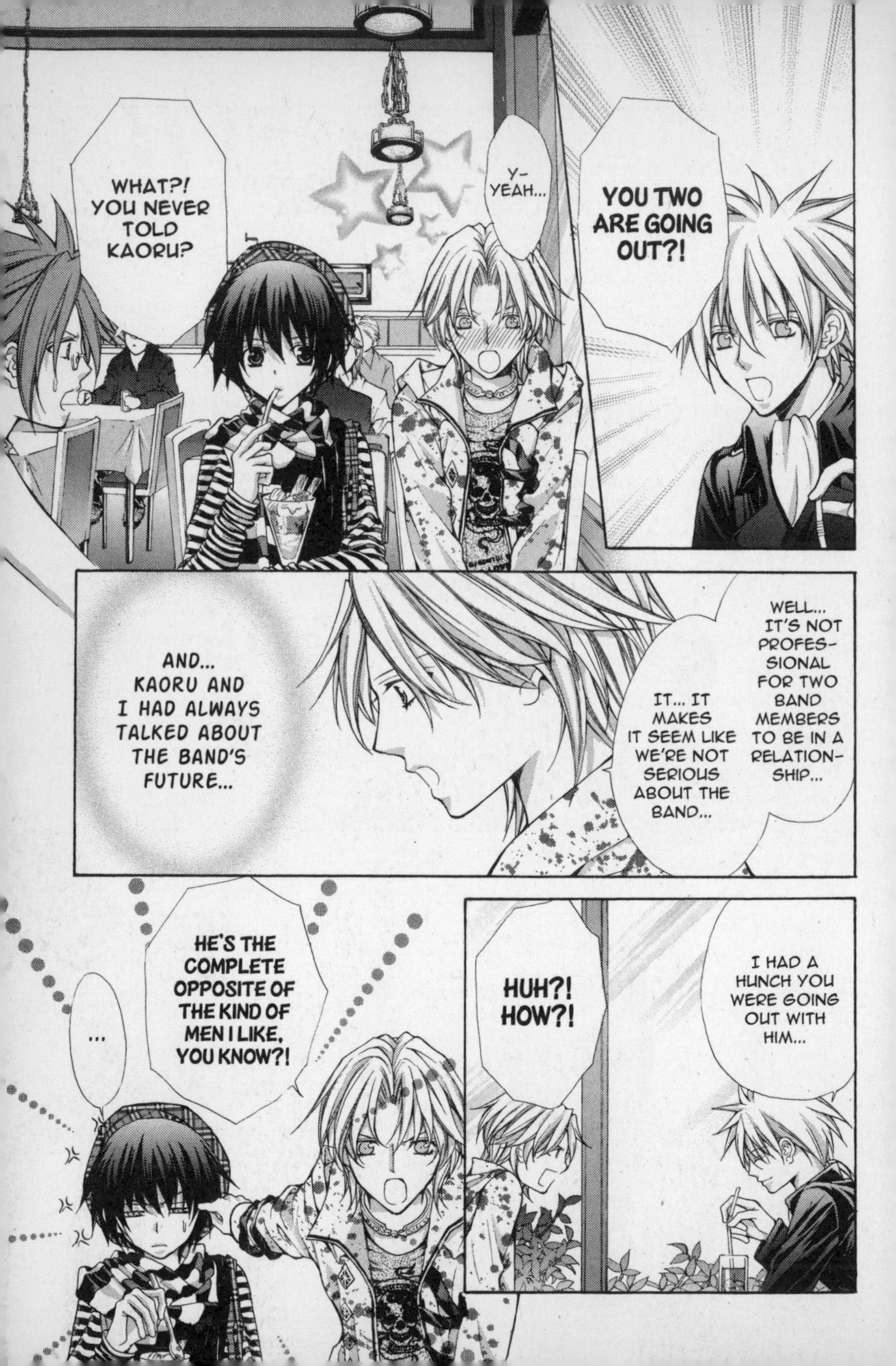
YOU TWO ARE GOING OUT?!
Y-YEAH...
WHAT?! YOU NEVER TOLD KAORU?
WELL... IT'S NOT PROFES-SIONAL FOR TWO BAND MEMBERS TO BE IN A RELATION-SHIP...
IT... IT MAKES IT SEEM LIKE WE'RE NOT SERIOUS ABOUT THE BAND...
AND... KAORU AND I HAD ALWAYS TALKED ABOUT THE BAND'S FUTURE...
I HAD A HUNCH YOU WERE GOING OUT WITH HIM...
HUH?! HOW?!
HE'S THE COMPLETE OPPOSITE OF THE KIND OF MEN I LIKE, YOU KNOW?!
...

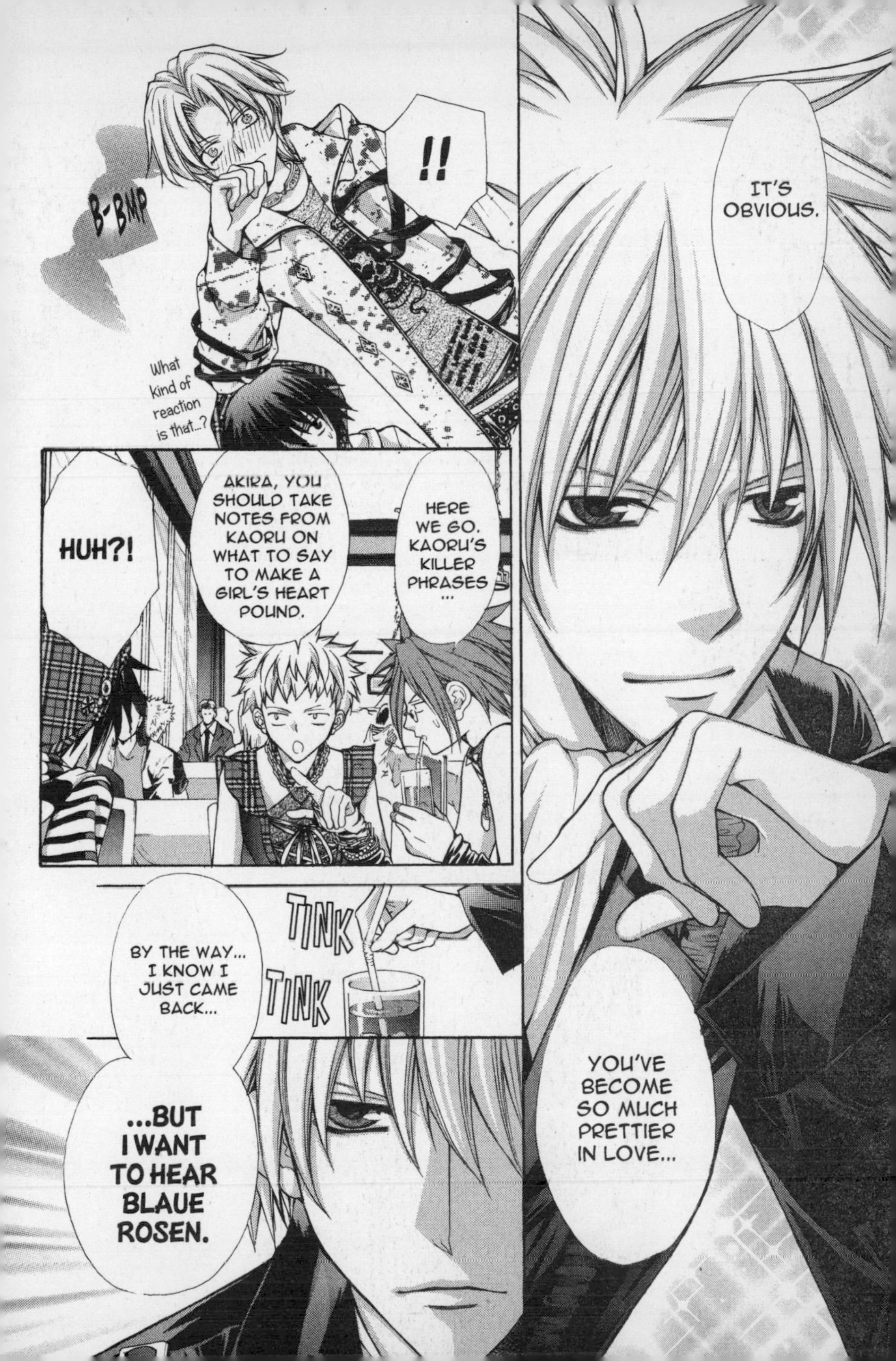
IT'S OBVIOUS.
YOU'VE BECOME SO MUCH PRETTIER IN LOVE...
!!
B-BMP
What kind of reaction is that...?
HERE WE GO. KAORU'S KILLER PHRASES ...
AKIRA, YOU SHOULD TAKE NOTES FROM KAORU ON WHAT TO SAY TO MAKE A GIRL'S HEART POUND.
HUH?!
TINK
TINK
BY THE WAY... I KNOW I JUST CAME BACK...
...BUT I WANT TO HEAR BLAUE ROSEN.

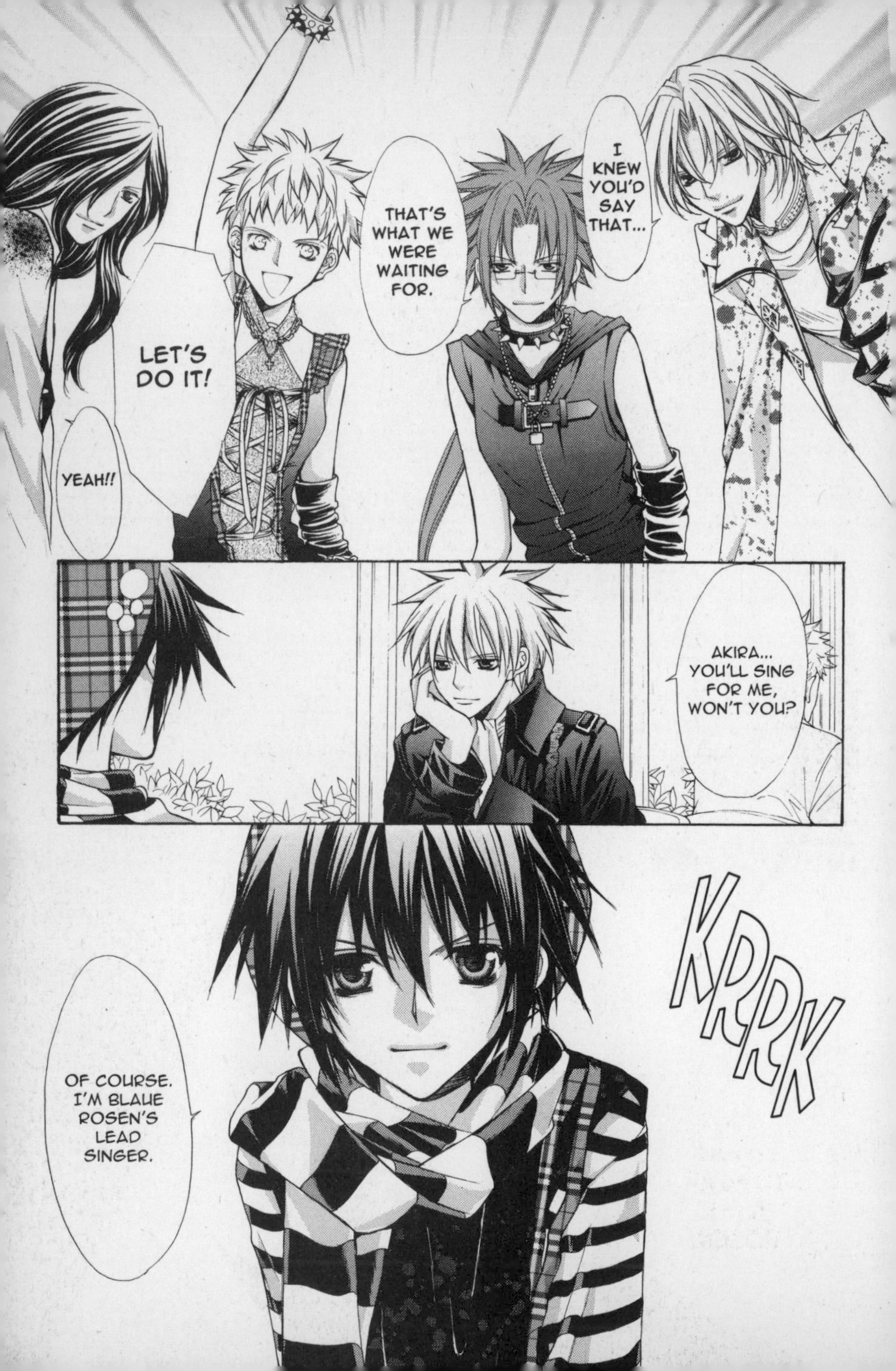
I KNEW YOU'D SAY THAT...
THAT'S WHAT WE WERE WAITING FOR.
LET'S DO IT!
YEAH!!
AKIRA... YOU'LL SING FOR ME, WON'T YOU?
KRRK
OF COURSE. I'M BLAUE ROSEN'S LEAD SINGER.

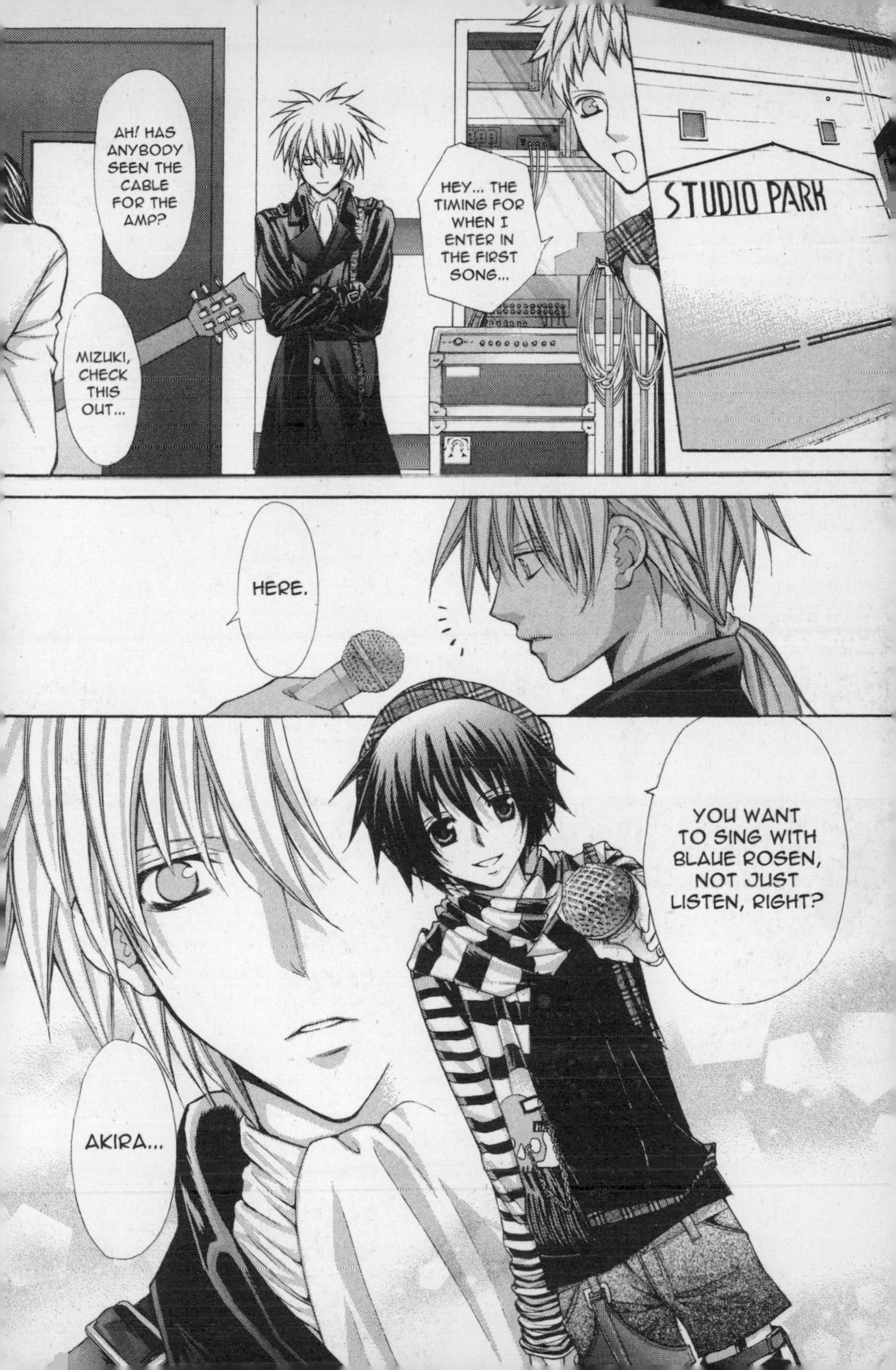
HEY... THE TIMING FOR WHEN I ENTER IN THE FIRST SONG...
AH! HAS ANYBODY SEEN THE CABLE FOR THE AMP?
MIZUKI, CHECK THIS OUT...
STUDIO PARK
HERE.
YOU WANT TO SING WITH BLAUE ROSEN, NOT JUST LISTEN, RIGHT?
AKIRA...

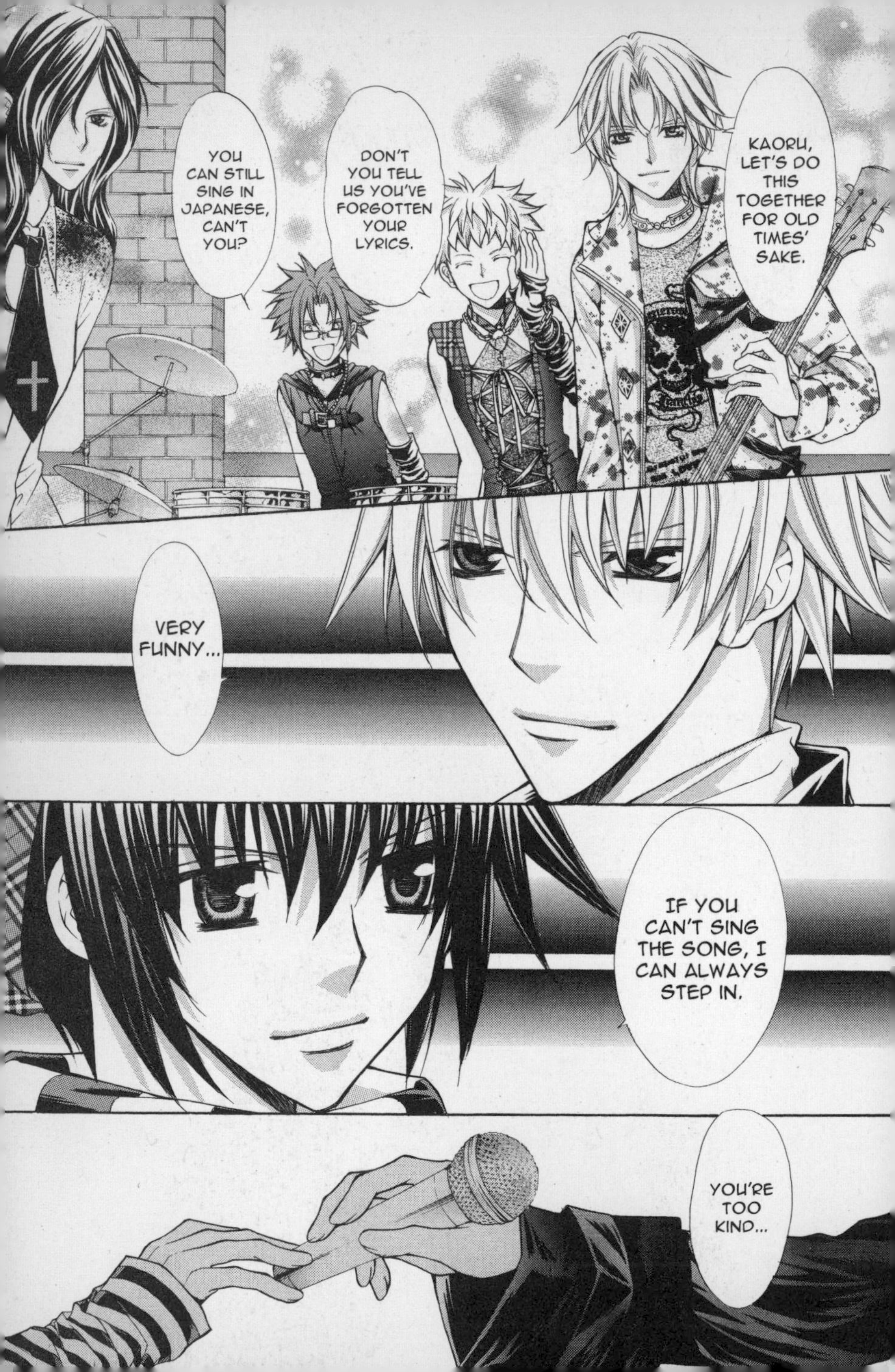
KAORU, LET'S DO THIS TOGETHER FOR OLD TIMES' SAKE.
DON'T YOU TELL US YOU'VE FORGOTTEN YOUR LYRICS.
YOU CAN STILL SING IN JAPANESE, CAN'T YOU?
VERY FUNNY...
IF YOU CAN'T SING THE SONG, I CAN ALWAYS STEP IN.
YOU'RE TOO KIND...

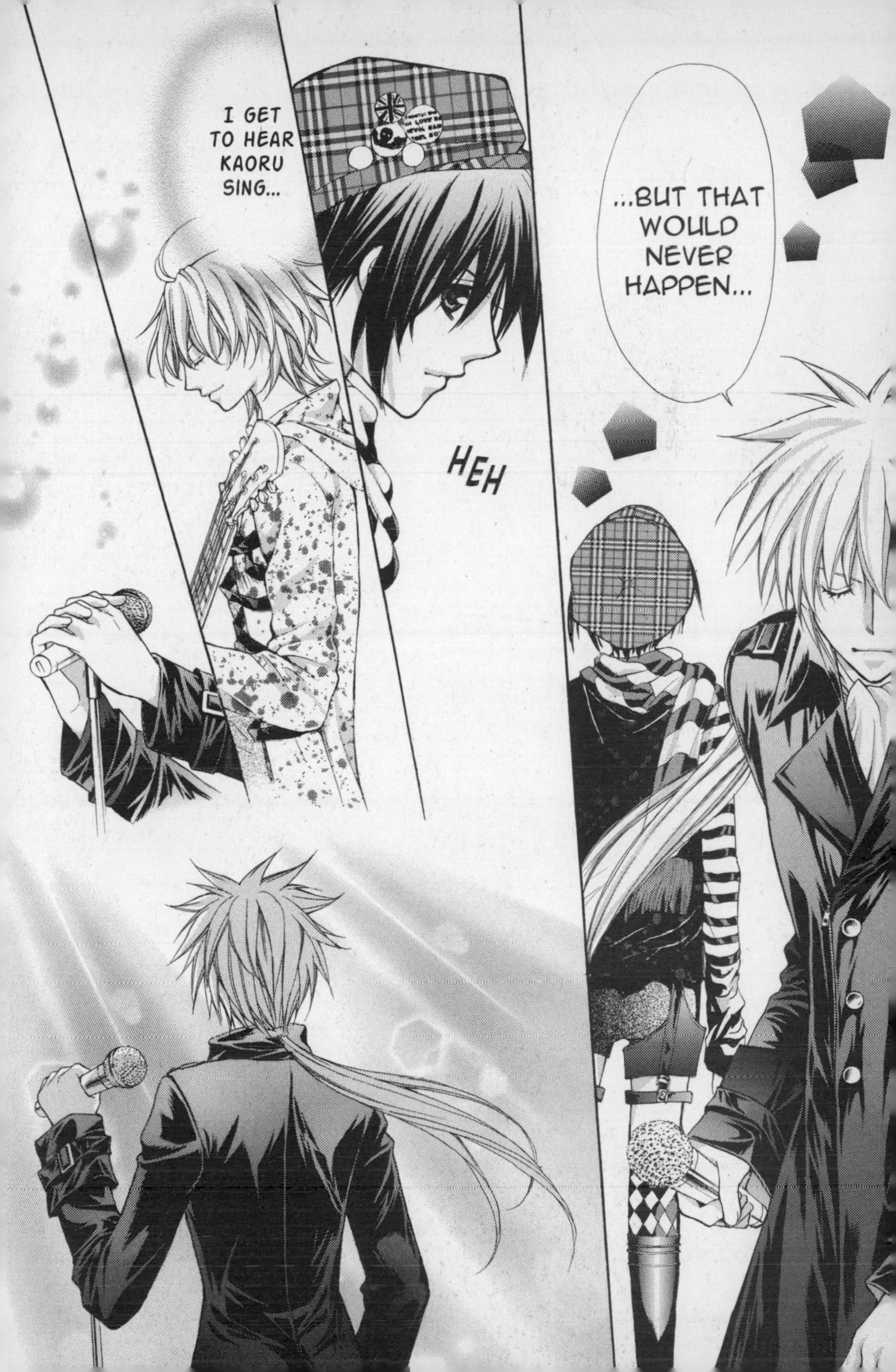
I GET TO HEAR KAORU SING...
HEH
...BUT THAT WOULD NEVER HAPPEN...

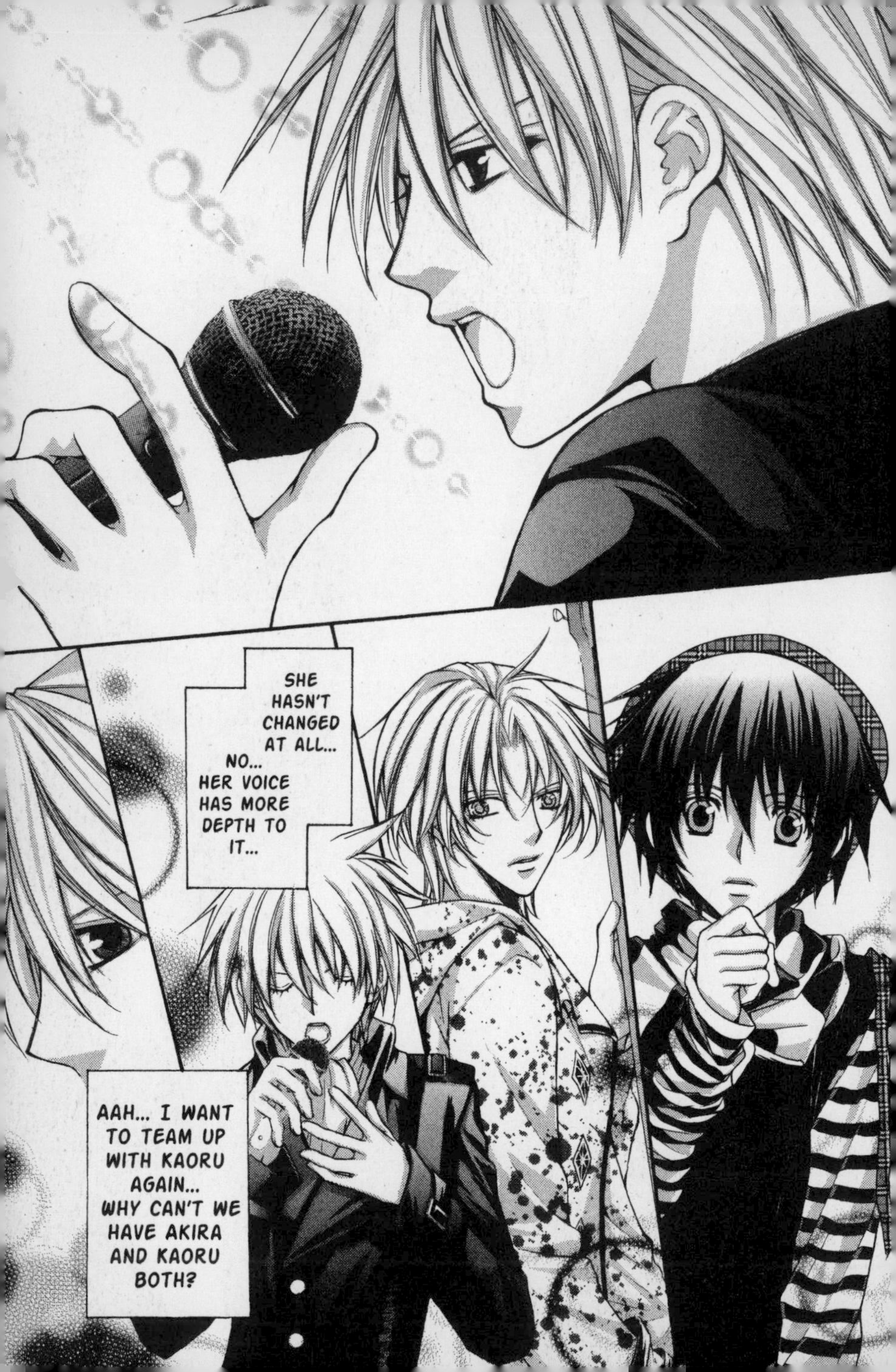
SHE HASN'T CHANGED AT ALL... NO... HER VOICE HAS MORE DEPTH TO IT...
AAH... I WANT TO TEAM UP WITH KAORU AGAIN... WHY CAN'T WE HAVE AKIRA AND KAORU BOTH?

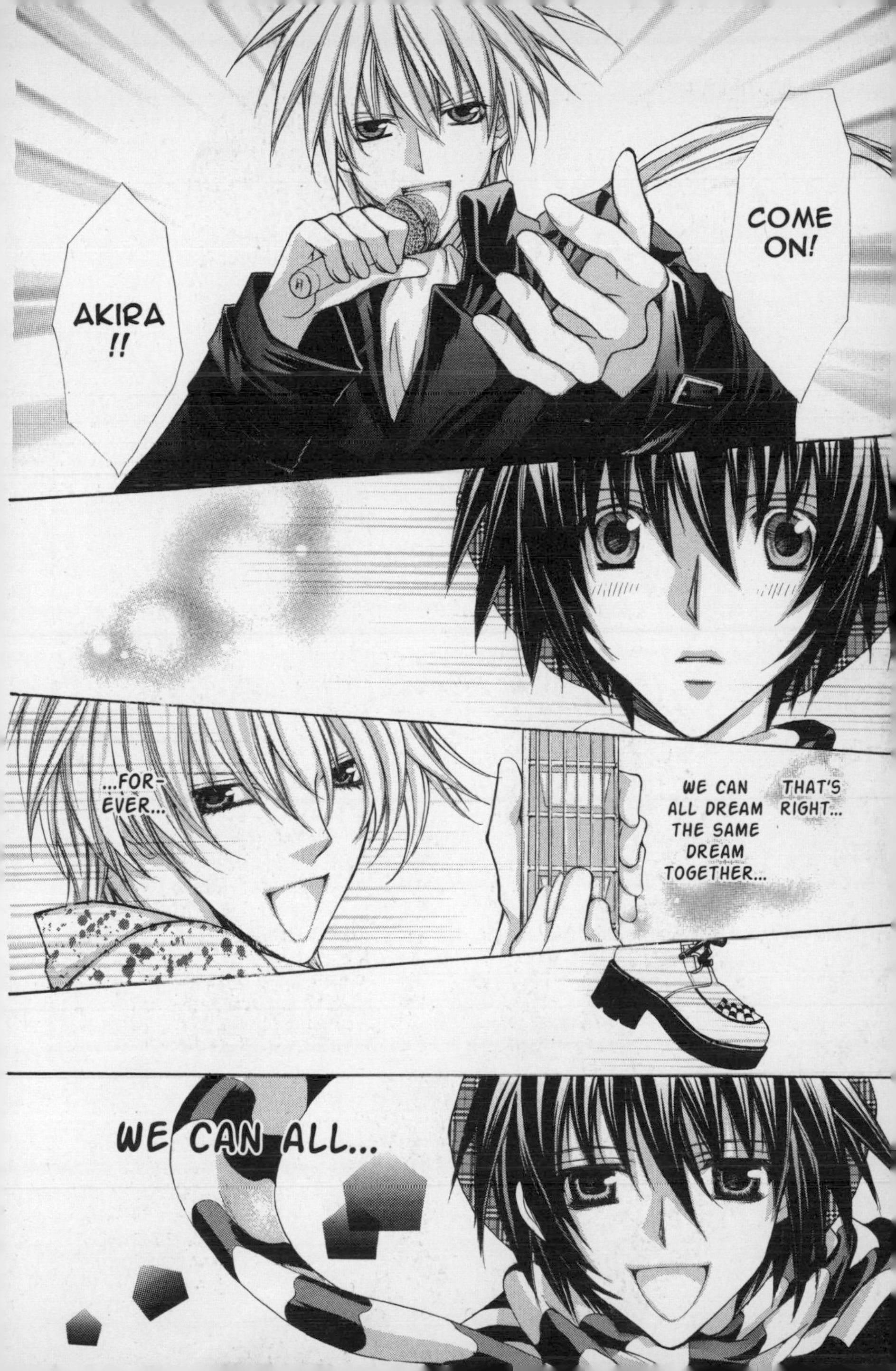
COME ON!
AKIRA !!
THAT'S RIGHT...
WE CAN ALL DREAM THE SAME DREAM TOGETHER...
...FOR-EVER...
WE CAN ALL...

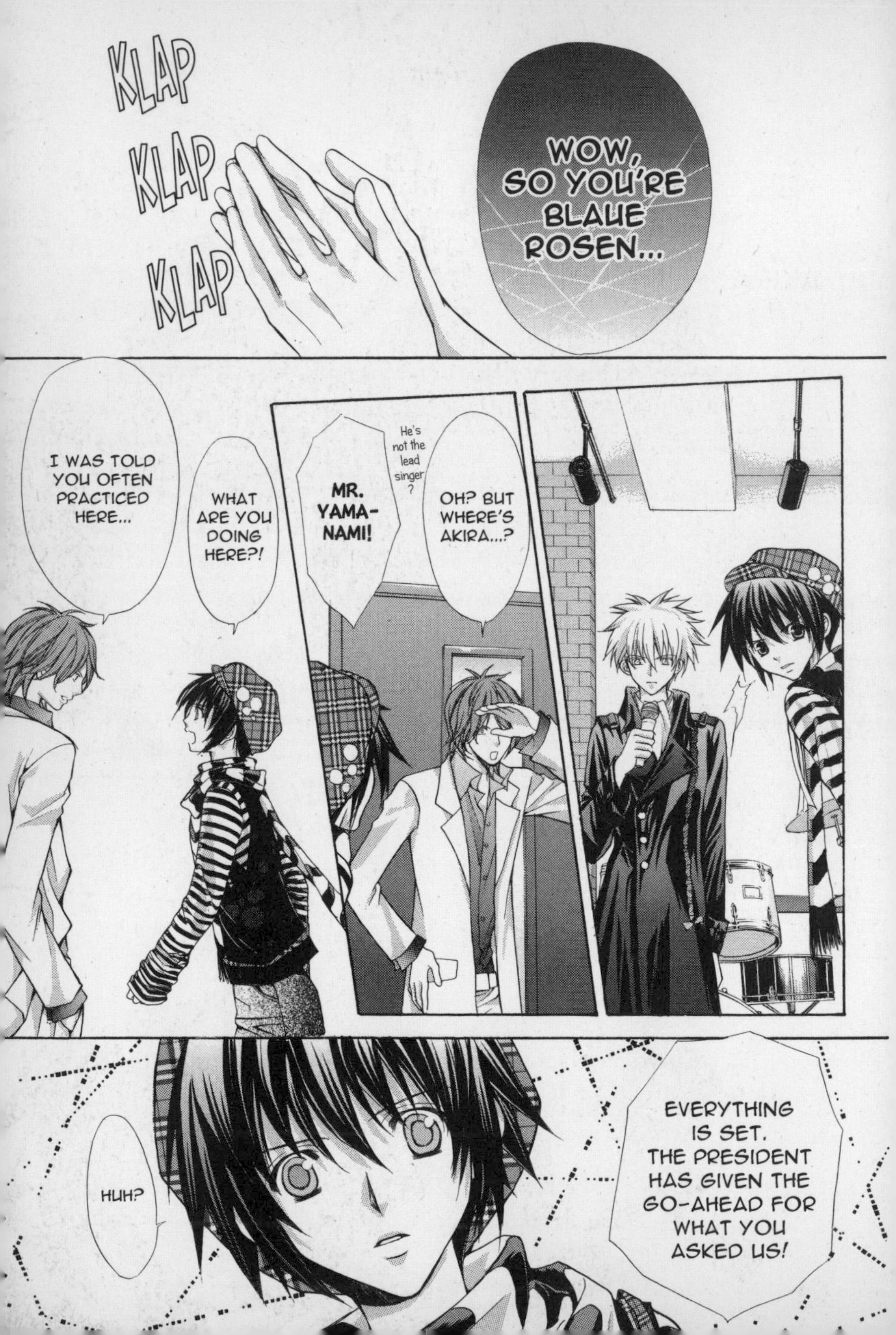
WOW, SO YOU'RE BLAUE ROSEN...
KLAP
KLAP
KLAP
OH? BUT WHERE'S AKIRA...?
He's not the lead singer?
MR. YAMA-NAMI!
WHAT ARE YOU DOING HERE?!
I WAS TOLD YOU OFTEN PRACTICED HERE...
EVERYTHING IS SET. THE PRESIDENT HAS GIVEN THE GO-AHEAD FOR WHAT YOU ASKED US!
HUH?

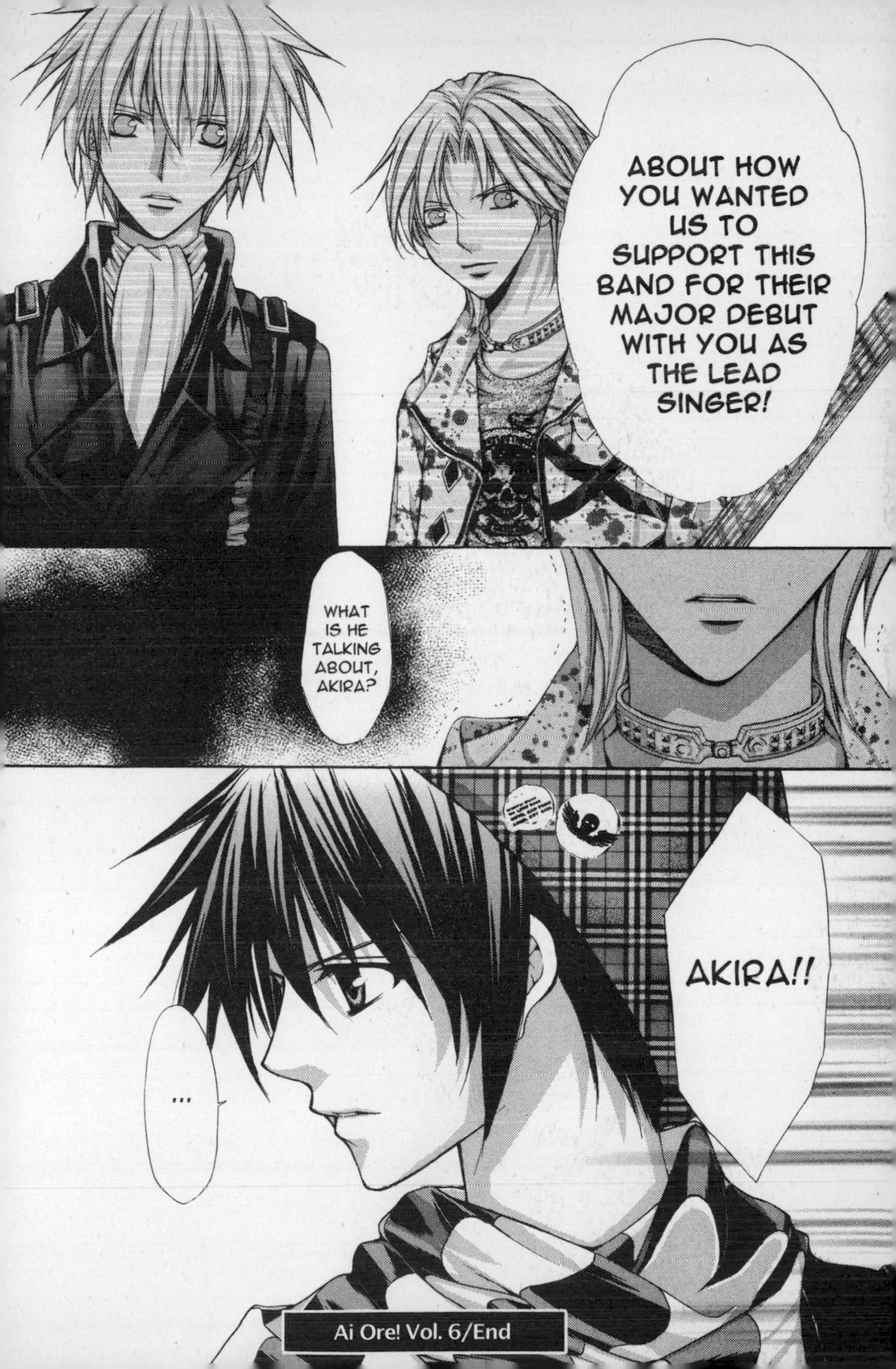
ABOUT HOW YOU WANTED US TO SUPPORT THIS BAND FOR THEIR MAJOR DEBUT WITH YOU AS THE LEAD SINGER!
WHAT IS HE TALKING ABOUT, AKIRA?
AKIRA!!
...
Ai Ore! Vol. 6/End

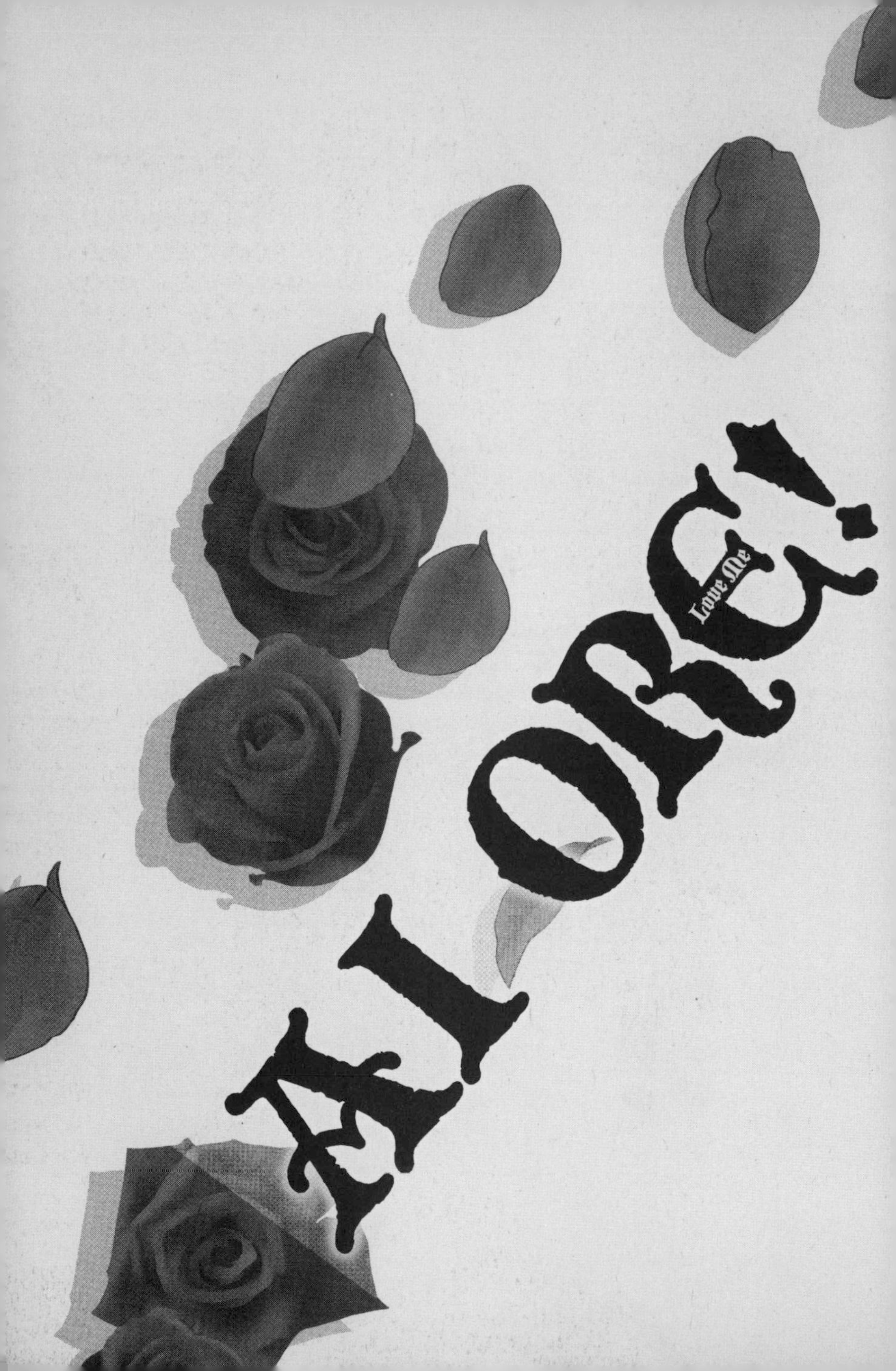
AI ORE!
Love Me

I'd like to tell you that the cover illustration was a request from my editor—it's not something I drew to meet my taste. I really mean it!! But, um... I did enjoy drawing it...

-Mayu Shinjo

Mayu Shinjo was born on January 26. She is a prolific writer of shojo manga, including the series *Sensual Phrase*. Her current series include *Ai-Ore!* and *Ayakashi Koi Emaki*. Her hobbies are cars, shopping and taking baths. Shinjo likes The Prodigy, Nirvana, U2 and Glay.

Ai Ore!

Volume 6
Shojo Beat Edition

STORY AND ART BY
MAYU SHINJO

Translation/Tetsuichiro Miyaki
Touch-up Art & Lettering/Inori Fukuda Trant
Design/Yukiko Whitley
Editor/Nancy Thistlethwaite

Ai Ore! ~Danshikou no Hime to Joshikou no Ouji~
Volume 3
© Mayu SHINJO 2009
First published in Japan in 2009 by KADOKAWA
SHOTEN Co., Ltd., Tokyo.
English translation rights arranged with
KADOKAWA SHOTEN Co., Ltd., Tokyo.

Printed in the U.S.A.

Published by VIZ Media, LLC
P.O. Box 77010
San Francisco, CA 94107

10 9 8 7 6 5 4 3 2 1
First printing, August 2012

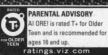

www.viz.com

www.shojobeat.com

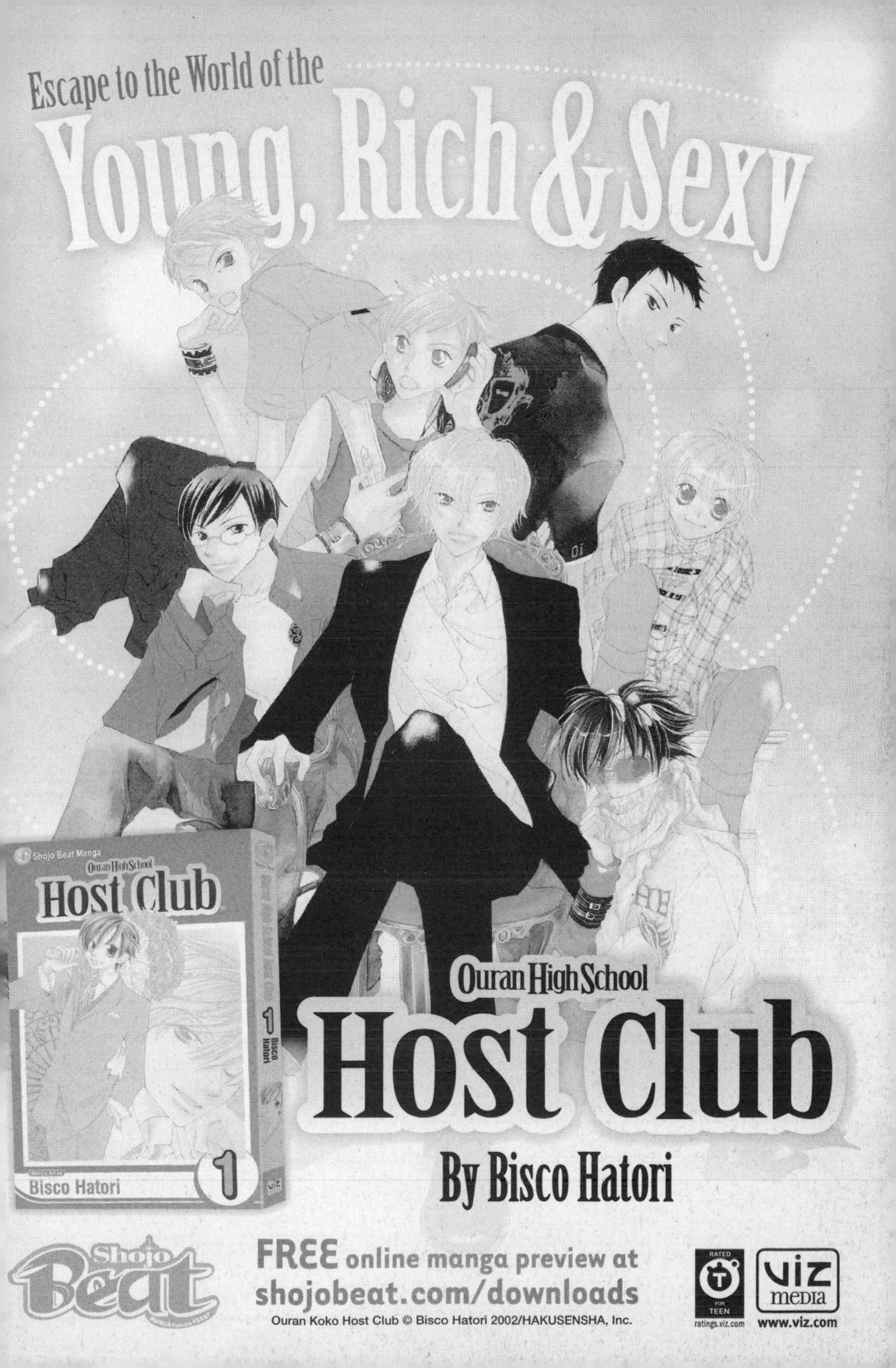
Escape to the World of the
Young, Rich & Sexy
Shojo Beat Manga
Ouran High School
Host Club
1
Bisco Hatori
Ouran High School
Host Club
By Bisco Hatori
Shojo Beat
FREE online manga preview at
shojobeat.com/downloads
Ouran Koko Host Club © Bisco Hatori 2002/HAKUSENSHA, Inc.
RATED T FOR TEEN
ratings.viz.com
VIZ media
www.viz.com

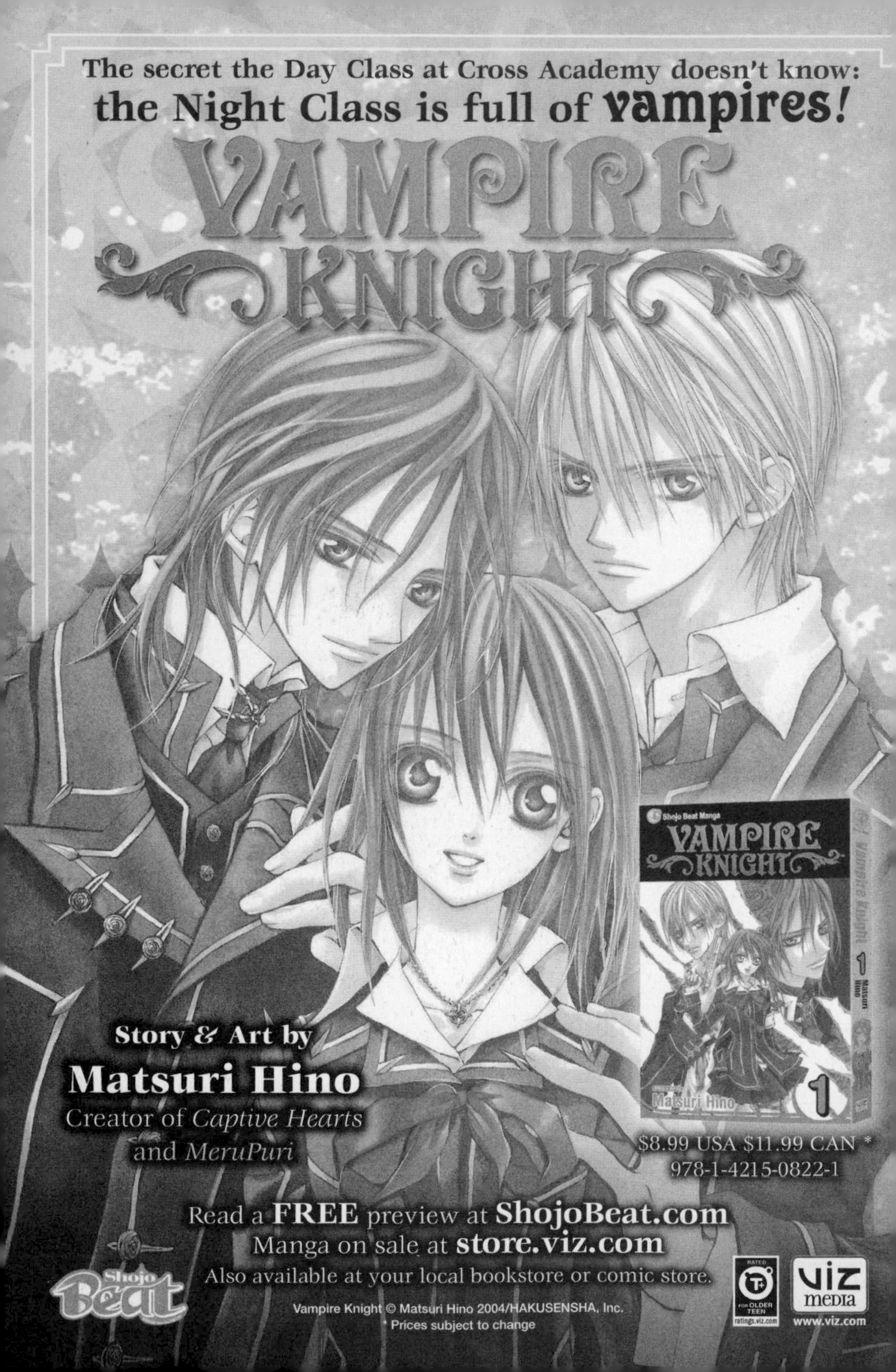
The secret the Day Class at Cross Academy doesn't know:
the Night Class is full of vampires!
VAMPIRE KNIGHT
Story & Art by
Matsuri Hino
Creator of Captive Hearts and MeruPuri
Shojo Beat Manga
VAMPIRE KNIGHT
1
Matsuri Hino
$8.99 USA $11.99 CAN *
978-1-4215-0822-1
Read a FREE preview at ShojoBeat.com
Manga on sale at store.viz.com
Also available at your local bookstore or comic store.
Shojo Beat
RATED T+ FOR OLDER TEEN
ratings.viz.com
VIZ media
www.viz.com
Vampire Knight © Matsuri Hino 2004/HAKUSENSHA, Inc.
* Prices subject to change

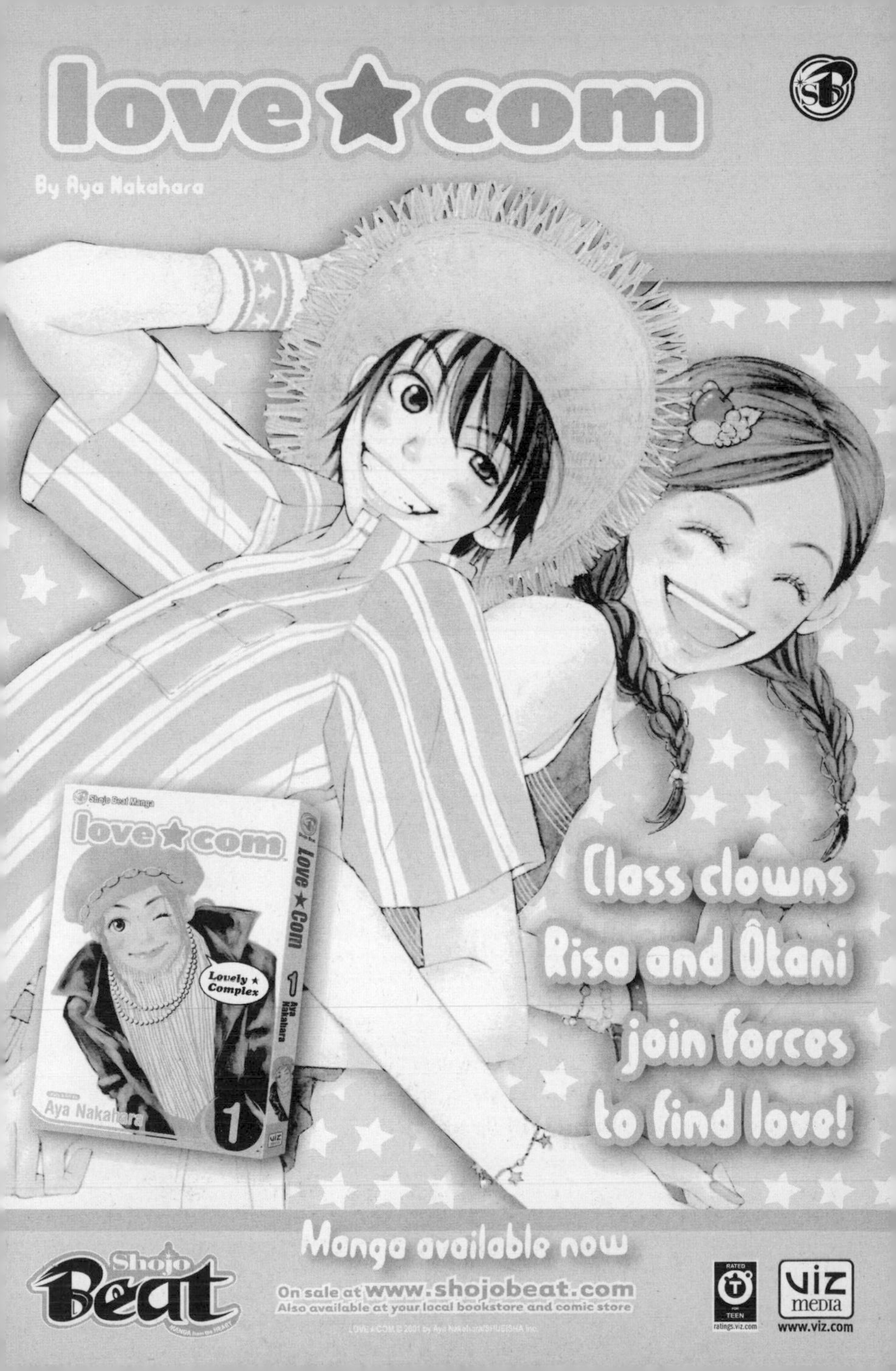

love★com
By Aya Nakahara
Shojo Beat Manga
love★com
Lovely ★ Complex
Aya Nakahara
1
Class clowns Risa and Ôtani join forces to find love!
Manga available now
Shojo Beat
On sale at www.shojobeat.com
Also available at your local bookstore and comic store
LOVE★COM © 2001 by Aya Nakahara/SHUEISHA Inc.
RATED T TEEN
ratings.viz.com
VIZ media
www.viz.com

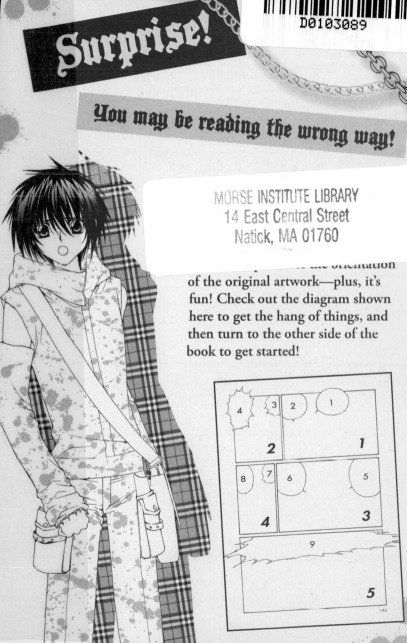

Surprise!

You may be reading the wrong way!

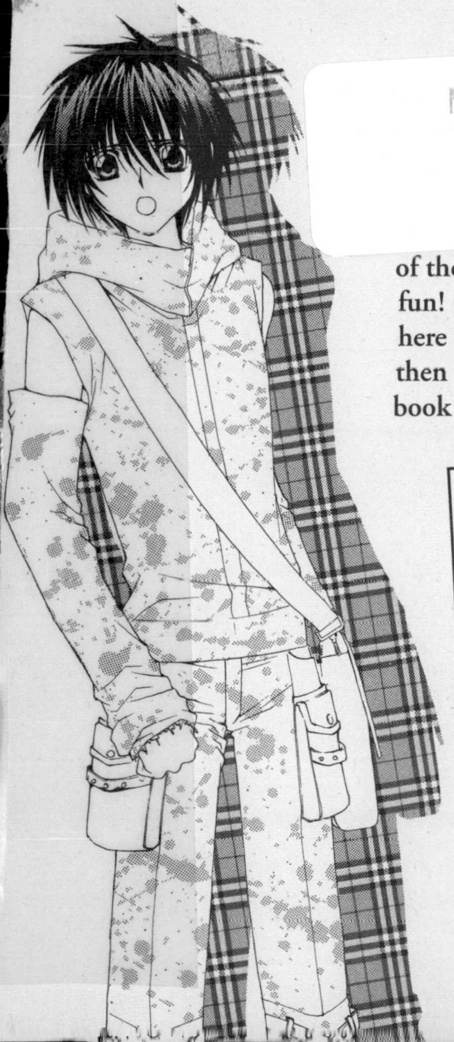

of the original artwork—plus, it's fun! Check out the diagram shown here to get the hang of things, and then turn to the other side of the book to get started!

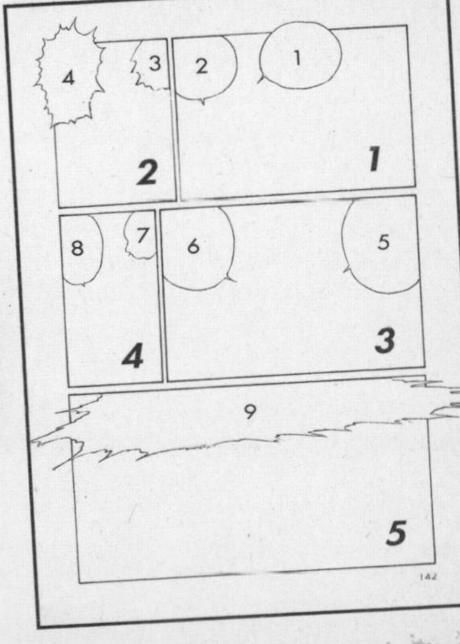
1
2
3
4
1
2
5
6
7
8
3
4
9
5
142